Masanobu Endo

Creation and Christology

A Study on the Johannine Prologue
in the Light of Early Jewish Creation Accounts

Mohr Siebeck

MASANOBU ENDO, born 1963; studied Social Science (Saitama University) and Theology (Japan Bible Seminary), besides other studies in USA (Gordon Conwell Theological Seminary), and in Scotland (University of St. Andrews); 2000 Ph.D. at the University of St. Andrews, Scotland; since 2000 Reader in New Testament at the Japan Bible seminary, Tokyo, and Minister at Kinugasa Central Church, Yokosuka.

Die Deutsche Bibliothek - CIP-Einheitsaufnahme

Endo, Masanobu:
Creation and Christology : a study on the Johannine prologue in the
light of early Jewish creation accounts / Masanobu Endo. - Tübingen :
Mohr Siebeck, 2002.
   (Wissenschaftliche Untersuchungen zum Neuen Testament : Reihe 2 ; 149)
   ISBN 3-16-147789-8

The book was printed by Druck Partner Rübelmann GmbH in Hemsbach on non-aging paper and bound by Buchbinderei Schaumann in Darmstadt.

Printed in Germany.

ISSN 0340-9570

Wissenschaftliche Untersuchungen
zum Neuen Testament · 2. Reihe

Herausgegeben von
Jörg Frey, Martin Hengel, Otfried Hofius

149

Preface

This book was originally produced as my Ph.D. dissertation, presented to the University of St. Andrews, Scotland, in 2000.

My special thanks are due to my supervisor, Prof. Richard Bauckham, Bishop Wardlaw Professor of St. Mary's College (University of St. Andrews). His guidance has always been so thorough and insightful that I have never lost my direction. I remember how excited I was when I was sitting before him and listening to his advice. I also am thankful for the sincere guidance of Prof. Francis Watson (University of Aberdeen) and Dr. Bruce Longenecker (University of St. Andrews) in the defense of my thesis.

I am privileged to present my study to the public forum of biblical scholars through the WUNT II series of Mohr Siebeck. I am grateful to Prof. Martin Hengel and Prof. Jörg Frey for this opportunity. Prof. Frey read my thesis in detail and gave me valuable comments at many points.

I wish to thank the Japan Evangelical Alliance Mission for having granted me a long term scholarship (1995-2000). I am also thankful to Ms. Yoko Saito, Ms. Miho Matsunaga, Mr. and Mrs. Nagahashi, Rev. Wakasa and the brothers and sisters of Tokumaru, Kasumicho, Kinugasa, Koga, and Martyrs Churches, for their prayers and many gifts. My sincere gratitude should be extended to my relatives, Mr. and Mrs. Iwasaki, Mr. and Mrs. Uchida, Mr. and Mrs. Yamada, and especially to my father and mother-in-law, Rikizo and Mariko Takakusa, for their encouragement and financial assistance. I want to give many thanks to Fiona and Ian Smith, who spent their precious time for proof reading. I am also grateful to Alexander and his spouse, who sent me a Slavonic manuscript from the Bulgarian Library.

In particular, I wish to thank my parents, Masuo and Reiko Endo, for their unfailing spiritual and financial support. I recognize how much I owe my father, who initially gave me a firm foundation through his biblical preaching.

My final but greatest gratitude is due to my wife, Kaoru. She has supported my study with her love and financially by working as an organist at Martyrs Church in St. Andrews and as a Japanese teacher in Edinburgh. I also thank my son, Masayoshi (Mercy) for his encouragement with his lovely smile. I really know that my study would not have been completed at all, without the assistance of my family and many friends. So I want to dedicate this book to all of them.

ἁγιασθήτω τὸ ὄνομά σου.

March 2002   Masanobu Endo, Tokyo

Table of Contents

Part II
The Johannine Prologue in the Light of Early Jewish Creation Accounts
(ca. 2nd Century BC to 1st Century AD)

Abbreviations

Abbreviations for Ancient Literature

Ab	Abot
Abr	De Abrahamo
Ant	Antiquities of the Jews
ApAbr	Apocalypse of Abraham
ApLao	Apollinaris of Laodicea
Aristob	Aristobulus
AsMos	Assumption of Moses
b.	Babylonian Talmud
1 Bar	1 Baruch
2 Bar	2 (Syriac Apocalypse of) Baruch
CD	Damascus Rule
Conf	De Confusione Linguarum
DeutR	Midrash Rabbah on Deuteronomy
1 En	1 (Ethiopic Apocalypse of) Enoch
2 En	2 (Slavonic Apocalypse of) Enoch
3 En	3 (Hebrew Apocalypse of) Enoch
4 Ezra	4 Ezra
Fug	De Fuga et Inventione
GenR	Midrash Rabbah on Genesis
Heres	Quis Rerum Divinarum Heres
JosAsen	Joseph and Aseneth
Jub	Jubilees
Ketub	Ketubot
LAB	Liber Antiquitatum Biblicarum
LadJac	Ladder of Jacob
Leg All	Legum Allegoriae
LXX	Septuagint
m.	Mishna
Mak	Makkot
Meg	Megilla
MT	Massoretic text of the Hebrew Bible
NumR	Midrash Rabbah on Numbers
Op Mund	De Opificio Mundi
Post	De Posteritate Caini
PrMan	Prayer of Manasseh

1QH[a]	Thanksgiving Hymns from Qumran Cave 1
1QM	War Scroll from Qumran Cave 1
1QS	Community Rule from Qumran Cave 1
4Q176	Tanhumin from Qumran Cave 4
4Q180	Ages of Creation from Qumran Cave 4
4Q216	Jubilees[a] from Qumran Cave 4
4Q381	Non-Canonical Psalms B from Qumran Cave 4
4Q392	Works of God from Qumran Cave 4
4Q400 - 405	Songs of the Sabbath Sacrifice[a-f] from Qumran Cave 4
4Q422	Paraphrase of Genesis and Exodus from Qumran Cave 4
4Q504	Works of the Luminaries[a] from Qumran Cave 4
11QPs[a]	Psalms[a] from Qumran Cave 11
11QPsAp[a]	Apocryphal Psalms from Qumran Cave 11
Quaest Exod	Quaestiones et Solutiones in Exodus
Quaest Gen	Quaestiones et Solutiones in Genesis
Det	Quod Deterius Potiori Insidiari Soleat
Quis Rer	Quis Rerum Divinarum Heres
Sacr	De Sacrificiis Abelis et Cain
Sanh	Sanhedrin
SibOr	Sibylline Oracles
SifDeut	Midrash Sifre on Deuteronomy
SifNum	Midrash Sifre on Numbers
Sir	Sirach (Ecclesiasticus)
Somn	De Somniis
Suk	Sukkah
t.	Tosephta
Ta 'an	Ta 'anit
TAb	Testament of Abraham
TargJon	Targum Jonathan
TargNeo	Targum Neofiti 1
Tim	Timaeus
TLev	Testament of Levi
TMos	Testament of Moses
y.	Jerusalem Talmud
Wisd	Wisdom of Solomon

Abbreviations for Serial Publications

AB	The Anchor Bible
ABR	*Australian Biblical Review*
APOT	Apocrypha and Pseudepigrapha of the Old Testament
ATR	*Anglican Theological Review*

BDB	Brown-Driver-Briggs, Hebrew and English Lexicon of the OT
BETS	*Bulletin of the Evangelical Theological Society*
Bib	*Biblica*
BJRL	*Bulletin of the John Rylands Library*
BT	*Bible Translator*
BZAW	*Beihefte zur Zeitschrift für die alttestamentliche Wissenschaft*
CBQ	*Catholic Biblical Quarterly*
CBQMS	Catholic Biblical Quarterly Monograph Series
CSCO	Corpus Scriptorum Christianorum Orientalium
DJD	Discoveries in the Judean Desert
DSD	*Dead Sea Discoveries*
ET	*Expository Times*
EQ	*Evangelical Quarterly*
Ex Auditu	*Ex Auditu*
HBT	*Horizon in Biblical Theology*
HR	*History of Religions*
HTR	*Harvard Theological Review*
HTS	*Harvard Theological Studies*
IOS	Israel Oriental Studies
JJS	*Journal of Jewish Studies*
JSHRZ	Jüdische Schriften aus hellenistisch-römischer Zeit
JSJ	*Journal for the Study of Judaism*
JSNT	*Journal for the Study of the New Testament*
JSNTSup	Journal for the Study of the New Testament, Supplement
JSOTSup	Journal for the Study of the Old Testament, Supplement
JSPSup	Journal for the Study of the Pseudepigrapha, Supplement
JTS	*Journal of Theological Studies*
LCL	Loeb Classical Library
NICNT	New International Commentary on New Testament
NTA	New Testament Apocrypha
NTS	*New Testament Studies*
NovT	*Novum Testamentum*
OTP	The Old Testament Pseudepigrapha
PAM	Photo of the DSS MSS in the Palestine Archaeological Museum
RB	*Revue Biblique*
RL	*Religion in Life*
RSR	*Recherches de science religieuse*
SBLASP	*Society of Biblical Literature, Abstracts and Seminar Papers*
ScrHie	*Scripta Hierosolymitana*
SE	*Studia Evangelica*
SHR	Photo of the DSS MSS in the Shrine of the Book Photographs
STDJ	Studies on the Texts of the Desert of Judah

SJT	*Scottish Journal of Theology*
TLZ	*Theologische Literaturzeitung*
VT	*Vetus Testamentum*
WBC	Word Biblical Commentary
WTJ	*Wesleyan Theological Journal*
WUNT	Wissenschaftliche Untersuchungen zum Neuen Testament
ZKT	*Zeitschrift für katholische Theologie*
ZTK	*Zeitschrift für Theologie und Kirche*
ZNW	*Zeitschrift für die neutestamentliche Wissenschaf*

Miscellaneous

AD	anno Domini
BC	before Christ
bk(s).	Book (s)
ca.	circa, about (with dates)
cf.	confer, compare
ch(s).	chapter(s)
ed.	edition, edited by, editor
e.g.	exempli gratia, for example
esp.	especially
frag(s).	fragment, fragments
i.e.	id est, that is
lit.	literally
MS, MSS	manuscript, manuscripts
§	section
tr.	translator, translated by
v(v).	verse(s)
vol(s)	volume(s)
<	root, or original form of the word

Chapter 1

Introduction

1.1 Purpose

This research project attempts to explore the hypothesis that the Johannine Christology in the prologue of the Fourth Gospel is developed on the basis of the biblical and early Jewish exegetical traditions of the Genesis creation account. Several bodies of literature have been read in relation to the Johannine prologue in the 20th century AD: (1) Mandaean literature (Iranian Gnostic tradition; ca. 3rd century AD thereafter [possibly to the 2nd century AD])[1]; (2) Hermetic literature (Egyptian Gnostic tradition; ca. 2nd to 3rd centuries AD); (3) Jewish wisdom literature (ca. 2nd century BC thereafter); (4) Philo's works (Hellenistic Judaism; 1st century AD); (5) Rabbinic (ca. 3rd century AD thereafter) and Targumic literature (ca. 2nd century AD thereafter). However, so far only a few attempts have been made to examine the early Jewish documents which are generally dated between the 2nd century BC and the 1st century AD. Therefore, this study will give a new perspective for understanding the background of the Johannine prologue.

1.2 Previous Discussions on the Background of the Johannine Prologue

1.2.1 Rudolf Bultmann: Gnostic Tradition

In the early 20th century, R. Bultmann set forth a hypothesis that the prologue was originally a pre-Christian cultic hymn, an ultimate source from Gnosticism, which is seen in the Odes of Solomon and some of the Mandaean writings. He argues that the λόγος of John 1:1 cannot be understood on the basis of the OT[2] since the notion of God's word in the OT is different from that of the λόγος in John.[3] He argues that the figure of wisdom which is found

---

[1] The discussion on the date of Mandaean literature has not been settled yet.

[2] R. Bultmann, *The Gospel of John: A Commentary*, tr. G. R. Beasley-Murray (Philadelphia: The Westminster Press, 1971) = *Das Evangelium des Johannes* (Göttingen: Vandenhoeck & Ruprecht, 1964), 21.

[3] R. Bultmann (*John*, 20-21) argues that (1) the word of God means God's temporal deed or event in the OT, while in John the λόγος is an eternal being; (2) it is not the essence of a

in Judaism (as well as the OT) is related to the Johannine λόγος.[4] The suggested similarities are as follows: (1) she is pre-existent, and is God's partner at creation (Prov 8:22-30; Sir 1:1-9; 24:3, 9; Wisd 8:3; 9:4, 9); (2) she seeks a dwelling on earth among men, but is rejected, so that she returns to the heavenly world (Prov. 1:20-32; Job 28; Sir 24:7; 1 Bar 3:10-13, 29-36; 1 En 42:1-3); (3) she reveals herself only to individual religious men, and makes them friends of God and prophets (Wisd 7;14, 27; Sir 1:15); and (4) she is simply designated 'Wisdom' (Prov 8:1; Sir 1:6; 24:1; Wisd 7:22; 1 Bar 3:2). Bultmann maintains that this wisdom myth does not have its origin in the OT nor Judaism at all, but in Gnosticism.[5] That is to say, Jewish wisdom took over the Hellenistic and Gnostic literature, and she was de-mythologised and transferred to the Torah. If there may be a connection between the Johannine prologue and Jewish wisdom, then both go back to the same tradition for their source, namely Gnosticism.[6] After an examination of the possibility of the influence from Alexandrian Jewish circles,[7] he accepted Reitzenstein's assumption, that the prologue was influenced from Iranian Gnosticism with its notion of the redeemed redeemer.[8]

1.2.2 Post Bultmann: from Gnosticism to Wisdom Tradition

Guided by Bultmann's hypothesis, his students, H. Becker[9] and E. Schweizer,[10] sought to reconstruct a typical archetype of the 'Gnostic Revealer Discourse' from parallels found in Mandaean texts and the Odes of

---

system of cosmic laws; (3) it has the idea of the relation of the chosen people to the word of God, while in John λόγος has the idea of the relation of the world to the Word; (4) a man cannot be designated as the bearer of revelation without an inspiration, while Jesus is not thought of such a bearer; and (5) the word of God has not become a hypostasis.

[4] R. Bultmann, *John*, 22.

[5] R. Bultmann ('Der religionsgeschichtliche Hintergrund des Prologs zum Johannes-evangelium,' in H. Schmidt (ed.), *EYXAPIΣTHPION: Studien zur Religion und Literatur des Alten und Neuen Testaments* [Göttingen: Vandenhoeck & Ruprecht, 1923], 12-13) states, 'Jedoch dürfte die Auffassung der Weisheit als eines Geschöpfes jüdische Umdeutung einer älteren mythologischen Anschaung sein, nach der die Weisheit eine selbständige göttliche Gestalt ist.'

[6] R. Bultmann, 'Religionsgeschichtliche,' 16-17. As for the de-mythology, it has been developed as follows: (1) the mythology has been severely pushed into the background; (2) Gnostic cosmology has been repressed and has given way to the belief of Creation; (3) and the concern for the relation of man to the revelation of God has become dominant ('Religionsgeschichtliche,' 30-31).

[7] R. Bultmann, 'Die Bedeutung der neuerschlossenen mandäischen und manichäischen Quellen für das Verständnis des Johannesevangeliums,' *ZTK* 24 (1925), 14-15.

[8] R. Bultmann, 'Bedeutung,' 19-20.

[9] H. Becker, *Die Reden des Johannesevangeliums und der Stil der Gnostischen Offenbarungsrede* (Göttingen: Vandenhoeck & Ruprecht, 1956).

[10] E. Schweizer, *Ego Eimi: Die Religionsgeschichtliche Herkunft und Theologische Bedeutung der Joh. Bildreden* (Göttingen: Vandenhoeck & Ruprecht, 1939).

Solomon. However, Bultmann's hypothesis has not always been accepted by other scholars. While examining another Bultmannian hypothesis which states that the prologue is a pre-Christian Gnostic hymn which stems from Baptist circles,[11] E. Käsemann[12] comments on Bultmann's former hypothesis by writing, 'The pre-Christian character of the hymn is more than problematical, the Aramaic original incredible, the alleged Baptist hymn a pure hypothesis.'[13] Following Käsemann, E. Haenchen also doubted Bultmann's Mandaean hypothesis[14] and argued that the prologue is, 'ein christlicher Hymnus.'[15] E. Yamauchi refutes Bultmann's hypothesis.[16] He argues that most of the Mandaic texts date between the sixth and the ninth century since there are many explicit references to Islam in these texts.[17] Moreover, the origin of the sect was at least the 3rd century AD and possibly even the 2nd century AD.[18] Rather, he holds that the early Jewish texts can surely provide a more satisfactory background for the Johannine prologue.[19] C. H. Dodd went another way. He examined the parallels between the Johannine prologue and the Poimandres tractate (Hermetic writings),[20] focusing on some distinct beings (the divine Revealer [Poimandres], the prophet, the heavenly Anthropos, and the Logos), and the concept of regeneration (new birth; cf. John 1:12-13). Since he could not ignore the date issue, he carefully stated that both the Johannine prologue and the Poimandres tractate do not necessarily borrow from one side or the other, but rather they share a common thought.[21]

Recent scholars who have worked on the Gnostic literature have pointed out the common milieu on which both the prologue and the Gnostic literature are drawing, i.e. the Jewish wisdom tradition.[22] The general arguments are as

---

[11] R. Bultmann, *John*, 16-17.

[12] E. Käsemann, 'The Structure and Purpose of the Prologue to John's Gospel,' in idem (ed.), *New Testament Questions of Today* (Philadelphia: Fortress Press, 1969), 138-167.

[13] E. Käsemann, *Structure*, 150.

[14] E. Haenchen, *John* (Hermeneia; Philadelphia: Fortress Press, 1984), 36.

[15] E. Haenchen, 'Probleme des Johanneischen 'Prologs',' *ZTK* 60 (1963), 307, 333.

[16] E. Yamauchi, 'Gnostic Ethics and Mandaean Origins,' *HTS* 24 (1970); idem, *Pre-Christian Gnosticism: A Survey of the Proposed Evidences* (Grand Rapids: Eerdmans, 1973); idem, 'Jewish Gnosticism? The Prologue of John, Mandaean Parallels, and the Trimorphic Protennoia,' in R. van den Brock and M.J. Vermaseren (eds.), *Studies in Gnosticism and Hellenistic Religions* (Leiden: Brill, 1981), 467-497.

[17] E. Yamauchi, *Pre-Christian Gnosticism*, 4-8.

[18] E. Yamauchi, *Pre-Christian Gnosticism*, 9.

[19] E. Yamauchi, 'Jewish Gnosticism,' 485.

[20] C. H. Dodd, *The Interpretation of the Fourth Gospel* (Cambridge: Cambridge Unversity Press, 1965), 10-53.

[21] C. H. Dodd, *Interpretation*, 53.

[22] G. W. MacRae, 'The Jewish Background of the Gnostic Sophia Myth,' *NovT* 12 (1970), 86-101; J. H. Charlesworth and R. A. Culpepper, 'The Odes of Solomon and the

follows: (1) the Johannine prologue does not necessarily depend upon Gnostic texts (cf. Odes of Solomon, and the Trimorphic Protennoia) because of the chronological difficulties; (2) there seems to be common ground in the wisdom tradition, upon which both the prologue and the Gnostic literature are drawing; (3) both texts were transformed (de-Christianized [the Johannine prologue], or more developed as Gnostic literature) from there. Many efforts have been made to read the Johannine prologue in accordance with the theological framework of the Jewish wisdom tradition. They give light to an idea that the Jewish wisdom was transformed and adapted into the Johannine Logos.[23] However, we should not ignore the fact that Jewish wisdom is associated with the motif of the word of God, and they each depict different aspects of the unique identity of God (e.g. 2 En 33:3-4; Sir ch. 42; Wisd 9:1-2; 4Q403).[24] It is thereby crucial to observe how these attributes function in each of their respective theological contexts.

1.2.3 Philo's Logos

The association of the Johannine Logos with Philo's Logos has long been discussed because of similarities in the personified figure.[25] Philo's Logos is

---

Gospel of John,' *CBQ* 35 (1973), 303, 306; H. Schenke, 'Die Neutestamentliche Christologie und der Gnostische Erlöser,' in K. Tröger (ed.), *Gnosis und Neues Testament: Studien aus Religionwissenschaft und Theologie* (Berlin: Evangelische Verlangsanstalt, 1973), 109-125; Y. Janssens, 'The Trimorphic Protennoia and the Fourth Gospel,' in A. H. B. Logan and A. J. M. Wedderburn (eds.), *The New Testament and Gnosis* (Edinburgh: T. & T. Clark, 1983), 229-244, esp. 235; J. Ashton, 'The Transformation of Wisdom: A Study of the Prologue of John's Gospel,' *NTS* 32 (2) (1986), 161-186; W. Carter, 'The Prologue and John's Gospel: Function, Symbol and the Definitive Word,' *JSNT* 39 (1990), 35-58; J. T. Sanders, 'Nag Hammadi, Odes of Solomon, and NT Christological Hymns,' in J.E. Goehring (ed.), *Gnosticism and the Early Christian World: In Honor of James M Robinson* (Sonoma: Polebridge Press, 1990), 51-66; G. Robinson, 'The Trimorphic Protennoia and the Prologue of the Fourth Gospel,' in J. E. Goehring (ed.), *Gnosticism and the Early Christian World* (Sonoma: Polebridge Press, 1990), 37-50.

[23] E.g. H. R. Moeller, 'Wisdom Motifs and John's Gospel,' *BETS* 6 (1963), 92-100; J. S. Ackerman, 'The Rabbinic Interpretation of Psalm 82 and the Gospel of John: Jn 10:34,' *HTR* 59 (1966), 186-191; E. Epp, 'Wisdom, Torah, Word: The Johannine Prologue and the Purpose of the Fourth Gospel,' in G. Hawthorne (ed.), *Current Issues in Biblical and Patristic Interpretation* (Grand Rapids: Eerdmans, 1975), 128-146; J. Dunn, *Christology in the Making: A New Testament Inquiry into the Origin of the Doctrine of the Incarnation* (London: SCM Press, 1980), 163-268; J. Ashton, 'Transformation,' 161-186; Ben Witherington, *John's Wisdom* (Louisville: Westminster, 1995), esp. its Introduction.

[24] R. Bauckham (*God Crucified: Monotheism and Christology in the New Testament* [Carlisle: Paternoster Press, 1999], 21) rightly argues that the personifications have been developed precisely out of the ideas of God's own wisdom and word, that is, aspects of God's own identity.

[25] Cf. C. Dodd, *Interpretation*, 54-73; P. Borgen, *Philo, John and Paul: New Perspectives on Judaism and Early Christianity* (Atlanta: Scholars Press, 1987), 77.

described as a divine mediator (as 'the healer of the soul' [Leg All 3:177-178], 'comforter' [Fug 5-6], 'mediator' [Quaest Exod 2:13], and 'ambassador' [Heres 205]). The Logos is associated with life (Leg All 2:86; Post 127-129; Somn 2:241-246; Leg All 3:174-178; Det 118; Heres 79, 191) and light motifs (Op Mund 31; Abr 47; Leg All 3:45). It is also linked to the water (Leg All 2:86; Post 127-129; Somn 2:241-246) and manna motifs (Leg All 2:86; Leg All 3:174-178; Det 118; Heres 79, 191), which are prominent in the Johannine Christology (John 4:14; 6:35). In some contexts, the Logos is called 'a God' (Somn 1:227-230) or 'the second God' (Quaest Gen 2:62).

However, once each context is carefully examined, it becomes clear that these mediator figures were basically vivid ways of speaking of God's own powers and activities (not as the hypostatic existence of these entities),[26] or the way of solving theological and exegetical problems (in particular against the polytheistic views), as will be discussed in the thesis.[27] Instead, our thesis will present a distinction between Philo's Logos and the Johannine Logos.

1.2.4 Jewish Exegetical Traditions of the Genesis Creation Account

Some scholars attempt to read the prologue against the background of the Jewish exegetical traditions of the Genesis creation account. P. Borgen assumes that the prologue of John is an exposition of Genesis 1:1-5, finding a similar exposition of Genesis 1:1-5 in the Midrash Rabbah Genesis (Gen 3:3) and the Targum Neofiti 1 (Gen 3:24)[28]: in the former, the word (רבר) is identified with light which was called good[29]; the latter exhibits a chiastic structure which is seen in the prologue.[30]

The Targumic interpretation (or paraphrase) of the Genesis creation account has been considered as well. In this exposition, 'the word (ממרא or מימר) of the Lord' and 'the glory (שכינה: lit. 'dwelling') of the Lord' function as the main agents of God's work of creation (TargNeo Gen ch. 1). On the one hand, some scholars have questioned the pre-Christian date of the tradition in Neofiti 1,[31] whereas on the other hand, M. McNamara maintains that its substance would go back to pre-Christian times, by showing an other

---

[26] Cf. L. Hurtado, *One God, One Lord: Early Christian Devotion and Ancient Jewish Monotheism* (Philadelphia: Fortress Press, 1988), 36-50; P. Davis, 'Divine Agents, Mediators, and New Testament Christology,' *JTS* 45 (2) (1994), 491.

[27] See Excursus, 'Philo's Cosmogonic Account.'

[28] P. Borgen, 'Observations on the Targumic Character of the Prologue of John,' *NTS* 16 (1970), 288-295.

[29] P. Borgen, *Logos was the True Light and other Essays on the Gospel of John* (Trondheim: Tapir Publishers, 1983), 15.

[30] P. Borgen, *Logos*, 18.

[31] P. Wernberg-Møller, 'An Inquiry into the Validity of the Text-Critical Argument for an Early Dating of the Recently Discovered Palestinian Targum,' *VT* 12 (1962), 312-330; A. York, 'The Dating of the Targumic Literature,' *JSJ* 5 (1974), 49-62.

Palestinian Targumic paraphrase (TargNeo Exod 12:42; Exod 15:18 in the
Paris MS 10), in which the word of the Lord is identified with the primordial
light in the Genesis creation account.[32]   Some scholars argue that the word
(ממרא) is only a nominal substitute for God's name (אהיה in TargNeo Exod
3:12, 14),[33] whereas D. Munoz and M. McNamara hold that the use of ממרא
in Neofiti 1 may have a more theological purpose.[34]   It seems undeniable that
the word in the Targum shows a link to the biblical (e.g. Ps 33:6-9; Isa 48:3,
13; 55:11) word tradition:

> The word (ממרא) of the Lord is not like the word of the sons of man; nor are the works
> of the Lord like the work of the sons of man; the sons of man say and do not act; they
> decree and fulfill not; and they go back and deny their words. God, however, says and
> does; he decrees and fulfills, and his prophetic words are established forever (TargNeo
> Gen 23:19).

Moreover, both ממרא and שכינה exhibit different aspects of the unique
identity of God: i.e. on the one hand, ממרא indicates the appearance of God
through his word by which the people could realize his dwelling among them
(TargNeo Gen 17:1; 18:1; 20:3, 6, 13: 35:11; TargNeo Exod 3:8; 11:4; 19:9;
20:24; TargNeo Num 11:17; 22:9, 12, 20; 23:4, 5, 12, 16), whereas on the
other hand, שכינה indicates the appearance of God through a visible sign (such
as light, cloud, and pillar of fire), by which the people could realize his
dwelling among them (TargNeo Gen 11:5; 22:14; TargNeo Exod 3:1; 19:11, 18,
20; 20:20, 21; 24:13).   TargNeo Exod 19:11 illustrates these distinctions:

> And the Lord said to Moses: 'Behold, my Memra will be revealed to you in the might of
> the cloud so that the people may hear when I speak with you' (TargNeo Exod 19:9); the
> Glory of the Shekinah of the Lord will be revealed to the eyes of all the people upon
> Mount Sinai' (TargNeo Exod 19:11).

In addition, we should note that the ממרא is not depicted as an autonomous
existence, but rather as the special way of the historical appearance of God to
the world.   Therefore, it seems possible to consider the ממרא to be an

---

[32] M. McNamara, Targum and Testament. Aramaic Paraphrases of the Hebrew Bible. A
Light on the New Testament (Granad Rapids/Shannon: Eerdmans/Irish University Press,
1972), 103; idem, 'Logos of the Fourth Gospel and Memra of the Palestinian Targum (Ex.
12.42),' ET 79 (1968), 116.

[33] G. F. Moore, 'Intermediaries in Jewish Theology,' HTR 15 (1922), 41-85; P. Vermes,
'Buber's Understanding of the Divine Name related to Bible, Targum and Midrash,' JJS 24
(1973), 147-166; R. Hayward, 'The Memra of YHWH and the Development of Its Use in
Targum Neofiti 1,' JJS 25 (1974), 412-418; idem, 'Memra and Shekhina: A Short Note,' JJS
31 (1981), 210-213.

[34] D. Munoz, Gloria de la Shekina en los Targumim del Pentateuco (Madrid: Consejo
Superior de Investigaciones Científicas. Instituto "Francisco Suarez", 1977), 525-527; M.
McNamara (ed.), Targum Neofiti 1: Genesis (The Aramaic Bible; Wilmington: Michael
Glazier, 1992), 37-38.

expanded biblical (prophetic and creational) word motif,[35] which may be associated with the Johannine Logos.[36]

1.3 New Approaches and Plan of Action

After the refutation of Bultmann's hypothesis, scholars' concerns have shifted to the Jewish wisdom tradition and the exegetical (Rabbinic and Targumic and Philonic) traditions of the Genesis creation account. In general, the former focuses on the personified figure of wisdom (originated from Prov 8:22-31) and its exposition tends to ignore the context of the Genesis creation account which is prominent in John 1:1-5. As for the latter investigation, only a few attempts have so far been made on the early Jewish literature which is generally dated between the 2nd century BC and the 1st century AD. Therefore, our thesis will focus on these sources, with the following new approaches.

First of all, our thesis will deal with *the creation accounts* of these sources and investigate mainly *the theological functions* of the Genesis creation account in each literary and thematic context. Since previous scholarship has searched for figure equivalent to the personified Logos, scholars have easily ignored the context in which the Genesis creation account is the focus. Secondly, the classification of the creation accounts will be made in accordance with the way that they are treated in each work of piece of literature (i.e. narrative and descriptive accounts and brief references to creation). This classification attempts to avoid an artificial division in our Jewish sources (e.g. the division between wisdom and apocalyptic literature, or between the so-called Pseudepigrapha and the Dead Sea Scrolls). Thirdly, our thesis will consider the aspect of how the OT or the biblical traditions were understood by a contemporary Jewish reader or one familiar with Jewish literature.[37] Fourthly, several creation motifs (such as light and life), as well as divine attributes (esp. the divine word and wisdom), will be examined in accordance with the theological functions of the Genesis creation account.[38] We cannot treat these Jewish texts as sources the NT writers used, but we can see them

---

[35] Cf. 4 Ezra 6:38, 43; 2 Bar 14:17; 21:4, 7; 48:2, 8; 54:1, 3; 56:4.

[36] Cf. C. Evans, *Word and Glory: on the Exegetical and Theological Background of John's Prologue* (JSNTSup 89; Sheffield: Sheffield Academic Press, 1993), 114-121.

[37] R. Bauckham, *Jesus and the Identity of God* (forth-coming, 2001).

[38] I am grateful to Professor R. Bauckham for sharing these points of view at the first stage of my work. In his forth-coming work, *Jesus and the identity of God* (provisional title), he has launched a hypothesis that John 1:1-5 is a retelling or interpretation of the beginning of the Genesis creation narrative (Gen 1:1-4), and that it belongs to a recognizable genre of Jewish retellings of the scriptural account of creation.

as evidence of the way that the Scriptures were read in the first century, with which NT writers were familiar.[39]

The plan of Part I (chs. 2-5) is to explore the Jewish exposition of the Genesis creation account (ca. 2nd century BC to 1st century AD), and to observe how the Jewish readers in our period understood the Genesis creation account in their theological context. In this part, the narrative accounts of creation (Chapter 2), the descriptive accounts of creation (Chapter 3), and the brief references to creation (Chapter 4) will be investigated. After the summary for Part 1 (Chapter 5), Philo's cosmogonic account will be considered (as an Excursus to Part I). The analysis takes its point of departure from literary considerations on these points: (1) the context in which the creation account appears and the main concern of the creation accounts; (2) a reconstruction of the text (if it is needed); and (3) the influence of key passages from the OT. Thematic (more theological) considerations will follow. The texts which will be examined in Part I are as follows: (1) *the narrative accounts of creation:* Jub 2:1-16; 2 En chs. 24-33; 4 Ezra 6:38-54; SibOr 1:5-35; 3:8-25; frag. 3; Ant 1:27-36; 1QM 10:8-18; 1QH[a] 9:7-20; 4Q381 frag. 1 1-12; (2) *the descriptive accounts of creation::* 1 En 69:16-25; 2 En chs. 47-48; 65-66; 4 Ezra 3:3-4; 6:1-6; 2 Bar 14:15-19; 21:4-8; 48:2-10; 54:1-3, 13; ApAbr 21:1-22:2; LAB 15:5-6; JosAsen 8:10-11; 12:1-2; Sir 16:24-17:14; 39:12-35; 42:15-43:33; 1QS 3:13-4:1; 4Q392 frags. 1-9; 4Q422 frag. 1 1-13; 4Q504 frag. 8 4-10; 11QPs[a] 26:9-15; (3) *brief references to creation::* Jub 12:4, 26; LAB 60:2-3; ApAbr 7:10-11; 9:3, 9; LadJac 2:10-14, 20; PrMan 1:2-3; Wisd 7:22; 8:5; 9:1-2, 9; 1 Bar 3:32-38; Sir 33:7-15.

Part II (chs. 6-9) attempts to explore the literary and thematic analyses of the Johannine prologue in the light of our research results of early Jewish creation accounts (Part I, chs. 2-5). First of all, Chapter 6 will briefly assess the recent surveys of both source (diachronic) and structural (synchronic) analyses of the prologue, and will propose a new structural understanding which will be the basis for later thematic analysis. Chapter 7 will examine the literary and thematic correspondences between John 1:1-5 and the Genesis creation account, and will argue that the Genesis creation account is alluded to in the first part of the Johannine prologue. While showing that these allusions to the Genesis creation account in John 1:1-5 have relevance to the early Jewish exegetical tradition, this chapter will suggest how the Genesis creation account functions to develop Christology in the Johannine prologue. Chapter 8 will show that several key christological motifs in the Johannine prologue (which are associated with the descriptions of 'the divine identity' and 'the role' of the Son [Logos]) are expanded in the rest of the Fourth Gospel.

---

[39] R. Bauckham, 'The Relevance of Extra-Canonical Jewish Texts to New Testament Study,' in J. Green (ed.), *Hearing the New Testament: Strategies for Interpretation* (Grand Rapids: Eerdmans, 1995), 95.

1.4 Limitations of this Investigation

The following investigation is not an attempt to study all the possible sources (from the Mediterranean world), but to focus on the creation accounts in Jewish literature which are generally considered to have been written around the Second Temple period (esp. 2nd century BC to 1st century AD). Some of the so-called OT Pseudepigrapha with which our thesis will deal are of uncertain date, but we will accept a general scholarly consensus that they preserve early Jewish traditions. Moreover, since most of the Pseudepigrapha were discovered outside Palestine, their original languages are uncertain. We thereby notice our limitations in accessing the original meanings, but we will make every effort to understand them in a preserved language. The fuller study of the textual criticism, as well as the date issue, lie outside the scope of this thesis.

As the title of the thesis has suggested, our study has deliberately been restricted to the understanding of the Johannine prologue in the light of the early Jewish exegetical traditions of the Genesis creation accounts. Therefore, our thesis will not include thorough discussions on all questions of the Johannine prologue, or its relation to the biblical traditions (OT and NT). In addition, the exposition of the Johannine prologue will be structured by a thematic analysis in accordance with our main theological concern (i.e. the Johannine Christology in the prologue).

Part I

Early Jewish Creation Accounts
(ca. 2nd Century BC to 1st Century AD)

Chapter 2

Narrative Accounts of Creation

This chapter focuses on the narrative accounts of creation in early Jewish Literature (ca. the 2nd century BC to the 1st century AD). It is a long retelling of the Genesis creation account, and generally follows the narrative order of Gen chs. 1-2; whereas, some accounts reorder the narrative in accordance with their concern and subject. Poetic narrative is also included in this category. Our analysis takes its point of departure from literary considerations on these points: (1) the context in which the creation account appears and the main concern of the creation account; (2) a reconstruction of the text (if it is needed); (3) the relation to the Genesis creation account (and influence of key passages from the OT). Thematic (a more theological) consideration will follow. The following texts will be examined: Jub 2:1-16; 2 En chs. 24-33; 4 Ezra 6:38-54; SibOr 1:5-35; 3:8-25; frag. 3; Ant 1:27-36; 1QM 10:8-18; 1QH^a 9:7-20; 4Q381 frag. 1 1-12.

2.1 The Book of Jubilees 2:1-16

2.1.1 Literary Considerations

Context and Main Concern

The prologue of Jubilees states, 'these are the words regarding "the divisions of the times of the law" (*'ūfālē măwā'ēlāt hĕg*) and of the testimony, of the events (*lăgbĕr*) of the years, of the weeks of their Jubilees throughout all the years of eternity.'[1] The author of Jubilees retells Israelite history which is recorded in the OT from Gen ch. 1 to Exod ch. 14, putting the date in each episode in accordance with the Solar calendar (7 day periods) and Jubilee years (49 year periods), in order to demonstrate how history is governed by the times of the laws.

The retelling of the Bible begins with the Genesis creation account (Jub 2:2-16), which is followed by exegetical supplements on the Sabbath law (Jub

---

[1] Similar expression is repeated in Jub 1:4. Our thesis mostly refers to VanderKam's English Translation (*The Book of Jubilees* [CSCO 88; Louvain: Peeters, 1989]), consulting VanderKam's Ethiopic edition (*The Book of Jubilees: A Critical Text* [CSCO 87; Louvain: Peeters, 1989]).

2:17-33) related to the creation account. The utterance of the angel who was appointed to tell the story of creation to Moses makes clear the purpose for the reference to the Genesis creation accounts.

> Write all the words about the creation (*fĕṭrăt*) - how *in six days* the Lord God *completed* (*fäṣăm*) all his works, all that he had created (*zăftăr*), and *rested* (*wă'äsnbăt*) *on the seventh day*. He *sanctified* (*wăkdsā*) it for all ages, and set it (as) a sign (*tĕ'ĕmrĕt*) for all his works (Jub 2:1).

This utterance alludes to the biblical creation account of Exod 20:11 and Gen 2:2-3 as follows:

> For *in six days* the Lord *made* (עשה) heaven and earth, the sea, and all that is in them but *rested* (וינח) *on the seventh day*; therefore the Lord *blessed* the Sabbath day and *consecrated* (ויקדשהו) it (Exod 20:11).

> And on the seventh day God *finished* the work that he had done, and he *rested* (וישבת) *on the seventh day* from all the work that he had done (Gen 2:2).

The focus is clearly on the sabbath law: i.e. God kept the first sabbath (*wă'äsnbăt*: cf. שבת) after all his work of creation, sanctified (*wăkdsā*: cf. קדש) it, and made it 'a sign' (*tĕ'ĕmrĕt*: cf. אות) for all his works. As for the term 'sign,' it may be related to the account of the creation of luminaries in Gen 1:14: 'let them (luminaries) be for signs (לאתת) and for seasons and for days and years.'

It is interesting that the Book of Jubilees states that God created a sign (i.e. luminaries) by which they might keep the Sabbath (Jub 2:21); moreover, it maintains that the Creator of all created (*zăftăr*: cf. Jub 2:1) the Sabbath as well (Jub 2:32). The Sabbath is considered to be 'the first law' (*wăḥĕg kădămī*: והתורה הראש[ונה] [4Q216 5:17]) (Jub 2:24), and 'the eternal law (*ḥĕg zăl'ălăm*) for their (Israelites) generations' (Jub 2:33). The author also argues that the solar calendar (365 days) is sacred, and that it governs the universe and human history, so that the Israelites are encouraged to be more conscious of this calendar, not to transgress it even unconsciously (Jub 6:32-33).

In the first chapter, the Book of Jubilees retells the story of Moses in Mount Sinai (cf. Exod 24:18), in which God predicts the ultimate restoration of his people. In this revelation God told Moses that what God would make known to him was concerning what is first (*zăkdămī*) and what is last (*wăzdăḥăr*) and what is to come (*wăzyĕmṣē'*) during all the divisions of time (Jub 1:26). It is also said, 'from [the time of creation until]² the day of the

---

² Our Ethiopic text does not have this section; however, we follow M. Stone's restoration ('Apocryphal Notes and Reading,' IOS 1 [1971], 125).

new creation (*fĕṭrăt hădās*) (Jub 1:29).[3] That is to say, the author of Jubilees argues that the restoration (as a new creation) will occur in accordance with the division of the times, a strict heavenly timetable (Jub 1:19). In this sense, the creation account of Jubilees might be associated with the former and later eschatological discussions.

Influence of Key Passages from the OT

The creation account of Jub 2:2-16 is mostly based on the Genesis creation account. However, the author of Jubilees picks up twenty two objects which were made in the six days, particularly counting seven objects (heaven, earth, water, all of the spirits, abysses,[4] darkness [evening[5]], light [dawn and daylight]) which were created on the first day.[6]

Day	Jubilees	Genesis (the OT)
1st	heaven, earth, water, Spirits, abysses, darkness, light	heaven, earth, light; light was separated from darkness
2nd	firmament	firmament
3rd	the separation of the water from dry land, sea, rivers, ponds, dew, seed, trees, and garden of Eden	dry land, seed, trees
4th	the sun, the moon, stars	the greater light, the lesser light,[7] stars
5th	great sea monsters, fish, birds	great sea monsters, fish, birds
6th	beasts of the earth, cattle, humankind	beasts of the earth, cattle, humankind

---

[3] Charles suggests that 'new' is inserted wrongly and it is possibly an interpolation, or a mistake of ὡς for ἕως; translate 'until.' VanderKam also comments, 'This relocation of "until" is now found in mss 21 35 38[c] 42[c] 58, but it appears to be a scribal attempt to solve the very problem that Charles was discussing.' However, this idea appears in Jub 1:26-28.

[4] VanderKam (*Jubilees*, 8) comments that the Ethiopic term lacks the accusative ending, and suggests the reading, 'There were also the depths.' However, it is apparent that 'abysses' is counted as created object. The Greek and Syriac versions take the accusative ending.

[5] 'Night' is restored from the Greek text of Ephiphanius in both translations (e.g. Wintermute [OTP II, 55] and Charles [APOT II, 14]).

[6] The narrative begins with the phrase, 'For on the first day (*bă'ĕlt ḳdămīt*) he created the heavens, which are above, and the earth' (Jub 2:2). The Book of Jubilees may understand the first word of Genesis, בְּרֵאשִׁית (Gen 1:1), as 'the first day (*bă'ĕlt ḳdămīt*).'

[7] J. van Ruiten (*Primaeval History Interpreted: The Rewriting of Genesis 1-11 in the book of Jubilees* [JTSSup 66; Leiden: Brill, 2000], 38 and 70) comments that the author of Jubilees uses the words 'sun' and 'moon' instead of 'the greater light' (Gen 1:16c) and 'the lesser light' (Gen 1:16d), because of special attention to the sun (i.e. solar calendar).

This is because he wants to extract the special number 'seven' (Jub 2:3) and 'twenty two' (Jub 2:16) from this order of creation. The former is the same as the number of days in one week, whereas the latter is the same as the number of chief men from Adam until Jacob (Jub 2:23).[8]

The book of Jubilees supplements the story of the creation of the Spirit (or the angels).[9] The book seems to understand the term רוח in Gen 1:2 as a spirit or an angel in order to solve the problem that the angels are on the scene at very early stages in Genesis (e.g. Gen 1:26; 3:22-24).[10] It is also possible that the author of Jubilees regards the plural in נעשה אדם בצלמנו כדמותנו (Gen 1:26) and כאחד ממנו (Gen 3:22) as an expression of the coexistence of the angels. This is why the 'we' section begins from the first day of creation (Jub 2:3): the angels blessed the creation work of the Lord (Jub 2:3); they kept the Sabbath with the people (Jub 2:21); they brought to Adam all of the living things so that Adam named all of them (Jub 3:1); they gave Adam work and taught him how to do everything which was appropriate for tilling (Jub 3:15); and the Lord told them what God wanted them to do (Jub 2:19; 3:4). J. van Ruiten proposes a possible influence from Job 38:7, where the angels praise God's work of creation.[11] Therefore the description of the creation of angels may have been influenced by an interpretation of Gen 1:2 and the plural sections in Genesis.[12]

2.1.2 Thematic Considerations

God's Utterance, Knowledge, and Hands in Creation

First of all, the motif of creation by God's utterance appears in Jub 2:5-6: 'On the third day He (God) did as He said to the waters. . . , and the water did so, as He told them.' This picture exhibits how the creatures obey God's creative command. This description of the work of creation is common in the biblical and Jewish creation accounts.[13] The motif of the creative word appears in Jub 12:4 and 26.[14]

---

[8] Charles (APOT II, 15) thought that there was a lacuna after Jub 2:22, 'Restored text = "as there were twenty-two letters and twenty-two sacred books and twenty-two heads of mankind from Adam to Jacob, so there were made twenty-two kinds of work."'

[9] In 4Q216 5, the list of angels can be recognized as the same as Ethiopic edition.

[10] VanderKam, 'Biblical Interpretation,' 118-119.

[11] J. van Ruiten, *Primaeval History*, 26 and 70.

[12] Cf. 1 En 60:19-22; 75:3; cf. 2 En 19:3-5.

[13] E.g. Pss 33:6-8; 89:11; 104:1-30; 135:7; 136:5-9; Job 36:22-38:38; Isa 40:28; 42:5; 44:24; 45:7; 48:12-13; Jer 10:12-13; Jub 12:4; SibOr bks. 1, 3, frag. 3; ApAbr 9:2; Wisd ch. 9; 1 Bar chs. 3-4; 2 En chs. 47-48, 65-66; 4Q176; 4Q381; 4Q392; 4Q403; 11QPsAp^a 2-3; 11QPs^a 24.

[14] See § 4.1.2 and § 4.2.2.

Secondly, Jub 2:2 hints at the wisdom motif, when it states that God prepared the depths, darkness and light, dawn and evening, 'through the knowledge of his mind (*bă'ă'ĕmrō lĕb*)' (Jub 2:2). The motif of God's knowledge seems to be associated with the description of his wonderful design or plan through which a wonderful contrast (darkness and light, dawn and evening) was made (Jub 2:3), as well as a meaning number (seven) of the work of creation on the first day (Jub 2:3).

As for the connection to Jewish sapiential tradition, the similarities between 4Q216 (4QJub[a]) 5:10 (which corresponds to Jub 2:2-3) and 11QPs[a] 26:11-12 are suggested.[15]

4Q216(4QJub[a]) 5:10 [16]	11QPs[a] 26:11-12 [17]
מאפלה ושחר ונ]אור וערב אשר הכין בד]עתו אז ראינו מעשיו ונברכהן]	מבדיל אור מאפלה שחר הכין בדעת לבו אז ראו כול מלאכיו וירננו
Darkness, dawn, [light, and evening which he prepared by] his [know]ledge. (cf. 'of his heart,' in Ethiopic text) Then we (angels) saw his works and we [blessed him]	Separating light from deep darkness he prepared the dawn by the knowledge of his mind When all his angels had witnessed it,

Both creation accounts mention that the Lord separates light from darkness through the knowledge of his heart. The plural 'we' indicates the plural existence of 'the angels' in Jub 2:3, so that it is also parallel to 'all his angels' in 11QPs[a] 26:11-12. Moreover, it is obvious that 'wisdom' is the focus in 11QPs[a] 26:11-15:

ברוך עושה ארץ בכוחו	Blessed be he who makes the earth by his power
מכין תבל בחוכמתו	established the world *by his wisdom*
בתבונתו נטה שמים	By his understanding he stretched out the heavens
ויוצא [רוח] מאו[צרותיו]	and brought forth [wind] from his st[orehouses].

In 11QPs[a] 26:12, the angels praise the Lord for his knowledge that was shown to them through his work of creation, which corresponds to the praise of the angels in Jub 2:3. Thus, there seems to have been a common tradition behind Jub 2:2-3 and 11QPs[a] 26:10-15, or a possible dependence of one on the other.

Thirdly, God's hand is also mentioned as a metaphor (or the divine attribute) to indicate the mighty power of God: 'these were made by his hands' (Jub 2:11; cf. 12:19). This idea appears in biblical creation accounts

---

[15] P. W. Skehan, 'Jubilees and the Qumran Psalter,' *CBQ* 37 (1975), 343-47.

[16] VanderKam, 'Jubilees,' in *Qumran Cave 4* (DJD 13), 13.

[17] J. A. Sanders (DJD 4), 89-90.

(Isa 45:12; Job 10:8; Pss 95:5; 119:73).[18] The implication of God's hands as his mighty power (Jub 2:11) may be associated with the context which tells of the creation of legendary creatures, 'the great sea monsters.'

In short, the creation account of Jubilees uses several images (God's utterance, knowledge, and his hands), and each imagery seems to exhibit a particular sense or an aspect of the identity of God: i.e 'the hands of God' are good to show God's mighty power; 'knowledge' is used to express the magnificence of his wonderful plan; and the word of God depicts his sovereign power in the work of creation.

Creation and Eschatology

God revealed to Moses the secrets of both the creation and the eschatological events (Jub 1:4, 26, 29), as previously observed. The author of Jubilees refers to the eschatological passages from the OT, and puts them into the discourse (between God and Moses) and the narrative.

JUBILEES	SCRIPTURES
I. 1st Discourse (1:15-18)	
Seeking the Lord with all heart and soul (15)	Deut 4:29 (cf. Deut 30:10; 1 Chr 28:9; Jer 29:13)
Planting[19] Israel in Jerusalem (16)	Jer 32:41 (cf. Jer 24:6; 31:28)
Blessing (16)	Zech 8:13
Restoration of National Dignity (16)	Deut 28:13
God's Dwelling in New Temple and New Covenant (God & People) (17)	Ezek 37:26-28 (cf. Jer 24:7)
Everlasting Grace for Israel (18)	Deut 31:6 (cf. Ps 94:14)
II. 2nd Discourse (1:22-26)	
Creation[20] of New Spirit and Heart (20-21)	Ezek 11:19 (cf. Ezek 36:26; Jer 24:7; 32:39)
Circumcision of Heart (23)	Ezek 11:19
New Covenant (Father & Sons) (25)	Cf. Jer 3:19; 31:9; Deut 14:1; 32:6.
God's Descent and Dwelling in His People (26)	Ezek 43:7, 9 (Zech 2:11; 8:3)

---

[18] The imagery of 'God's hands' is employed elsewhere in the OT to show the mighty power of God (Exod 15:17; Deut 3:24; 4:34; 6:21; 7:8, 19; 9:26; 11:2; 26:8; 1 Kgs 8:42; 2 Chr 6:32; Pss 20:6; 89:13; Isa 5:12; 62:8; Ezek 20:33,34).

[19] Wintermute (OTP II, 53) comments on the translation of 'transplant': 'The Ethiopic word means to "remove." It has the sense of moving away from one's home and is hardly suitable in this context.'

[20] The Ethiopic edition renders, 'to create,' rather than 'to give.' This rendering may come from Ps 51:10 (12 [MT]), and it is possible that the author may have wanted to express it in a more eschatological sense. The words 'new creation' occur in Jub 1:29.

III. Narrative (1:27-29)

New Temple (27)	Ezek 37:26
Theophany (28)	Zech 9:14 (cf. Zech 2:5;Isa 60:2)
God's Eternal Kingship and	Isa 24:23
Sanctification of Jerusalem (28)	
New Creation (29)	Isa 65:17 (cf. Jer 5:21)
New Creation of Lights (29)	Isa 30:26 (cf. Isa 58:8, 10-12;
	60:1-3, 19-21)

It is interesting that three topics (creation of a new heart, new covenant, and new temple) are reiterated in the first (Jub 1:15-18) and second (Jub 1:22-26) sections in the same order, and these topics also appear in the narrative section (Jub 1:27-29). The author's concern is directed, not only to the past, but also to the future, i.e. 'from the first creation until the eschaton' (Jub 1:27, 29). It should be noted that the eschatological event is regarded as the renewal of creation, which is associated with the rebuilding of the Jerusalem Temple, sanctification of Jerusalem, theophany, and new creation of light(s) (cf. Ezek 37:26, Isa 30:26 and 65:17).

As has already been argued, the author of Jubilees states that the restoration will occur according to the division of the times, a strict heavenly timetable (cf. Jub 1:19). Although the eschatological account does not reach the full number of jubilees, and it closes with the narrative of the Sinai event (forty-nine jubilees in Jub 50:1-13), he may also have looked further.

Lights: A Symbol of New Creation

The Book of Jubilees states the role of 'lights' in Jub 2:8-10 as follows:

to give light on the earth (8a)
to rule over the day and the night (8b)
to divide light from darkness (8c)
to be a sign for days, Sabbaths, months, feasts (days), years, Sabbaths of years,
    jubilees, and for all of the (appointed) times of the years (9)
to divide the light from the darkness (10)
to prosper everything which sprouts and grows upon the earth (10)

'To prosper everything upon the earth' (Jub 2:10, 12) is an interpretation of Gen 1:15 and 16: 'to give light upon the earth.' In Gen 1:14-15, there are three divine commands (with היה saying): 'Let there be lights'; 'Let them be for signs'; and 'Let them be light upon the earth.' The author of Jubilees may understand the first command 'Let there be lights' as the creation of lights, and the second and third as an appointment of roles to the lights: the first role as the basis for the covenant, and the second as God's blessing to his creatures.[21] The latter role is referred to in Moses' prayer (Jub 1:29):

---

[21] The term, 'to prosper' (Jub 2:10, 12; cf. צלח in Hebrew), is often used as God's blessing in the OT (e.g. Gen 24:40, 42, 56; 39:2, 3, 23).

And all of *the lights* will be renewed for *healing* and peace and blessing for all of *the elect of Israel* and in order that it might be thus from that day and unto all the days of the earth (Jub 1:29).

This passage alludes to Isa 30:26.

The light of the moon will be like the light of the sun, and the light of the sun will be sevenfold, like the light of seven days, on the day when the Lord *binds up the injuries* of *his people*, and *heals* the wounds inflicted by his blow.

The author of the Book of Jubilees summarizes the first section of Isa 30:26 as 'all of the lights will be renewed,' and takes the last temporal clause as the purpose clause for the renewal of the lights, adding the blessing motif which may come from author's exegesis of Gen 1:15 and 16.

In the next paragraph, the author discusses the law of 'the Sabbath' again in relation to the work of creation (Jub 2:17-33), and argues that God created a sign by which they (the Israelites) ought to keep the Sabbath on the seventh day (Jub 2:21a).[22] In other words, God created lights (luminaries) as a sign for the times of the law (including the Sabbath) so that the Israelites would be separated from the nations to be blessed by the Creator. Furthermore, the author expects these lights to be recreated in the eschatological time, as a symbol of the new creation.

2.2 2 (Slavonic Apocalypse of) Enoch chs. 24-33

2.2.1 Literary Considerations

Context and Main Concern

After the narrative of Enoch's heavenly journey (chs. 1-22), Enoch was told the great secrets,[23] which were the accounts of creation (chs. 24-33) and of the eschatological event. The motif of creation is associated with eschatology in 2 Enoch: 'I (Enoch) have been sent today to you (his antecedent) . . . whatever has been and whatever is now and whatever will be until the day of judgment' (39:5); 'I (Enoch) know everything, for either from the lips of the Lord or else my eyes have seen from the beginning even to the end, and from the end to the recommencement' (2 En 40:1). The appeal to the divine plan which was thought up before creation (23:5; 24:5; 25:3) enforces the certainty of the coming eschatological judgment.

---

[22] The OT also states that the Sabbath was given to Israel as a sign (Exod 31:13; Ezek 20:12, 20), and it separates Israel from all the nations (1 Kgs 8:53).

[23] 2 En 23:1; 24:1.

The creation account in a 'quasi-scientific manner'[24] is regarded as one part of 'the great secrets of God' (24:1[J]), in which the people expected to learn the divine order.   Moreover, the creation accounts of 2 En chs. 24-33 emphasize that God is the sole ruler (33:7) in the universe, and that there is no other God except himself (33:8; cf. 2:1; 10:6). The people are encouraged to learn from this fact, so that they might not perish in the future flood which God will create in their generation (33:12). The final judgment is prepared (34:3) because they are inclined to be idol worshippers and sodomite fornicators (33:12), so that they reject God's commandments (34:1). Thus, the creation account is employed in a sapiential framework to teach the way of life.

Influence of Key Passages from the OT

2 En chs. 24-33 is based on the creation narrative of Genesis (as well as its order), while it adds the account of the creation of the throne of God (2 En 25:4), the creation of the angels (2 En 29:3), and the creation of Paradise which was created as the garden of Eden on the third day (2 En 30:1).

Day	2 Enoch	Genesis (the OT)
1st	light, darkness, throne, water, earth	heaven, earth, light; light was separated from darkness
2nd	heavens, angels[25]	firmament, division of waters
3rd	trees, fruits, mountains, seed, Paradise (Garden)	dry land, seed, trees
4th	sun, moon, stars	sun, moon, stars
5th	fish, birds, reptile	great sea monsters, fish, birds
6th	humankind	beasts of the earth, cattle, humankind

---

[24] F. I. Andersen (OTP I, 91).

[25] God created Angels (or the bodiless armies, or ten myriad angels) from the fire; the fire is from the rock. Andersen (OTP I) comments that 'fire' is not an element in Gen ch. 1, and that the derivation of fire from the rock does not accord with other Cannanite (e.g. the Chaldean oracles) nor with the Greek belief. The shorter recention (A) reads, 'From the rock I cut off a great fire, and [from] the fire I created all the armies of the bodiless ones, and all the armies of the stars and cherubim and seraphim and ophanim, and all these from the fire I cut out.' It is interesting that 'the armies of the stars' are paralleled with Hebrew names of the angels.

2.2.2 Thematic Considerations

God's Command and the Word

Non-biblical materials can be seen in the creation accounts of the heavens and the earth: i.e. the cosmogonic figures, Adoil[26] (25:1-2) and Arkhas[27] (25:5-26:3), are mentioned as the basic elements which produce the heavens and the earth. Adoil may be equivalent to 'the age of creation' (вѣка тварнаго: *věka tvarnago*) of 2 En 65:1 [A].[28] It is established before all things existed, and before all creation came out (65:1 [A]).

Developing non-biblical materials, however, the creation account in 2 Enoch chs. 24-33 describes how God founded the heavens and the earth by his command. Throughout the account, 2 Enoch follows the formula of the Genesis creation account, 'God commanded (< повелѣти: *povelěti*) . . ., "Let . . .," and . . . came out' (25:1; 26:1, 3; 27:1, 2; 28:1; 30:1, 2, 7, 8). God commanded the lowest things (преисподинх: *preicpodinik*) to let one of the invisible things (невидимых: *nevidimĭk*) descend, and Adoil did. He had a great age (or light)[29] in his belly, from which the great age (вѣка велкаго: *věka velikago*)[30] came out (25:1-3). God called again to let one of the invisible things (невидимых: *nevidimĭk*) come out solid and visible (видимо: *vidimo*); Arukhas did and became an age (вѣкъ: *věkŭ*) and darkness (25:5-26:3). The former age, which came out from Adoil, became the foundation (шснование: *wsnovanie*) for the highest things; the latter, which came out from Arukhas, became the foundation for the lowest things. The water was made by the combination of them both (27:1-3), and was placed between the light and the darkness (27:3-4). Both Adoil and Arkhas are personified and function as those who obey the command of God; however they are not described as the agents, but rather as the objects which are transformed and created.

---

[26] See C. Böttrich's comments on Adoil (*Apokalypsen: Das slavische Henochbuch* [JSHRZ V/7; Gütersloher Verlagshaus, 1995]): Charles suggested יד אל (God's hand); Loisy suggested האור (the Light); Gry, אוראל (the Light of God) ; Fischer, עדואל (God of eternity).

[27] See Böttrich's comments on Arkhas (JSHRZ 5/7): Charles, רקיע (sky) or ἀρχή; Loisy, הארץ (the earth).

[28] The division of the Texts, [A] and [J], is by Charles: [A] is the shorter, and [J] is the longer recension. Our thesis uses Vaillant edition for [A] (*Le Livre des Secrets D' Hénoch* [Paris: Institut D' 'Etudes Slaves: Texte Slave et Traduction Française, 1952]), and Sokolov edition for [J] (*Slavyanskaya kniga Enoha Pravednage: Tekst', latinskij perevod i izsledovanie* [Moscow: The Inperial Society for Russian History and Antiquities, 1910]).

[29] MSS A, U, B, Chr read *věka velikago*, 'great age'; V, N, B[2] read *kamyka prěvelikaago*, 'very large stone'; J, P, R read *světa*, 'light.' It seems possible that the great age which came out from Adoil is related to the light imagery and the great age which came out from Arukhas is related to the darkness imagery. So that 'the great age' may have been considered to be 'light' in several MSS.

[30] Charles suggests that 'the age' should refer to the heavenly world (APOT II, 445).

In the epilogue of the creation account, it is emphasized that God is the sole Creator, and that there is no adviser and no successor to his creation (нѣст свѣтника ни слѣдника: *nĕst svĕtnika ni slĕdnika*) (33:4 [J], [A]). In the same context, God's wisdom and his word are mentioned as the agents of creation: 'My thought (мысль) is without change; My wisdom (мѫдрость) is my adviser and my agent (lit. дѣло: deed) is my word (слово)' (33:4 [J], [A]).[31] It should be noted that wisdom is summoned as an agent for the creation of man: 'I commanded my wisdom to create man (повекъх моеи премоудрости чловѣка: *povekŭx moei premudrosti stvoriti člověka*) (30:8 [J], [A]). This may be because several arrangements (i.e. the composition of the seven invisible and other seven visible substances) were required to create human beings (30:8-9 [J]).

Light and Darkness

In the creation account, light is not depicted as a creational product, but as the thing which is pre-existent.[32]　　Before any visible things had come into existence, and light (свѣт: *svĕt*) had not yet opened up, God existed in the midst of light (свѣта: *svĕta*) (24:4 [A]; 25:3).[33] As for the creation of light, it was given as the result of the disintegration of Adoil who had a great age (or light)[34] in his belly (25:1), and it became the foundation of the highest things (вышним: *vĭiwnim*) (25:4b), which is called, 'the light' (свѣта: *svĕta*) (25:5). Light is placed highest over all creation (25:5), and it is separated from darkness, the lowest of things (долнимь: *dolnimĭ*) (27:4). The creation of the luminaries on the fourth day is stated in accordance with the narrative order of the Genesis creation account (2 En 30:1-6). The light is also depicted as a symbol of paradise (65:10), which is never darkened (31:2), whereas darkness is described as a symbol of judgment (34:3).

Darkness is pre-existent at the beginning of creation (24:5), and it is the foundation of the lowest things (26:3). There is a division between light and darkness (27:4), and both function as the primary elements for the composition of the work of creation which follow (27:1).

Life as a Symbol of Paradise

2 Enoch explains how death and life came to human beings from various points of view. Firstly, Adam was created out of the seven components (earth, the sun, the bottomless sea, stone, the mobility of angels and clouds, grass of the earth, and spirit and wind), and from the invisible and visible

---

[31] Cf. 1 En 14:23; Wisd 9:4, 10.

[32] The idea that the visible things appear from the invisible things may come from Platonic cosmological understanding.

[33] Cf. 4Q392 frag. 1 4-7.

[34] Cf. the above footnote (no. 27).

substances (30:10a). They were also given seven properties (hearing, sight, smell, touch, taste, endurance, and sweetness) (30:8-9). The nature of both death and life came from the mixture of both invisible and visible substances (30:10b). Secondly, like biblical and Jewish traditional understanding, 2 Enoch argues that God gave Adam free will and pointed out to him the two ways, namely light and darkness (30:15). However, Adam was inclined to the latter, so that sin and death became unavoidable (30:16). Moreover, 2 Enoch states that death was brought to Adam through his wife (30:17). It is an expanded interpretation of Gen 3:6.

As for the life motif, Enoch seems to focus on life as an eschatological blessing. Enoch saw the paradise of Eden at the 3rd heaven (42:3), and the righteous is said to have been given joy and happiness with eternal light and life (42:6). That is to say, life, as well as light, is depicted as one of the symbols of Paradise.

New Revelation

God spoke with Enoch face to face (23:6). Enoch is allowed to see God's face (22:1) and to listen to his voice coming from his very mouth (22:2, 5). Enoch is guided to sit at the left side of God (24:1), and God himself wanted to speak to Enoch (24:2). The secrets, which God explained, were never revealed to his angels (24:3). Enoch told the message from God to his sons after his descent by saying;

> I have been sent from the lips (шт оустъ: *wt ustŭ*) of the Lord to you, . . .
> It is not from my own lips, . . . but from the lips of the Lord who has sent me to you. . .
>
> I have heard (the words) from the fiery lips (шт оустъ: *wt ustŭ*) of the Lord . . .
> I am one who has seen the face (лице: *live*) of the Lord . . .
> I have gazed into the eyes of the Lord . . .
> I have seen the right hand of the Lord . . .
> I have seen the extent of the Lord . . .
> I have heard the words (глаголы: *glagoľii*) of the Lord (2 Enoch 39:1-6 [A])

It is emphasized that Enoch admonished his children in all things, which his eyes had seen from the beginning even to the end (40:1), truthfully from the lips of the Lord, just as he saw them and heard them and wrote them down (39:8). 2 Enoch seems to mention that the revelation of Enoch is superior to the revelation of Moses (cf. Ex 33:20).

Wisdom as God's Thought (or Thought-Up Plan)

Before anything existed at all, God thought up the idea of establishing a foundation (24:5). The theme, that there was a thought-out plan before all creation, is repeated throughout this creation account.

> It (the great age) revealed all the creation which I *had thought up* (ломыслп: *lomïisli*) to create (25:3 [J]).

> Cf. [A]: It carried all the creation which I *had wished* (хотѣх: *xotêx*) to create.

> By my *wisdom* (прѣмѫдростіѧ: *prĕmôdrostia*) all these things I *planned* to accomplish (33:3 [J]).

> Cf. [A]: By my supreme *wisdom* (премоыдростию: *premudrostju moeju*), I *have planned* (оухитрихъ: *uxitrixŭ*) it all.

> There is no adviser and no successor to my creation. . . My *thought* (мысль: *mïislï*) is without change. My *wisdom* (мѫдрость: *môdrostï*) is my adviser and my agent (lit. дѣло: deed) is my word (слово) (33:4 [J]).

> Cf. [A]: There is no counselor and no successor, . . . My unchanging *thought* (веслремѣнна мысль: *veslremĕnna mislï*) is (my) counselor, and my word (слово) is (my) agent (дѣло).

The idea that God had a plan before he took action can be seen in the Old Testament (e.g. Isa 40:13; 46:10; Ps 33:11), and this theme appears in several Jewish creation accounts as well (e.g. 4 Ezra 6:1-6; 7:70; 8:52; 2 Bar 14:17). It highlights that God's work is perfect, and that he rules history from beginning to end. Wisdom is considered the perfect thought of God (2 En 33:3), through which the work of creation was planned or designed, and realized by his word (2 En 33:4). It is interesting that both wisdom and the word function as the agents, and each takes its own part: i.e. to think up a perfect plan (by wisdom) and to realize this plan (by the word).[35]

2.3   4 (The Fourth Book of) Ezra 6:38-54

2.3.1 Literary Considerations

Context and Main Concern

4 Ezra can be divided into seven sections (I. 3:1-5;20; II. 5:21-6:34; III. 6:35-9:25; IV. 9:26-10:59; V. 11:1-12:51; VI. 13:1-58; and VII. 14:1-48),[36] based on its constituent literary units (the narrative introduction [i.e. 3:1-3; 5:21-22; 6:35-36; 9:26-28; 11:1a; 13:1; 14:1a]; dialogues with the angel [4:1-47; 5:31-6:16; 7:1-9:25], and visions or revelatory experiences [9:38-10:27a; 11:1-12:3a; 13:2-13a]). The main concern of 4 Ezra is the question why Israel

---

[35] In prophetic tradition, both roles are frequently assigned to the divine word (cf. Jer 11:8; 25:3-14; 28:6-9; 33:14, 15; 39:16; 44:29; Isa 24:3; 31:2; 45:23; 46:10; 48:3; 58:14).

[36] See T. Willett, *Eschatology in the Theodicies of 2 Baruch and 4 Ezra* (JSPSup 4; Sheffield: JSOT Press, 1989), 54-58.

should be handed over to the unrighteous, and why salvation should be delayed (4 Ezra 3:28-36; 5:28-30; 6:55-59). 4 Ezra deals with this question from the viewpoint of theodicy (3:3-26) and divine providence (or the divine time table) (5:41-49). 4 Ezra also provides a hope that salvation is at hand, beginning with several signs of the coming of the eschatological events (5:1-14), followed by the restoration of the human sinful heart [6:26-27], the coming of the Messiah, and the final Judgment (7:26-43; 8:51-54). In the latter part of 4 Ezra, several apocalyptic messages are also given: the new Jerusalem (9:38-10:59); the destruction of Rome (11:1-12:35); the Judgment by the Son of Man (13:1-53). The Book of 4 Ezra has been given as a restoration of the law which had been burned (after the fall of the Temple[37]) in order to give light to the people who dwelt in darkness.

The third section (4 Ezra 6:35-9:25) begins with a long narrative creation account (6:38-54). Its length may correspond to the weight of the following section: i.e. God promises Ezra, ahead of this account, to reveal greater things than before (4 Ezra 6:31). The first part of this section (6:35-7:25) functions as a prologue for the rest of the eschatological account. The author of 4 Ezra anticipates the God who alone has the authority over his creation from the beginning of the world until the end, and who assigned a part of his authority to the Israelites to complete his eschatological works immediately. Thus, the creation account is obviously associated with eschatological expectations.

Influence of Key Passages from the OT

4 Ezra understands בראשית in Gen 1:1 as 'the beginning of God's work of creation' (cf. 4 Ezra 6:38, *ab initio creaturae*).[38] 4 Ezra states that God's utterance was at the beginning, through which the heavens and the earth were created (esp. 4 Ezra 6:38).

4 Ezra is mostly based on the Genesis creation account as follows:

Day	4 Ezra	Genesis (the OT)
1st	heaven, earth; light was brought from God's treasuries	heaven, earth, light; light was separated from darkness
2nd	firmament, division of water	firmament, division of waters
3rd	separation of the water from dry land; fruit, flowers	dry land, seed, trees
4th	sun, moon, stars	sun, moon, stars
5th	great sea monsters, fish, birds	great sea monsters, fish, birds

---

[37] So long as Pseudonym pretends to be Ezra, the Temple means the First Temple; however, it clearly overlaps with the picture of the destruction of the Second Temple.

[38] Cf. 4 Ezra 6:1, *Initio terreni orbis*, 'In the beginning of the circle of the earth.'

6th	beasts of the earth, cattle, humankind	beasts of the earth, cattle, humankind

The idea, that the word comes from God's mouth and it immediately realizes God's plan or his will, alludes to Isa 48:3 and 55:11

Your word accomplished the work (4 Ezra 6:38)	So shall *my word* be, which goes out from my mouth, it shall by no means turn back in vain, until *it accomplishes* what I desire and makes succeed what I sent it (Isa 55:11).
Your word went forth, and *immediately*	They (the former things which I foretold long ago) *go out of my mouth*, and I made known them,
the work was done (4 Ezra 6:43).	and I accomplish *immediately*, and *they came to pass* (Isa 48:3).

In both 4 Ezra 6:38-43 and Isa 55:11 (and Isa 48:3), the word of God is personified and functions as an agent to accomplish the will or the plan of God. The idea that God accomplished his works at once with his word may allude to Isaiah (e.g. Isa 48:3, 12, 13; Isa 44:24-28; 45:7-8).

2.3.2 Thematic Considerations

Creation and New Creation of Israel

4 Ezra suggests that God put the divisions in the world: i.e. God commanded the spirit to divide and to make a division (*divideret et divisionem*) between the waters (4 Ezra 6:41); God preserved (*conservasti*) the six parts (of the waters) so that some of them might serve (*ministrantia*) before you (6:42); God preserved (*conservasti*) two living creatures, . . . you separated (*separasti*) the one from the other (6:49-50). This motif is possibly related to later arguments on the original status of Israel as the chosen people. 4 Ezra also refers to the role of Adam as an administrator of the rest of the creatures (6:46; 54). These two points are associated with the main question of why Israel can not possess their world as an inheritance (6:59) although this world was originally created for them (6:55).

Moreover, 4 Ezra argues that the world was created for Israel, and that God the Creator bears the responsibility for his most important creature, i.e. the Israelite. 4 Ezra restates that all creatures were the workmanship of God's hands and of his word. In particular, Israel is said to be created as God's own people (4 Ezra 5:23-30; 6:54, 59; 8:24, 45). The creation motif is employed here in order to demonstrate the special relationship between God and Israel, while other nations are said to be nothing (*nil*) and like spittle (*salivæ*) or a drop from a bucket (*stillicidium*) (4 Ezra 6:56). In particular, the latter idea alludes to Isa 40:15 and 17: 'the nations are like a drop from a bucket' (Isa 40:15); 'the nations are as nothing before him' (Isa 40:17).

The Word of Creation

4 Ezra expands the beginning of the Genesis creation account by clearly mentioning that God accomplished his work of creation by his utterance and his word.

> *O Domine, **loquens locutus**[39] **es ab initio creaturæ, in primo die dicens:** Fiat cælum et terra; et tuum verbum opus perfectum* (4 Ezra 6:38).

> O Lord, *you indeed spoke from the beginning of creation, and said on the first day,* 'Let heaven and earth be made,' and *your word accomplished the work.*

> Cf. Gen 1:1
> In the beginning God created the heavens and the earth.

The same motif of the creative word (or command) is repeated in the rest of the creation account.

> Then you *commanded* (*dixisti*) that a ray of light be brought forth from your treasuries, so that your works might then appear (4 Ezra 6:40).

> On the third day you *commanded* (*imperasti*) the waters. . . For *your word went forth, and at once the work was done* (*verbum enim tuum processit, et opus statim fiebat*) (4 Ezra 6:42-43).

> On the fourth day you *commanded* (*imperasti*) the brightness of the sun, the light of the moon, and the arrangement of the stars to come into being (6:45).

> On the fifth day you *commanded* (*dixisti*) the seventh part to bring forth living creatures, birds, and fishes, and so it was done (6:47).

> The dumb and lifeless water produced living creatures, as God *commanded* (quæ Dei nutu jubebantur)[40] (6:48).

The personification of the divine word can be seen in these verses: 'the word of God accomplished the work (4 Esra 6:38); 'the word went forth, and the work was done' (4 Ezra 6:43).[41] It is an expression to depict the actuality (or reality) of God's mighty work in creation. It is noteworthy that the last two examples (6:47, 48) describe God producing living things out of inanimate objects (i.e. the dry land and the dumb and lifeless water) by his word (or by

---

[39] Note its emphatic expression.

[40] However, the text of this verse is uncertain (Cf. Metzger's note in OTP I, 536), and this phrase is omitted by all MSS except Latin MS.

[41] Cf. 4 Ezra 8:22-23.

his command). In other words, the word of God is depicted as an important agent to produce life from lifeless things.[42]

Light

The creation of light (4 Ezra 6:40) and luminaries (4 Ezra 6:45-46) is referred to in accordance with the narrative order of the Genesis creation account. Both light and luminaries are given by God's utterance (or by his command). It should be noted that 4 Ezra states that a ray of light was brought forth from God's treasuries (4 Ezra 6:40).[43]   G. Box comments that the Rabbinic tradition[44] tells that light was created on the first day before the creation of luminaries, and this light was afterwards withdrawn and reserved by God for the righteous in the world to come.[45] That is to say, light itself existed before the work of creation, and it is described as a divine thing. The role of light is to let God's works of creation appear (4 Ezra 6:40) and to serve human beings (6:46). It is a comment or brief summary of Gen 1:14-18.

2.4 Sibylline Oracles 1:5-35

2.4.1 Literary Considerations

Context and Main Concern

The author of SibOr Book 1 gives a prophecy of all things from the past, present, and future (SibOr 1:1-4). The author explains how the world which was created as a good thing declined to evil (e.g. SibOr 1:46, 73-74, 101-103), and how the wrath of God (the flood) came upon the world (people) as he had declared (1:165), or as he planned it (1:216). Based on the event that people were punished by the water (or the flood) in the past, the author gives warning that the final judgment (2:149-347) and destruction by fire (2:196-214) will truly come.

The first few verses allude to the purpose of Book 1 (and Book 2[46]): i.e. 'so that you may never neglect my commands' (SibOr 1:6-7). The first section (the accounts of creation and of the first generation) tells that because

---

[42] Cf. J. Cook, 'Creation in 4 Ezra,' 134.

[43] Cf. 2 En 25:1-3; 4Q392 frag. 1 4-7.

[44] Cf. t. b. Ḥag. 12a.

[45] G. H. Box in APOT II, 578.

[46] The first two books of the Sibyline Oracles are considered to be a unit, by sharing the same division of world history into ten generations (J. J. Collins, OTP I, 330); however it contains Christian material as J. J. Collins says (OTP I, 330). J. J. Collins refers to the work of J. Geffcken, *Komposition und Entstehungszeit der Oracula Sibyllina* (Leipzig; Hinrichs, 1902), 47-53.

the first man neglected God's command, human beings received the fate of death (SibOr 1:40-46, 50-55, 73-86), and they were removed from life, and Hades received them (SibOr 1:80). The author also tells that there will be a great contest for entry to the heavenly city (SibOr 2:39). This is the gate of life and entry to immortality which the heavenly God has appointed (SibOr 2:150). Book 1 and 2 divide world history into ten generations (lacking the eight and ninth generations), and the creation account functions as a prologue for these two books. It tells about the beginning of world history (the first generation) and the beginning of the course of the decline of human history (the fate of death).

Influence of Key Passages from the OT

The author briefly summarizes the Genesis creation account, and reconstructs it by using his own expressions: ἤδρασε γὰρ γῆν Ταρτάρῳ[47] (draping it [earth] around with Tartarus[48]) (1:9-10); οὐρανὸν ὕψωσεν (elevated heaven) (1:11a); γλαυκὴν δ᾽ ἤπλωσε θάλασσαν (stretched out the gleaming sea) (1:11b); πόλον ἐστεφάνωσεν ἅλις πυρισαμπέσιν ἄστροις (amply crowned the vault of heaven with bright-shining stars) (1:12); and γαῖαν κόσμησε φυτοῖς (decorated the earth with plants) (1:13).

He does not mention each day of creation, but mostly follows the order of the Genesis account, except for the account of the creation of stars (SibOr 1:12).

Day	SibOr 1:5-37	Genesis (the OT)
1st	earth, light, heaven	heaven, earth, light; light was separated from darkness
2nd	sea, stars	firmament, division of waters
3rd	plants	dry land, seed, trees
4th		sun, moon, stars
5th	fish, birds, beasts, creeping serpents	great sea monsters, fish, birds
6th	humankind	beasts of the earth, cattle, humankind

---

[47] The Greek text is of Geffcken's edition (*Die Oracula Sibyllina* [Leipzig: J. C. Hinrichs'sche Buchhandlung, 1902]).

[48] It indicates the nether world (J.J. Collins, OTP I, 335). Gehenna is regarded as a part of Tartarus or identical with it (M. Terry, *The Sibylline Oracles* [El Paso, Texas; Selene Books, 1991 [org. ed. 1890], 33); usually Tartarus is the lowest part of Hades, sometimes the lowest part of Gehenna, or equivalent to Gehenna.

The author distinguishes the account of the creation of Adam from the rest of the creation account: the account pauses at SibOr 1:22, with the words, 'He himself made these things with a word and all came to be, swiftly and truly' (αὐτὸς ταῦτ' ἐποίησε λόγῳ καὶ πάντ' ἐγενήθη ὦκα καὶ ἀτρεκέως); then it restarts from v. 23, by saying, 'and then later he again fashioned an animate object' (καὶ τότε δὴ μετέπειτα πλάσεν πάλιν ἔμπνοον ἔργον) (SibOr 1:22). This may be because the author focuses on the creation of human beings as a prologue for later accounts of human history.

2.4.2 Thematic Considerations

The Word of Creation

At the beginning and the ending of the first part of the creation account (SibOr 1:8-22),[49] the author mentions that God created the whole world with his word.

> ὅς ἔκτισε κόσμον ἅπαντα εἴπας, γεινάσθω' καὶ ἐγείνατο (SibOr 1:8-9).
> It was he who created the whole world, *saying*, 'let it come to be' and it came to be.

> αὐτὸς ταῦτ' ἐποίσε λόγῳ καὶ πάντ' ἐγενήθη ὦκα καὶ ἀτρεκέως (SibOr 1:19-20).
> He himself made these things *with a word* and all came to be, swiftly and truly.

God's utterance, 'Let it come to be' and it came to be (γεινάσθω' καὶ ἐγείνατο), which is mentioned in the first example, is a variation of the Genesis creation account formula, 'Let there be . . . and there was . . .' (...ויהי ... יהי אלהים ויאמר). SibOr 1:8 and 1:19-20 may be influenced by a psalmic account of creation (Ps 33:4-9, 13):

Ps 33:4-9, 13	SibOr 1:8, 19-21
For *the word of the Lord* is upright, and all his work is done *in faithfulness* (וכל־מעשהו באמונה)[50] . . .	(All came to be) swiftly and *truly* (ἀτρεκέως < ἀτρεκής)
By the word of the Lord the heavens were made. . .	He himself made these things with *a word*.
For he spoke, and it came to be;	*Let it come to be and it came to be,* he commanded,
The Lord *looks down from heaven* . . .	*looking down from heavem* . . .

---

[49] The division of the creation account is given above.

[50] The LXX translates it as πάντα τὰ ἔργα αὐτοῦ ἐν πίστει.

The idea of the creative word emphasizes the points that God created the whole world swiftly and truly (ὦκα καὶ ἀτρεκέως),[51] that he is self-begotten (αὐτολόχευτος[52]) and that under him the world has been brought to completion (ὑπὸ τῷ τετέλεστο δὲ κόσμος) (SibOr 1:20-22). It is a strong expression of the sovereign power of God.

The Gate of Life and Entry to Immortality

God is called 'immortal' (ἀθάνατος) and he is contrasted to the 'mortality' of human beings, which came to them because of their transgression of God's commands. Eve was deceived to the fate of death (τοῦ θανάτου) by the snake (SibOr 1:40-41), and Adam also forgot about his immortal Creator (ἀθάνατος κτίστης) and neglected clear commands (SibOr 1:44-45). The Immortal became angry with them and expelled them from the place of immortals (ἀθανάτων χώρου) (SibOr 1:50-51), and decreed that they remain in a mortal place (θνητῷ < θνητός) since they had not kept the command of the great immortal God (SibOr 1:51-53). The author of Book 2 of SibOr then announces that there is a last great contest for entry to immortality (ἀθανασίης) (2:39-41). The reward is 'life' (ζωή) and 'immortality' (ἀθανασίης) (2:150), and the righteous who are concerned with justice, noble deeds, piety, and most righteous thoughts, will be brought to light (φῶς) and to life (ζωή), in which is 'the immortal path of the great God' (τρίβος ἀθάνατος μεγάλοιο θεοῖο) (2:315-317). In short, life (ζωή) is considered to be life in the place of immortals (ἀθανάτων χώρου). Adam and Eve were once favored with it, and it will be given to the righteous as a final reward. It should be noted that light and life are parallel in meaning (i.e. the eschatological rewards) in SibOr 2:316.

2.5 Sibylline Oracles 3:8-25

2.5.1 Literary Considerations

Context and Main Concern

The creation account (SibOr 3:8-28) appears in the first forty-five verses of Book 3. Although the connection between the first forty-five verses and the

---

[51] See the emphasis on the immediacy of God's creation with the word of God motif in 4 Ezra 6:38, 43; 2 Bar 14:17; 56:4; cf. 21:7.

[52] From αὐτο + λοχεύω

rest of the book is not necessarily clear,[53] the former seems to give a reason why the eschatological destruction is to come, which is the subject of the rest of the Book. The author denounces the sins against the immortal God (in particular against idolatry). The reference to creation is associated with the argument to the idolatry, by making a contrast between the Creator and the idols which were made by a sculptor's hand (SibOr 3:8-35). The creation account is also referred to here in order to recall the sovereignty of God who rules over the eschatological judgment (SibOr 3:34-35).

Influence of Key Passages from the OT

The creation account in SibOr 3:20-28 does not necessarily follow the narrative order of the Genesis creation account. However, it mentions the whole creation account of Genesis 1:1-25.[54] In a context which highlights the identity of God, references to several biblical texts which emphasize the sovereignty of God (in a monotheistic emphasis) are made. For example, firstly the idea of contrast between the Creator and the idols may be taken from Isa 40:18-26. Interestingly, both SibOr and Isaiah have the same expression, 'God lives in the sky' (SibOr 3:11; Isa 40:22). Secondly, Exod 33:20 is referred to in SibOr 3:17-19 in which the invisibility of God is mentioned. Thirdly, Ps 33:6 is possibly recalled in SibOr 3:20 in which the motif of the creative word is employed to emphasize the mighty power of God.

2.5.2 Thematic Considerations

The Sovereign God and the Word

There is speculation about the identity of God in the creation context. God is introduced as the 'one God' (εἷς θεός), 'the sole ruler' (μόναρχος), 'the one who lives in the sky' (αἰθέρι ναίων), 'the one who himself sees all things' (ὁρώμενος αὐτὸς ἅπαντα). He is 'self-begotten' (αὐτοφυής[55]), 'ineffable' (ἀθέσφατος), 'invisible' (ἀόρατος), and 'immortal' (αἰώνιος) (SibOr 3:11-15). In this context, God is depicted as the sole Creator, who created everything by his word (λόγῳ) and fashioned Adam (SibOr 3:20-28). On the one hand, the idols were made *by the sculptor's hand* and *revealed* by a cast of gold and ivory in the crafts of humankind (SibOr 3:13-14), whereas on the other hand, God created the universe *by his word* (SibOr 3:20) and he *revealed* (ἀνέδειξεν

---

[53] The first ninety-six verses of Book 3 of the Sibylline Oracles are considered to be dissociated from the rest of the book, and vv. 1-45 is also separated from the rest of the material because of its contextual difference (See J. J. Collins [OTP I, 359]).

[54] See § 2.6.1.

[55] ἀυτος (self) + φύω (with passive voice, 'to be born').

< ἀναδείκνυμι) himself as the one who is and was before, and shall be hereafter (SibOr 3:13).

The God of Creation and the God of Salvation

In the context of assailing idolatry, SibOr 3:33-35 denounces the sins against monolatry: 'You never revere nor fear God, . . . forgetting the judgment of the immortal Savior who created the heavens and the earth.' It is worth noting that in the last sentence, 'the judgment of the immortal Savior' is paralled with the description of the identity of God as Creator. The identity of God as Creator (SibOr 3:35; cf. vv. 20-28) and Sustainer (SibOr 3:33) is associated with his status as an eschatological Savior (SibOr 3:34-35).

2.6 Sibylline Oracles Fragment 3

2.6.1 Literary Considerations

Context, Main Concern, and Textual Considerations

SibOr frags. 1-3 are found in Theophilus (Ad Autolycum 2:3 and 2:36), and they are thought to be a part of the lost Book 2 with some connection to SibOr 3:1-45.[56] Although it is uncertain whether the fragments and SibOr 3:1-45 are Jewish writings or Christian redactions, it is undeniable that they contain a Jewish tradition that emphasizes monotheism and denounces idolatry. Frag. 3 has the character of supplementation of SibOr 3:1-45: both share similar terminology as shown below, and frag. 3 has a tendency to supplement SibOr 3:1-45. For example, frag. 3 mentions the assignment of a human role (frag. 3:12-14; cf. Gen 1:26-28); the names of idols, dogs and birds are supplemented (frag. 3:26-27); and the final rewards are mentioned not only as judgment to the idolaters but also as the blessing to the good (frag. 3:46-49). The correspondences between 3:1-45 and frag. 3 are as follows:

SibOr 3:1-45	SibOr frag. 3
God	*God*
one God (εἷς θεός)	One God (θεὸς εἷς)
sole Ruler (μόναρχος)	sole (μόνος)
	Highest (πανυπέρτατος)
ineffable (ἀθέσφατος)	incorruptible (ἄφθαρτος)
	eternal in corruptible (αἰθέρα ναίων)
self-begotten (αὐτοφυής)	
invisible (ἀόρατος)	
eternal (αἰώνιος)	eternal (αἰώνιος)

---

[56] See J. J. Collins (OTP I, 360, 469); C.A. Kurfess (NTA II, 707).

who lives in the sky	who lives in the sky
who himself sees all things	God the king who oversees all
who created all by his word	He has made . . .

<Narrative Order>	<Narrative Order>
Heaven	Heaven
Sea	Luminaries
Luminaries	Earth
Springs, Rivers	Sea
Fire, Days, Nights	Mountains, Springs
Man	Water Creatures
Wild Beasts	Serpents, Birds
Serpents, Birds	Wild Beasts, Cattles
	Man was made Ruler of all

God and Man	*God and Man*
No one can see God	No one can know, but God

Denunciation of idolatry	*Denunciation of idolatry*
worshipped Gods	worshipped Gods
Snakes	Snakes
Cats	Cats
	Dogs
	Birds
Idols	Idols

Rewards	Rewards
Judgment to Idolaters	Judgment to Idolaters
	Blessing to the good

Influence of Key Passages from the OT

Needless to say, the creation account in frag. 3:21-33 follows the creation account in SibOr 3:20-28 as shown above. However, it is distinct for the creation account in frag. 3:21-33 to refer to Ps 8:5-8 which mentions the status of human beings as the rulers of all creation (frag. 3:13-14). The reference to the divine knowledge of God who alone knows of all creation is obvious in the OT (e.g. Job chs. 38-42).

2.6.2 Thematic Consideration: the Sovereignty of God

SibOr frag. 3 shares a common theme with SibOr bks. 1 and 2, i.e. monotheism and the denunciation of idolatry as previously observed. In retelling the Genesis creation account, the unique identity of God as the sole Creator is emphasized. SibOr frag. 3:16-20 depicts the sovereignty of God not only as the Creator (frag. 3:16-17) but also as the one who is preparing for the final judgment and reward (frag. 3:18-20). It should be noted in this account, that

God is depicted as 'life' (ζωή) and 'imperishable eternal light' (ἄφθιτον ἀέναον φῶς) (frag. 3:34; cf. frag. 3:46-49).

2.7 Josephus Antiquitates Judaicae 1:27-36

2.7.1 Literary Considerations

Context and Main Concern

The second longest work of Josephus, Jewish Antiquities, narrates Jewish history from creation to the administration of the last procurators before the wars with Rome (20:252-268). Allusion to the purpose of this book is made in the preface of the first book:

> On the whole, one who would wish to read through it would especially *learn from this history* that those who comply with *the will of God* and do not venture to transgress *laws* that have been well enacted succeed in all things beyond belief and that happiness lies before them as a reward from God. But to the extent that they dissociate themselves from *the scrupulous observance of these laws* the practicable things become impracticable, and whatever seemingly good thing they pursue with zeal turns into irremediable misfortunes (1:14).[57]

Josephus attempts to introduce Jewish history into the Greek-speaking world (1:5), and encourages people to conform to the will of God and not to transgress the laws (1:14). In this sense, his historical viewpoint is akin to the biblical historiography of the Deuteronomist and the Chronicler.[58]

Josephus begins with restating the Genesis creation account (1:27-36) as the first historical narrative of Moses (1:26). The lesson to be learnt from this account is that because Adam transgressed the command of God (1:46), he was brought into a calamitous condition (1:49).

Influence of Key Passages from the OT

It should be noted that Josephus begins with the opening words of the Genesis creation account: Ἐν ἀρχῇ ἔκτισεν[59] ὁ θεὸς τὸν οὐρανὸν καὶ τὴν γῆν (Ant 1:27). The LXX translation seems to be in Josephus' mind: e.g. the expression, ταύτης δ' ὑπ' ὄψιν οὐκ ἐρχομένης (Ant 1:27a), comes from the LXX translation of Gen 1:2a (ἡ δὲ γῆ ἦν ἀόρατος καὶ ἀκατασκεύαστος), which

---

[57] Translation of L. Feldman (*Judean Antiquities 1-4: Translation and Commentary* [*Flavius Josephus* 3; Leiden: Brill, 2000]).

[58] Cf. H. W. Attridge, 'Josephus and his Works,' in M. Stone, *Jewish Writings*, 218.

[59] The LXX renders ἐποίησεν here; however, the LXX renders κτίζω in the context of God's creational work (cf. Gen 14:19, 22; Exod 9:18; Deut 4:32; 32:6; Pss 32:9 [MT 33:9]; 88:13, 48 [MT 89:12, 47]; 103:30 [MT 104:30]; 148:5).

cannot be seen in the Masoretic tradition. He shortens or embellishes several portions with his own words. L. Feldman comments that Josephus adds information to the meager and even telegraphic account of the Bible, in order to make it more intelligible to his Greek audience.[60]

> 'This latter (the earth) had not come into sight but was hidden in deep darkness' (βαθεῖ μὲν κρυπτομένης σκότει) (Ant 1:27b) for σκότος ἐπάνω τῆς ἀβύσσου (Gen 1:2b); ' inspecting the whole of matter, He divided the light from the darkness' (κατανοήσας τὴν ὅλην ὕλην διεχώρισε τό τε φῶς καὶ τὸ σκότος) (Ant 1:28) for διεχώρισεν ὁ θεὸς ἀνὰ μέσον τοῦ φωτὸς καὶ ἀνὰ μέσον τοῦ σκότους (Gen 1:4b); 'separating it from the rest, He deemed it proper for it to receive a certain place by itself' (ὅτ᾽ αὐτὸν ἀπὸ τῶν ἄλλων διακρίνας καθ᾽ αὐτὸν ἠξίωσε τετάχθαι) (Ant 1:30b) for διεχώρισεν ὁ θεὸς ἀνὰ μέσον τοῦ ὕδατος ὃ ἦν ὑποκάτω τοῦ στερεώματος καὶ ἀνὰ μέσον τοῦ ὕδατος τοῦ ἐπάνω τοῦ στερεώματος (Gen 1:7); ' He established the earth, pouring out the sea around it' (ἵστησι τὴν γῆν ἀναχέας περὶ αὐτὴν τὴν θάλασσαν) (Ant 1:31a) for Gen 1:9-10; 'plants and seeds sprouted straightway from the earth' (εὐθὺς φυτά τε καὶ σπέρματα γῆθεν ἀνέτειλε) (1:31b) for Gen 1:11-13; 'he adorned the heaven with the sun and the moon and the other stars' (δὲ διακοσμεῖ τὸν οὐρανὸν ἡλίῳ καὶ σελήνη καὶ τοῖς ἄλλοις ἄστροις) (Ant 1:31c) for Gen 1:14-15; 'assigning movements and courses for them by that the revolutions of the seasons might be signified' (κινήσεις αὐτοῖς ἐπιστείλας καὶ δρόμους, οἷς ἂν αἱ τῶν ὡρῶν περιφοραὶ σημαίνοιντο) (Ant 1:31d) for Gen 1:16-19; 'He sent forth in the deep and through the air the creatures that swim and fly' (ζῷά τε κατ᾽ αὐτὴν νηκτὰ καὶ μετάρσια τὰ μὲν κατὰ βάθους τὰ δὲ δι᾽ ἀέρος ἀνῆκε) (Ant 1:32b) for Gen 1:20-23; 'He created the race of the four-footed creatures, making both male and female. On this day He also fashioned humanity' (δημιουργεῖ τὸ τῶν τετραπόδων γένος ἄρρεν τε καὶ θῆλυ τοιήσας. ἐν ταύτῃ δὲ καὶ τὸν ἄνθρωπον ἔπλασε) (1:32c) for Gen 1:24-27; 'He injected breath (πνεῦμα) and soul (ψυχή) into him' (1:34) for Gen 2:7.[61]

As a whole, however Josephus simply restates the Mosaic account of creation (Gen 1:1-2:3), and follows the division of the days of the Genesis creation account.

2.7.2 Thematic Consideration: the Fall, a Historical Discipline

Josephus understands that Moses gives a simple account of creation in Gen 1:1-2:3, and that he gives a theological explanation from Gen 2:4 by writing, 'In particular, Moses began, after the seventh day, to discuss nature (φυσιολογεῖν)[62], speaking thus about the formation of humanity' (Ant 1:34). Josephus focuses on the fall of human beings and the reward which was given

---

[60] L. Feldman, *Judean Antiquities 1-4*, 11).

[61] The Greek text of H. Thackeray (*Josephus*, vol. 4 [London: William Heinemann Ltd, 1926]).

[62] See Feldman's comment (*Judean Antiquities 1-4*, 13): 'He (Josephus) explains that in chapter 2 of Genesis Moses begins to interpret nature (φυσιολογεῖν), just as he had declared in his proem (*Ant*. 1:18) that much of Moses' work is devoted to natural philosophy (φυσιολογία).'

to them because of their disobedience to the divine commandment. According to his account, the serpent who grew jealous of the blessings misled the woman to scorn the commandment of God (τῆς ἐντολῆς τοῦ θεοῦ καταφρονῆσαι) (Ant 1:43). Josephus repeats the incident of their disobedience in Ant 1:46 (παραβάντι τὴν τοῦ πρόσταξιν) and 1:47 (παρακούσας τῶν ἐμῶν ἐντολῶν). As a result of this disobedience, they were kept away from a happy life (βίον εὐδαίμονα) and from a long life (τὸ ζῆν ὑμῖν μακρὸν) (1:46). While the blessings were destined for them in case they obeyed God's command (παράγγελμα τοῦ θεοῦ), disobedience (παρακούσαντας < παρακούω) will bring trouble upon them (Ant 1:41). Josephus emphasizes that the disobedience to the will of God or his command would remove them out of eternal life.

Thus Josephus introduces Jewish history into the Greek-speaking world in order to encourage them to conform to the will of God and not to transgress his laws. That is to say, Josephus restates the Mosaic account of creation (Gen 1:1-2:3), particularly focusing on the narrative of human creation and fall, in order to draw a historical lesson that disobedience to the will of God or his command will remove the people from the possibility of eternal life.

2.8 1QM (War Rule from Qumran Cave 1) 10:8-18

2.8.1 Literary Considerations

Preliminary Remarks: Is the War Eschatological?

There are at least three major opinions concerning the date of the War Rule: the Seleucid period hypothesis[63] (2nd century BC); the Roman period hypothesis[64] (1st century BC to 1st century AD); and the redaction hypothesis[65] (2nd century BC to 1st century AD). The key issues here are

---

[63] K.M.T. Atkinson, 'The Historical Setting of the "War of the Sons of Light and the Sons of Darkness",' *BJRL* 40 (1957), 286; P. von der Osten-Sacken, *Gott und Belial* (Göttingen: Vandenhoeck & Ruprecht, 1969), 62-72; M. Treves, 'The Date of the War of the Sons of Light,' *VT* 8 (1958), 422; M. H. Segal, 'The Qumran War Scroll and the Date of its Composition,' in Ch. Rabin and Y. Yadin (eds.) *Aspects of the Dead Sea Scrolls* (ScrHie 4; Jerusalem: Magnes, 1965), 140, etc.

[64] Y. Yadin, *The Scroll of the War of the Sons of Light against the Sons of Darkness* (Oxford: Oxford University Press, 1962), 243-246; F. M. Cross, *The Ancient Library of Qumran* (New York: Anchor Books, 1961), 124; Geza Vermes (ed.) *The Dead Sea Scrolls in English* (4th [ed.]; London: Penguin Books, 1995), 123; G. R. Driver, *The Judaean Scrolls* (Oxford: Basil Blackwell, 1965), 196, etc.

[65] See Duhaime's note ('War Scroll,' in J. H. Charlesworth [ed.], *The Dead Sea Scrolls: Hebrew, Aramaic, and Greek texts with English translations* [The Princeton Theological

whether the War is theological or more practical, whether it is the eschatological war against the Roman Empire or the Maccabean revolt.

The portrayal of the war in 1QM can be acknowledged as 'the holy war.'[66] Firstly, the war is characterized by dualistic, metaphorical words: 'the sons of light' (בני אור) and 'the lot of the sons of darkness' (גורל בני חושך). The enemy is guided by 'Belial' (בליעל) who is a figure of evil angel in Jewish tradition, and they are also supported by 'the ungodly of the covenant' (ברית מרשיעי) (1QM 1:1-17). On the other hand, God will support 'the sons of light' (בני אור), sending everlasting aid by the power of the majestic angel (1QM 17:6), and he will ultimately subdue all his enemies (1QM 1:15). Secondly, the instructions which the War Rule provides are not only tactical but also ritualistic: the combatants should be pure and perfect men (1QM 7:3-6; cf. Deut 20:8; 23:10; Lev 15:16; 21:17-20; Num 8:25-26); there are sets of regulations which were originally taken from the OT (trumpet: 1QM 3:1-11, cf. Num 10:1-10; the banner: 1QM 3:12-5:2, cf. Num 17:17-18). Thirdly, the war will be conducted with ritual prayers and blessings (1QM 9:17-14:15). Fourthly, the time and the phases of the war are also predetermined (1QM 15:5, 12; 17:5; 18:10), and the victory of the sons of light has already been declared (1QM 18:10-19:14). Some other parallels in contemporary Hellenistic and Roman tactics and military organizations may support the Roman period hypothesis.[67]

Seminary Dead Sea Scrolls Project; Tübingen: J. C. B. Mohr, 1995]). He points out these discrepancies in 1QM: (1) the content of the hymn (12:8-16 and 19:1-8); (2) the period of the war (col. 1, 15-19 and col. 2); (3) the numbers and names of trumpets (2:16-3:11, 7:9-9:9 and 16:3-18:6); (4) the cavalry (6:8-18 and cols. 15-19). P. Davis (*The Literary Structure of 1QM* [Ph. D. Thesis; University of St. Andrews, 1973]) suggests five stages of its redaction: A. Cols. 2-9 (War Rule for the twelve tribes redacted in the Hasmonean period on the basis of material composed in the Maccabean period); B. Col. 14:2-16a (fragment of a non-dualistic War Rule); C. Cols. 15-19 (dualistic War Rule that developed from an earlier non-dualistic War Rule partly preserved in col. 14:2-16a); D. Cols. 10-12 (Complex of liturgical pieces, many of whose component compositions come from the Maccabean period); and E. Col. 1 (introduction composed for and prefixed to the final form of the War Rule [ca. 50 AD]).

[66] The similarities between 1QM and 1 and 2 Maccabees have been pointed out (see Duhaime, 'War Scroll,' 88-89). It is possible to assume that both the War Rule and 1 and 2 Maccabees might have followed the OT traditions of the holy war. D. Wenthe ('The Use of the Hebrew Scriptures in 1QM,' *DSD* 5 [3] [1999]) points out the influence of the OT in 1QM. Otherwise, 1 and 2 Maccabees might have inspired the Jewish resistance movements against Rome in the first and second centuries AD (cf. R. Bauckham, *The Climax of Prophecy: Studies on the Book of Revelation* [Edinburgh: T. & T. Clark, 1993], ch. 8).

[67] So Vermes, *The Dead Sea Scrolls*, 123; Treves, 'The Date of the War,' 219.

Context and Main Concern

The text can be divided into four sections by an indicator which breaks up the text (i.e. the vacant at the end of each section) and also by its thematic change: (1) the introduction (1:1-16); (2) the rule of the war (2:1-9:16); (3) the war prayers (10:1-14:18); and (4) the instructions in each phase of the final war against Kittim (15:1-19:14).

At the beginning of the section of war prayers, the author of 1QM instructs Israel by citing Deut 20:2-5 and Num 10:9 to remind them that God goes with them to do battle for them, as they approach the battle. The section of war prayers consists of three parts: (a) the prayers at the beginning of the war by the priest (10:1-12:18); (b) the prayers at the moment of victory by the priests, the levites, and all the elders (13:1-18); and (c) the thanksgiving hymn by all community members (14:1-18). The creation account appears in the first prayer (1QM 10:8-18). The main themes of the hymn are given in the opening section: the God of Israel is awesome and none of the other gods can be compared with him (10:8-9a); God's Israel is special because it is chosen from all the other nations by the unique God (10:9b-11a). On account of the unique relationship between the sovereign God and Israel, they can assume that God will listen to their prayers (1QM 10:17-18).

Influence of Key Passages from the OT

The opening section (10:8-11a) consists of two parallel sentences in the form of a rhetorical question which emphasizes the unique identity of God[68] and of Israel.

מיא כמוכה אל ישראל בשׁמיִם ובאריץ
אשר יעשיכה הגדולים וכגבורתכה החזקה
ומיא כעמכה ישראל
אשר בחרתה לכה מכול עמי הארצות

These sentences may allude to Moses' prayer in Deut 33:26-29[69]: 'There is no one like the God of Jeshurun . . . O Israel, who is like you . . .'

The hymn lists God's works of creation, not rejecting all the narrative of the Genesis creation account (by mentioning the works of creation of the 1st, 3rd, 5th, and 6th days), but also showing certain similarities to the other biblical (Job chs. 37-38) and Jewish traditions of the creation account (Jub ch. 2; 1 En chs. 60, 75-80; 2 En ch. 19). The creation hymn can be divided into

---

[68] The idea, 'the divine identity,' is that of R. Bauckham. He defines it as 'a label for a concern with who God is' (*God Crucified*, 7-8). See its application to Christology (*God Crucified*, 21-22, 35-36, 45-79; idem, 'The Throne of God and the Worship of Jesus,' in J. Davila and C. Newman (eds.), *The Jewish Roots of Christological Monotheism* [Leiden; E. J. Brill, 1999], 43-69).

[69] Cf. Exod 15:11; Pss 35:10; 89:5-18; 113:5; Isa 44:7; Mic 7:18.

three parts: the creation which belongs to the heavenly domain (10:11b-12a); the creation which belongs to the earthly domain (10:12b-14a); and an expansion of the creation account (14a-15a).

THE LITERARY STRUCTURE OF 1QM 10:11b-15a

I. The Works of Creation which are in the Heavenly Domain (11b-12a)

> The expanse of the skies (מפרש שחקים)
> The host of luminaries (צבא מאורות)
> The tasks of the winds (or spirits) (משא רוחות)
> The dominion of the holy ones (ממשלת קדושים)
> The treasures of glo[ry] (אוצרות כב[נוד])
> [The expansion of] clouds ([מפרשי] עבים)[70]

II. The Works of Creation which are in the Earthly Domain (12b-14a)

> The division of land and all its products
>   the earth
>   the laws dividing it (the earth) into desert and steppe
>   (וחוקי מפלגיה למדבר וארץ ערבה)
>   all its products, fruits, seeds

> The division of waters
>   the circle of the sea (חוג ימים)
>   the reservoirs of the rivers (מקוי נהרות)
>   the divisions of the abyss (מבקע תהומות)

> Animals and Human beings
>   the beasts, birds,
>   the shape of human beings
>   the genera[tions of] his [seed] (ותול[ד]ות זר[עו])

III. The Expansion of the Creation Account (14b-15a)

> The division of the nations
>   the division of tongues (בלת לשון)
>   the separation of peoples (מפרד עמים)

---

[70] Y. Yadin (*The Scroll of the War of the Sons of Light against the Sons of Darkness* [Oxford: Oxford University Press, 1962]) suggests the readings, '[expanses of] clouds' ([מפרשי] עבים), and '[and the dew of] clouds' ([וטל] עבים); García Martínez (*The Dead Sea Scrolls Study Edition* [Leiden: E. J. Brill, 1997]) suggests, '[in the darkness] of the clouds' ([באפ]ל עבים). García Martínez may have taken a small dot, which is seen between Line 11 and 12, as the head of ל which belongs to Line 12, but it seems to be a misreading. The Photo of SHR 3374 (E. Tov [ed.] *The Dead Sea Scrolls on Microfiche: A Comprehensive Facsimile Edition of the Texts from the Judean Desert: Companion Volume* [Leiden: E. J. Brill and IDC, 1993]) clearly suggests that the dot belongs to Line 11. Although the Photo of SHR 3396 might show a small possibility that the dot belongs to Line 12, nevertheless, it cannot be read as a part of ל.

the dwelling of the clans (מושב משפחות)
the inheritance of the lands (נחלת ארצות)

The division of the times
the sacred seasons (מועדי קודש)
the cycle of the years (תקופות שנים)

the ages of eternity (. . . וקצי עד)
. . . (ה[. . .])

The idea of the task of the winds (or spirits) (משא רוחות) (1QM 10:12; cf. 1QH 9:12[71]) can be seen in the meteorological account of Job ch. 37 and the Book of Jubilees (ch. 2), as well as in the Ethiopic (chs. 60, 75-80) and the Slavonic Apocalypses of Enoch (ch. 19). The parallel words, 'the dominion of the holy ones' (ממשלת קדושים), seem to mention the assignment of the divine role which governs the meteorological phenomena to the angels (cf. Jub 2:1-2).[72] Similar expressions to 'the treasures of glory' (אוצרות כב]וד]) appear in 1QS 10:2-3: 'when he (God) unlocked his store (אוצרו) and spread them (darkness) out . . .'; 'when the lights (מאורות) shine out of the holy dwelling-place (מזבול קודש), when they (the heavenly lights) retire to the place of glory' (למעון כבוד). They describe the astronomical phenomena, by employing the notion of the heavenly storehouse, which can be seen in 1 En ch. 75-80.[73] If the reading, 'the expanse of the clouds' (ומפרשי עבים), is possible, then it alludes to the meteorological account of Job chs. 36-38.

In the second part (12b-14a), the idea of 'the laws of the divisions' (lit. חוקי מפלגיה) is highlighted. The desert and steppe are separated, and the boundaries of waters are fixed for the sea, the rivers and the abyss. This idea is prominent in the creation accounts of biblical (Job 38:8-12; Ps 104:8-9; Prov 8:28-29) and Jewish literature (Sir 16:26-28; 1 En 69:18; 2 En 47:5, etc.). The idea of the division of times undoubtedly comes from Gen 1:14: 'And God said, "Let there be lights (מאות) . . . to separate (בדל < להבדיל) the day from the night; and let them be for signs (אתת) and for seasons (מועדים < מועד) and for days and years (לימים ושנים).' These ideas are developed in Ps 104 which emphasizes the sovereignty of God, and mentions both the division of space (Ps 104:8-9) and the creation of luminaries (Ps 104:19-23). The idea of the creation of the divisions of space and time is developed into the understanding of the divisions of the nations and of the appointed times in the third part (1QM 10:14b-15a), and these ideas appear in the rest of the book as

---

[71] See the combination of רוחות (winds) with משא (tasks): סערה] למשאם זקים וכול רוחות].
[72] Cf. 1QH[a] 9:11: למלאכי קודש . . . בממשלותם
[73] Cf. Deut. 28:12 (treasures of rain); Jer 10:13 (of wind); Ps 135:7 (of wind); Job 38:22 (of snow and hail). See 1QH[a] 9:12: 'well-designed treasures (אוצרות).'

well: Israel as the chosen people (cf. 1QM 13:9); the time for the restoration or the war and the victory of Israel (1QM 11:8, 11; 13:14; 15:3, 5, 6; 17:5; 18:10).

In short, the creation account of 1QM seems to have been influenced by the creation accounts in the Book of Jubilees and Enochic literature, as well as by the OT (mainly from Job chs. 37-38).

2.8.2 Thematic Consideration

Unique God and Unique People

God is remembered as a unique God because of his great works (lit. הגדולים מעשיכה) and his mighty strength (lit. גבורתכה החזקה) (1QM 10:8-9a; 13:13). He is unique because he is the Creator of the heavens and the earth. He is the God of mysteries: the creation hymn refers to several mysteries which are often cited in the biblical and Jewish literature, such as the role of winds and spirits, and the ways of luminaries and lightnings, and the divisions of spaces, nations, and times. Nothing is comparable to him (1QM 13:13-14; 14:4-15), and God is the God of all gods (1QM 14:16). In the victory of the eschatological war, God is revealed as the most high, the glorious king who shall reign forever (1QM 6:6; 11:8; 19:1; cf. 4QM[a] frag. 11, 2:11; frag. 15 7; 4QM[b] frag. 1 13).

The uniqueness of Israel is also emphasized in 1QM. It is the chosen and holy nation, and many privileges in seeing God's revelation were provided for the people throughout history (1QM 10:9b-11a, 15b-18). The reference to the mysteries of several divisions in the universe (1QM 10:12b-15a) may have been connected to the emphasis on the unique status of Israel (cf. Sir 33:7-12).

The Division of the Nations: the Dualism of 1QM

The light/darkness dualism gives a significant framework to the whole book of 1QM.[74] The War Rule states that there are two kinds of lots (גורל[75]): one is the lot which belongs to God (13:5), and can be called 'the lot of light' (אור

---

[74] P. Davis thinks of 14:2-16a as a non-dualistic War Rule, based on his literary and redaction critical analysis.

[75] In the biblical Hebrew, גורל generally means the lot by which the land was allotted; it can imply 'the portion' (Ps 125:3; Dan 12:13), and in some contexts it is paralleled with חלק and מנת (Isa 17:14; 57:6; Ps 16:5). The Greek renderings in the LXX are κλῆρος (e.g. Isa 57:6; Jer 13:25) and κληρονομία (e.g. Isa 17:14; Ps 16:5). It should be noted that the chosen people are called, κληρονομία Ιακωβ (Sir 23:12) and μερὶς κυρίου κληρονομία ἀυτοῦ (Sir 24:12) in the sense of 'the generation.' Yadin (*The Scroll*, 256) gives a definition of the term, as 'preordained segment of humanity, of time, of an event, of a collection of objects.' Concerning the conception of two lots, Yadin (*The Scroll*, 242) argues that the scroll does not intend to explain the theory of light and darkness to the sect, but is concerned with defining who were the sons of light and the sons of darkness.

גורל) (13:9) or 'the lot of his [co]venant' (גורל ב[רי]תו) (17:6); the other belongs to Belial (1:5, 15; 4:2; 13:2, 4, 12), and it is called 'the lot of darkness' (גורל חושך) (1:11; 13:2, 5). It is noteworthy that in the context of 1QM col. 13, גורל is used in the sense of the 'eternal portion' which Israel is allotted through God's covenant with their fathers: 'We are an eternal people,[76] and you established a covenant with our fathers and ratified it with their offspring for eternal times' (13:7b-8a); 'You, God, have redeemed us to be for you an eternal nation, and you have made us fall into the lot of light' (גורל אור) (13:9). The remnant of Israel who were allotted to this portion are called 'the sons of light' (בני אור) (1:1, 3, 9, 11, 13, 14); on the other hand, the Gentiles and their Israelite Supporters (Kittim and their allies) are called 'the sons of darkness' (בני חושך) (1:1, 16; 13:16; 14:17; 16:11).[77] Thus the self-identity of Israel as the chosen people, which is common in Judaism, is illustrated by this dualistic language (i.e. light/darkness imagery).

The idea of the angels as sustainers is also seen in early Jewish literature: in particular, the archangel is assigned the role of guardian and defender of Israel (1 En 9:1[Greek]; 40:9; 44:6; 61:8); Belial's role is as the chief of demons (Jub 10:8; 11:5, 11; 17:16; 18:9, 12; 19:28; 48:1-15; 49:2).

THE DIVISION OF THE NATIONS

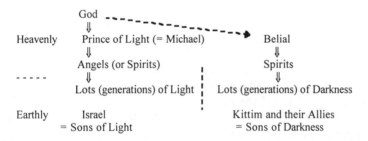

According to the Book of Jubilees, God created both good angels and evil angels, and they were able to intervene in human history: the Lord gave evil spirits the authority to rule over the Gentiles (Jub 15:31); however, the Lord did not permit them to touch the Israelites (Jub 15:32). Likewise, in the War Rule the host of holy angels, who consist of 'the prince of light' (שר מאור)[78] and all the angels of justice (מלאכי צדק) or the spirits of truth (רוחי אמת) (13:10), will assist the sons of light (1:16; 12:1-5, 8-9; 13:10; 17:6-7). On the

---

[76] García Martínez suggests the reading, נח[ל]לת[כ]ה] (cf. Deut 4:20), but the microfiche photos (SHR 3377 and 3399) suggest that the ending of the word is not likely ה, but ם or כ or ת; Yadin reads ע[ו]ללם] (cf. עם־עולם [Isa 44:7; Ezek 26:20]; עם מולמים [1QM 13:9]).

[77] Cf. Sir 33. This passage compares the division of time with the division of the nations.

[78] Cf. 1QM 9:15. Yadin (*The Scroll*, 322) thinks of him as Michael.

other hand, the sons of darkness are guided by Belial who is called 'the prince of the dominion of evil' (שר ממשלת רשעה) (17:5-6), and all the spirits of his lot (13:2, 4, 11-12; 15:14) who work in accordance with the law of darkness (חוקי חושך) (13:12).

The expiration of the eschatological war is depicted by the light/darkness imagery. It is said that the sons of justice shall shine (יאירו) to all the edges of the earth (קצוות תבל הלוך) (geographical expansion), and they shall go on shining (ואור) to the end of all the appointed times of darkness (מועדי חושך עד תום כול) (historical expansion), and in the end God's exalted greatness (רום גודלו) is expected to shine (lit. יאיר) for all the et[ernal] times ([ע[ולמים לכול קצי) (1QM 1:8). The extermination of all the sons of darkness (lit. לכלות כול בני חושך) (1QM 13:16) is depicted by the light/darkness imagery that (God) is going to humiliate (or to bring low) darkness (להשפיל חושך) and strengthen light (להגביר אור) (1QM 13:15). In other words, at the end of the eschatological war, the generation which is symbolized as 'light' is anticipated to overcome the lot of darkness which implies the generations of darkness. Therefore, it seems possible to say that the dualistic view of the War Rule is mostly based on Judaism (such as the division of the people and the assignment of the tasks of the angels). 1QM develops this view (the wholly negative view of all Gentiles) by employing a more dualistic language. It should be noted that both ideas (the division of the people and of the tasks of the angels) appear in the creation hymn (1QM 10:8-18) as well.

The Division of Times: Creation and Eschatology

The creation account of 1QM 10:8-18 refers to the division of times as previously mentioned: i.e. the appointed times (מועדי קודש), the cycle of the years (תקופות שנים), and the times of eternity (קצי עד) (1QM 10:15-16). This idea of the division of time may be related to the understanding of the eschatological time in the War Rule: i.e. 'From old (מאז) (You) proclaimed the appointed ([מ]ועד) time of your mighty hand against Kittim (1QM 11:11)[79]; 'From old (מאז) You appointed (יערתה) the day of the great battle' (1QM 13:14)[80]; 'From old (מאז) (God) appointed the Prince of light to assist us (Israel)' (1QM 13:10). The eschatological time is called, 'the appointed time of God' (מוער אל).[81] The glory of God is blessed because of his holy plan (מחשבת קודשו) (1QM 13:2; 14:14). Thus the creation account of 1QM 10:8-18 which particularly focuses on the divine order, such as the division of creation, the division of the nations, and the division of the times, gives a theological basis for encouraging the people to trust in God the Creator.

---

[79] Cf. Isa 31:8.

[80] Cf. 1QM 4:7; 17:5-6; 18:10-11; 1QS 3:18; 4:18, 20, etc.

[81] Cf. Dan 8:19; 11:27, 29, 35. The eschatological time is considered to have been appointed by God (e.g. עת קץ [the time of the end]; למוער [the appointed time]).

2.9 1QHᵃ (Thanksgiving Hymns from Qumran Cave 1) 9:7-20[82]

2.9.1 Literary Considerations

Preliminary Remarks: Reconstruction of the Text

A few lines from the top and from the bottom of plate 35 which contains
1QHᵃ 9:1-39 (Sukenik 1:1-39) have rotted away, and a long lengthwise lacuna,
which misses two or three words in each line, runs from the top to line 20. So
a reconstruction of the text with its literary analysis must be proposed.

RECONSTRUCTION OF 1QHᵃ 9:7-20

	[Stanza A]
7	ובחכמתכנ[ה] [83]ה{נ}כינותה [עולם
7 - 8	ובטרם בראתם ידעתה כול מעשיהם לעולמי עד
8	[84]מבלעדיכה לא[ן יעשה כול
8	ולא יודע בלוא רצונכה

	[Stanza B]
8 - 9	אתה יצרתה כול רוח
8 - 9	[85]ו{נ}פ[ע]ו{ל}תה הכינותה]
9	ומשטם לכול מעשיהם
9 -10	ואתה נטיתה שמים לכבודכה
10	כול [86]אשר בם הכינו[ח]תה לרצונכה

---

[82] The numbering of column and line follows García Martínez's. It corresponds to col. I
of Sukenik's original numbering (E. Sukenik, *The Dead Sea Scrolls of the Hebrew
University* [Jerusalem: Magnes, 1955]). Several scholars attempted to reconstruct the
original hymn book, by putting other fragmental texts into the lost sections. E. Stegemann
reconstructed the Hodajot, and put other two lines at the beginning of column 9. Therefore,
our text obtains the numbering 9:9-22 (A. Lange, *Weisheit und Prädestination: Weisheitliche
Urordnung und Prädestination in den Textfunden von Qumran* [STDJ 18; Leiden: E.J. Brill,
1995], 204).

[83] Stanza A and F constitute an inclusio, and it suggests this reading.

[84] Cf. 1QHᵃ 1:20; 18:9.

[85] The photo of Plate 35 suggests that ב, כ, מ, or פ may come after ו and before ע.
1QHᵃ 7:25 (Sukenik, 15:22) suggests the reading, ופעולתה הכינותה ('and he organized
its task'): אתה יצרתה רוח ופעולתו הכינותה (1QHᵃ 7:25). Licht (Jacob Licht [ed.],
מגילת ההודיות [Jerusalem: Bialik Institute, 1957]) and Carmignac (*Les Textes de
Qumran* [Paris: Letouzey et Ané, 1961]) also agree with this reading (sec. Holm-Nielsen,
Hodayot, 21).

[86] Stanzas B and C compose a thematic unit which narrates the creation of the heavenly
things and their course; Stanzas D and E compose a unit which narrates the creation of the
earthly things and the destiny (or the course) of human beings. The phrase, לרצונכה

[Stanza C]

10 - 11   ורוחות עוז לחוקיהם בטרם היותם למלאכי ⁸⁷[קודש]

11   לרוחות עולם בממשלותם

11   מאורות לרזיהם

12   כוכבים לנתיבותן

12   וכול רוחות סערה] למשאם

12   זקים וברקים לעבורתם

12 - 13   ואוצרות מחשבת לחפציהם

13   ⁸⁸ומפרש עבים] לרזיהם

[Stanza D]

13   אתה   בראתה ארץ בכוחכה

14   ימים ותהומות ⁸⁹[עם נהרות

14   וכול יוש]ביהם

14   הכינותה בחוכמתכה

14 - 15   וכול אשר בם תכנתה לרצונכ]ה[

[Stanza E]

15   ⁹⁰[והפלתה גורל] לרוח אדם אשריצרת בתבל

15 - 16   לכול ימי עולם ודורות נצח ⁹¹[למו]עד הפקודה] בקציהם

16   פלגתה עבודתם בכול דוריהם

16 - 17   ומשפט במועדיה ⁹²[לממשל]ת כול מעשיהם עולם] לדור ודור

17 - 18   ופקודת שלומם עם עם כול בנעיהם ⁹³[ומועדי צרה]

18 - 19   ותפלגה לכול צאצאיהם למספר דורות עולם

19   ולכול שני נצח]   ה[

כול אשר בם הכינותה, may come from Exod 20:11; Ps 146:6, functions as a literary insertion (i.e. as a refrain). This occurs between Stanzas D and E, as well as B and C. Therefore, the reading, אשר בם הכינותה in 9:10 is quite possible.

⁸⁷ Cf. 1QSª 2:8; 1QM 7:6; 10:11.

⁸⁸ A. Dupont-Sommer (*Le Livre des Hymnes découvert près de la mer Morte (1QH). Semitica VII* [Paris: Librairie d'Amérique et d'Orient Adrien Maisonneuve, 1957]) reads ברד ושלג ואבני with the reference to Job 38:22 and Jos 10:11; Licht takes the reading, עבים ומפרש, from Job 36:29 (cf. 1QM 10:12). In Job 36:26-30, clouds and lightning and thunder are paralleled, and its context emphasizes the knowledge of God the Creator.

⁸⁹ Dupont-Sommer reads עם נהרות וכול יושביהם; Licht reads וכול יושיהם היבשה; Carmignac reads בטובכה after ותהומות (sec. Holm-Nielsen).

⁹⁰ Cf. 1QS 4:26.

⁹¹ Cf. 1QS 3:18; 4:19-20. Licht למלא פעולותיהמה (cf. 1QS 3:16); Dupont-Sommer למשול במעשי ידיכה (sec. Holm-Nielsen).

⁹² Dupont-Sommer reads שתי רוחות כמעשיהם שמתה (cf. 1QS 3:18, 22); Licht ודרכיהם תכנתה (sec. Holm-Nielsen). My reading is from Ps 145:10-13: it has a similar expression, כל־מעשיך, and וממשלתך בכל־דור ודור is used in the meaning of 'all your creatures.'

⁹³ Dupont-Sommer proposes מעולם ידעתה; Licht לקציהם תכנתה; however, H. Bardtke's reading ('Die Loblieder von Qumran,' *TLZ* 81 [1956]) seems probable according to the similar expression of 1QS 3:23 (sec. Holm-Nielsen).

[Stanza F]

19 ובחכמת דעתכה הכי[נ]ותה תע[ו]דתם בטרם היותם

19 - 20 ועל פי [94ר]צונכה יה[י]ה כול ומבלעדיך לא יעשה

LITERARY STRUCTURE OF 1QHᵃ 9:7-20

Stanza A: Opening - corresponds to Stanza F (Inclusio)

In his wisdom God designed everything.
God knew all their deeds before creating them.
He is the sovereign God to achieve everything and to reveal his mysteries.

Stanza B: *Creation of Heavenly Things*

God created winds and determined their tasks and rule.
God stretched out the heavens.

Refrain: God designed (everything which is in them) according to his will.

Stanza C: Creation of heavenly things and their rule (course)

Powerful Spirits (the holy angels)
Astronomical elements: luminaries and stars, and their circuits
Meteorological elements: stormy winds, lightning, thunder, (clouds),
storehouse, and their roles and tasks.

Stanza D: *Creation of Earthly Things*

God created the earth, seas, depths with his strength.
God created their inhabitants in his wisdom.

Refrain: God designed everything which is in them according to his will.

Stanza E: Creation of Human beings and their destiny (course)

God created human beings and determined their course.
God allotted their tasks, rule, reward, affliction, and the time of suffering.

Stanza F: Closing - corresponds to Stanza A (Inclusio)

In the wisdom of his knowledge God designed their course before they came to be.
He is the sovereign God to achieve everything according his will.

---

[94] H. Bardtke reads כבודכה נהיה; Dupont-Sommer רצונכה נהיה; Licht נהיה (רברכה sec. Holm-Nielsen); and Martínez רצונכה יהיה. 1QHᵃ 9:20 clearly corresponds to 1QHᵃ 9:7.

Context and Main Concern

A composition of an *inclusio* between Stanza A and Stanza F, and two or three words which are blank after v. 20 indicate that 9:7-20 is composed as a large unit. The whole creation account is indicated by the demonstrative pronoun, אלה, at the beginning of the next paragraph, and it is also called רזי פלא, 'wondrous mysteries' (9:21), as a whole. In vv. 1-6, although most part of this paragraph has been lost, the ending part mentions God's greatness by citing a biblical formula[95] which indicates God's compassion toward sinful human beings: וארוך אפים במשפטן ואתה] צדקתה בכל מעשיכה (9:7). After the creation account, the emphasis is again on God's greatness in his justice and compassion, which contrast with the lowly and the finite nature of human beings (9:21-33a). Then it moves to sapiential instruction (9:33b-39).

Stanzas B-C and Stanzas D-E have a similar structure. The former narrates the creation of heavenly things, and the latter focuses on the creation of earthly things. The author of this creation hymn attempts to figure out a mystic correspondence between the rule (משפט) of the heavenly and earthly realms. That is to say, God created the heavenly things (and beings) and designed their courses, just as he created human beings and designed their destinies (or courses) with his wisdom. In this hymn, a general expression of God's work of creation, 'God created the heavens and the earth,' is divided into two parts (the creation of the heavenly things and the earthly things), and compared in order to argue that everything which happens in human history is in the knowledge of the sovereign God.

Influence of Key Passages from the OT

In the beginning and end sections of this creation hymn, the author refers to divine wisdom (1QH[a] 9:7-8; 19-20), and demonstrates God's providential plan. There are several examples of God's providential plan in the Old Testament (e.g. Isa 40:13; 46:10; Ps 33:11). This idea appears in the creation context of other Jewish writings as well.[96] Wisdom (or his knowledge) is mentioned in the context where the motif of God's arrangement or his perfect design is highlighted (1QS 3:15; 11:11; 4Q 402 frag. 4 12-14; 4 Ezra 5:49; 6:7-10; 2 En 33:3-4; Sir 42:21). Likewise, 1QH[a] 9:7-20 emphasizes God's perfect design both in the universe and in human history.

The list of the creation of astronomical and meteorological things (1QH[a] 9:8b-13) may be influenced by Job chs. 36-38 (cf. Pss chs. 104, 135; Sir 43:1-25).[97] The idea of the creation of the winds (רוח) and the assignment of their tasks is common in the OT (Job ch. 37; Ps ch. 104; cf. Ps ch. 33) and Jewish exegetical tradition (4 Ezra 6:1-6; 1 En 18:1-5a; 69:16-25; 76:1-14; JosAsen

---

[95] Cf. Exod 34:6; Pss 145:8; 103:8; 86:15; Joel 2:13; Jon 4:2, etc.

[96] See § 3.17.1 and § 3.17.2.

[97] Cf. 1 En chs. 72-77; 34-36; 2 En 40:4-11; Jub 2:1-2.

12:1-2; 1QM 10:12; 11QPs^a 26:14). The creation of the angels appears in some creation accounts as well (Jub 2:2; 2 En 29:1; LAB 60:2-3; 1QS 3:15-18, etc.).

2.9.2 Thematic Considerations

Creation of Adam

The account of the creation of Adam and his destiny (1QH^a 9:15-19) should be compared with a similar account in 1QS 3:15-26. In both contexts, human beings were created in order to rule (ממשלת) God's entire creation (1QS 3:17; 1QH^a 9:16-17) and they were allotted their tasks (עבורתם) until the end time (1QS 3:26; 1QH^a 9:16-17). They were allotted reward (שלומם) with afflictions (בגעיהם) and suffering (צרה) (1QS 3:13-14; 1QH^a 9:15b-19a) as well. The point is that the creation hymn of 1QH^a col. 9 emphasizes God's sovereignty over human history, by referring to the unshakable order of God, which is compared with the order (or course) in the astronomical and meteorological phenomena.

Wisdom in Creation

Wisdom language appears three times (1QH^a 9:7, 14, 19) in this hymn. The context in which the first wisdom appears (9:7) is not certain because there is a word missing in the middle of the sentence. Wisdom in the second example is paralleled with כוחכה (lit. your strength). In the Old Testament, wisdom (תושיה; חכמה) and strength (כח; גבורה) are sometimes used as a word pair to express the total activity of God (Jer 10:12; 51:15; Isa 10:13; Prov 8:14; Job 12:16): i.e. wisdom is depicted as his deep consideration, and strength or power as his mighty deeds. The creation account is mentioned as wonderful mysteries (רזי פלא) (1QH^a 9:21; cf. 9:11, 13), and its focus is on God's perfect design to rule the courses of his creatures which are in the heavens and on the earth. The third wisdom establishes the course of God's creatures (תעורדתם), and it is also paralleled with 'the will (of God)' (רצונכה). Therefore, the wisdom language is most probably employed here in relation to the author's concern with God's perfect design in creation.

The last part of 1QH^a 9:1-39 has a similar framework to the creation account in Sir ch. 17 and ch. 18. Sirach contrasts the weakness and the transient life of human beings (Sir 17:1-2, 30-32; 18:9-10) with the greatness of God's mercy and his majesty (Sir 17:21, 22b, 26b[GII], 29; 18:1-7, 11-14). In spite of the lawlessness of human beings, God endowed them with his wisdom: the fear of God (Sir 17:8); discretion, tongue, eyes, ears, and a mind for thinking (Sir 17:3-6; cf. 1QH^a 9:21-23a; 31b-33a). God wanted to show them the majesty of his works (Sir 17:8), so that they will praise his holy name (Sir 17:10) and will proclaim the grandeur of his works (Sir 17:9; cf.

1QH[a] 9:27b-31).[98]   Therefore, the poetic narrative of the creation account
(1QH[a] 9:7-21) is used in sapiential contexts where the sovereignty of God is
emphasized, and all of creation is expected to bear witness to his glory.

2.10 4Q381 (Non-Canonical Psalms B from Qumran Cave 4) frag. 1 1-12

2.10.1 *Literary Considerations*

Preliminary Remarks: Reconstruction of the Text

Both the top of the fragment and the right side have enough space to assume
that it must have been an upper margin. The left margin must be wider than
the fragment (perhaps more than the width of one word). The bottom of the
column has rotted away, and it cannot be established. There are large holes in
the right side of Line 4 to 8, and in the left side of Lines 4 to 5. Most parts of
Lines 9 to 11 are lost. Here is an attempted reconstruction of the text.

RECONSTRUCTION OF 4Q381 frag. 1 1-12

1		הגדתי ונפלאתו אשיחה
1		והיא תהיה לי למורה
1-2		משפט ["על] פי [99]
2		ולפתאים ויבינו
2		ולאין לב ידעון
2-3	נפלאות]	יהוה כמה גבור
3		הוא ביומי עשה שמים וארץ
3-4		ובדבר פיו [100] [כל צבאם]
4		ואפיקים [102] שך[ח][101] אור
4		ותיה אגמים וכל בלעה
4-5		[לילה וככנבי[ם וכסילים [103] ו]נ[אר] ל[ן

---

[98] These arguments may have originated from Ps 145:8-13, as well as Ps 139:4.

[99] See an idiomatic use in 1QH[a], 1QS, 11QT, and CD, etc.

[100] So E. Schuller ('4Q380 and 4Q381: Non-Canonical Psalms from Qumran,' in D.
Dimant and U. Rappaport [eds.], *The Dead Sea Scrolls: Forty Years of Reserch* [Studies on
the Texts of the Desert of Judah vol. X; Leiden: E. J. Brill, 1992]). Ps 33:6; 4Q422 1 6.

[101] E. M. Schuller (DJD 11) proposes אורותיה for אור ותיה, by assuming that there
seems to be a bad patch on the leather that led the scribe to break אורותיה into two words.
However, 2 mm blank seems too wide to take this reading, and the photo (PAM 43.224)
does not seem to give clear evidence for a bad patch on the leather.

[102] Schuller (DJD 11, 93, 95) comments that it is virtually impossible to reconstruct a
letter before שך, and suggests the root, שוך. However, the photo (PAM 43.224) clearly
indicates the space for one letter before שך, and ink marks can be seen.

5	ויהיר [¹⁰⁴] [מ]ן [ ] לאו]נת לדורות]
5-6	[ויצמח] עץ וכל פרי כרם וכל תבואות שדה¹⁰⁵
6-7	ולפי דבריו [ל]כל [האדם] את א]נ]כלה]¹⁰⁶
7	וברוחו העמידם למשל בכל אלה באדמה ובכל [במשים]
8	[לח]רש בנח]רש למועד במועד ליום ביום
8	לאכל פריה תנובב [הארץ]
9	[לכל חית הארץ] ועוף וכל אשר להם לאכל חלבי כל¹⁰⁷
9-10	וגם [כל בהמה וכל הארץ וכל ר]מש בהם¹⁰⁸
10	וכל צבאיו ומלא]ניו [
11	ולעבד לאדם ולשרתו ו] [
12	[ ]ל[[

TRANSLATION WITH LITERARY STRUCTURE

[Opening]
 I proclaimed and reflected on his wonders.
  And that shall be instruction for me.
   the law [on] my mouth
   for the small, so that they would understand
   for the senseless, so that they would know
    the Lord is gre[at] wondrous.

[General Creation Account]
 He, by his oath, created the heavens and the earth.
  with the word of his mouth, he (created) [all the hosts]

 and he lighted the channels of darkness.
 and he enclosed the pools and every whirlpool.
 and [he lighted] by night, and the stars and the constellations.
 and he caused [ ] to shine as a si[gn for the generations].

 and [he made to grow] the tree, all fru[it of the vineya]rd, and all the produce of the field.

 and according to his words, [(he provides) food to all humankind].
 and by his spirit, he appointed them to rule over all on the earth and over all [in the air]
    [mo]nth by [mo]nth, feast by feast, day by day

 and he made flourish [the earth] for all living things on the earth and birds
  to eat its fruit of produce [of the earth]
 and all that is theirs to eat the best of everything.
 and also [all beasts in all the earth and all the creep]ing things among them.

---

[103] Schuller proposes וידבר or ויאמר; however, it does not make sense in this context.
[104] Cf. 4Q422 frag. 2 10.
[105] Cf. Gen 2:9.
[106] Cf. Gen 1:29-30. Schuller (DJD 12) proposes [את א]נ]שתו   [ ]כל[ ];
however it seems to be out of context.
[107] Cf. Gen 1:30.
[108] Cf. Gen 1:26; Ps 8:6-8.

and all his hosts and angels [   ]
    and to serve humankind and to help them and [   ]

Context and Main concern

The opening words may suggest that this hymn represents sapiential teaching: the hymn reflects God's greatness and wonders which were manifested in the work of creation (1:1-3). In particular in the rest of the hymn, it is emphasized that God nourishes his creatures in his greatness. The mentioning of the angels as the sustainers in the last part of the fragment may indicate that the hymn might go on to emphasize God's generosity for human beings.

Influence of Key Passages from the OT

The words from the opening phrase of the hymn, ונפלאתו אשיחה, are used in biblical and extra-biblical psalms (cf. Pss 105:2; 119:27; 145:4-5; Sir 16:24-25; 39:29; 1QH^a 9:7 [Sukenik, 17:7]; 4Q381 frag. 31 2) to emphasize the sovereignty of God, and in many cases they are followed by the creation account. The idea that the great God revealed his knowledge to small, worthless beings (i.e. human beings) (4Q381 frag. 1 2), is Sirach's important argument (Sir chs. 17-18).[109]

The narrative order of the creation account of 4Q381 seems to be dependent on the Genesis creation account. In the creation account (4Q381 frag 1 3-11), firstly, the general creation account is stated (v. 3), and like other Jewish creation accounts, the divine attributes (the divine oath and the word of God) are mentioned. Following this statement, the Genesis creation account (i.e. Gen 1:1-26) is referred to as follows[110]:

4Q381 frag. 1 3-10	Genesis Creation Account
light and firmament (Lines 4-5)	Gen 1:1-8, 14-18
Plants (Lines 6)	Gen 1:11-12
Human Role (Lines 7-8)	Gen 1:26-28
Beasts and creeping things (Line 8-10)	Gen 1:20-25, 30

---

[109] 1QH^a (cols. 5 and 9) also takes it from the creation hymns of Sirach.

[110] I am grateful to Prof. R. Bauckham for suggesting this structural understanding. He thinks further that Lines 7-8 might be mentioning the creation of luminaries (Gen 1:14-18) because of the reference to the division of time ('[mo]nth by [mo]nth, feast by feast, day by day'). However, these words might be taken as an expression of 'the duration of time' (in the sense of eternity). Lines 6-7 seem to compose a parallelism (e.g. 'according to his words . . .' and 'by his spirit . . .'), and both lines seem to be concerned with the life of human beings (cf. 4 Ezra 3:4-5a). That is to say, the former indicates God's nourishment for human beings, whereas the latter indicates the assignment of the human role. The reference to the assignment of a human role in the creation context is very important for Jewish literature (cf. Sir 17:2-4; 1QS 3:17; 4Q422 frag. 1 9; 4Q423 frag. 2 2; 4Q504 frag. 8 6; 4 Ezra 6:54; 2 Bar 14:18; Jub 2:14).

The reference to the divine attributes at the beginning of the creation account (4Q381 frag. 1 1:3) may refer to Ps 33:6 (cf. SibOr 1:19-20; 2 Bar 14:17; 21:4; ApAbr 22:2; 8:10-11; JosAsen 12:2; Sir 39:17; 4Q422 frag. 1 6).[111]

4Q381 frag. 1 3	Ps 33:6
הוא ביומי עשה שמים וארץ	בדבר יהוה שמים נעשו
ובדבר פיו]כל צבאם[	וברוח פיו כל־צבאם

It is not a direct citation from Ps 33: וברוח פיו is changed to ובדבר פיו, and בדבר יהוה is replaced by הוא ביומי. ביומי in verse 3 should be translated as 'by an oath,'[112] rather than as 'in the day.'[113] This idea, the creation by a divine oath, can be understood as another exposition of the word of creation (cf. 1 En 69:16-25; Leg. All. 3:204).[114]

4Q381 frag. 1 6-10 refers to the assignment of human dominion over the created realm, based on the account of Gen 1:26 and 28. The wording of 4Q381, such as, למשל (1:7), and the list of created beings (1:9-10), may have been influenced by Ps 8:6-9. It is also interesting that 4Q381 describes the event of this assignment of the human role with the motif of the spirit (4Q381 frag. 1 6-7). The parallelism between 'according to his words' (ולפי דבריו) and 'by his spirit' (וברוחו) may suggest the reference to Ps 33:6.

The description of the role of the angels as supporters of humans in the rest of the fragment may reflect a Jewish tradition (cf. 1 En 9:1[Greek]; 40:9; 44:6; 61:8; Jub 15:32; 1QM 1:16; 12:1-5, 8-9; 13:10; 17:6-7). God's nurture of his creatures to his creatures (4Q381 frag. 1 9-10) is mentioned as it is in Sir chs. 16-17 (esp. Sir 16:26-30).

2.10.2 Thematic Consideration: God's Sovereignty and the Word

4Q381 portrays the sovereignty of God from several points of view. Firstly, it praises God who reveals his wonderful knowledge to human beings (1:1-2). The greatness of God is compared to the worthlessness of human beings. Secondly, the account of the creation of heavenly things which govern the astronomical and meteorological phenomena (1:3-5) is given as enigmatic

---

[111] The word of creation (not necessarily Ps 33:6) is mentioned in Sir 42:15; Jdt 16:14; Wisd 9:1; 4 Ezra 6:38; 7:69; 2 Bar 21:4; 48:8; Jub 12:4; SibOr 3:17-19; 2 En 33:4.

[112] So Shuller, and Martínez ('aduration' in *The Dead Sea Scrolls Study Edition* [1998], 755). 'The right hand' (ימין) is used in a divine oath (see BDB), so that the oath and the right hand may have been synonymous. Shuller (DJD 12, 95) comments that יומי is from the Aramaic root of ימי 'to swear' in a *Qutl* form.

[113] So M. Wise (*The Dead Sea Scrolls: A New Translation* [London: Harper Collins, 1996]), and the former translation of Martínez (*The Dead Sea Scrolls Translated* [1996], 312).

[114] See § 3.1.2 and § 4.6.2.

knowledge, and it elucidates how wonderful God is (1:2).   Thirdly, it
emphasizes that God carefully established the world in which human life is
sustained (1:7-11). Fourthly, the reference to the divine attributes (the word
of God, the oath of God, and the spirit of God) in the context of creation (1:3)
seems to emphasize the idea of the sovereignty of God.[115] Thus, the function
of the creation account here is to characterize the identity of the sovereign
God.

2.11 Summary (for Chapter 2)

We may now sum up some of our findings in the narrative accounts of
creation in early Jewish literature (ca. the 2nd century BC to the 1st century
AD):

(1) The narrative account of creation is a long retelling of the Genesis
creation account. It generally follows the narrative order of Gen chs. 1-2 (Jub
ch. 2; 2 En chs. 24-33; 4 Ezra ch. 6; Ant ch. 1; 4Q381), whereas some creation
accounts rearrange the order of the creation narrative in accordance with their
focus and point of view (SibOr bks. 1, 3, frag. 3; 1QM col. 10; 1QH^a col. 9).
Some creation accounts supplement the extra-biblical accounts of creation (e.g.
the creation of the angels [Jub 2:2; 2 En 29:3], the winds [1QM 10:11-12;
1QH^a 9:11-12], Paradise [2 En 30:1], and the throne of God [2 En 30:1]). 2
En chs. 25-26 exhibits a unique (i.e. quasi-scientific) interpretation of the
Genesis creation account by employing non-biblical ideas (i.e. the cosmogonic
figures, Adoil and Arkhas).   However, the narrative accounts of creation
mostly follow the Genesis creation account.

(2) The Jewish creation narratives also take several important ideas from
the biblical texts (mainly from Psalms, Job, and Isaiah). Ps 33:6-8 (SibOr bks.
1, 3; 4Q381) and Isa 48:3 and 55:11 (4 Ezra 6:38-43) are referred to in the
context which highlights the sovereign power of God. Reference to Isa 40:18-
26 is made in a context which makes a contrast between God the Creator and
the idols (or other gods) which were made by human hands (SibOr bks. 1, 3,
frag. 3; 2 En 33:12). Ps 8:5-8 is mentioned for the affirmation of the status of
human beings as ruler of all creation (SibOr frag. 3; 4Q381). The cosmogonic
account in Job chs. 38-43 is linked to the Genesis creation account, and the
account speculates on the mystic knowledge of God who alone knows all of
creation (SibOr frag. 3; 1QH^a 9:8-13).

(3) As mentioned above, the unique identity of God is described in
accordance with his status as the Creator. He is the only God since he is the
Creator of all things (space and time) (2 En 33:7-8; SibOr bks. 1, 3, frag. 3;
1QM 10:8-9a). This speculation on the unique identity of God in relation to

---

[115] Cf. Sir 39:17-18; 42:15; 43:5, 10, 13, 23, 26; 2 En 33:4.

his status as the Creator is expanded into a more salvific and eschatological sense. 4 Ezra 6:38-54 understands that the sole Creator who has sovereignty over all creation can alone fulfill the eschatological salvation. Similarly, SibOr finds a link between the identity of God as a Savior, who is preparing for the final judgment and reward, and the description of God as Creator (bks. 1, 3, and frag. 3). The creation accounts in 1QM col. 10 and 1QH^a col. 9 focus on the creation of the division of space and time (cf. Gen 1:4, 6, 9, 18). This motif is mentioned in the biblical (Job 38:8-12; Ps 104:8-9; Prov 8:28-29) and other Jewish writings (4 Ezra 6:49-50; Sir 16:26-28; 1 En 69:18; 2 En 47:5) in which the sovereignty of God over human history is highlighted. The Qumran Sectarians developed this motif in a more deterministic sense. They thought that God had already established every human course: the division of the nations and the division of the appointed times. Therefore, they strongly expected that the nation of Israel would be restored to its original status as ruler of the nations at the exact appointed time (cf. 4 Ezra 6:38-54). It is an eschatological interpretation of the Genesis creation account.

(4) The description of the work of creation accompanies the motifs of the divine attributes (such as the word of God [or command, oath], wisdom [or knowledge], right hand [or hands], and spirit). Each imagery seems to exhibit a particular sense or an aspect of the identity of God. For example, 'the word of God' seems to be associated with the description of the sovereign power in God's work of creation (2 En 33:4; 4 Ezra 6:38, 43; SibOr 1:19; 3:20; 4Q381 frag. 1 6-7). Wisdom (or knowledge) expresses God's perfect design or magnificent plan for the created world and for his people (2 En 33:3-4; 1QH^a 9:7, 14, 19). The hands of God are mentioned in a context which highlights the mighty power of God (Jub 2:11). The spirit of God is also mentioned as an agent of creation which gave human beings their role (4Q381 frag. 1 7; cf. Gen 2:7). In 2 En 33:3-4, both wisdom and the word appear in the same creational context; the former implies the perfect design or plan of God, whereas the latter depicts the reality of God's deeds or his works. It should be noted that the creational word in 4 Ezra 6:38 and 43 is personified and depicted as an agent to produce life from lifeless things. Therefore, the divine attributes play very important roles in the Jewish creation accounts (as well as in the biblical accounts [Ps 33:6; Prov ch. 8]) in accordance with the description of the unique identity of God.

(5) The creation account also speculates on human history which was recorded in the books of Moses. The Book of Jubilees retells Israelite history from Gen ch. 1 to Exod ch. 14, dividing each important period by the Jubilee years (49 year periods). SibOr bks. 1-2 divides Israelite history into ten generations and begins with the retelling of the Genesis creation account. Jewish Antiquities narrates history from creation to the administration of the last procurators before the wars with Rome. They attempted to learn from

history as to how the transgression of Adam brought about a calamitous condition (Ant 1:49; SibOr 1:38 thereafter). Secondly, they attempted to affirm the original status of human beings (or Israel) as the rulers of all creation (4 Ezra 6:46, 54; SibOr frag. 3; 1QM col. 10; 1QH[a] col. 9; 4Q381 frag. 1 6-7), by referring to the Genesis account of the creation of human beings (cf. Gen 1:26, 28; Ps 8:5-8). Thirdly, their recognition of time was associated with the expectation of the immediate coming of the eschatological salvation (4 Ezra ch. 6; 1QM col. 10; 1QH[a] col. 9).

(6) As for the life motif in the context of creation, it is associated with the identity of God: i.e. he is the sovereign God who has the authority to produce life with his word *ex nihilo* (4 Ezra 6:47, 48); God is said to be 'life' itself (SibOr frag. 3:34). When eschatological salvation is mentioned in relation to God's work of creation, life is depicted as an eschatological reward in terms of immortality (SibOr frag. 3:47) and as a symbol of Paradise (2 En 42:6).

(7) The light imagery is used in various ways. 4 Ezra focuses on the roles of light to enlighten God's creational works (6:40), as well as to serve human beings (6:46). Jub ch. 2 understands the role of lights as a sign for the times of the laws (the Sabbath), so that it became the basis for the covenant between God and Israel (2:8-10. Jub ch. 2 also understands it as a blessing for human beings (Jub 2:10, 12). This motif is extended to an eschatological meaning as the final blessing: i.e. 'All of the lights will be renewed for healing and peace and blessing for all of the elect of Israel' (Jub 1:29; cf. Isa 30:26). It is also interesting that in the picture of creation, light is depicted as the dwelling place of God (2 En 24:4 [A]; 25:3). Similarly, SibOr frag. 3:34 depicts God as 'imperishable eternal light' in the same context which depicts God as 'life.'

Chapter 3

Descriptive Accounts of Creation

This chapter treats the descriptive accounts of creation in early Jewish Literature (ca. the 2nd century BC to the 1st century AD). It is a shorter account which may focus on particular events of creation (i.e. selective reference to the Genesis creation account), and it is more interpretative than the narrative creation account. The following texts will be located in this category: 1 En 69:16-25; 2 En chs. 47-48; 65-66; 4 Ezra 3:3-4; 6:1-6; 2 Bar 14:15-19; 21:4-8; 48:2-10; 54:1-3, 13; ApAbr 21:1-22:2; LAB 15:5-6; JosAsen 8:10-11; 12:1-2; Sir 16:24-17:14; 39:12-35; 42:15-43:33; 1QS 3:13-4:1; 4Q392 frags. 1-9; 4Q422 frag. 1 1-13; 4Q504 frag. 8 4-10; 11QPs^a 26:9-15. Like the previous chapter, our analysis begins with the literary considerations on these points: (1) the context in which the creation account appears and the main concern of the creation account; (2) a reconstruction of the text (if it is needed); (3) the influence of key passages from the OT. Thematic (more theological) considerations will follow.

3.1 1 (Ethiopic Apocalypse of) Enoch 69:16-25

3.1.1 Literary Considerations

Context and Main Concern

1 En ch. 69 is part of the Book of Similitudes (chs. 37-71), so that the date issue has yet to be settled.[1] However, as far as 1 En ch. 69 is concerned, it shares important ideas with other Jewish writings. The idea of 'the oath of God' is conspicuous in this text; it also appears in the creation account of 4Q381 (frag. 1 3) and in Philo's Leg All 3:204.[2] The cosmogonic idea, 'the

---

[1] Cf. Milik (*The Book of Enoch Aramaic Fragments of Qumrân Cave 4* [Oxford: Clarendon, 1976], 91-92) argues that the Book of Similitudes is a late Christian work; however, the SNTS Pseudepigrapha Seminar (1977 and 1978) (the report was published in *NTS* 25 [1979], 315-27) concluded that the Book was Jewish and that it can be dated from the late first century AD.

[2] See § 2.10.2 (4Q381 frag. 1 1-11) and § 4.6.2 (PrMan 1:2-3).

divine order,' is also prominent in other Books of 1 En (2:1, 3; 5:2; 18:15-16; 72:3; 75:2, 3; cf. 21:6; ch. 80).[3]

The Book of Similitudes (1 En chs. 37-71) is composed of three parables concerning the eschatological judgment (I. 38:1-44:1; II. 45:1-57:3; and III. 58:1-69:29). Each parable argues for a future judgment which will come to both sinners and righteous ones (cf. 1 En 38:1-5; 41:1-2; 45:1-6). In the final parable, the judgment is declared to the angels (chs. 64-69), to the kings, to the mighty, and to those who possess the earth (chs. 62-63). Referring to heavenly and astronomical secrets, the author of the Similitudes argues that there is an absolute and perfect destiny which was given before the creation of the world (1 En 41:3-9; 43:1-44:1):

> And (I saw) how they do not leave their courses and neither lengthen nor reduce their courses, but they keep faith (*wăhāymānōtō mū yā'ăkĕbū*) with one another in the covenant (*bămăḥlā*) by which they abide (41:5b).

> No angel hinders and no power is able to hinder (the judgment of luminaries for blessing or for course) (41:9).

> (And I saw that) they (lightnings and the stars of heaven) hearkened unto him (43:1).

> And I saw how they are weighed in a righteous balance (*lămṣālĕw ṣĕdĕk*) according to their amount of light, according to the width of their spaces and the day of their appearing, and how their movement produces lightning, and their motions according to the number of the angels, and (how) they keep faith (*wăhāymānōtō mū yā'ăkĕbū*) with each other (43:2).[4]

Similarly, the creation account which appears in 1 En 69:16-25 depicts the divine order that is sustained by the divine power of the oath from the beginning until the end (1 En 68:2).

---

[3] Enoch is commanded to examine all divine order in the heavens and the earth, and he is encouraged to know how they do not alter their ways how they do not divert from their appointed order (1 En 2:1), and how all the works of God, as being manifested, do not change (1 En 2:3). All of his work prospers and obeys him as his servant (1 En 75:2, 3), and it does not change; but everything functions in the way in which God has ordered (1 En 5:2), and it is expected to obey (cf. 1 En 18:15-16; 'all of them (which are arranged) one after another in a constant order' (1 En 72:3); and 'for those luminaries scrupulously render service to the fixed positions in the cosmos' (1 En 75:3); if those luminaries transgress the order of God, they are bound in a chaotic and terrible place (or Sheol) (1 En 18:15; 21:6), and the judgment against the sinners comes when this order collapses (1 En ch. 80).

[4] English Translation is of Matthew Black (ed.) *The Book of Enoch or I Enoch: A New English Edition with Commentary and Textual Notes* (Leiden: E. J. Brill, 1985). Our thesis consults M. Knibb's Ethiopic edition as well (*The Ethiopic Book of Enoch: A New Edition in the Light of the Aramaic Dead Sea Fragments* [Oxford: Clarendon Press, 1978]).

Influence of Key Passages from the OT

1 En 69:16-25 uses a poetic form by echoing similar phrases (such as, 'by that oath,' and 'from the creation of the world and forever'). After the reference to the creation of the heavens, earth, sea, and depths, the poem cites the compact form of 1 En chs. 72-77 (or ch. 80) which tells of the ordinances of the universe (i.e. the ordinances of the luminaries [1 En chs. 72-75], the winds and meteorological phenomenon [1 En 76], the mountains and rivers [1 En ch. 77]). The idea of 'the ordinances of heavens' seems to be taken from Job chs. 37-38, in which God rules the meteorological (Job 37:1-18; 38:22-30) and astronomical (Job 38:31-32) phenomena with the winds (Job 37:9, 17-18) and his commands (Job 37:6, 12, 15). Job also mentions the laws of the heavens (חֻקּוֹת שָׁמַיִם) (cf. Job 38:33) in these contexts.

3.1.2 Thematic Consideration: The Divine Oath in Creation

The idea of the divine oath is reminiscent in this creation account:

> Through *his oath* (*bămăḥlā*) the firmament and the heavens were suspended before the world was created and for ever (1 En 69:16; cf. Gen 1:6-7)

> And through it (*the oath*) the earth was founded upon the waters, . . . and through that *oath* (*bămăḥlā*) the sea was created and its foundations, . . . and through that *oath* (*bămăḥlā*) are the depths made fast (1 En 69:17-19; cf. Gen 1:9-10; Ps 33:7).

> And through that *oath* (*bămăḥlā*) the sun and moon complete their course, . . . And through that *oath* (*bămăḥlā*) the stars complete their course (1 En 69:20-21; cf. Gen 1:14-16).

> And likewise, with regard to the waters, to their winds, and to all spirits and their courses from all regions of spirits. . . And by it (*the oath*) they shall be kept, and they shall keep to their paths, and their course shall not be spoiled (69:16-25).

In 4Q381 frag. 1 3-4, the divine oath parallels the word of God in the context of creation: 'He, by his oath (ביומי), created the heavens and the earth; with the word of his mouth (בדבר פיו), he (created) [all the hosts].'[5] J. Fossum observes that the creative and sustaining oath would have been the יהי 'let it be . . .' of Gen ch. 1.[6] Referring to J. Fossum's works, S. McDonough discusses how the divine oath is connected with the name of Yahweh (יהוה).[7]

---

[5] § 2.10.2 (4Q381 frag. 1 1-11).

[6] J. E. Fossum, *The Name of God and the Angel of the Lord* (WUNT 36; Tübingen: J. C. B. Mohr [Paul Siebeck], 1985), 78. Cf. Both TargNeo and TargJon to Exod 3:14 begin their explanation of the YHWH name with the words, 'The one who spoke and the world was . . .'

[7] S. McDonough, 'The One who is and who was and who is to come: Revelation 1:4 in its Hellenistic and Early Jewish Setting' (Ph. D. Thesis: University of St. Andrews, 1997), 110-112; the published title is *YHWH at Patmos* (WUNT II/107; Tübingen: Mohr Siebeck, 1999). See our discussion in § 4.6.2.

The verb 'to be' (היה) might be associated with God's revealed name 'I am who I am' (אהיה אשׁר אהיה; cf. Exod 3:14). It might be possible that the name of God as 'I am who I am' (אהיה אשׁר אהיה; cf. Exod 3:14) is associated with the unique identity of God who is the origin of all things so that he alone can let everything be (exist). That is to say, the name of God also indicates his identity as the Creator. Interestingly, 1 En 69:13-15 states that the oath was given through the secret name (*săm hĕbū'*) (of God?).[8] According to Philo, the oath is a proof of the exceeding power of God, and whatever he says is sure to take place (Leg All 3:204). The divine oath indicates the power of divine authority of Yahweh, through which the heaven and the earth were made and sustained. The idea of 'the divine oath' that the oath which is given through God's mouth produces a destiny or order in the universe obviously originated from the motif of the Genesis creation account (i.e. the motif of the word of creation).

3.2 2 (Slavonic Apocalypse of) Enoch chs. 47-48

3.2.1 Literary Considerations

Context and Main Concern

After the narrative of Enoch's descent (2 En chs. 36-38) and a brief summary of his testimony[9] (2 En chs. 39-42), a sapiential disciplinary section (2 En chs. 43-66) begins with an introductory account which teaches the principle of instruction, i.e. the fear of God.[10] Two creation accounts (chs. 47-48 and 65-66) appear in the context where that principle (the fear of God) recurs.

> And [among] all nations who are discerning (смыслать: *smyslêti*) so that they may *fear* (воятса: *voôtsê*) God (2 En 48:7 [J]).[11]
>
> Cf. [A]: who discern (съмысле: *sŭmysle*) and *fear* (воат: *voêt*) the Lord.
>
> And walk in front of his face *with fear* (съ страхш: *sŭ straxw*) and worship him *alone* (единомоу: *edinomu*) (2 En 66:2 [J]).
>
> Cf. [A]: Walk in front of the face of the Lord, and worship him *alone* (единомоу: *edinomu*).

---

[8] Cf. 'the name' in the creational context (PrMan 1:3; LAB 60:2; Jub 36:7).

[9] The great secrets of God which 2 Enoch picks up are as follows: the composition of the heaven and the earth, and their contents (2 En 40:1-2, 7, 12); the astronomical (40:4-6) and meteorological phenomena (40:8-11); Adam's fall (41:1-2); and Paradise and Hell (42:1-14).

[10] The framework of this section is similar to Sir 33:7-13 (See the section on Sir 33:7-19 in this chapter).

[11] Our thesis uses Sokolov's edition for [J], Vaillant' edition for [A].

Influence of Key Passages from the OT

The biblical passages which emphasize God's sovereignty over his creation (monotheism) are taken from Job, Isaiah, and the Psalms.

2 En 47[12]	Biblical Passages
There is no one except the Lord alone (Господа единаго: *gospoda edinago*), neither in the heaven, nor on the earth,	If I ascend to heaven, you are there;
nor in the deepest places, nor in the one foundation (47:3).[13]	if I make my bed in Sheol, you are there (Ps 139:8-12).
God laid the foundation[14]; spread out the heavens (47:4).	God, the Lord who created the heavens and stretched them out (Isa 42:5 cf. 40:22; 44:24).
Solidified the earth above the waters . . .	(The Lord of lords) who spread out the earth on the waters (Ps 136:6)
and he alone (единъ: *edinŭ*)[15] created the uncountable creatures . . .	The earth is full of your creatures. . . creeping things innumerable are there, living things both small and great (cf. Ps 104:25).
the God who has counted the dust of the earth or the sand of the sea or the drops of	He gave to the wind its weight, and apportioned out the waters by measure (Job
rain or the dew (of the clouds) or the blowing of the wind (47:5)	28:25); who has wisdom to number the clouds? or who can tilt the waterskins of the heavens (Job 38:37) (cf. Isa 40:12; Sir 1:2; 16:26-28).
The God who gave the indissoluble bonds between the land and the sea . . .	and prescribed bounds for it, and set bars and doors (Job 38:10) (cf. Ps 104:9; Prov 8:28-29; 1 En 69:18, etc.).
and made stars of fire in the sky (47:6)	You make the winds your messengers, fire and flame your ministers (Ps 104:4).

It should be noted that these biblical references stress God's uniqueness and his sovereign power in each context:

---

[12] Translation is mostly based on F. I. Andersen (OTP I, 174).

[13] This statement seems to have a thematic connection to 2 En 66:4: it points to the heavens, the earth, the depths of the ocean (for 'the deepest places' of 2 En 47:3), and all that is beneath the earth (for 'the foundation' of 2 En 47:3), and states that the Lord is there because he created all things. In other words, since he is the sole Creator of all things, there is no place where the Lord is absent.

[14] Cf. 2 En 24:5; 26:3; 33:3.

[15] The shorter recension (A) has this reading (but [J] does not have 'alone').

Text: Who has measured the waters in the hollow of his hand . . . (Isa 40:12); (It is he)
        who stretches out the heavens . . . (Isa 40:22).
Context: To whom then will you compare me (תדמיוני), or who should be like him
        (ואשוה)? (Isa 40:25).

Text: Who created the heavens and stretched them out, who spread out the earth . . .
        (Isa 42:5).
Context: I am the Lord, that is my name, and I do not give my glory to another
        (Isa 42:8).

Text & Context: I am the Lord, who made all things, who alone (לבדי) stretched out
        the heavens, who by myself (אתי) spread out the earth (Isa 44:24).

Text: When he gave to the wind its weight, and meted out the waters by measure . . .
        (Job 28:25).
Context: And he said to humankind, 'Truly, the fear of the Lord (יראת אדני), that is
        wisdom . . .' (Job 28:28).

Text & Context: Who has wisdom to number the clouds? (Job 38:37).

Text: You set a boundary (גבול) that they may not pass, so that they might not again
        cover the earth (Ps 104:9).
Context: O Lord my God, you are very great (גדלת מאד) . . . (Ps 104:1);
        O Lord, how manifold (מה־רבו) are your works (Ps 104:24).

3.2.2 Thematic Consideration: Creation and Monotheism

As shown above, 2 En chs. 47-48 develops a monotheistic understanding of
God, by mentioning several imageries which may have been taken from the
OT: there is no other besides the Lord (2 En 47:3) since he is the sole Creator
of all things (2 En 47:4-5a). The uniqueness of the Lord is emphasized (2 En
47:5b; 47:6).

   2 Enoch gives a shorter account of the solar movement (2 En 48:1-4; cf.
chs. 13-15), and focuses on God's thoughtful arrangement of it: 'He fixed it
by measure, by his own wisdom' (2 En 48:4 [J]; cf. 2 En 33:3).   Moreover,
the Lord is described as the God who created everything from the invisible and
the visible (ш невидимы видѣние всѣ сътвори: *w nevidimy viděnie vsě
sŭtvori*),[16] and as the God who is invisible (невидимь: *nevidimĭ*) (2 En 48:5).
Concluding these arguments, 2 Enoch encourages the readers to accept these
books and to fear the Lord (2 En 48:6-9) in order to gain the way to Life (2 En

---

[16] According to the Sokolov edition (cf. 2 En 25:1; 51:5; 65:1). Cf. In 2 En ch. 24 the
visible is described to have come out from the invisible things. In 2 En ch. 65, on the one
hand, the visible and invisible were created (65:1), whereas, on the other hand the context
suggests that the visible came out from the invisible (see § 2.2.2). That is to say, God is
depicted as the Creator of all (invisible and visible); however, the visible things seem to be
considered to have come out from the invisible.

48:9). Thus the creation account of 2 En chs. 47-48 functions as a theological basis for sapiential instructions.

3.3 2 (Slavonic Apocalypse of) Enoch chs. 65-66

3.3.1 Literary Considerations

Context and Main Concern

The second creation account (2 Enoch chs. 65-66) is placed in the final section of the first part of 2 Enoch (chs. 1-68). When the Lord calls Enoch up, the people were coming to kiss him (2 En 64:1), and Enoch gave the last instructions to them (chs. 65-66) before he was taken up to the highest heaven (ch. 67). 2 En chs. 65-66 goes back to the principal instruction (to fear the Lord) (e.g. 66:1-2), which is mentioned at the beginning of the disciplinary section (2 ch. En 43) and in the former creation account (2 En chs. 47-48), and recalls the instructions, i.e. the appreciation of the laws (65:5), the prohibition of idolatry, and the worship of the sole Creator (monolatry) (66:1-2, 5 [J]; cf. 2:2; 10:6). In these arguments, it is highlighted that God is the Creator of all creation (65:2, 3, 6; 66:1, 3, 4, 5).

Influence of Key Passages from the OT

For the argument of the appreciation of the laws (65:1-5), 2 Enoch develops the creation motif of Ps 90:12 in a quasi-scientific manner: Firstly, it mentions that human beings are created according to God's image, having been given the special knowledge to think and to argue, as well as to see and to hear (65:2); secondly, it mentions the division of times (65:3-4); and finally, it concludes by saying, 'a person might think about time, . . . and so that he might keep count of his own life from the beginning unto death, and think of his sins, . . . and so that he might not transgress anything of God's commandments' (65:4-5) [cf. 'So teach us to count our days so that we may gain a wise heart' (Ps 90:12)].

In the same context, allusion is made to Ps 139, in which the omniscience of the Lord is highlighted.

2 En 66:3-4	Ps 139 [trans. of the LXX (Ps 138)]
For the Lord sees whatever man meditates in his heart, and what counsel he plans.[17]	You discern my thoughts long before (139:2b).
[For] every thought is presented before the	Behold, O Lord, you have known all

---

[17] Translation of Charles.

Lord who made the earth firm and settled all the creatures upon it.

things, the last and the first: you had fashioned me . . . (139:4b-5a).[18]

If you look upon the sky, behold, the Lord is there; for the Lord created the sky.

If I should go up to heaven, you are there (139:8a);

If you look upon the earth, then the Lord is there; for the Lord founded the earth, and placed upon it all his creatures.

If you meditate upon the depths of the ocean and on all that is beneath the earth, then the Lord is there; for the Lord created all things.

If I should go down to Hades, you are present (139:8b).[19]

3.3.2 Thematic Considerations

Creation and Monolatry

Enoch instructs his sons and all the elders of the people how they should walk with fear in front of the Lord (2 En 66:2, 5-7), from whom no kind deed is hidden (2 En 66:5c). The monotheistic instruction is extended into monolatry (to worship him alone) as well.

And *worship* (томоу: *tomu*) him *alone* (единомоу: *edinomu*) (2 En 66:2 [J]).

Cf. [A]: and *worship* (том8: *tomu*) him *alone* (единомоу: *edinomu*).

Do not *bow down to* (иоклонитеса: *ioklonitesê*) anything created by man, nor to anything created by God, so *committing apostasy* (оставивиіе: *ostaavivije*) against the Lord of all creation (2 En 66:5 [J]).

In 2 En 66:5 [J], it is forbidden to worship the idols because the true God is 'the Lord of all creation' (га въсаѫ твари: *ga vŭsêô tvari*). Thus 2 En chs. 65-66 takes the form of a sapiential instruction which exhibits monotheism, and it is extended into monolatry, based on the understanding of God's mighty work of creation.

Creation and the Eschaton: the Age of Creation

One of the key ideas in these accounts is 'the age of creation' (вѣка тварнаго: *věka tvarnago*) (2 En 65:1[A]),[20] by which the author explains how the eschaton would be realized. The shorter recension in [A] (in Andersen), or in [B] (in Charles) states, 'Before all creation came about, the

---

[18] Cf. the MT trans., 'O Lord, you know it all. You enclosed me behind and before.'

[19] Cf. the MT trans., 'If I make my bed in Sheol, behold, you are there.'

[20] Adoil (2 En 25:1) may be equivalent to 'the age of creation' of 2 En 65:1 [A].

Lord established the age of creation (вѣка тварнаго: *věka tvarnago*),[21] and after that he accomplished all his creation' (2 En 65:1).[22] Then the Lord divided the age of creation into times (years, months, days, week, seven, and hours) (2 En 65:3 [A]), so that human beings came alive in the world where the times existed (2 En 65:4). The expression, 'so that he might keep count of his own life from the beginning unto death, and think of his sins,' may allude to life in the mortal world. This age is said to be 'the age of suffering' (волѣзнаго вѣка сего: *voléznago věka sego*) (2 En 66:6) as well. When the Lord's great judgment comes, all time (времена: *vremena*) (years, months, days, and hours) will perish (2 En 65:7), and 'a single age' (вѣк единъ: *věk edinŭ*) (2 En 65:8a), which is called 'the great age' (вѣсе велисѣм: *věce velicěm*) (2 En 65:8b) and 'the never-ending age'[23] (2 En 66:6), will come out. It is given as if it were reappointed. Thus the author attempts to explain how the eschaton will be realized by using the idea of 'the age of creation.' In other words, eschatology finds its relation to the creation account.

Light as an Eschatological Blessing

After the Lord's great judgment, the great age is to come with a great light (свѣт великъ: *svět velikŭ*) and an indestructible wall (стена: *stena*)[24] and Paradise (2 En 65:10), where there is no darkness (2 En 65:9). During the great age, the righteous who shall escape God's great judgment will be made to shine seven times brighter than the sun (2 En 66:7 [J]). In this case light is depicted as one of the eschatological blessings and as a symbol of Paradise.

3.4 4 (The Fourth Book of) Ezra 3:4-5

3.4.1 Literary Considerations

Context and Main Concern

Ezra retells the biblical account from creation to the event of the giving of the Torah (4 Ezra 3:4-19). B. Longenecker understands that this section can be divided into two parts (3:4-12 and 13-19), and that in particular the first part follows the general structure of Gen chs. 1-11, which is particularly concerned

---

[21] MSS B (R. H. Charles [ed.], *The Book of the Secrets of Enoch: Translated from the Slavonic by W. R. Morfill* [Oxford: Clarendon Press, 1896]) reads, 'The Lord made the world and then created.'

[22] The longer recension ([J] in Andersen, or [A] in Charles) renders, 'the Lord . . . created the whole of his creation.' However, it seems clear that 'the age of creation' is contrasted to 'the great age' (2 En 65:7) and 'never-ending age' (2 En 66:6).

[23] Charles renders, 'you shall be heirs of eternity.'

[24] Cf. [J]: стѣна here.

with the relationship between God and creation: (1) God acts and all is good; (2) humanity acts and all turns bad; (3) God destroys and begins again.[25]

The creation account appears in 4 Ezra 3:4-5.

O Dominator Domine, tu dixisti[26] ab initio, quando plantasti[27] terram, et hoc solus, et imperasti populo, Et dedit[28] Adam corpus mortuum; sed et ipsum figmentum manuum tuarum erat, et insufflasti in eum spiritum vitæ, et factus est vivens coram te

(4 Ezra 3:4-5).[29]

> O Ruler, Lord, you spoke at the beginning, when you formed the earth, and by you alone, and you commanded the dust so that it gave Adam, and dead body. However he was the creation of your hands, and you breathed into him the breath of life and he was made alive in your presence.

God is called *Dominator Domine* (lit. 'Ruler, Lord'). This title is used in the rest of the book as well (5:23; 7:17, 58; 12:7; 13:51), and it seems to be related to the context which demonstrates God's sovereignty over human history (cf. 4 Ezra 3:3-4; 4:1-11; 5:36; 6:1-6; 38-54; 8:22-23). God is the sole Creator who alone (*solus*) established (*plantasti*) the earth, and created Adam with his (lit. your) hands (*manuum tuarum*).

Based on the understanding of the sovereignty of God, the relationship between God and Israel is remembered: i.e. Adam was created by his word and by his spirit of life, so that they would not be abandoned without God's grace and mercy. This account goes on to Theodicy, and it refers to the fact that sinful human nature came down from the first generation. Moreover, this argument is extended into a pessimistic eschatological understanding that salvation cannot be expected in this world but in the world to come. Thus, the creation account of 4 Ezra 3:4-5 focuses on the identity of the people of Israel and their destiny in relation to the understanding of the identity of God as the Creator.

---

[25] B. Longenecker, *Eschatology and the Covenant: A Comparison of 4 Ezra and Roman 1-11* (JSNTSup 57; Sheffield: Sheffield Academic Press, 1991), 51.

[26] Codices Complutensis (C) (9th-10th AD) and Mazarinaeus (M) (11th AD) have *nonne* ; it is omitted by Sangermanensis (S) (822 AD) and Ambianensis (A) (9th AD) (sec. J. Myers, *I and II Esdras: Introduction, Translation and Commentary* [Garden City, NY: Doubleday, 1974], 159).

[27] C and M takes this reading; S and A read *plasmasti* (tr. fixed) (sec. Myers, 159).

[28] Several MSS read it *dedisti* (pf 2nd person); Syriac and Mazarinaeus read it *dedit* (pf 3rd person of *do*) (sec. Myers, *I and II Esdras*, 159). Comparing to 2 Bar 6:53, the latter rendering seems reasonable: *Sexto autem die imperasti terræ, ut createt coram te . . .* (On the sixth day you commanded the earth so that it should bring about before you . . .).

[29] Latin Text is from VIII Clementis (ed.) *Biblia Sacra* (Paris: Apud Garnier Fratres, Bibliopolas, 1868).

Influence of Key Passages from the OT

The narrative of the creation of Adam is based on Gen 2:7 and Isa 42:5. It is worth noting that 4 Ezra also puts the motif of the word of creation in this account, and his people are called 'those who were created by his word' (4 Ezra 7:69[139]).[30] The expression, 'the creation by the hands of God' (4 Ezra 3:5), seems to be taken from Job 10:8: 'Your hands fashioned and made me, and now you turn and destroy me,' with similar motivation.

3.4.2 Thematic Considerations

God's Word and Hands in Creation

4 Ezra 3:4-5 focuses on the creation of Adam. The opening phrase, 'O sovereign Lord, you spoke at the beginning (*tu dixisti ab initio*) . . . and commanded the dust' (*et imperasti populo*) (4 Ezra 3:4), gives a nuance that Adam was created by God's command or his word. In the later sections, it is clearly indicated that human beings were created by his word and by his command.

> *Et judex si non ignoverit his qui curati sunt **verbo ejus**, et deleverit multitudinem contentionum, non fortassis derelinquerentur in innumerabili multitudine, nisi pauci valde* (4 Ezra 7:69 [139]).

> And the judge, if he did not pardon those who were created *by his word* and annul the multitude of their contempts, there would probably be left only very few of the innumerable multitude.

> *Si ergo perdideris eum qui tantis laboribus plasmatus est, **tuo jussu** facile ordinari, ut et id quod fiebat servaretur.*

> If therefore you destroy the one, who was molded with so great labor, *by your command* with easy order, to what purpose was he made? (4 Ezra 8:14).

The attempt to employ the motif that God created Adam by his own word is in a sense to emphasize the distinguished status of Israel as the chosen people (4 Ezra 3:4-6; 7:69[139]; 8:14) and the fact that God's special care has never been absent from them, even though Israel had been in tribulation.[31]

The expression, 'the creation by the hands of YHWH' (4 Ezra 3:5) is used here as well. The metaphor of God's hands is used in several biblical texts to

---

[30] The idea that God by his word brings about the thing which does not exist appears in other Jewish texts: 'And with the word you arise that which does not exist (2 Bar 48:2)'; 'For you, Lord, spoke and they were brought to life, because your word, Lord, is life for all your creatures' (JosAsen 12:2).

[31] Cf. 'He (Adam) was the workmanship of your hands, and you breathed into him the breath of life, and he was made alive in your presence. And you led him into the garden which your right hand had planted before the earth appeared' (4 Ezra 3:5b-6).

highlight the mighty power of God (e.g. Isa 45:12; Ps 95:5) and to demonstrate God's care for his works of creation (e.g. Job 10:8; Ps 119:73). Thus 4 Ezra seems to mention that since human beings were created by God's word or by his hands, they will not be abandoned easily by their God the Creator.

Life and the Divine Word

God is described as the life giver to lifeless beings (4 Ezra 3:5). 4 Ezra states that the living things were made by his utterance on the fifth day (in the air and in water) (4 Ezra 6:47-48) and on the sixth day (on the land) (4 Ezra 3:4-5). It emphasizes God's sole work in creation (3:4; 6:6) and his mighty power to produce life from lifeless objects (6:48). As for the creation of Adam, 4 Ezra states that his (lifeless) body was made by the word of God (3:4-5a), and then it was made alive when God breathed into it the breath of life (3:5b). However, it could be said that Adam was created by the word of God (4 Ezra 7:69 [139]) as a whole.

Creation and Theodicy

The first section explains how sinful human nature existed from the beginning of the world. Adam transgressed the command which was given by God (3:7), and his descendants did ungodly things before the Lord (3:8). After the flood, Noah's descendants began to be more ungodly than their ancestors (3:12), and the descendants of Abraham and Jacob (3:20) and David (3:26) possessed the same evil heart. 4 Ezra takes up this subject at the end of section III, and focuses on the people's sinful nature and their attitude to the Mosaic law.

> *O Domine, te nobis ostendens, ostensus es patribus nostris in deserto, . . . Ecce enim ego semino in vobis legem meam, . . . Nam patres nostri accipientes legem, non servaverunt, et legitima mea non custodierunt, et factus est fructus legis non parens: nec enim poterat, quoniam tuus erat* (4 Ezra 9:29-32).

>> O Lord, you indeed showed yourself to us, through our fathers in the wilderness . . . For behold, I sow my law in you, . . . But though our fathers received the law, they did not keep it, and did not observe the statutes; yet the fruit of the law did not perish, it was impossible, because it is yours (4 Ezra 9:29-32).

4 Ezra understands that the evil seed which was sown (*seminatum*) in Adam's heart remains in the people's hearts (4:30) together with the seeds of the law which were sown at Mount Sinai (cf. 3:22: 9:32-36). 4 Ezra concludes that the diseases became 'permanent . . . what was good departed, the evil remained' (5:22), and that the ancestors who received the law perished (9:33), and those who have received it will perish (9:36) since God did not hinder their sinful nature (3:8) and did not take them away from their evil hearts (3:20). This argument of theodicy alludes to the author's expectation that

salvation will be given through the new creation of human hearts and that it should be anticipated in the right path (i.e. the Mosaic law).

Light Imagery and Revelation

4 Ezra understands that the world lay in darkness after the fall of the First temple (586 BC), and its inhabitants were without light (4 Ezra 14:20) since the law was burned (4 Ezra 14:21). What was good departed and evil remained (4 Ezra 3:22), and that age was full of sadness and infirmities (4 Ezra 4:27). Ezra was assigned to restore it through the new revelation. For this purpose the Lord lit in the author's heart the lamp of understanding (4 Ezra 14:25), and his heart was filled with wisdom (4 Ezra 14:40) so that he could complete his writings (4 Ezra 14:40-44). In these books there is the spring of understanding, the fountain of wisdom, and the river of knowledge (4 Ezra 14:27). In this context, the light imagery is associated with the revelation of the law. It was restored through the Holy Spirit (4 Ezra 14:22) as a provisional light for the people who lived in darkness before the coming of the eschatological era.

3.5 4 (The Fourth Book of) Ezra 6:1-6

3.5.1 Literary Considerations

Context and Main Concern

There is a major subject change between 4 Ezra 5:56-6:6 and the rest of the second section (4 Ezra 6:7-34): the former part argues that the eschatological event (salvation) will be brought about by God alone, not through another Messianic figure, whereas the latter is concerned with the eschatological times (cf. the notion of the organized age in the sense of the time order [5:49]; the final age [5:50-55]; the division of history [6:7-10]; and the signs for the end of the world [6:11-28]).[32] The purpose of the reference to the creation account thereby is to demonstrate that God had already made a plan for the eschatological salvation with his deep thought (cf. 4 Ezra 5:49; 6:6, 7-10).

---

[32] M. Stone (*Fourth Ezra: A Commentary on the Book of Fourth Ezra* [Minneapolis: Fortress Press, 1990], 144-145) understands that a major new question begins in 4 Ezra 5:56-6:6, which is distinguished from previous questions.

Influence of Key Passages from the OT

The entire framework of this section may be taken from Prov 8:22-29,[33] in which many temporal subordinate clauses (with מֵרֹאשׁ, עַד, and בְּ) are juxtaposed. The main clause is concerned with the pre-existent plan for the past (creation) and the future event (the eschaton) (4 Ezra 6:6a).

> In the beginning of the circle of the earth (*terreni orbis*),
> before the portals of the world (*exitus sæculi*) were established,[34]
> before the assembled winds (*conventiones*[35] *ventorum*) blew,
> before the rumblings of thunder resounded,
> before the flashes of lightning glittered,
> before the foundations of paradise (*fundamenta paradisi*) were laid,
> before the beautiful flowers (*decori flores*[36]) appeared,
> before the powers of motion *(motæ virtutes)* were established,
> before the innumerable hosts of angels were gathered together,
> before the heights of the air (*altitudines æris*) were raised up,
> before the measures of the firmaments (*mensuræ firmamentorum*) were named,[37]
> before the footstool (*camini*) was established in Zion,[38]
> before the present years were tracked out,
> before those who now sin were removed,[39]
> and those who stored up (*thesaurizaverunt*) faith were sealed (*consignati*),
> *Then, I thought, and these things were made through me alone* (4 Ezra 6:1-6).

The content of the creation account is obviously influenced by several biblical and extrabiblical texts as Myers and Box have suggested[40]:

> 'In the beginning' (Prov 8:23; Ps 90:2; 1 En 48:6b; 60:11-12; 2 Bar 48:7-10; 59:5-12); 'the terrestrial world' (*terreni orbis*) (Ps 89:2 [90:2] in Vulgate; Prov 8:26); 'portals of the world' (1 En 34, 35); 'the wind-blasts' (2 Bar 59:5; 1 En chs. 17, 34); 'crashes of thunder' (Pss 77:18; 104:7); 'beauty of the flowers' (cf. Sir 43:9; 2 Ezra 6:44); 'innumerable hosts of angels (1QM 7:6; 12:1, 8; Job 25:3); 'measures of the firmaments' (2 En 3; 21:6; 22:1).

---

[33] Cf. H. Kee, "'The Man' in Fourth Ezra: Growth of a Tradition,' *SBLASP* 20 (1981), 200-201.

[34] S, A, C, reads *starent*, 'stand' (sec. Myers).

[35] Syriac reads *ywqrhyn*, 'weighs' (sec. Myers).

[36] Syriac reads, 'beauty of the flowers' (sec. Myers). Gunkel thinks that they are the flowers of the heavenly paradise which were originally stars (sec. Myers).

[37] A, C, M, reads *numerarentur*, 'were numbered,' instead of *nominarentur*, Syriac renders, *nštmhm*, 'named' (sec. Myers).

[38] Syriac read *nštrr*, 'appointed,' or 'designated' (sec. Myers).

[39] Our text reads, *antequam abalienarentur eorum qui nunc peccant adinventiones*; cf. Metzger, 'the imaginations of those . . . were estranged'; Myers, 'the tricks of those . . . were thwarted.'

[40] Cf. Myers notes (196) and Box (574).

3.5.2 Thematic Considerations

Monotheism and Eschatology

Monotheistic expression is prominent in 4 Ezra 6:6: 'I thought, and these things were made through me alone (*per me solum*), and not through another; and the end [will come] through me (*per me*) and not through another.'[41] This argument is related to the principal question, 'By whom will you visit your creation?' (4 Ezra 5:56). If our textual reading of 4 Ezra 6:6 is reasonable, then 4 Ezra emphasizes that the end time will be brought about by God alone. Moreover, the point is that eschatological salvation is discussed on the recognition of the unique identity of God who thought out the plan for the creation of the world.

Wisdom in Creation

The entire account illustrates how God designed the world, preparing 'the powers of motion,' 'innumerable hosts of angels,' and 'the measures of the firmaments.' This motif may be related to the main subject of the second section, which refers to God's design of the times or the order of the historical stages (the arranged time order [5:49] and the division of the times [6:7-10]). Thus, the wisdom motif in this context highlights God's sovereignty over human history.

3.6 2 (Syriac Apocalypse of) Baruch 14:15-19

3.6.1 Literary Considerations

Context and Main Concern

After Baruch's lamentation about the miserable state of Israel (2 Bar chs. 10-12), the new section (which is the second dialogue between God and Baruch) begins from ch. 13. In the dialogue, firstly God proclaims thorough 'destructive' judgment upon the nations (the Gentiles) (2 Bar 13:5-8, 11-12), which is contrasted to the 'instructive' punishment for Israel, the punishment for their repentance and forgiveness (2 Bar 13:10). Responding to it, Baruch complains that the (sinful) Gentiles still live in happiness (2 Bar 14:2-3). This question is dealt with through the rest of the dialogue (2 Bar 15:1-20:2), and

---

[41] The Syriac edition lacks the last part, 'and the end [will come] through me and not through another.' See M. Stone's note (*Fourth Ezra*, 143). However, Ezra's question which follows, 'What will be the dividing of the times? Or when will be the end of the first age and the beginning of the age that follows?,' may suggest that Ezra is concerned with the sovereignty of God over the eschatological events.

the fairness of God's judgment against Israel is emphasized.[42] The creation account (2 Bar 14:15-19) is employed to recall the original status of Israel as the chosen people.

Influence of Key Passages from the OT

The expression, 'You devised and spoke with the word' (2 Bar 14:17), gives a nuance that God made a plan before his work of creation and then carried it out with his word. The interaction between the word of God and wisdom in the context of creation is seen in 2 Bar 56:4: 'It came to pass, when the word had gone from before him, . . . and it was established according to the multitude of the intelligence (ܣܘܟܠܐ: sūkāleh) of the one who sent it.' That interaction may come from the unification of the two biblical traditions: one is from Ps 33:6 (cf. Ps 33:9; 148:5; Isa 45:12; 48:13), the other from Prov 8:30; 2:19-20 [which is cited in Jer 10:12; 51:15-16]; and Ps 104:24).[43] The idea that the works of creation stood (ܩܡܘ: qāmw < qm[44]) at once (ܡܚܕܐ: šāʿtē) before God is alluded to Isa 48:3, 13, or Ps 33:6, 9.

2 Bar 14:17	Isa 48:3, 13; Ps 33:6, 9
You . . . spoke (w'emmart) with the word (bmelṭā)	he spoke, (Ps 33:9) . . . With the word of the Lord the heavens were made (Ps 33:6).
and at once (šāʿtē) the works of your creation stood (qāmw) before you.	then at once I did (Isa 48:3). I call to them, they stand forth together (Isa 48:13); it stood forth (Ps 33:9).

The idea of the immediacy of God's work of creation, which is related to the word motif, cannot be seen in the OT except in Isa 48:3. In the case of 4 Ezra 6:43, Isa 48:3 is clearly referred to as shown above.

---

[42] Baruch understands that (1) although the holy city was delivered up for a time, the real holy city which has been in heaven from the beginning of creation is never destroyed (2 Bar 4:1-6); (2) the new world is prepared for the righteous (2 Bar 15:7-8); (3) the (temporal) punishment for Israel is for the sake of forgiveness (2 Bar 13:10), but there will be the (final) judgment of the nations (2 Bar 13:12-14:1); (4) the responsibility rests with the unrighteous who trespassed the law (2 Bar 15:5-6; 19:3); and (5) the fall of Jerusalem is said to be a sign that God will visit the world sooner (than expected) (2 Bar 20:1-2).

[43] Cf. TargNeo Gen 1:1: 'From the beginning with wisdom (בחכמה) the word of the Lord (מימרה דייי) created and perfected the heavens and the earth'; 2 En 33:3-4: 'By my supreme wisdom all these things I planned to accomplish; my wisdom is my adviser and my deed is my word' (2 En 33:4).

[44] The Syriac, qm is used in 2 Bar 48:8 in aph'el form, mqīm (ptc act), in the sense that God raises or brings about that which does not exist.

The understanding of the human status as guardian (ܡܦܪܢܣܢܐ: *mparnsānā*) over the creatures of God seems to be an exposition of Gen 1:26, 28, and Ps 8:6-8.

3.6.2 Thematic Considerations

Creator and Israel

The creation account is employed to describe the relationship between the people (Israel or the righteous) and the world.

The creation motif appears in a context which contrasts the existing condition of Israel with their original status as the chosen people (2 Bar 14:15-19): 'you (God) said that you would make a man (ܒܪܢܫܐ: *barnāšā*)[45] for this world as a guadian (ܡܦܪܢܣܢܐ: *mparnsānā*)[46] over your works so that . . . he was not created for the world, but the world for him' (2 Bar 14:18). Baruch questions, 'Why are Israelite people going to depart, and the world remain?' (2 Bar 14:19). The Lord answers this question, by directing Baruch's attention to 'the coming world' (lit. 'that again which is to come' [ܕܥܬܝܕ ܗܘ ܬܘܒ: *haw tūb da'tīd*]), not to 'this world' (ܗܢܐ ܥܠܡܐ: *hānā 'ālmā*), which is prepared (at the beginning) for the righteous (2 Bar 15:7-8).

There is a similar account in 4 Ezra 6:55-59 that raises the question of why Israel cannot possess their world, although the world was created for Israel, not for other nations.[47] Thus both 4 Ezra and 2 Baruch share a similar understanding of the relationship between the people (or Israel) and the world, or the relationship between Israel and God the Creator. This is an interpretation of Gen 1:26, 28.[48]

The Word and Wisdom in Creation

> O Lord, my Lord, when of old there was no world with its inhabitants, you *thought* ('*sthassabt* [49]) and spoke (*w'emmart*) *with the word* (*bmeltā*)[50] and *at once* (*šā'tē*) the works of your creation stood (*qāmw < qm*) before you (2 Bar 14:17).

---

[45] Cf. 4 Ezra 8:1, 44 (for man); 6:55, 59; 7:11; AsMos 1:12 (for Israel); 2 Bar 14:19; 15:7; 21:24 (for the righteous in Israel) (See Charles' note in APOT II, 491). The Syriac Text is of M. Kmosko (ed.) *Epistola Baruch Filli Neriae*, Patrologia Syriaca (Paris: Instituti Franciti Typographi, 1907).

[46] It means 'steward,' 'caretaker', 'guardian,' or 'administrator' (J. P. Smith, [ed.] *A Compendious Syriac Dictionary* [Oxford: Clarendon Press, 1903], 292).

[47] In the account of 2 Baruch, the righteous (15:7) and patriarchs (21:24) are said to be the possessors of this world (2 Bar 15:7).

[48] See the later Rabbinic tradition (m. Sanh. 4:5).

[49] Ethpa'al, reflexive use: 'to think,' 'to plan,' 'to design' (Smith, *Syriac Dictionary*, 161).

[50] Emphatic form of *meltā*. The original verbal form is *mll*.

The literary form of this creation account, as well as its function in the context, is similar to 4 Ezra 6:38-43.

2 Bar 14:17	4 Ezra 6:38-43
O Lord, my Lord,	*O Lord*,
you devised and *spoke* . . .	*you spoke*
when of old there was no world, . . .	*at the beginning* of creation, . . .
with *the word* . . .	and *your word* accomplished the work. . .
	For *your word* went forth,
and *at once* the works of your creation	and *at once* the work was done.
stood.	

Both invoke the name of the Lord in the dialogue with God and confirm the sovereignty of the Lord, the Creator of the world. God is described as the one who accomplished the work of creation with his word, and the immediacy[51] of God's deed is emphasized. The differences are firstly, that the word of God in 2 Baruch is not personified; secondly that 2 Baruch employs the wisdom motif together with the word motif: 'you thought (ܐܬܚܫܒܬ: *'sthassabt*) and spoke (ܘܐܡܪܬ: *w'emmart*) with the word (ܒܡܠܬܐ: *bmeltā*).' The Syriac rendering, *'sthassabt*, which comes from *ḥsb*, has the meaning of 'making a plan,' or 'designing something,' which alludes to the nature and the role of wisdom.

3.7 2 (Syriac Apocalypse of) Baruch 21:4-8

3.7.1 Literary Considerations

Context and Main Concern

The second dialogue begins with Baruch's (as Pseudonym) long prayer (from ch.21). The literary pattern is similar to three other descriptive sections (chs. 14, 48, 54): i.e. (1) God's name is addressed; (2) Baruch refers to the creation account; and (3) he develops his theological themes on the basis of the creation account. The main concern of this section is the fulfillment of God's promise to Israel (cf. 2 Bar 21:25).

Influence of Key Passages from the OT

There are several textual correspondences between 2 Bar 21:4-7 and Ps 33:6, 9 and Isa 48:3, 13: (1) both have the ideas of the creation 'by the word of the Lord' and 'by the spirit' (2 Bar 21:4 and Ps 33:6); (2) *daqrā* < *qr'* in Syriac (2

---

[51] The idea that the work was accomplished at once by the word of God may come from Isa 48:3, as in 4 Ezra 6:38-43.

Bar 21:4) and *qōrē* < *qr'* in Hebrew (Isa 48:13); (3) the creative command (2 Bar 21:5 and Ps 33:9); and (4) the motif of the immediacy of his deed (2 Bar 21:7 and Isa 48:3).

2 Bar 21:4-7	Pss 33:6-9 & Isa 48:3,13
O (Lord) one who made the earth, hear me, the one who fixed the firmament *by the word* (*bmeltā*) and fastened the heaven *by the spirit* (*brūḥā*).	*By the word* of the Lord the heavens were established; and all the host of height of them *by the spirit* (וברוח) of his mouth. For he *spoke*, and they were made (Ps 33:6)
the one who from the beginning of the world *called* (*daqrā* < *qr'*) that which did not yet exist and they obeyed you (21:4).	When I *call* (καλέσω [LXX]; *qōrē* < *qr'* [MT]) to them, they stand forth together Isa 48:13).
You who *commanded* (*pqaḏt*) to the air *with your sign* (*bremzāk*) and have seen the things which are to come as well as those which have passed (21:5).	and he *commanded* (*ziwwā*), and they were created (Ps 33:9).
. . . you may create *immediately* *barsā'ṯē*) all that you want (21:7)	I (God) did *immediately*, and they (the events) came to pass (Isa 48:3).

The reference to τὸ πνεύμα in the context of creation (although it is not necessarily certain whether it should be translated as 'wind' or 'spirit') appears in Ps 33:6 as well.[52] The idea of the immediacy of God's work of creation in 2 Bar 21:7 may also come from the same source in 4 Ezra 6:38-43 as shown above, that is, Isa 48:3.

3.7.2 Thematic Considerations

Creation and Eschatology

It should be noted that the realization of the eschatological plan is expected on the basis of the sovereign power of God, which was manifested in his work of creation.

< God of Creation >	< God of the Eschaton>
You can create *immediately* (*barsā'ṯē*) all that you wanted (21:7);	*Not to postpone* that which was promised by you (21:25
You who *rule with great thought* (*bḥbuššābā rabbā*) the hosts and holy beings that stand before you (21:6).	You alone can *sustain* all who are,[53] and those who have passed away (21:9).

---

[52] Cf. Isa 42:5; Ps 104:30.

[53] Emphasis is on God's sovereign rule over all human history.

| You *know* the number of the drops (21:8); | You *know the number*[54] of mankind of rain (21:11) |
| | You alone *know* the consummation of the times before they come (21:8); and you *know* where you preserve the end of those who sinned or the consummation of those who have been righteous (21:12). |

2 Bar 21:4-8 gives a vivid picture of the sovereign power of God in the work of creation. He summoned (ܩܪܐ: *daqrā* < *qrʿ*) that which did not exist (2 Bar 21:4) and he can create at once what he wants (2 Bar 21:7). He alone knows the end of the times (21:8), and he counts exactly the number of people who will gain and lose eternal life (21:10; cf. 23:4). He has seen those things which are to be (ܕܥܬܝܪܢ: *daʿtīrān*) as those things which have passed over (ܕܥܒܪ: *daʿbar*),[55] and he rules over the heavenly beings (2 Bar 21:6).

2 Baruch highlights the unique identity of God by repeating the same phrase, 'You, you alone' (ܐܢܬ ܒܠܚܘܕܝܟ: *ʾat balhūḏayk*) (2 Bar 21:7, 9a, 9b, 10): he alone creates all he wants at once (2 Bar 21:7); he alone rules over the heavenly beings (21:9a); he alone is life (ܚܝܐ: *ḥayā*) who is unsearchable (21:9b) and who never dies (ܡܐܬ: *māʾet*) (21:10). He is also the one who prepares for the eschatological judgment of the righteous and unrighteous (21:12).

The unique relationship between God and his people as 'a beloved people' (ܥܡܐ ܚܒܝܒܐ: *ʿamā ḥabbībā*) (2 Bar 21:21) is also recalled: 'those (patriarchs) on whose account you have said you have created the world' (2 Bar 21:24).

The Word and Thought (Wisdom) in Creation

The divine word figure, as well as the spirit and thought (in the sense of wisdom?), gives a vivid picture of God's sovereignty over his works of creation and also of the reality of the accomplishment of his eschatological work.

Creation by the word (ܒܡܠܬܐ) (2 Bar 21:4a), and similar expressions, 'the one who from the beginning of the world called (ܩܪܐ) that which did not yet exist' (2 Bar 21:4b), and 'you who commanded (*pqart*) . . . with your sign' (ܒܪܡܙܟ) are restated (2 Bar 21:5). In this text, the word of God is not personified but described as an instrument of God's work of creation. 2 Baruch seems to understand the role of the divine word in this context as a

---

[54] Perhaps in an eschatological meaning.

[55] Peʿal ptc of ʿ*br*. Kmosko corrects the MS' reading, *daʿbad* (to do), to *daʿbar* (to pass over).

divine sign (ܪܡܙܐ: *remzā*)[56] (2 Bar 21:5) which gives a certain command. This imagery demonstrates the immediacy of God's work of creation (2 Bar 21:8), and it may be associated with later eschatological discussions: e.g. 'And, now, show your glory *soon* and *do not postpone* that which was promised by you' (2 Bar 21:25).

The wisdom motif appears in this context to depict the aspect of the reign of God over the celestial beings: 'You who reign with great thought (ܒܚܘܫܒܐ ܪܒܐ: *bḥbuššābā rabbā*) over the hosts that stand before you' (2 Bar 21:6).[57]

Life

God alone can sustain all who live, and who have passed away, and who are to be, because of the fact that he is life (ܚܝܐ: *hayā*) (or the one who lives) and the never searchable being (ܕܠܐ ܡܬܥܩܒ: *dlā metʿaqab*) (2 Bar 21:9). He also supervises the number of humankind[58] (lit. 'He knows the number of humankind') since he alone is life (ܚܝܐ: *hayā*) who never dies (ܕܠܐ ܡܐܬ: *dlā maʾet*) and is unsearchable (2 Bar 21:10). God is described, therefore, as the one who supervises the whole of human life (the past, present, and future) since his spirit is the Creator of life (ܒܪܝܐ ܚܝܐ: *bāryā hayyeh*) (2 Bar 23:5).

3.8 2 (Syriac Apocalypse of) Baruch 48:2-10

3.8.1 Literary Considerations

Context and Main Concern

2 Baruch 48:2-24 is the long prayer of Baruch.[59] This section functions as the opening of a large unit (48:1-77:26) which is composed of dialogue (48:26-52:7), vision (53:1-12), and other related prayers and dialogues on eschatological events (the tribulation, judgment, and final reward). Baruch addresses his prayer to the God who rules over history from creation to the eschaton (48:1-10), and expects immediate visitation of the final judgment and the immediate realization of salvation (48:12-19). Responding to his prayer,

---

[56] 'Sign,' or 'gesture'; as a metaphor, it means the divine will or command (Smith, *Syriac Dictionary*, 543). See the argument on 2 Bar 48:8 (§ 3.8.2).

[57] Cf. 2 Bar 48:9.

[58] In 2 Bar 23:4-5, this number implies the numbers of people who are counted for Paradise and for Sheol. See also 2 Bar 48:6: 'You command (*pāqer*) the number (*lmenyānā*) which pass away, and which will be preserved, and you prepare a house for those that are to be.'

[59] The other three are 21:4-25, 38:1-4, and 54:1-22. See Willett's (*Eschatology*, 80-95) argument on the literary structure of 2 Baruch.

the Lord highlights the reality of his eschatological promise (48:25-41), and his immediate visitation (48:25-41). Thus the main concern is directed to the expectation of the eschatological salvation.

Influence of Key Passages from the OT

Like other descriptive creation accounts in 2 Baruch, the author takes a creation motif from Isa 48:13 (cf. Ps 33:9), and applies it to an eschatological context. God who called out 'the beginning' of time with his word prepares to summon the end time through his word (48:2a).[60] The correspondences are as follows:

<table>
<tr><td align="center">2 Bar 48:2-10</td><td align="center">Ps 33:9; Isa 48:13</td></tr>
<tr>
<td>You *summon* (*qārē*) the coming of the times, and they *stand* (*wqāimīn* < *qām*) before you (48:2a).</td>
<td>When I *call* (קֹרֵא *qōrē*) to them, they *stand* forth together (Isa 48:13).</td>
</tr>
<tr>
<td></td>
<td>For he spoke, and it came to be; he *commanded* (צִוָּה) and it *stood* firm (Ps 33:9).</td>
</tr>
<tr>
<td>*With signs* ((*bremzē*) of fear and threat you *command* the flames, and they change into *spirits* (*lrūḥē*).</td>
<td>(Ps 104:4)</td>
</tr>
<tr>
<td>And *with the word* (*wameltā*) you *raise* (*mqīm*) that which does not exist (48:8a-b).</td>
<td>When I *call* to them, they *stand* forth (Isa 48:13).</td>
</tr>
<tr>
<td>Innumerable hosts . . . serve quietly at *your sign* (*lremzāḵ*) (48:10).</td>
<td></td>
</tr>
</table>

The creation of spirits (or angels) from the fire are seen in the LXX rendering of Ps 104:4[61] and several Jewish writings: 'the angels of the spirit of fire' in Jub 2:2; 'from the rock I cut off a great fire, and from the fire I created the ranks of the bodiless armies - ten myriad angels - and their weapons were fiery and their clothes are burning flames, and I gave orders that each should stand in his rank' (2 En 29:3).

3.8.2 Thematic Considerations

Creation and Eschatology

Like other previous sections, the eschatological account of 2 Bar ch. 48 is based on the understanding of the sovereignty of God, which was shown from the beginning of the world.

---

[60] Cf. 2 Bar 59:8: 'the beginning of the day of judgment.'

[61] Ps 104:4: ὁ ποιῶν τοὺς ἀγγέλους αὐτοῦ πνεύματα καὶ τοὺς λειτουργοὺς αὐτοῦ πῦρ φλέγον (Who makes his angels spirits, and his ministers a flaming fire).

THE MOTIFS OF CREATION AND THE ESCHATON IN 2 BAR 48:2-10

< God of Creation >	< God of Eschaton>
	You summon (*qārē*) the coming of the times, and they stand (*wqāymūn* > *qām*) before you (48:2a).
	You make (*ma'bar* < *'br*) the power of the ages to pass away, and they do not resist you (48:2b).
	You arrange (*mp̄arnes* < *prns*) the course of the periods, and they obey you (48:2c).
You alone *know the length* of the generations, . . . you made known the multitude of the fire, and you weigh the lightness of the wind. You explore the limit of the heights, and you scrutinize the depths of darkness (48:3-5).	You *command (pakkar) the number* which will pass away, and which will be preserved. You prepare a house for those who will be (48:6).[62]
You *remember the beginning* which you made (48:7a).	And you *do not forget the destruction* that is to be (48:7b).
With signs (*bremzē*) of fear and threat you command the flames, and they change into spirits (*lrūhē*). And with the word (*wabmeltā*) you raise (*mqīm*) that which does not exist (48:8a-b).	
	And with mighty power you hold that which has not yet come (48:8c).
You instruct the creation with your intelligence (*bsakkūltānūtāk*), and you make the spheres wise (*wamhakkem*) so that they minister according to their orders (*bteksarhūn*) (48:9).	
Innumerable hosts . . . serve quietly at your sign (*lremzāk*) (48:10).	

It is God the Creator who can control and arrange the times (48:2) and can summon the end time (2 Bar 48:2), since he is the one who called out the beginning of time. He knows exactly the number which will pass away and those who will be preserved (48:6), as he alone knows the length, the number, the weight, and the depths of his creation (48:3-5). While he remembers the

---

[62] Cf. 2 Bar 21:10.

beginning of it (48:7a), God prepares for the judgment of the world (48:6-8). 2 Baruch thereby attempts to give encouragement to the people who were suffering (52:6), and to direct their concerns to the sovereign power of God and to the final reward which had already been preserved for them by the Creator (52:7).

God is described as the sole Ruler over human history (2 Bar 48:3), who remembers the beginning of the world, as well as the end (48:7). Everything which has existed and which has not existed yet obeys his word (or his sign in the sense of the divine command) (48:8) and his order which had been given by his wisdom (48:9-10). Therefore the motifs of the word of God and wisdom support the unique identity of God as the sole Creator and sole Ruler over the world, as will be discussed in the next section.

The Word, Power, and Instruction (Wisdom?) in Creation

> You *summon* (*qārē*) the coming of the times, and they *stand* (*wqāimīn*) before you (48:2a).

> With *signs* (*bremzē*) of fear and threat you command the flames, and they change into spirits (*lrūḥē*). And *with the word* (*waḥmelta*) you raise (*mqīm*) that which does not exist (48:8a-b)

> Innumerable hosts . . . *serve quietly at your sign* (*lremzāk*) (48:10).

The first example, 'You summon (ܩܪܐ: *qārē*) the coming of the times, and they stand (ܘܩܝܡܝܢ: *wqāimīn*) before you' (48:2a), alludes to the scene of the Genesis creation account. As for the third example, the parallel phrases, 'with signs' (ܒܪܡܙܐ) and 'with the word' (ܘܒܡܠܬܐ), were already observed in 2 Bar 21:4-5. The 'sign' is the signal to express a particular command.[63] In this case, it is modified by 'the fear and threat' (ܘܕܙܝܥܘܬܐ ܕܕܚܠܬܐ: *ddeḥltā wdaz'īpūtā*) which gives a nuance of divine authority so that the sign has authority to govern the heavenly beings (2 Bar 48:10). Likewise, the word is regarded here as a divine signal that raises at once the thing which does not exist.[64]

'The mighty power' (ܚܝܠܐ ܪܒܐ: *ḥaylā rabbā*) of God is also paralleled with the divine word:

> And *with mighty power* (*ḥaylā rabbā*) you hold (*w'aḥīd* < *'ḥd*) that which has not yet come (48:8c).

This power is for the holding of the things which have not yet come. So, it is an expression that God governs the course of the periods (cf. 2 Bar 48:2c).

---

[63] See Smith, *Syriac Dictionary*, 543.

[64] Cf. 2 Bar 21:4.

The verb, *w'aḥīr* (aph'el ptc act of *'ḥr*), corresponds to the noun, *ḥaylā rabbā*, in the sense of ruling power.[65]

2 Baruch refers to God's ruling power over the universe with his intelligence and wisdom, which gives them an order.

> You *instruct* the creation with your *intelligence* (*bsakkūlṭānūṭāk*), and you *make wise* (*wamhakkem*) the spheres (*mawzlē* < *mawzalṭa*[66]) so that they *minister according to their orders* (*ḫṭeksarhūn* < *taksā* cf. τάξις) (48:9).

Each metaphor describes several aspects of God's mighty activities: i.e. the divine word (or the divine sign to validate God's commands) raises that which has not yet existed (2 Bar 48:8a-b); the divine power governs the course of the periods (2 Bar 48:8c); and his wisdom gives the universal order.

The motif that the divine command created the things which did not exist before[67] appears in 2 Bar 48:8: God raised (ܡܩܝܡ: *mqīm* < *qām*) that which did not exist by the divine word. The verb, *mqīm* (aph'el ptc act of *qām*) may correspond to *wqāimīn* (pe'al ptc act of *qām*) in 2 Bar 48:2: i.e. both 48:2 and 8 share the same understanding that God summons with his word that which does not exist nor has yet come. This motif is applied to the account of the creation of Adam: 'You commanded (ܦܩܪܬ: *pqart*) the dust one day so that it would produce (ܕܢܬܠ: *dnettel*[68]) Adam' (2 Bar 48:46).

Moreover, 2 Baruch explains the eschatological will of God by using this word motif. God prepares a house (*beyt*) (the new life in heaven) for those who will be (2 Bar 48:6b), and he knows the number of humankind who will lose their life, and those who will gain eternal life (2 Bar 48:6a). Further God commands (ܦܩܪ: *pakkar* < *pkr*) the number of humankind to have eternal life (2 Bar 48:6), as he commanded (ܦܩܪܬ: *pkart*) the dust to produce the first of humankind (2 Bar 48:46).

The Law and Wisdom

The law is Israel's hope for salvation, and it ought to be kept from unrighteousness[69]: 'Your law (ܢܡܘܣܟ: *nāmūsāk* < *nāmūsā*) is with us, and we know that we shall not fall so long as we keep your statutes (or covenant) (ܕܩܝܡܝܟ: *daqyāmayk* < *qyām*)[70]' (2 Bar 48:22); 'the law (ܢܡܘܣܐ: *nāmūsā*)

---

[65] In 2 Bar 51:11 the divine word or the command takes the same role: 'those who (the hosts of the angels) are held *by my word* now lest they show themselves, and those who are withheld *by my command* so that they may stand at their places until their coming has arrived.'

[66] 'A sphere, an orbit, the globe, the poles, a zone of the heavens' (Smith, *Syriac Dictionary*, 257).

[67] Cf. 2 Bar 21:4.

[68] Pe'al impf of *ntl*.

[69] The law is said to be life (*ḥayyē*), and wisdom is right guidance in 2 Bar 38:2.

[70] Smith, *Syriac Dictionary*, 504.

which is among us will aid us' (2 Bar 48:24a); and 'To all time are we blessed at all events in this that we have not mingled with the Gentiles' (2 Bar 48:23). The law is thereby an assurance that they are the chosen people: 'For this is the nation which you have chosen, and these are the people, to whom you do not find equal' (2 Bar 48:20); 'for we are all one celebrated people, who have received one law (ܚܕ ܢܡܘܣܐ: *har nāmūsā*) from One (ܚܕ: *har*) (God)' (2 Bar 48:24). The point is that the law is paralleled with wisdom in this context: 'And surpassing wisdom (ܚܟܡܬܐ: *hekmtā*) which is in us will help us' (48:24b).[71] As the law is among the people to help them, so is wisdom among them.

The motif, 'hiding of wisdom from the people,' can be seen both in biblical (Prov. 1:26-28; 14:6; Job 28:14-22; Jer 49:7) and other Jewish literature (1 En 42:1-2; Wisd 7:22; 8:1). In particular, 2 Baruch, as well as 4 Ezra (5:9b-10), applies this motif to the eschatological context, i.e. as one of the signs of the approaching end of the age or as an aspect of the time of tribulation which will come before the final judgment: 'And many shall say to many at that time, "Where has the multitude of intelligence (ܣܘܟܠܬܢܘܬܐ: *sakkūltānūtā* < *sakkūltān*) hidden (ܐܬܟܣܝ: *'etkasyat* ethpa'al of *ks'*) itself, and whither has the multitude of wisdom (ܚܟܡܬܐ: *hekmtā*) removed itself?" (2 Bar 48:36).' It corresponds to the previous verse, 'For there shall not be found many wise (ܚܟܝܡܐ: *hakkīmē*) at that time, and the intelligent (ܣܘܟܠܬܢܐ: *sakkūltānē*) shall be but a few; moreover, even those who know (ܝܕܥܝܢ: *dyād'īn* < *yd'*) shall most of all be silent (ܢܫܬܩܘܢ: *neštqūn* < *štq*)' (2 Bar 48:33).[72] It should be noted that in 4 Ezra it is described only as the personified wisdom, whereas in 2 Baruch the personified wisdom (ܚܟܡܬܐ: *hekmtā*) or intelligence (ܣܘܟܠܬܢ: *sakkūltān*) (2 Bar 48:36) indicates real personal figures, i.e. 'the wise' (ܚܟܝܡܐ: *hakkīmē* pl of *hakkīm*) and 'the intelligent' (ܣܘܟܠܬܢܐ: *sakkūltānē*) (2 Bar ch. 48) who have knowledge of the law (cf. 2 Bar 48:24; 51:3, 7). The silence or the absence of the wise men (2 Bar 48:33) is described by the motif of a hidden wisdom. Moreover, it is said that at the final judgment God will come as the Judge and examine their hearts according to their deeds in the light of the divine law (2 Bar 48:38-41, 47).[73]

Light

Light is depicted as a symbol of the final reward for the righteous, which shall be given with eternal life in Paradise: 'So in the world where there is no end, you shall receive great light (ܢܘܗܪܐ ܪܒܐ: *nūhrā rabbā*)' (2 Bar 48:50b; cf.

---

[71] Cf. 2 Bar 38:1-4; 51:3, 4, 7.

[72] Cf. 2 Bar 39:6.

[73] In 4 Ezra 13:38, the judgment by the fire corresponds to the judgment by the law.

51:3, 9,10, 11). It is also said that their shape will be changed into light (ܢܘܗܪܐ: *nūhrā*) (2 Bar 51:3) and stars (ܠܟܘܟܒܐ: *lkawkbē*) (2 Bar 51:10).[74]

3.9 2 (Syriac Apocalypse of) Baruch 54:1-3, 13

3.9.1 Literary Considerations

Context and Main Concern

The last prayer of Baruch in Ch. 54 asks for the interpretation of the apocalypse which was revealed earlier (2 Bar 54:6). It functions as a literary intermission between the apocalypse (2 Bar 53) and its interpretation (2 Bar 56-76). Its content is summarized in 2 Bar 55:2, 'regarding the multitude of goodness which sinners who are upon the earth have rejected, and regarding the great torment which they have despised.' The first creation account (2 Bar 54:1-3) appears at the beginning of the first half of the prayer (54:1-11) which is mainly composed of praises for the Mighty God. The second creation account (54:13) is given at the beginning of the latter half (54:12-22) which is concerned with the great torment to which the people have not subjected themselves.

Influence of Key Passages from the OT

The notion that God summons the coming of the eschatological time (cf. 2 Bar 48:2a) appears in 2 Bar 54:1 with the modifier, 'by your word.' In 2 Bar 54:3, it is restated with a metaphorical expression: i.e. 'the beginning of the ages serves the word.' This motif of the divine word is applied to the eschatological context. That is to say, the word of God which worked in creation is strongly expected to work in the eschaton (2 Bar 54:1). This figure of personified word (2 Bar 54:3)[75] hints at Isa 55:11 and 48:13. The fact that creation came into being by the right hand of God, which occurs only in Isa 48:13 in the Old Testament, is evidence that 2 Baruch refers to Isa 48:13.

2 Bar 54:1-3; 13	Isa ch. 48
You *bring about* (or summon) (*maytē*) the things which will happen in the times *by your word* (*bmelṭāk*)	They (what God declared) went out from my mouth, . . . then suddenly I did them, . . . and they *came to pass* (Isa 48:3; cf.

---

[74] Cf. 2 En 69:9; 66:7 [J].

[75] In 2 Bar 56:4, the word of creation is personified, which is the reading of Isa 55:11 in the context of creation: 'It came to pass, when the word had gone from before him the length of the world was established (to be) something short (*wahwā dkar nepqaṭ hwāṭ melṭā men qrāmaw[hy], qām hwā ʾūrkeh dʿālmā merem zʿūr*).

(2 Bar 54:1c);   44:24-28; 46:10-11); so shall *my word*
The beginning of the ages *serve*   be that goes out from my mouth, . . . it
(*mšamšīn*) *the word* (*lmelṭāk*)   shall *accomplish* that which I purpose
(2 Bar 54:3).   (Isa 55:11).

all creation which *your right hand*   *My hand* laid the foundation of the earth,
yammīnāk) has created (2 Bar 54:13b)   *my right hand* (< *yāmîn*) spread out the
                                                  heavens (Isa 48:13a).

3.9.2 Thematic Considerations

Creation and Eschatology

In the first section, God's infinite knowledge and his sovereign rule over the times and ages are emphasized. God knows beforehand (מקדם: *mqaddem*) the things which will happen in history and at its end, and God alone can control the course of the times (2 Bar 54:1). Baruch praises the Mighty one who reveals his apocalypse in order to comfort[76] the chosen people (54:4).

O Lord, you alone, *beforehand* (*mqaddem*) *know the histories* (*yawmaw[hy]*[77]) of the world, and you bring about (or summon[78]) (*maytē*) the things which will happen in the times (*dabzabne* < *zabnē*) by your word (*bmelṭāk*) (2 Bar 54:1bc).

And against the works of the inhabitants of the earth *you hasten* (*msarhbaṭ* < *rhb*) *the beginning of the times* (*riššayhūn dzabnē*), and *the ends of the periods* (*sawphūn d'edānē*) you alone know (2 Bar 54:1d).

You are the one to whom both the depths and the heights come together, and *the beginning of the ages* (*rīšay 'ālmē*) *serves* (*mšamšīn* pa'el ptc of *šmš*) *the word* (*lmelṭāk*) (2 Bar 54:3).

The second section argues that the perishing of the people is unavoidable because of their ignorance against the knowledge and the sovereign power of God. It is their responsibility to choose their way with regard to the final reward. 2 Baruch argues that Adam is not the cause of the coming torment, except only for himself, but each of them is expected to prepare for the coming of glory (2 Bar 54:14-19).

The creation motif is related to the eschatological arguments since it is based on the exposition of Isaiah. God, who brought about the things which did not exist in the beginning, will be able to summon the coming of the

---

[76] Cf. Isa 50:4.

[77] M. Muraoka's (*The Old Testament Pseudepigrapha* [Apocrypha and Pseudepigrapha 3; Tokyo: Kyobunkan, 1976], 124) rendering of *yawmaw*[hy] instead of *rawmaw*[hy] seems reasonable, since it fits well with *mqarem* (beforehand: the meaning of foreknowledge) and *wmerrem dabzabnē* (the things which will happen). Cf. Charles' rendering, 'deep'; Klijn's, 'heights.'

[78] Smith, 32.

eschatological times (2 Bar 54:1c); and in the metaphorical expression, the word of God is considered to be served by the times of the world (2 Bar 54:3). God is also described as the sole Ruler over human history (2 Bar 54:1). God is the one who alone knows the histories of the world beforehand (2 Bar 54:1a) and can bring about its end (2 Bar 54:1b).[79] He is the Creator and Ruler over all created things (2 Bar 54:12), since he created the world by his right hand (ܝܡܝܢܟ: *yammīnāk*), and since he reigns over all creation with his intelligence (or counsel) (ܒܬܪܥܝܬܟ: *btarʿītāk*) (2 Bar 54:13).

God's Right Hand in Creation

God's right hand (lit. ܝܡܝܢܟ: *yammīnāk*) is said to create the whole creation (2 Bar 54:13). In the biblical tradition, the right hand is used as a metaphor to describe God's glorious power to support the people (cf. Pss 17:7; 18:35; 63:8; 139:10) as well as to bring about victory (cf. Pss 20:6; 48:10; 60:5; 78:54; 98:10) and salvation (cf. Pss 44:3; 108:6; 138:7). The right hand (as God's instrument of his work of creation) appears only in Isa 48:13 in the OT[80]: i.e. 'My hand laid the foundation of the earth, and my right hand (וימיני < ימין [*yāmîn*]) spread out the heavens; when I call to them, they stand forth together.' Thus it is obvious that 2 Baruch alludes to this text.

The Word in the Eschaton

A similar expression in the previous creation account (2 Bar ch. 48) in which God summons (*qrʾ*) the coming of the eschatological times and the things which have not existed by his word, is restated in 2 Bar 54:1-3. There are the correspondences of the motifs of creation and the eschaton between 2 Bar 48:2-10 and 2 Bar 54:1-3:

THE MOTIFS OF CREATION AND THE ESCHATON IN 2 BAR CHS. 48 AND 54

2 Bar 54:1-3	2 Bar 48:2-10
CREATION	
	And *with the word* (*waḇmelṭā*) you raise (*mqīm*) that which does not exist (48:8b)
ESCHATON	
You *bring about* (or summon) (*maytē* < *ʾet*) the things which will happen in the times by your word (*bmelṭāk*) (2 Bar 54:1c)	You *summon* (*qārē*) the coming of the times, and they stand (*wqāimīn*) before you (48:2a).

---

[79] 'You alone (*balḥūḏayk*)' is repeated twice in 2 Bar 54:1.

[80] The creation by God's hands (plural) appears in the poetic section of the OT (Pss 95:5; 119:73; Job 10:8; Isa 45:12).

The beginning of the ages *serve* (*mšamšīn*) *the word* (*lmelṭāk̠*) (2 Bar 54:3).	Innumerable hosts . . . *serve* quietly at *your sign*[81] (*lremzāk̠*) (48:10).
You are the one who easily *performs* (*ʿāb̠ed̠* < *ʿbd̠*) all *by a sign* (*bremzā*) (54:2).	*With signs* (*bremzē*) of fear and threat you *command* the flames, and they change into spirits (*lrūḥē*) (48:8a).

There is a clear correspondence between the two sections concerning the idea that God summons the coming of the eschatological times. This idea seems to be associated with the creation motif that God raises that which does not exist by God's word, as in 2 Bar 48:8b. In short, the eschatological role of the divine word is found in the Genesis creation account (also influenced by Isaianic exposition of it). The expression, 'The beginning of the ages serves (*mšamšīn*) your word,' can be understood as an indirect personification of 'the word of God.'

Light and Wisdom

God is said in 2 Bar 54:13b to have established the whole fountain of light (ܟ݁ܠ ܡܒܘܥܐ ܕܢܘܗܪܐ: *kōl mabbūʿā dnūhrā*) beside him and to have prepared the treasures of wisdom (ܐܘܨܪܐ ܕܚܟܡܬܐ: *wʾawṣrē dnūhrā*) beneath his throne (2 Bar 54:13). The latter part of this verse constructs the following parallelism:

w'aṭ kōll mabbūʿā	dnūhrā	lwāṭāk̠	taqent
(a)	(b)	(c)	(d)

w'awṣrē	dhekmṭā	theyt trawnāws dīlāk̠	ʿatteḍt
(a')	(b')	(c')	(d')

You	whole fountain and the treasures	of light of wisdom	beside you[82] beneath your throne	established prepared.

A similar parallelism is seen in 2 Bar 59:11 (with several other components): 'the root of wisdom' (ܥܩܪܗ ܕܚܟܡܬܐ: *wʿeqārāh dhekmṭā*), . . . 'the treasures[83] of the light' (ܐܘܨܪܐ ܕܢܘܗܪܐ: *wʾawṣrē dnūhrā*). Both light and wisdom are described as God's possessions and they are located beside God who sits on the heavenly throne.[84]

---

[81] See the argument on the relationship between word and sign.

[82] Klijn translates it, 'with yourself'; however, Charles' rendering, 'beside you' (*lwāṭāk̠*), seems more reasonable because of the parallel correspondence between the fountain of light and the treasures of wisdom 'beneath his throne.'

[83] Note that 'the treasures' (*wʾawṣrē*) is used here for the light: cf. 'the treasures of wisdom' in 2 Bar 54:13.

[84] Cf. Prov 8:22-31.

Light and Revelation

The apocalypse (lit. 'vision [ܚܙܘܢ: *ḥezwānā*]' [54:6], 'what is hidden [ܟܣܝܬܐ: *kasyāṭā* < *ks*']' [54:5]) and its interpretation (ܦܘܫܩܗ: *pūšāqeh* < *pūšāq*) [2 Bar 54:6]) are illustrated as the event in which God shines (ܘܡܢܗܪ: *wmanhar* < *nhr*) upon the darkness (ܚܫܘܟܬܐ: *ḥeššūkāṭā* < *ḥeššūkā*) (2 Bar 54:5b). In the rest of 2 Baruch, the giving of Mosaic law, or the law itself, is described as the event of the giving of light.

> He (Moses) brought *the law* (*nāmūsā*) to the descendants of Jacob and *he lighted* (*w'anhar* pe'al ptc act of *nhr*) *a lamp* (*šrāgā*) to the generation of Israel (2 Bar 17:4).

> *The lamp of the eternal law* (*šrāgeh dnamūsā dal'ālam*) shone (*'anhar* < *nhr*) on all those who were sitting (*hwaw + yāṭbīn* [periphrastic use of ptc) in darkness (*bḥeššūkā*)' (2 Bar 59:2).[85]

> The shepherds of Israel have perished, and *the lamps* which *were shining* ((*hwaw + manhrīn* [periphrastic) are extinguished, and the fountains from which we used to drink have withheld their streams. We, however, have been *left* (Ethpe'al pf of *šbq*) *in the darkness* (*bḥeššūkā*), . . Shepherds and *lamps* and fountains *came from the law* (*nāmūsā*). If you, therefore, look upon *the law*, . . . *the lamp* will not be wanting. . .
> (2 Bar 77:13-16).

In particular, the second example (2 Bar 59:2) alludes to Isa 9:2: 'The people who walked in darkness have seen a great light; those who dwelt or sat (יֹשְׁבֵי) in a land of deep darkness light has shined on them.' The LXX renders the first phrase as 'those who are living' (οἱ κατοικοῦντες). Therefore, 2 Baruch may take the Hebrew rendering here and translate יֹשְׁבֵי as 'those who are sitting' (cf. Isa 9:2). The point is that 2 Baruch expands the term, 'light' in Isa 9:2, as the law in the social context of the Second Temple period. That is to say, after the fall of the Second Temple, rather than after the fall of the First, since the shepherds (i.e. the prophets in this context) of Israel were considered to have perished, and the people thought that they had been in darkness. Baruch found encouragement in the fact that they would still be able to receive the light, if they looked upon the existing law (2 Bar 77:16).

---

[85] Perhaps, it is the exposition of Isa 9:2.

3.10 Apocalypse of Abraham 21:1-22:2

3.10.1 Literary Considerations

Context and Main Concern

ApAbr can be divided into two parts. Chs. 1-8 constitutes a story of Abraham's search for God, whereas the rest of the book (chs. 9-32) narrates the apocalypse in which Abraham saw a picture of the creation and the eschaton. God also reveals the work of creation, and the age which was prepared after it (ApAbr 21:1). There were seven visions: (1) the light and fiery angels (15:5-7); (2) the fire (17:1-3); (3) the throne (18:1-14); (4) the firmaments (19:4-9); (5) the world (21:2-7); (6) the seven sins of the world (24:3-25:2); and (7) the destruction of the Temple (27:1-3). ApAbr finally gives an announcement of the judgment against the Gentiles, by expecting God's mighty works which echo the signs and wonders of the Exodus event (ch. 29). Therefore, the main purpose is to encourage the Israelites (after the destruction of the Temple) to expect the ultimate victory in the end time.

Influence of Key Passages from the OT

Answering Abraham's question, 'What is this picture of creation?' (ApAbr 22:1), God replies by saying, 'This is my will (вола моіа: *volê moja*) with regard to what is in the counsel (съвѣтъ: *sŭvětŭ*) (or light [свѣтѣ: *světě*])[86] and it was good before my face; then, afterward, I gave them a command (повелѣтъ: *povelětŭ*) by my word (словомъ моимъ: *slovomŭ moimŭ*) and they came into existence; whatever I had decreed to exist had been outlined (начертаса: *načertasê*)[87] in this; and all the created things stood before me (сташа предъ мною: *stawa predŭ mnoju*)' (ApAbr 22:2). This account refers to Ps 33:6-12.

ApAbr 22:2	Ps 33:6-12
This is my will with regard to what is in *the counsel* (*sŭvětŭ*)	The *counsel* of the Lord (עצת יהוה) stands firm forever (33:11).
I gave them *a command* *by my word* (*slovomŭ moimŭ*) and *they came into existence.*	He *commanded*, (33:6: *by the word* of the Lord), and it came to be (33:9)
All the previously created you have seen *stood* (*stawa*) before me	It *stood* fast (33:9).

---

[86] This thesis uses Slavonic text of N. S. Tikhonravov (C. H. Van Schooneveld [ed.] *Slavistic Printings and Reprintings* [Paris: Mouton, 1970]).

[87] It is the reading of S (Sil'vestrovskij sbornik, Moscow, 14th AD).

3.10.2 Thematic Considerations

Eschatological Interpretation of Ps 33:6-12

ApAbr reads Ps 33:9-12 together with the creation account of Ps 33:6-8, and emphasizes that God had a picture of creation before his work was done. It was good in his will[88] or in his counsel (съвѣтъ: *sŭvĕtŭ*), and it had already been outlined (начерта: *načerta*). This interpretation seems to be associated with the eschatological statement: 'I (God) will tell you (Abraham) what I have kept in my heart' (ApAbr 23:3); 'As the counsel (съвѣтъ: *sŭvĕtŭ*)[89] of your father (Terah) is in him, as your (Abraham) counsel is in you, so also the counsel of my will is ready' (ApAbr 26:5); and 'I (God) will judge with justice those whom I previously created' (ApAbr 27:11). Thus ApAbr argues that the eschatological event has already been prepared in God's will or in his counsel, and it will stand, as the picture of creation had already been outlined in his will (and it came into existence by his word). This is the eschatological interpretation of Ps 33:6-12.

Creation and Eschatology

The apocalypse which is shown to Abraham is said to comprise, 'the great things which you (Abraham) have not seen' (ApAbr 9:6). These ages were founded by God (lit. my) word, and made firm, and created, and then renewed (ти вѣкы гломъ моимъ създаниıа и оутвержениıа сътворениıа и поновениıа: *ti vĕky glomŭ moimŭ sŭzdanija i utverženija sŭtvorenija i ponevenija*) (9:9).[90] It is the message of what will come upon those who have done evil and just things in the human race (9:10), and what is in the heavens, on the earth, and in the sea, in the abyss, and in the lower depths, in the garden of Eden and in its rivers, in the fullness of the universe . . . its circles in all (12:10). The last example (AbAbr 12:10) corresponds to the picture of creation in ApAbr 21:1-7.

THE PICTURE OF THE CREATION (ApAbr 21:1-7)

[Heavens]

[Earth]
    Fruit
    Moving things and the things that had souls

---

[88] The mentioning of God's will in accordance with creation occurs in 1QS 11:17-18; 1QH[a] 9:13-15; 4Q 404 4:1-2; 4Q 405 4-5:2-3.

[89] Text K (Solovec, Leningrad, 16th-17th) takes this rendering; S, D, A, C takes *svĕtŭ* (light); B takes *sŭvĕt* (H. Lunt).

[90] R. Rubinkiewicz (OTP I, 693) translates, 'I will show you the things which were made by the ages and by my word . . . ,' by taking вѣкы as instrument. However, this suffix can be taken as accusative in plural form, which our reading takes.

Its host of humankind: the impiety of their souls and justification and their pursuit of their works

[Abyss, Lower Depths]
Torments
Perdition

[Sea & Islands]
Its cattle and its fish
Leviathan: his realm and his bed and his lairs and the world which lay upon him, and his motions and the destruction he causes the world

[Rivers]

[Garden of Eden]
Its fruits and trees
The source and the river
The men who are doing justice, and their food and their rest

[Final Judgment]
A great crowd of men and women and children
Right side: some have been prepared for judgment and order;
other for revenge and perdition at the end of the age
Left side: who have been set apart from the people with Azazel

The description of the earth in this picture corresponds to the Genesis creation account: i.e. ApAbr chooses the living creatures which are made on the 3rd (fruit), 5th (moving things), and 6th days (men) (ApAbr 21:3a) in accordance with the narrative order of Gen ch. 1.[91]

In this picture, ApAbr depicts the present reality of this world (the impiety of human souls and their pursuit of their works) (ApAbr 21:3b), and the present reality[92] of that world (torments and perdition in the abyss and lower depths [ApAbr 21:3c], along with the rest in Paradise [AbApr 21:6]). The portrait of this picture is extended to the eschatological judgment as well. For example, God shows Abraham a great crowd of men and women and children (ApAbr 21:7): the half of them on the right side of the portrayal, have been prepared for revenge and perdition, whereas the half of them on the left side of the portrayal have been prepared for judgment and order[93] (AbApr 22:4). It is also followed by the picture of God's redemptive works: the punishment of the Gentiles (29:15; 30:2-8; 31:2); the coming of the Messiah (31:1); and the restoration of the Temple and the sacrifices (29:17). Thus Abraham was shown the picture which portrayed the whole universe (heaven and the earth, abyss and paradise) and all ages (from creation to the eschaton). In other words, Abraham was guided to affirm the sovereignty of God over

---

[91] The creatures which are made in the 1st, 2nd, and 4th days are lifeless beings.

[92] In the Jewish tradition, both abyss and paradise are made in creation and exist.

[93] See H. Lunt's note (OTP I): *ustrojenie*, 'ordering, being put in order, restoration,'

space (universe) and time (history). It is interesting that after viewing this picture, Abraham calls God 'sovereign, mighty and eternal' (влдко крѣлкъии и прѣвѣчныи: *vldko krělkŭyi i prěvečnyi*)[94] (ApAbr 22:3). And it should be noted that God is called, 'the God of gods, the Creator' (ва во и творца: *va vo i tvorca*) (ApAbr 8:3); '(the God) who created previously the light of the age' (иже первѣие створихъ свѣта вѣка: *iže pervěje stvorixŭ světa věka*) (ApAbr 9:3); and 'God, the Creator of heavenly things and earthly things' (ва творца нвнхъ и ꙁемнъıхъ: *va tvorca nvnxŭ i zemnyixŭ*) (ApAbr 10:6).[95] That is to say, the unique identity of God is associated with his status as the Creator.

3.11 Liber Antiquitatum Biblicarum 15:5-6

3.11.1 Literary Consideration: Context and Main Concern

LAB assumes a character of 'retelling' or 'the rewritten Bible,'[96] which covers the history of Israel (from Adam to David). The narrative of the Exodus events begins in ch. 10, and our text (ch. 15) tells the story of the rebellion of the people who were guided by unfaithful spies (excluding Caleb and Joshua). God shows his anger and he remarks that everything was done as he had planned (LAB 15:5; cf. Isa 55:11[97]; Ezek 6:10), and the judgment which had already been planned would be done against their sins (LAB 15:6). LAB also expresses God's sovereign power which fulfills his promised words, referring to the Exodus events (LAB 15:5-6). In this context, the account of the creation of waters (Gen 1:9) appears in connection with the event of the Red Sea (Exod 14:22).

3.11.2 Thematic Considerations

Creation and New Light (the Law)

LAB recalls the two Exodus events: the crossing of the Red Sea (LAB 10:5-6; 15:5-6a; 23:10a; 32:17) and the giving of the eternal law at Mount Sinai (11:1-

---

[94] This expression occurs just one time here, and others are said, 'eternal, mighty one' (ApAbr 17:8, 13; 20:6; 22:1; 23:9, 12, 14; 26:1, 4; 27:4, 6, 8; 28:1; 29:1, 7).

[95] See also monotheistic assertion in ApAbr 19:4.

[96] Cf. Jubilees, the Genesis Apocryphon, and Josephus' Jewish Antiquities.

[97] Compare LAB 15:5, 'The plan of action that has issued from me will not be in vain,' and Isa 55:11, 'So shall my word be that goes out from my mouth, and it shall not return to me in vain.'

5: 15:6b; 23:10b; 32:7-8). It is interesting that LAB ch. 15 associates the
Exodus events with God's work of creation as follows.[98]

> *Et precepi mari, et diruptis ante faciem eorum abyssis, steterunt muri aquarum, et
> nichil simile factum est verbo huic, **ex qua die dixi ad eos: Congregentur aque sub
> celo in unum locum**, usque in hunc diem* (15:5b-6a)[99]

> And I commanded the sea and the abyss was divided before them, walls of water
> stood forth. And there was never anything like this event *since the day I said 'Let
> the waters under the heaven be gathered together into one place,'* until this day.

> . . . *et inclinavi celos et descendi incendere lucernam populo meo, et **creature
> ponere terminos*** (15:6b).

> . . . and I bent the heavens and came down to kindle a lamp for my people
> and *to establish laws (or boundaries) for creation.*

On the third day of creation, God commanded the waters under the heaven to
be gathered together into one place (LAB 15:6; Gen 1:9); likewise, he
commanded the Red Sea and the abyss to be divided (LAB 15:5; Exod 14:22)
and the walls of water stood forth. LAB comments that there was never
anything like this event since creation (LAB 15:6). Following this event at the
Red Sea, Israel was brought to Mount Sinai and received the eternal law. It is
worth noting that the giving of the law is described as the giving of light to the
world.

> *Dabo lumen mundo, et illuminabo habitabilia* (11:1b)

> I will give a light to the world and illumine their dwelling places.

> *et inclinavi celos et descendi incendere lucernam populo meo* (15:6b).

> and I bent the heavens and came down to kindle a lamp for my people.

> *Deus revelabit finem orbis ut vobiscum disponat super excelsa sua et in cendet in vobis
> sempiternalem lucernam* (19:4b).

> God has revealed the end of the world so that he might establish his statutes with
> you and kindle among you an everlasting light.

If Ps 18 (in particular 18:9 and 18:15) is in the author's mind,[100] then there
could be an allusion to Ps 18:28 ('It is you who light my lamp; the Lord, my

---

[98] This may belong to LAB's interest in finding parallels between God's acts in the OT:
e.g. Jephthah's daughter and sacrifice of Isaac (LAB ch. 40); the victory of Deborah and
Exodus event (LAB ch. 32).

[99] Latin text of Kisch's edition (*Pseudo-Philo's Liber Antiquitatum Biblicarum* [Notre
Dame, Indiana: University of Notre Dame, 1949]).

God, lights up my darkness'). It seems possible that while the third day of creation is recalled in relation to the Red Sea event (LAB 15:6), there might be an allusion to the fourth day of creation, when the luminaries were created (Gen 1:14-19), in relation to the Sinai event. In other words, the sequence of events from the Red Sea to Mount Sinai, which are actually described in sequence (LAB 15:5-6 and 23:10), may have been considered typologically[101] to correspond to the sequence of creation (the division of the waters on the third day and the creation of luminaries on the fourth day).

The laws (lit. *terminos*, 'boundaries') are given for the created beings (LAB 15:6), which is said to have been prepared from the origin of the world (lit. *ex nativitate seculi*) (LAB 32:7). The law is given as 'an everlasting law' (*legem sempiternam*) (LAB 11:2) in order to enlighten God's people (11:2; 19:6; 23:10) and in order that by obeying the law they might live (23:10).

Eschatology: Light and Life

Eschatological implication is also prominent in LAB. It is said that God's providence might be on them, and their land might be renowned over all the earth, and they might be restored (23:12-13). This salvation or the renewal of creation (*innovatio creatur*) (32:17) will reach its climax at the eschatological time: the present dimension of light and darkness will end; the dead will be brought to life; and there will be another earth and another heaven (*terra alia et caelum aliud*), an everlasting dwelling place (*habitaculum sempiternum*) (3:10), and they will have eternal life (*vita eterna*) (23:13). That is to say, light and life are depicted to be the eschatological blessings.

3.12 Joseph and Aseneth 8:10-11

3.12.1 Literary Considerations

Context and Reconstruction of the Greek Text

Joseph and Aseneth is a long narrative of Jewish legend which tells of the marriage of Joseph and Aseneth, the daughter of the idolatrous Priest of On (Gen 41:45). Jewish theologians provide reasons for the possibility of this

---

[100] R. Bauckham, 'The Liber Antiquitatum Biblicarum of Pseudo-Philo and the Gospels as 'Midrash',' in *Gospel Perspectives III* (Sheffield: Sheffield Academic Press, 1983), 43.

[101] We use the term of 'typology' in the sense of a perspective which is concerned with the revelatory connection between two historically distinct but religiously significant persons or events, so that it should be distinguished from allegory which is concerned with the hidden, spiritual meaning of a narrative (cf. R. N. Soulen, *Handbook of Biblical Criticism* [Atlanta: John Knox Press, 1981], 206).

marriage, highlighting the story of Aseneth's conversion to the God of Israel (JosAsen chs. 1-21). In this narrative, Joseph is portrayed as a discreet person who is not fond of paganism and foreign girls (JosAsen 7:1-6; 8:5-7[102]), and Aseneth is also introduced as a virgin who stayed away from adultery (1:4; 7:7-8) and in every respect is similar to the daughters of the Hebrews (1:5). Praying to God the Creator to bless Aseneth, Joseph intercedes for her conversion (8:10-11). The creation account is cited at the beginning of this prayer in which God is remembered as the Creator. The reconstruction of the Greek text with a structural analysis on JosAsen 8:10-11 is as follows:

Joseph's Prayer (JosAsen 8:10-11)[103]

[v. 10]
a   Κύριε ὁ θεὸς τοῦ πατρός μου Ἰσραήλ,

b   ὁ ὕψιστος,
c   ὁ δυνατός,[104]

d   ὁ ζωοποιήσας τὰ πάντα
e   καὶ καλέσας ἀπὸ τοῦ σκότους εἰς τὸ φῶς
f   καὶ   ἀπὸ τῆς πλάνης   εἰς τὴν ἀλήθειαν[105]
g   καὶ   ἀπὸ θανάτου   εἰς τὴν ζωήν,

h   σὺ αὐτὸς κύριε

[v. 11]
i   ζωοποίησον
j   καὶ εὐλόγησον τὴν παρθένον ταύτην.

k   καὶ ἀνακαίνισον   τῷ πνεύματί σου[106]
l   καὶ ἀνάπλασον αὐτὴν τῇ χειρί σου
m   καὶ ἀναζωοποίησον   τῇ ζωῇ σου

n   καὶ φαγέτω ἄρτον ζωῆς σου
o   καὶ πιέτω ποτήριον εὐλογίας σου,

---

[102] Chapter and verse numbering follows the longer recension of Burchard's edition (C. Burchard, ed. *Unterweisung in erzählender Form, Joseph und Aseneth* [JSHRZ 2; Gütersloh: Gütersloher Verlagshaus Gerd Mohn, 1983]). OTP II follows Riessler's numbering (*Altjüdisches Schrifttum ausserhalb der Bibel* [Augsburg, 1928; repr. Darmstadt, 1966).

[103] The Greek text is of Philonenko's edition (*Joseph et Aséneth: Introduction Texte Critique Traduction et Notes* [Leiden: E. J. Brill, 1968]).

[104] Syr, Arm, 436, Ngr (Modern Greek) have Ιακωβ. Cf. יַעֲקֹב אֲבִיר (Isa 49:26; 60:16; Ps 132:2, 5); LXX trans. is not always ὁ δυνατός.

[105] MSS B (Palatinus Graecus 17) and D (Baroccion Greek 147) omit this sentence.

[106] MSS D and E (600) add τῷ ἁγίῳ, 'holy.'

p   καὶ συγκαταρίθμησον αὐτήν τῷ λαῷ σου

q   ὃν ἐξελέξω πρίν γεννηθῆναι τὰ πάντα[107]

r   καὶ εἰσελθάτω εἰς τὴν κατάπαυσίν σου,

s   ἣν ἑτοίμασας τοῖς ἐκλεστοῖς σου.

Influence of Key Passages from the OT

God is also remembered as the one who gave life (ὁ ζωοποιήσας[108]) to all and as the one who called them out ([ὁ] καλέσας) from darkness to the light (JosAsen 8:10). It should be noted that God's work of creation is summarized by those two metaphorical expressions. The former seems to be an expanded exegesis[109] of Gen 2:7 which narrates the creation of Adam who became a living thing (חיה נפש; ψυχὴν ζῶσαν [LXX]) and received the breath of life (נשמת חיים; πνοὴν ζωῆν [LXX]). The illustration of God as the Life-Giver (Gen 2:7; cf. Isa 42:5) may be expanded to his whole work of creation (see JosAsen 8:3; 12:1, 2; 21:15).[110] The latter expression is also an expanded exegesis of Gen 1:1-3 (esp. the LXX trans.). According to the LXX translation, the created earth was invisible (ἀόρατος) and unfurnished (ἀκατασκεύαστος)[111] and was covered with darkness (σκότος); then God commanded light to appear (γενηθήτω). That is to say, the role of light here is thereby to let the invisible earth appear.[112] JosAsen 8:10 expands this imagery of light in creation and applies it to the ethical (or salvific) meaning.

---

[107] MSS B (11th AD) and D (15th AD) read ἣν ἐξελέξω πρὶν γεννηθῆναι; MSS (Greek 966; 17th AD) and A (Vaticanus Graecus 803; 11th-12nd AD) read our text.

[108] MSS A, C (Baroccio Greek 148), F (Greek 1796), W (Greek 1976) read the text; MSS E (600), L1 (Latin 1), L2 read ζωοποιῶν, 'gives life to'; MSS P (14), Q (Palatinus Graecus 364) read ποιήσας, 'made.' In the LXX, ζωοποιέω (orig.) is rendered for וּלְהַחֲיוֹת (hif inf const. in 2 Kgs 5:7[MT]), מְחַיֶּה (pi ptc in Neh 9:6 [MT]), תְּחַיֵּינוּ (pi impf in Ps 71:20 [MT]). These may mean 'to sustain life' rather than 'to give life' in the sense of continuation (cf. imperfect tense in Hebrew, and present in Greek); in JosAsen 8:10 it takes 'aorist tense' as the parallel participle καλέσας does, which clearly refers to the creation context. Thus ζωοποιήσας may imply God's work of creation to give life to all living things. See our comments on the similar expression of JosAsen 12:1-2.

[109] See Isaiah's illustration of God the Creator: i.e. God is depicted as the one who created the heavens and the earth, and the one who gave breath (נתן נשמה; διδοὺς πνοήν [LXX]) and spirit (רוח; πνεῦμα) to the people who live upon the earth (Isa 42:5).

[110] Cf. 4 Ezra 6:48; 2 Bar 21:9; 23:5.

[111] The MT renders תהו ובהו, 'formless and empty.'

[112] See the similar expression of 4 Ezra 6:40.

3.12.2 Thematic Consideration

Creation and Salvation

In the prayer, the God of Israel is called ὁ ὕψιστος, 'the Most High,' and ὁ δυνατός, 'the Powerful one.' Both terms are associated with the unique identity of God in the biblical tradition. In the LXX, ὁ ὕψιστος expresses the sovereignty of God over the earth (cf. Pss 83:18; 97:9 [LXX]), and it is paralleled with his mighty work of creation (cf. Gen 14:19, 22; Jdt 13:19), whereas ὁ δυνατός expresses God's mighty salvific works (Pss 23:8; 89:8 [LXX 88:9]; Job 36:5; Zeph 3:17; Jer 32:19 [LXX 39:19]; cf. Isa 49:26; 60:16).

Two short or summarized creation accounts (Lines d-e) are connected to Joseph's intercession for Aseneth's conversion (or salvation):

Thematic Flow of JosAsen 8:10-11

A　Lord God of Israel (ὁ θεὸς τοῦ πατρός μου 'Ισραήλ)

　　　　B　who gave life (ζωοποιήσας) to all
Creation
　　　　　　C　who called (them) out from the darkness to the light
- - - - - -

　　　　　　C'　1　who (called) (the people) from the error to the truth
　　　　　　　　　2　who　　　　　　　　　　　from the death to the life
Salvation
　　　　B'　1　Give life (ζωοποίησον) (to Aseneth)
　　　　　　2　Renew (ἀνακαίνισον) (Aseneth) by your spirit (τῷ πνεύματί σου)
　　　　　　3　Form a new (ἀνάπλασον) her by your hand (τῇ χειρί σου)
　　　　　　4　Make alive (ἀναζωοποίησον) by your life (τῇ ζωῇ σου)

　　　　　　5　Let her eat God's bread of life
　　　　　　6　Let her drink of God's cup of blessing

　　A'　Aseneth's Acceptance as an Israelite
　　　　1　Number her among God's people
　　　　2　Let her into God's rest which has been prepared for God's chosen people

As shown above, Joseph's prayer forms a chiasm (A, B, C, C', B', A'), and the two creation motifs (B and C) are developed in the salvific context (C' and B'). The same verb, ζωοποιέω, is used in the context of both creation (B) and salvation (B'); it is reiterated in other ways, ἀνακαινίζω 'to renew' (cf. Ps 104:30 [LXX 103:30]), ἀναπλάσσω 'to form anew,' and ἀναζωοποιέω 'to make alive again' (cf. JosAsen 15:5). It is important to notice the adverbial phrases ('by your spirit[113]'; 'by your hand[114]'; and 'by your life[115]') which are attached to these verbs, since they allude to the biblical and Jewish exegetical tradition of the Genesis creation account. The second creation account (Light imagery in the context of creation) (C) is developed into ethical ('from the error to the truth') and salvific ('from the death to the life': cf. JosAsen 15:12,[116] 14-15; 19:10-11; 21:21) meanings. Thus it seems appropriate that the salvific idea is deeply associated with the exegesis of the Genesis creation account.

Life as a New Creation

Joseph asks the God who gave life (ζωοποιήσας) to all creatures and called out them from the death to the life (ἀπὸ θανάτου εἰς τήν ζωήν), to give life (ζωοποίησον) to Aseneth. Joseph's intercession for her conversion (or salvation) can be divided into three sections (B' 1-4; B' 5-6; A' 1-2).[117] The first intercession (B' 1-4) is a development of the creation account (B) as previously argued, and the salvation is explicated as a new creation. The second part (B' 5-6) is, in a sense, an ocular confirmation of her salvation. When Aseneth had ceased making confession to the Lord, a chief of the angels visited her (JosAsen 14:1) and declared God's acceptance of Aseneth's conversion. Her name was (just) written (ἐγράφη: aorist passive) in the book of life (ἐν βίβλῳ ζωῆς) (15:4), whereas the angel announced that from that day (lit. ἀπὸ τῆς σήμερον) she would be renewed and formed anew and made alive again, and that she would eat the bread of life (ἄρτον ζωῆν) and drink the cup of immortality (ποτήριον ἀθανασίας). She then anointed herself with ointment of incorruptibility (ἀφθαρσίας) (15:5), and the angel let her eat from a honey comb (κηρίον μέλιτος) (16:1) which the angel provided (16:11), and which emitted the breath of life (ὀσμὴ ζωῆς) (16:8). This is the eternal life (οὐκ ἀποθανεῖται εἰς τὸν αἰῶνα) which all the angels and the chosen people and all the sons of God ate (16:14). The third section (A' 1-2) is an intercession on behalf of Aseneth to count her as one of God's chosen people for Joseph wanted her to share the heritage and promise of Israel (lit. εἰςελθάτω εἰς τὴν

---

[113] Cf. Ps 33:6; 2 Bar 21:4.

[114] Cf. Isa 45:12; 48:13; Job 10:8; Pss 95:5; 119:73; Jub 2:11; 12:19; 4 Ezra 3:5; 2 Bar 54:13.

[115] Cf. 2 Bar 21:9; 23:5.

[116] Angels were sent to rescue (τοῦ ῥύσασθαι) Aseneth from the darkness (ἐκ τοῦ σκότους) and to bring (ἀναγαγεῖν) her into the light (εἰς τὸ φῶς) (MSS A, P).

[117] Firstly, ζωοποίησον and ἀναζωοποίησον compose an *Inclusio*; secondly, φαγέτω and πιέτω are parallel; and thirdly, the last two imperative sentences have a thematic correspondence : i.e. Aseneth's acceptance as an Isralite, and sharing the blessing and promise of the chosen people.

κατάπαυσίν σου),[118] which God had prepared from the beginning of creation (lit. ὃν ἐξελέξω; ἣν ἑτοίμασας). Thus life (in the sense of salvation) is given from the God who gave life to all creation (JosAsen 8:10), which had been prepared for the chosen people (8:11; 16:14). It is given to the people who repent sincerely (15:7-8), and whose conversion is accepted and confirmed by God (chs. 14-17). He is the God who alone can call all creation from darkness to the light (8:10; 15:12).

3.13 Joseph and Aseneth 12:1-2

3.13.1 Literary Cosiderations

Context and Reconstruction of the Greek Text

After leaving Joseph (JosAsen 9:1-10:1), Aseneth set about her repentance (chs. 10-13): throwing away her valuables and idols (10:10-13), putting herself in sackcloth and ashes (10:14-17). JosAsen expresses Aseneth's heartfelt repentance by her soliloquy (11:3-14, 16-18) and long prayer (12:1-13:15). In the beginning of her prayer (12:1-2), Aseneth bears in mind that God to whom she addresses her prayer is the God who created all things and the one who governs them by his ordinances.

The reconstruction of the Greek text and structural analysis of JosAsen 12:1-2 is as follows:

Aseneth's Prayer (JosAsen 12:1-2 and after)

[v. 1]
a   Κύριε ὁ θεὸς τῶν αἰώνων[119]

    b   ὁ κτίσας τὰ πάντα καὶ ζωοποιήσας[120]
    c   ὁ δοὺς τᾶσι πνοὴν ζωῆν

    d   ὁ ἐξενέγκας τὰ ἀόρατα εἰς τὸ φῶς
[v. 2] e   ὁ ποιήσας τὰ πάντα καὶ φανερώσας τὰ ἀφανῆ

---

[118] Κατάπαυσις (rest or resting place) means promised land of God: i.e. Israel (Deut 12:9; 1 Kgs 8:56; Ps 95:11[94:11 LXX]); Zion (Ps 132:14); and Jerusalem Temple (Isa 66:1).
[119] The text is read by the old MSS (Arm, Syr), 436 (<L2), E, G (<b), d; other readings are διλαίων (A, F, W, c L1) and δυνάμεων (P, Q?).
[120] MSS F,W, (Syr?), Arm, L1 read the text; MSS a (A, C, P, Q [Graecus 365], R [Greek 530]), c (H [PanhagiosTaphos 73], J [Saba 389], K [Saba 593]), and G (McKell) take ὁ κτίσας τοὺς αἰῶνας καὶ ζωογονῶν (G ποιήσας) τὰ πάντα; 436 (< L2) reads qui creasti seculum et uiuificasti; 435 (<L2) reads qui creasti omnia. Thus the oldest (Arm 6th-7th AD; Syr 6th AD) and full and reliable (L2) MSS include or allude to this sentence.

f ὁ ὑψώσας τὸν οὐρανὸν
g ὁ θεμελιώσας αὐτόν ἐν τῷ στερεώματι ἐπί ἀνεμῶν[121]

h καὶ θεμελιώσας τὴν γῆν ἐπὶ τῶν ὑδάτων
i ὁ πήξας τοὺς λίθους τοὺς μεγάλους ἐπὶ τῆς ἀφύσσου τοῦ ὕδατος

j οἵτινες οὐ βυθισθήσονται
k ἀλλά εἰσιν ὡς φύλλα δρυὸς ἐπάνω τῶν ὑδάτων

l καὶ εἰσι οἱ λίθοι ζῶντες καὶ τῆς φωνῆς σου ἀκούουσι
m καὶ φυλάσσουσι, κύριε, τάς ἐντολάς σου ἅς ἐνετείλω αὐτοῖς

n καὶ τὰ προστάγματά σου οὐ μή παραβαίνουσιν[122]
o ἀλλ᾽ εἰσὶν ἕως τέλους ποιοῦντες τὸ θέλημά σου

p γὰρ σύ, κύριε, ἐλάλησας καὶ πάντα ἐζῳογονήθησαν
q γὰρ ὁ λόγος σου, κύριε, ἡ ζωή ἐστι πᾶσι κτισμάσι σου[123]

r Κύριε, ὁ θεός μου,

s πρὸς σὲ κεκράξομαι,
t πρόσσχες τὴν δέησίν μου

u Καὶ σοὶ ἐξομολογήσομαι τὰς ἁμαρτίας μου
v καὶ πρὸς σὲ ἀποκαλύψω τὰς ἀνομίας μου

(Italic Alphabet indicate that they are omitted by shorter recention)

---

[121] This sentence is our Greek reconstruction (cf. Syriac Text of Brooks' edition [*Historia Ecclesiastica Zachariae Rhetori Vulgo Adscripta vol. 1* (CSCO 38; Louvain: Imprimerie Orientaliste L. Durbecq, 1953], 34). Latin translation (E. W. Brooks [ed.] *Historia Ecclesiastica Zachariae Rhetori Vulgo Adscripta I: Interpretatus est* [CSCO 41; Louvain: Imprimerie Orientaliste L. Durbecq, 1953], 24), is *et caelum erexit et fundamenta eius porro venti dorso imposuit*. This sentence is reserved in the old MSS (Syr, Arm) and L2; a and d omit it. The author of JosAsen seems to use a poetic device: i.e. 'parallelism' which states each topic twice as shown in my reconstruction of the text, although several MSS did overlook it. If the shorter recension is taken here, it seems to break the literary flow. Thus several omissions of MSS d seems to be an epitome.

[122] MSS a and d omit from Line k to n; the old MSS (Arm, Syr) and L2, as well as F, W, take the text. Lines p-q play an important role to turn back to the previous topic (to demonstrate God's sovereignty: Lines a-i; cf. JosAsen 8:10) in order to specify again the God to whom Aseneth prays (Lines r-t). The second topic, which shows how God's creatures are obedient to God's ordinances (Lines j-o), seems to be contrasted to Aseneth's confession of sin (from Line u). Thus it seems possible to take the longer recension here (i.e. my reconstruction; C. Burchard) rather than the shorter recension (M. Philonenko's Greek edition, etc.).

[123] This sentence is our Greek reconstruction: cf. the paraphrastic expression of Syr and Latin MSS (Brooks' edition).

Influence of Key Passages from the OT

The literary and thematic flow of JosAsen 12:1-3 is similar to the previous prayer (JosAsen 8:10-11) as follows.

Joseph's Prayer (JosAsen 8:10-11a)	Aseneth's Prayer (JosAsen 12:1-3)
κύριε	κύριε
ὁ θεός	ὁ θεὸς
τοῦ πατρός μου ᾿Ισραήλ	τῶν αἰώνιων
ὁ ζωοποιήσας τὰ πάντα	ὁ κτίσας τὰ πάντα καὶ ζωοποιήσα
καὶ	ὁ δοὺς τᾶσι πνοὴν ζωῆν
καλέσας	ὁ ἐξενέγκας
ἀπὸ τοῦ σκότους εἰς τὸ φῶς	τὰ ἀόρατα εἰς τὸ φῶς
	ὁ ποιήσας τὰ πάντα καὶ φανερώσας
	τὰ ἀφανῆ
σὺ αὐτὸς κύριε	κύριε, ὁ θεός μου
Joseph's intercession for Aseneth	Aseneth's Confession of Sin

Both prayers begin by addressing God's name which is modified with the genitive modifiers (τοῦ πατρός μου ᾿Ισραήλ; τῶν αἰώνων), and the subordinate clauses which refer to the Genesis creation narrative (with relative pronouns and participial clauses). Then Joseph and Aseneth address their prayers (Joseph's intercession for Aseneth; Aseneth's confession of sin) to the Creator, calling God's name again (σὺ αὐτὸς κύριε; κύριε, ὁ θεός μου). In JosAsen 12:1, God is called ὁ θεὸς τῶν αἰώνιων (< αἰῶνος).[124] These opening words may correspond to the idea of Lines 10-15 which refer to God's eternal rule over all creation. The opening of Joseph's prayer (JosAsen 8:10, ὁ θεός τοῦ πατρός μου ᾿Ισραήλ) thereby plays an important role to make clear the theme of the rest of the prayer.[125] The descriptions of God as the Creator are restated in Aseneth's prayer with a more detailed account: the first participial clause, 'giving life (ζωοποιήσας) to all' (8:10) is restated in 12:1, 'giving breath of life (πνοὴν ζωῆν) to all'; the second participial clause, 'calling (them) from darkness to the light,' is restated in JosAsen 12:1-2, 'bringing the invisible (τὰ ἀόρατα) out into the light.' It should be noted that the creation account in JosAsen 12:1-2 borrows closer expressions of the Genesis creation accounts (esp. of the LXX): i.e. 'giving breath of life (πνοὴν ζωῆν) to all' alludes to Gen 2:7: ἐνεφύσησεν εἰς τὸ πρόσωπον αὐτοῦ **πνοὴν** ζωῆς καὶ ἐγένετο ὁ

---

[124] See similar expressions: τοῦ βασιλέως τῶν αἰώνων (JosAsen 15:16), τὸν θεὸν τῶν αἰώνιων (JosAsen 16:21); cf. ὁ θεός τῶν αἰώνων (Sir 36:17), τὸν βασιλέα τῶν αἰώνων (Tob 13:7).

[125] See our arguments on JosAsen 8:10-11.

ἄνθρωπος εἰς ψυχὴν ζῶσαν; 'bringing the invisible (τὰ ἀόρατα) out into the light' alludes to Gen 1:2-3: ἡ δὲ γῆ ἦν **ἀόρατος** . . . καὶ εἶπεν ὁ θεός γενηθήτω φῶς καὶ ἐγένετο φῶς.

3.13.2 Thematic Considerations

The Divine Order and Human Lawlessness

Aseneth's prayer refers to the creation of heaven and earth with four participial clauses, preceded (except Line h) by a relative pronoun (Lines f-i). These accounts are not a simple retelling of the Genesis creation account, but they employ some biblical and extra-biblical material: in particular JosAsen refers to the winds which are placed in front of heaven (Line g) and it also refers to big stones as well (Line i). Both appear in cosmogonic accounts of Job chs. 37-38 and 1 En 18:1-5a: the winds stand between heaven and earth (1 En 18:3), and obey God's commands to perform his will (Job 37:9-13; 1 En 69:22; Sir 43:16-22), and rule over the astronomical (1 En 18:4-5) and meteorological phenomena (1 En chs. 34-36); the stones are described as the foundation of the dry land (or the earth) (2 En 28:1-4), and the sea is commanded not to transgress the eternal boundary (2 En 28:4). Thus references to the winds and the big stones (JosAsen 12:1) may not be incidental, but could be taken from the biblical (cf. Job) and Jewish (cf. Enoch) traditions of cosmological understanding (i.e. the divine order of universe). The obedience of the creatures (i.e. the big stones in this context) seems to be contrasted to Aseneth's lawless deeds (lit. τὰς ἀνομίας μου) (JosAsen 12:4).[126]

The Word of Life in Creation

The life-giving motif (JosAsen 8:10; 12:1) is taken up again in Lines p-q, but in another way.

JosAsen 8:10 ὁ ζωοποιήσας τὰ πάντα

JosAsen 12:1 ὁ κτίσας τὰ πάντα καὶ ζωοποιήσας
ὁ δοὺς πᾶσι πνοὴν ζωῆν

JosAsen 12:2 σύ, κύριε, ἐλάλησας καὶ πάντα ἐζῳογονήθησαν
ὁ λόγος σου, κύριε, ἡ ζωή ἐστι πᾶσι κτισμάσι σου

JosAsen 12:2 takes other biblical and Jewish exegetical traditions of Gen ch. 1 which focuses on the word of creation.[127] In this context, it functions as an

---

[126] See the comparision between the obedience of the creatures and the attitude of human beings and angelic beings in 1 En 18:1-16; 21:6; 41:1-9; 43:4; 69:15-29; 101:1-9, etc.

[127] Cf. Pss 33:6, 9; 148:5; Isa 48:13b; 4 Ezra 3:4-5; 6:38, 42-43; 7:69; 2 Bar 14:17; 21:4; 48:8, 54:1; SibOr 1:19-20; 3:20; 2 En 33:4; Jub 12:4, 26; Sir 39:17; 42:15; WisdSol

agent to give life to lifeless beings (cf. 2 Bar 48:2-10; 4 Ezra 3:4-5; 6:38-54). The life-giving motif (JosAsen 8:10) may come from the generalizing of God's work of creation (Gen 2:7 [esp. LXX]) (see JosAsen 12:1). JosAsen 12:2 links it to the motif of the word of creation (ἐλάλησας καὶ πάντα ἐζῳογονήθησαν [< ζῳογονέω: to produce life]) since God accomplished all his work of creation by his word, which means that God gave life to all creation, as he actually gave the breath of life to Adam (Gen 2:7; Isa 42:5; 4 Ezra 3:5b; Ant 1:34). His word was easily understood as an agent (in a metaphorical sense) which produces life in the context of creation.

3.14 Sirach 16:24-17:14

3.14.1 Literary Consideration: Context and Main Concern

Sir 14:20-23:27 seems to comprise a large unit: (1) the introductory section: the blessedness of the people who search for wisdom (14:20-15:10); (2) the initiatory argument: the illustration of sinful human nature (15:11-16:16); (3) the kernel argument: God's mercy which prevails over human sinful nature (16:17-17:14); (4) the exhortation (17:15-32); (5) the summary (18:1-14); and (6) the ethical disciplines (18:15-23:27). The creation account (Sir 16:26-17:1-8) appears in the kernel argument, as an accurate knowledge (lit. ἐν ἀκριβείᾳ ἀπαγγελῶ ἐπιστήμην) (Sir 16:25), which focuses on the creation order (16:26-30), and on the creation of human beings (17:1-8).

3.14.2 Thematic Considerations

Creation Order

In the former section, God is depicted as the Creator who established the eternal order in the universe, referring to the creation account of Ps 104:5-23: God assigned their boundaries (διέστειλεν μερίδας αὐτῶν) (Sir 16:26; cf. Ps 104:5-9); God ordered (them) in eternity (ἐκόσμησεν εἰς αἰῶνα) and their realm in their generation (τὰς ἀρχὰς αὐτῶν εἰς γενεὰς αὐτῶν) (Sir 16:27; cf. Ps 104:10-23). God's grace and his dominion are upon the creation (Sir 16:29-30; cf. Ps 104:28-29, 32), so that they never lack that which they need (Sir 16:27; cf. Ps 104:10-16), obeying the divine order (Sir 16:28). Thus Sirach highlights the sovereignty of God who rules the world by his divine order (Sir 18:1; cf. Sir 18:3 [GII]).

9:1; PrMan 1:3; Aristob 4:3; ApAbr 9:9; 22:2; TAb 9:6 [A]; 4Q176 frag. 16-53:2; 4Q381 3 6; 4Q404 frag. 4 1.

Wisdom and the Law in a Sapiential Context

The latter section of the creation account (Sir 17:1-8) focuses on the creation of human beings. On the one hand, the weakness and the transient life of human beings (Sir 17:1-2, 30-32; 18:9-10) are contrasted with the greatness of God's mercy and his majesty (Sir 17:21, 22b, 26b[GII], 29; 18:1-7, 11-14). On the other hand, human beings (Israel is the focus in this context) are described as the people who are endowed with wisdom: firstly, they were given the fear of God in their hearts (Sir 17:8), together with other attributes (discretion, tongue, eyes, ears, and a mind for thinking) (Sir 17:3-6), since they were created in God's own image; secondly, they gained the knowledge and understanding to discern good and evil[128] (Sir 17:7); and thirdly they were allotted the law of life (Sir 17:11) at Mount Sinai.[129] Therefore, if human beings desire to live in accordance with the law and wisdom (and perhaps the divine order), they reach for the way of life (Sir 17:11b[GII]; 23-24; 18:13-14). In short, the creation account is developed in a sapiential context.

3.15 Sirach 39:12-35

3.15.1 Literary Considerations

Context and Main Concern

Sir 38:24-43:33 composes a unit, and this section is concerned with the sovereignty of God who provides for every need of his creation (Sir 39:33). In this section, first of all, the importance of those who devote themselves to the study of the law of God is contrasted with other vocations of the skilled worker (Sir 38:24-34). Similarly, the activity of the Scribes is introduced as seeking for the wisdom of all ancients (σοφίαν πάντων ἀρχαίων), hidden meanings of proverbs (ἀπόκρυφα παροιμιῶν), prophecies (προφητείαις) (Sir 39:1-3), meditation (διανοηθήσεται) on the Creator (lit. κύριον τὸν ποιήσαντα αὐτὸν) (39:5), and his mysteries (τοῖς ἀποκρύφοις αὐτοῦ) (39:7). Afterwards, God's work of creation are mentioned in the two sections (39:12-35; 42:15-43:33), in which the greatness of God is emphasized, being contrasted with human wretchedness (40:1-42:14).

Influence of Key Passages from the OT

The creation account of Sir 39:12-20 is clearly based on Ps 33:

---

[128] This may allude to Gen 3:1-7, 22, and it is taken in a positive sense here.
[129] Sir 17:11-13 allude to the Sinai event.

Sir 39:14-20, 33	Ps 33

Ascribe majesty to his name and give thanks to him with praise, with songs on your lips, and *with lyres* (ἐν ᾠδαῖς χειλέων καὶ ἐν κινύραις / נבל וכל מיני שׁוֹר] / [שׁ]ירות [B] [with songs of the harps and of stringed instruments) (39:15).

Praise the Lord with the harp (בכנור) of ten *lyres* (בנבל עשׂור) (33:2).

All *the works* (τὰ ἔργα / [מעשׂי] [B]) of the Lord are very *good* (καλὰ / טובים [B]), and whatever he commands (πᾶν πρόσταγμα / כל צורך [B][130]) will be done at the appointed time (ἐν καιρῷ αὐτοῦ / בעתו [B]) (39:16).

The word of the Lord (דבר־יהוה) is *right* (ישׁר), and all his *works* (מעשׂהו) (is done) in faithfulness (באמונה) (33:4)

By his word (ἐν λόγῳ αὐτοῦ) the waters stood (ἔστη) like a heap of water and with the word *of his mouth the reservoirs* water (ובמוצא פיו אוצרות) [B] [with the utterance of his mouth the reservoirs]) (39:17b).

By the word of the Lord (יהוה בדבר) the heavens were made; all their host by the breath of his of *mouth* (וברוח פיו).
He gathered the waters of the sea as in a bottle, and he put the depths in the ***reservoirs*** (באצרות) (33:6-7).

When he *commands*, his every will (is done) (ἐν προστάγματι αὐτοῦ πᾶσα ἡ εὐδοκία / תחת[י]ין רצונו יצליח [B] [In [his] place he makes his will prosper]) (39:18a).

For he spoke, and it came to be (ויהי הוא אמר); he *commanded*, and it stood firm (הוא־צוה ויעמד) (33:9).

And there is none who limits his salvation (καὶ οὐκ ἔστιν ὃς ἐλαττώσει τὸ σωτήριον αὐτοῦ / ואין מעצור לתשועתו [B] [and there is no restraint to his salvation]) (39:18b).

Cf. Ps 33:16-20

The works of ***all flesh*** (ἔργα πάσης σαρκὸς / מעשׂה כל בשׂר [B]) *are before him*, and can hidden from his eyes (39:19).

The Lord looks down from heaven, and he *sees all the sons of* nothing *humankind* (בני האדם) (33:13).

All the works of the Lord are good (ἀγαθὰ), and he will supply (χορηγήσει) every need in time (ἐν ὥρᾳ αὐτῆς) (39:33).

Pss 33:4; 104:27

---

[130] MS B reads וכל צורך בעתו יספיק (and every need at appointed time he provides); MS Bmarg (marginal glosses B) reads לכל עריך בעתו יספיקו.

3.15.2 Thematic Considerations

Creation and Eschatology

Two themes are mainly discussed here in relation to the Genesis creation account: (1) the works of God are good; and (2) everything he commands will be done at the appointed time. These themes are repeated at the beginning and the ending of the account: τὰ ἔργα κυρίου πάντα ὅτι καλὰ σφόδρα καὶ πᾶν πρόσταγμα ἐν καιρῷ αὐτοῦ ἔσται (39:16); τὰ ἔργα κυρίου πάντα ἀγαθὰ καὶ πᾶσαν χρείαν ἐν ὥρᾳ αὐτῆς χορηγήσει (39:33). As for the former theme, on the one hand, it is emphasized that God's work is perfect and everything has been created for its own purpose (39:17) and its need (39:21, 33), and the doctrine of equilibrium in creation is spelled out.[131] On the other hand, a dualistic idea is developed. That is to say, whereas God's blessing overflows and enriches the earth (39:22), his wrath is to be on the nations (39:23). From the beginning, good things were created for the good, and bad things for the sinners[132] (ἀγαθὰ τοῖς ἀγαθοῖς ἔκτισται ἀπ' ἀρχῆς οὕτως τοῖς ἁμαρτωλοῖς κακά) (39:25); all the needs for human life (39:26) are good for the good (τοῖς εὐσεβέσιν εἰς ἀγαθα), but for the wicked they turn out evil (τοῖς ἁμαρτωλοῖς τραπήσεται εἰς κακά) (39:27). Thus Sirach argues for Theodicy, highlighting the sovereignty of God over the whole creation (39:19-20).

As for the latter theme, it may be associated with the understanding of the prophetic tradition that what God declared would be fulfilled at the appointed time (cf. Isa 14:24; 31:2; 34:16; 45:23; 46:10, 11; 48:3; 55:11; Jer 1:12; 33:14; 39:16; Ezek 12:25, 28). Also it seems to be linked to the interpretation of Ps 33:9 in Sir 39:16, 18, and 33, as it will be discussed below.

Sirach 39:28-31 mentions the day of judgment ('the day of fury' עברה בעת) [B][133]; 'the final judgment' (ἐν καιρῷ συντελείας [39:28]):

> There are winds (πνεύματα / [ר[וחות] [B]) created for vengeance (εἰς ἐκδίκησιν ἔκτισται / נו[צרו] [B] / נבראו [Bmarg]), and in their anger they can dislodge mountains; on the day of consummation (ἐν καιρῷ συντελείας) they will pour out their strength and calm the anger of their Maker (τοῦ ποιήσαντος). Fire and hail and famine[134] and death (θάνατος / ודבר (pestilence) [B]), all these have been created for vengeance (εἰς ἐκδίκησιν ἔκτισται / למשפט נו[צרו] [B]). The fangs of wild animals (lit. beasts of tooth) and scorpions and vipers, and the sword that punished the ungodly

---

[131] See the comment of Di Lella (P. Skehan and A. Di Lella [eds.] *The Wisdom of Ben Sira* [AB 39; New York: Doubleday, 1987], 460).

[132] The Hebrew text from the Cairo Geniza (I. Lévi il, Facsimiles of the Fragments hitherto Recovered of the Book of Ecclesiasticus in Hebrew, Oxford-Cambridge, 1901) reads 'for the wicked, good things and bad' (לרעים טוב וריע) (MS B).

[133] The similar words, יום עברה, is used in the sense of the 'coming judgment' (e.g. Ezek 7:19; Zeph 1:15; Prov 11:4; Job 21:30; cf. Prov 11:23; see BDB).

[134] MS B reads רע (evil) instead of רעב.

with destruction.   They take delight in his bidding (ἐν τῇ ἐντολῇ αὐτοῦ / יְשִׂישׂוּ בְּצַוֹתוֹ אוֹתָם [when he commands them, they rejoice] [B]), always ready for the need (εἰς χρείας) on earth; and on their time (ἐν καιροῖς αὐτῶν / בְּחֻקָם [in their task] [B]) they never disobey the word (λόγον / פִּיו [his word] [B] / פִּיהוּ [Bmarg]).

The winds (Sir 39:28), fire, hail, famine, death (or disease [B]) (39:29), the fangs of wild animals, scorpions, vipers, and sword (39:30) are listed as the instruments for the (eschatological) judgment. The list of nine instruments for the punishment of the wicked is contrasted to the list of ten good things for human life (water, fire, iron, salt, wheat, milk, honey, grape, oil, and cloth) (Sir 39:26). The idea of each symbol of punishment may be taken from several biblical texts, as Di Lella summarizes:

> The Creator can remove mountains directly (as in Job 9:5) or indirectly through the fury of storm winds (39:28ab). These winds cause destruction, when called for, and so 'appease the anger of their Maker' (39:28cd); cf. 5:6d. 'Fire and hail' (39:29a) are found in a different context in Ps 148:8. Yahweh rained down sulfurous fire to destroy Sodom and Gomorrah (Gen 19:24). Hail was the seventh plague to afflict the Egyptians prior to the Exodus (Exod 9:13-26). Famine and disease (39:29a) are mentioned as possible punishments for David's census of the people (2 Sam 24:13); since he was given the choice, David chose pestilence (2 Sam 24:15). In Jer 29:17-18, sword, famine, and pestilence are mentioned together as punishments for infidelity to Yahweh. Famine and pestilence were the usual accompaniments of a prolonged siege; cf. Lev 26:25-26; Jer 21:2-9; Ezek 5:12; 7:15. 'Ravenous beasts' (lit. beasts of tooth) and reptiles (39:30a) are agents of destruction also in Deut 32:24. 'Scorpions' (39:29a) are an image of chastisement in 1 Kgs 12:11, 14 (= 2 Chr 10:11, 14). 'The avenging sword' (39:30b) is an allusion to Lev 26:25.[135]

Eschatological Interpretation of Ps 33:6-12

Sirach understands that God created (Sir 39:28-30) the tools of the final judgment and they are always ready for their task (39:31). It should be noted that these instruments (or agents in the weak sense) are expected to obey 'the word of God' or 'his command' (lit. λόγον / פִּיו [his word] [B] / פִּיהוּ [Bmarg]) at the final judgment (ἐν καιροῖς αὐτῶν). This expression seems to be related to the previous argument that the word of God (or what God commands) would be fulfilled at the appointed time.

A: The word of prophecy   πᾶν πρόσταγμα ἐν καιρῷ αὐτοῦ ἔσται (39:16b).[136]

B: The word of creation   ἐν λόγῳ αὐτοῦ ἔστη ὡς θιμωνιὰ ὕδωρ
                                καὶ ἐν ῥήματι στόματος αὐτοῦ ἀποδοχεῖα
                                ὑδάτων (39:17b).

---

[135] Di Lella (*Wisdom*, 460-461).

[136] The Greek text is of Vattioni's edition (F. Vattioni [ed.] *Ecclesiastico: Testo ebraico con apparato critico e versioni greca, Latina e siriaca* [Napoli: Istituto Orientale di Napoli, 1968]).

The word of creation
C: &   ἐν προστάγματι αὐτοῦ πᾶσα ἡ εὐδοκία (39:18a).
The word of prophecy

A: The word of prophecy   ἐν τῇ ἐντολῇ αὐτοῦ εὐφρανθήσονται . . .
                          καὶ ἐν καιροῖς αὐτῶν οὐ παραβήσονται λόγον
                          (39:31).

Therefore, Sirach understands that God who accomplished his work of creation by his word (Sir 39:17b) can realize and accomplish his eschatological judgment through his word. This is an eschatological interpretation of Ps 33:6-12.[137]

3.16 Sirach 42:15-43:33

3.16.1 Literary Considerations

Context and Main Concern

The opening phrase, 'I will now recall the works of the Lord' (μνησθήσομαι δὴ τὰ ἔργα κυρίου / אזכר נא מעשי אל [B]), may allude to Ps 77:12a: אזכיר מעללי־יה. It also corresponds to Sir 39:12: 'Once more I will meditate and describe' (ἔτι διανοηθεὶς ἐκδιηγήσομαι). After some ethical instructions (Sir 40:1-42:14) which are given between the two creation accounts (39:12-35; 42:15-43:33), the sovereignty of God is recalled in the meditation on God's mighty works.

Influence of Key Passages from the OT

Sirach may allude to Job chs. 37-38 with the following correspondences: 'the ordinances of the heavens' (Sir 43:1-10 and Job 38:31-33), 'thunders' (Sir 43:13, 17 and Job 37:5), 'snow' (Sir 43:13 and Job 37:6), 'north wind' (Sir 43:17b, 20-21 and Job 37:9-10), 'south wind' (Sir 43:16b and Job 37:17a), 'hail' (Sir 43:15 and Job 38:22), 'frost' (Sir 43:19 and Job 38:29), and 'ice' (Sir 43:20 and Job 38:30). These metaphors highlight God's mighty power of judgment: i.e. none can withstand the sun's burning heat (Sir 43:3); God sends snow and speeds the lightnings of his judgment (κρίματος αὐτοῦ) (43:13); the north wind consumes the mountains and burns up the wilderness and withers the tender grass like a fire (43:21). These metaphors are also linked to God's salvific power: A mist quickly (κατὰ σπουδὴν) heals (ἴασις) all things and the falling dew gives refreshment from the heat (Sir 43:22). There is also an

---

[137] Cf. ApAbr also interpretes Ps 33:6-12 in the eschatological framework (see § 3.10.2).

allusion to Isa 40:13 in Sir 42:21, in which the sovereignty of God is highlighted, as will be discussed later.[138]

3.16.2 Thematic Considerations

Sovereignty of God: His Knowledge and Power

Arguing that God's work of creation is full of his glory (τῆς δόξης κυρίου πλῆρες τὸ ἔργον αὐτοῦ) (42:16), and stand firm in his glory (στηριχθῆναι ἐν δόξῃ αὐτοῦ) (42:17b),[139] and that they are desirable (ἐπιθυμητα) (42:22a) and perfect (lit. He has made nothing incomplete' [οὐκ ἐποίησεν οὐδὲν ἐλλεῖπον] (42:24b), Sirach contends that the Lord's magnificence is more than this: 'Many things greater than these lie hidden' (πολλὰ ἀπόκρυφά ἐστιν μείζονα τούτων ὀλίγα) (43:32); 'We could say more but could never say enough, and the final word is "He is the all" (πολλὰ ἐροῦμεν καὶ οὐ μὴ ἀφικώμεθα καὶ συντέλεια λόγων τὸ πᾶν ἐστιν αὐτός)' (43:27); and 'He is greater than all his works' (ὁ μέγας παρὰ πάντα τὰ ἔργα αὐτοῦ) (43:28). Sirach praises God who is omniscient (Sir 42:18-20) and omnipotent (Sir 43:1-25): God searches out (ἐξίχνευσεν) the human heart (42:18, 20) and history (42:19), and even the deepest part of creation (lit. ἄβυσσον) (42:19); he rules over both the astronomical (Sir 43:1-10) and meteorological (Sir 43:11-25) phenomena. Sirach also refers to God's composition of the universal order:

Sir 42:21a
    τὰ μεγαλεῖα τῆς σοφίας αὐτοῦ ἐκόσμησεν
    He arranged the splendors of his wisdom

    וּנ̇בורת הכמ̇תו חכן[140] (B)
    [The might of his wisdom] he regulated

Sir 42:23
    πάντα ταῦτα ζῇ καὶ μένει εἰς τὸν αἰῶνα ἐν πάσαις χρείαις καὶ πάντα ὑπακούει
    All things live and remain forever and all respond to all needs

    הוא ה . . . יקים . . . ל . . . (Bmarg)
    He established [all things for ever]

Sir 43:26
    δι' αὐτὸν εὐοδοῖ ἄγγελος αὐτοῦ καὶ ἐν λόγῳ αὐτοῦ σύγκειται τὰ πάντα
    Through him each of his angels succeeds and by his word, all things hold together

---

[138] See § 3.16.2.
[139] MS B reads אימץ אלהים צבאיו להתחזק לפני כבודו, 'God gave strength to his hosts, so that they may endure firmly before his glory.'
[140] MS Bmarg reads גבורות, 'mighty acts,' for גבורת.

(B) ¹⁴¹למענו יצלח מלאך ובדבריו יפעל רצון

By his reason [his] angels prospers and by his words he performs (his) pleasure

Thus Sirach highlights God's sovereignty over all creation by referring to his knowledge (Sir 42:18-20) and his power which rules over all creation through the universal order (Sir 43:21, 23).

Sovereignty of God: His Word and Wisdom

The motif of the creative word which accomplished God's work of creation (cf. Sir 39:17b, 18a) is restated in Sir 42:15b:

Sir 42:15b
> ἐν λόγοις κυρίου τὰ ἔργα αὐτοῦ
> By the word of the Lord his works (are done)

> באומר אלהים רצ[ו]נו
> By the word of God his will [B]

> באומר אלהים מעשיו
> By the word of God his works [Bmarg].¹⁴²

Sirach argues that both the astronomical (Sir 43:1-10) and meteorological (Sir 43:11-25) phenomena are ruled over by God's word and his command:

Sir 43:5
> ἐν λόγοις αὐτοῦ κατέσπευσεν πορείαν
> By the words it [sun] hurries on its course

> (B) ובדבריו ינצח אביריו
> And (with) his words he makes his mighty ones

Sir 43:10
> ἐν λόγοις ἁγίου στήσονται κατὰ κρίμα
> By the words of the Holy one they stand in their appointed places [lit. according to the decision]

> (B) בדבר אל יעמד הק
> By the word of God a statute is established

Sir 43:13
> προστάγματι αὐτοῦ κατέσπευσεν χιόνα
> By his command he sends snow

> (B) ותנצח זיקות [במשפט]

---

¹⁴¹ MS Bmarg reads למענהו, 'for his own purpose,' for למענו.

¹⁴² Some Greek texts have καὶ γέγονεν ἐν εὐδοκίᾳ αὐτοῦ κρίμα, 'and (his) decision had come in his will,' following this text; MS B reads ופועל רצונו לקחו, 'he accepts the one who does his will.'

And makes brilliant the flashes [in judgment]

(Bmarg) ותנצח זיקים [במשפט]
And casts off the living substance [in judgment]

Sir 43:23

λογισμῷ αὐτοῦ ἐκόπασεν ἄβυσσον
By his plan he stilled the deep

(B) מחשבתו ... שיק רבה
His counsel burns up the deep

(Bmarg) משובתו ... שיק רבה
From his quietness the deep is burnt up

Sir 43:26

ἐν λόγῳ αὐτοῦ σύγκειται τὰ πάντα
By his word, all things hold together

(B) ובדבריו יפעל רצון
And by his words he performs (his) pleasure.

Wisdom is also mentioned in the context where God's perfect arrangement
or design (cf. ἐκόσμησεν in Sir 42:21a; perfect and eternal order of creation in
Sir 42:23-25) is highlighted.

Sir 42:21a

τὰ μεγαλεῖα τῆς σοφίας αὐτοῦ ἐκόσμησεν
He arranged the splendors of his wisdom

(B) גנבורת הכמ]תו חכן[143]
[The might of his wisdom] he regulated

It is important to notice that Sir 42:21a is followed by the statement which
strongly exhibits monotheism, with an allusion to Isa 40:13b-14a and 28:

Sir 42:21b

ὡς ἔστιν πρὸ τοῦ αἰῶνιος καὶ εἰς τὸν αἰῶνα
οὔτε προσετέθη οὔτε ἡλαττώθη
καὶ οὐ προσεδεήθη οὐδενὸς συμβούλου

> Who is he, from all eternity, 'One' (lit. from eternal to eternal);
> nothing can be added or taken away;
> and he needs no one to be his counselor

אחר הוא מעולם [Bmarg]) מהעולם)
לא ... [ו]לא נאצל
(B) ולא צריך [Bmarg]) צרך) לכל מבין

---

[143] MS Bmarg reads גבורות, 'mighty acts,' for גבורת.

He is 'One' from everlasting;
nothing (had been added [to him], or) diminished (from him);
and he had no need (Bmarg) of any instructor

Cf. Isa 40:13b-14a, 28b [LXX]

τίς αὐτοῦ σύμβουλος ἐγένετο ὃς συμβιβᾷ αὐτόν
ἢ πρὸς τίνα συνεβουλεύσατο καὶ συνεβίβασεν αὐτόν (Isa 40:13b-14a)

Who has been his counselor who instructs him?
Or with whom has he taken counsel, and he has instructed him?

θεός αἰώνιος ὁ θεός ὁ κατασκευάσας τὰ ἄκρα τῆς γῆς
οὐ πεινάσει οὐδὲ κοπιάσει
οὐδὲ ἔστιν ἐξεύρεσις τῆς φρονήσεως αὐτοῦ (Isa 40:28b)

The eternal God, the God who formed the ends of the earth,
shall not hunger, nor be weary,
and there is no searching of his understanding

Thus the mentioning of wisdom in the context of creation is related to the description of the identity of God with monotheistic emphasis: 'He had no need of any instructor' (Sir 42:21). The repeated expression that the universe is ruled by God's word (Sir 42:15b; 43:5, 10, 26) should be understood in the same context. Thus Sirach depicts God's identity by referring to the exegetical tradition of the Genesis creation account in which God is depicted as the Creator and Ruler over the whole universe. It should be noted that in this description, the divine word and wisdom motifs are employed. Because of the context in which Ps 33 is referred to (Sir 39:16-20), Sir 42:15-43:33 seems to focus on the word motif rather than wisdom. It is an example of the creation account choosing between the word motif or that of wisdom in accordance with its context.

3.17 1QS (Community Rule from Qumran Cave 1) 3:13-4:1

3.17.1 Literary Considerations

Context and Main Concern

1QS is one of the old Qumran scrolls which contain the community's beliefs of an earlier stage (the 2nd to the 1st century BC).[144] It seems probable that

---

[144] J. Charlesworth (*The Dead Sea Scrolls: Hebrew, Aramaic, and Greek texts with English translations vol. 2* [Tübingen: J. C. B. Mohr, 1995]) comments that the date of the Community Rule from Qumran Cave 1 is considered to be from 100 to 75 BC, based on Cross' palaeographical study (F. M. Cross, 'The Development of the Jewish Scripts,' in G.

the text of 1QS is composed of several separate units since these are clearly divided by marginal signs and blank lines and spaces,[145] as well as some literary indicators (למשכיל [1:1; 3:13], ואלה [4:2; 6:24; cf. 4:15], וזה [5:1; 6:8b]). However, there seems to be some thematic connection between them. For example, in the first section, the aim of the rule of community is said 'to seek God' (לדרוש אל) with all one's heart and with all one's soul and to do what is good and just 'in his presence' (לפניו) (1QS 1:1b-2). In the second section, a similar sapiential teaching is given: 'to enlighten' (להאיר) the heart of man, to straigthen out 'in his presence' (לפניו) all the paths of true justice, 'to establish fear' (לפחד) in his heart 'for the precepts of God' (במשפטי אל) (1QS 4:2-3a). Several wisdom languages can be found in this context (1QS 4:3-6, 18, 22, etc.). This sapiential theme is treated through the rest of 1QS: e.g. 'No-one should walk in the stubbornness of his heart' (5:4); 'of the many in order to walk in the stubbornness of his heart' (7:25); 'They should not depart from any counsel of the law in order to walk in all stubbornness of their heart' (9:10). The account of the identity of human beings (3:13-4:26) also seems to be an expanded argument of sapiential teachings. It instructs the community members to walk according to the laws or with wisdom (e.g. 1QS 4:24). The brief outline of 1QS is as follows.

THE OUTLINE OF 1QS

I. The rule of entry into the community (1:1-3:12)
   a. The aim of entry into the community and priests' and levites' blessings (1:1-20)

   b. The liturgy for entry into the community (1:21-2:18)
   c. The rule of renewal ceremony, denunciation, and atonement (2:19-3:12)

E. Wright [ed.] *The Bible and the Ancient Near East* [Garden City, New York: Anchor Books, 1965], 170-264, esp. 169-171), and that the oldest copy of the Community Rule from Cave 4 is derived from the end of the second century BC (so J. T. Milik, ''Prière de Nabonide' et autres écrits d'un cycle de Daniel: Fragments araméens de Qumrân 4,' *RB* 63 [1956], 61) ; G. Vermes, 'Preliminary Remarks on Unpublished Fragments of the Community Rule from Qumran Cave 4,' *JJS* 42 [1991], 250).

[145] Basically both the Rule of the Congregation (1QS[a]) and the Rule of Benedictions (1QS[b]) are regarded as supplements to 1QS, since they derive not only from the same scroll, but they also have the same date and handwriting (so J. T. Milik, in DJD 1, 107). Because of several duplicate passages (the aims of the community: 1:1-15, 5:1-7a, 8:1-4a; the admission of new members: 5:20b-23a, 6:13b-23; two lists of punishments: 6:24-7:25, 8:16b-9:2) and a thematic contradiction (e.g. about priests' authority: 9:7, 5:2b-3a), reduction criticism has been attempted for 1QS. See Martínez (*The People of the Dead Sea Scrolls: their writings, beliefs and practices, transl. by W. G. E. Watson* [Leiden: E. J. Brill, 1995 (1993)], 51); M. A. Knibb, *The Qumran Community* (Cambridge: Cambridge University Press, 1987), 77; Murphy-O'Connor, 'Community, Rule of the, (1QS),' in David Noel Freedman et al. (eds.) *Anchor Bible Dictionary*, vol. 1 (New York: Doubleday, 1992), 1110-1112.

II. Two paths of human beings and their destiny: wisdom instruction (3:13-4:26)
   a. The nature of all human beings (3:13-4:1)
   b. The paths of humility and stubbornness to the laws and their rewards (4:2-14)
   c. The nature of all human beings and their destiny (present and future) (4:15-26)

III. The rules for the congregation (5:1-10:8)
   a. The rules for life in the community (5:1-6:23)[146]
   b. The rules for punishment (6:24-7:27)
   c. The rules for the holy congregation (8:1-9:26)

IV. The Hymn of Praise (10:1-11:22)

Section two (1QS 3:13-4:26) argues that there are two paths in human history, and that they are exclusively separate and have their own destiny. So, the members of congregation are expected to choose the path of truth.[147] In particular, this section deals with two theological issues: (1) the division of the two generations; and (2) the reality of sin and suffering in the community members (at the present time). The descriptive creation accounts appear at the beginning of the main arguments (1QS 3:15b-18a) and at the ending of the first part (1QS 3:25) as follows:

Thematic Flow of 1QS 3:13-4:24

Heading for Section 2 (3:13-15a): The description of 'the nature of human history' (תולדות),[148] i.e. their kinds,[149] deeds, and final rewards

I. 3:15b-4:1
   A. *Descriptive creation account* (3:15b-18a)
       God's perfect design (or plan)
       God's perfect dominion
       Creation of the human and the two spirits
   B. Two paths in history of mankind (3:18b-21)
       Two Spirits: רוחות והעול / רוחוא האמת
       Two Generations: תולדות העול / תולדות האמת
       Two Angels: מלאך חושך / שר אורים
       Two Paths: דרכי חושך / דרכי אור
   C. Present Reality: Sins and suffering exist in the present community (3:22-25a)

---

[146] (1) the rules for community life (6:1-8a); (2) the rules for a session of congregation (6:8b-13a); and (3) the rules for candidates (6:13b-23).

[147] Compare with the idea of human choice in Sir 15:11-20.

[148] This terminology may allude to אלה תולדות in the OT (e.g. Gen 2:4; 5:1; 6:9; 10:1; it occurs 13 times in Gen; 9 times in 1 Chr; 13 times in Num; 3 times in Exod; and 1 time in Ruth). 1QS may attempt to write a comprehensive genealogy of human beings with an expanded chronical view point. Concerning the translation of תולדות, A. Leaney (*The Rule of Qumran and its Meaning: Introduction, translation and commentary* [London: SCM Press, 1966], 146) comments, 'To write therefore the 'generations' or history of mankind is to give an account of men's nature.'

[149] García Martínez translates it as 'the ranks of their spirits'; however, מיני (< מין) may allude to the terminology of Gen ch. 1 (e.g. 1:11, 12, 21, 25) in the sense of 'kind.'

A.' *Descriptive creation account* (3:25b-26)
    God's creation of two spirits
    God's design of their deeds

II. 4:2-14
    B'. The nature of the two spirits and final reward
        Humble spirit (רוח ענוה)
            and its reward in eternal light (באור עולמים)
        Stubborn heart (כובוד לב)
            and its reward in the abysses (בהויות חושך)

III. 4:15-24
    C'. The present and end time reality of the two spirits
        Present situation:
            The division of the two spirits (אמת and עולה)
            The two spirits feud in believers' spirits
        End time situation: אמת goes up / עולה goes down

The creation account functions as an important theological basis which highlights the point that the present and eschatological situations of community members are under the perfect dominion of God.

Influence of Key Passages from the OT

The creation account in 1QS col. 3 seems to have relevance to the Jewish exegetical tradition of creation[150] from several points of view: (1) God's

---

[150] The dualism of 1QS 3 has been compared with that of the Zurvan myth: K. G. Kuhn, 'Die Sektenschrift und die iranische Religion,' *ZTK* 49 (1952), 312; C. T. Fritsch, *The Qumrân Community* (New York: Anchor Books, 1956), 73; W. F. Albright, 'The Bible After Twenty Years of Archeology,' *RL* 21 (1952), 549; F. M. Cross, *The Ancient Library of Qumran* (New York: Anchor Books, 1961), 98; A. Dupont-Sommer, *The Essene Writings from Qumran* (New York: Meridan Books, 1962), 118-119; D. Winston, 'The Iranian Component in the Bible, Apocrypha, and Qumran: A Review of the Evidence,' *HR* 5 (1966), 200; J. M. Allegro, *The Dead Sea Scrolls* (Baltimore: Vallentine, Mitchell, 1956), 128; H. Ringgren, *The Faith of Qumran* (E. T. Sander [trans.]; Philadelphia: Fortress Press, 1963), 78 (See brief summary of their arguments in J. H. Charlesworth, 'A Critical Comparison of the Dualism in 1QS 3:13-4:26 and the "Dualism" Contained in the Gospel of John,' in *John and the Dead Sea Scrolls*, ed. J. H. Charlesworth [New York: Crossroad Publishing Company, 1990], 76-106, esp. 87-89). Charlesworth's argument is mainly based on R. C. Zaehner's work on the Zoroastriarism: *Zurvan: A Zoroastrian Dilemma* [Oxford: Clarendon Press, 1955); *The Dawn and Twilight of Zoroastrianism* (London: Weidenfeld and Nicolson, 1961). However, there seems to be chronological difficulties particularly in the textual investigation, since the textual evidence for the idea of monotheistically flavored dualism, which depicts Zurvan as the sole Creator, and through whom two spirits (those dwelling in the light and darkness) came out, is limited to a few written texts (i.e. *Yasna* 72:10; *Vidēvdt* 19:13; 19:16; and *Nyāyisñ* 1:8). The evidence from the citations of the Greek writers is not necessarily clear (see Zaehner, *Zurvan*, 447-450), and it is also uncertain whether Zurvan is really regarded as a personal being either, since in several contexts it means an infinite time and space (e.g. even in *Dubitationes et solutiones de Principiis of*

perfect design before the work of creation; (2) the creation of the spirits (or angels)[151]; and (3) the establishment of the divisions in the world.[152]

Firstly, a similar expression to 1QS 3:15b-16, 'the perfect knowledge of God to make a plan before it happened,' is seen in other Qumran sectarian texts (1QS 3:15; 11:11, 17; 1QH[a] 5:6; 7:17; 9:7-8, 19-20; 21:12-13; 4Q176 frags. 16, 17, 18, 22, 23, 33, 51, 53, 1:2-3; 4Q180 frag. 1:1; 4Q402 frag. 4 1:12-14; 4Q404 frag. 4 1:1-2, etc.). It can be seen in other Jewish writings (1 En 2:1-5:2; 9:11; 2 En 25:3; 33:3; 4 Ezra 6:1-6; 7:70; 8:52; 2 Bar 14:17; 54:1; TMos 1:12-13, etc.). In these contexts, Prov 8:22-31 is more or less mentioned. The expression, 'And when they have come into being at their appointed time, they will accomplish all their deeds according to his glorious design without altering anything' (1QS 3:16), seems to share the idea with 1 En 2:1-5:2, in which God's perfect universal order is highlighted.

Damascius, 125 [it is known as the evidence from Eudemus, Aristotle's pupil]). As far as the doctrine of Zoroastriarism is concerned, the universe is from the beginning divided into dual domains (i.e. light [the hights], in which Ohrmazd is dwelling, and darkness [the depths], in which Ahriman is dwelling). The question is what historical factors made Zurvan myth different from orthodox Zoroastriarism: in other words, 'Should we simply regard the similarity between the monotheistically oriented dualism of 1QS col. 3 and the Zurvan myth as the evidence of 1QS's dependence on the Zurvan myth? More or less, the problem may occurs from complexity of the idea of 'Dualism.' J. Frey ('Different Patterns of Dualistic Thought in the Qumran Library: Reflections on their Background and History' in M. Bernstein, F. García Martínez, and J. Kampen [eds.] *Legal Texts and Legal Issues* [Leiden: Brill], 1997], 282-285) gives a clear definition and classification of 'Dualism': *Metaphysical dualism* which signifies the opposition of two dominating causal powers of equal rank; *Cosmic dualism* which denotes the division of the world and of humanity into two opposing forces of good and evil (non coeternal nor strictly causal), darkness and light; *Spatial dualism* which signifies the division of the world in two spatialy divided parts such as heaven and earth, above and below; *Eschatological dualism* which signifies the division of the world in two temporally divided parts (the rigid division of time between the present aeon and the future one); *Ethical dualism* which signifies the bifurcation of mankind into two mutually exclusive groups according to virtues and vices; *Soteriological dualism* which denotes the division of mankind caused by faith or disbelief in a saviour; *Theological dualism* which contrasts between God and humanity, or creator and creation, etc.; *Physical dualism* which denotes the absolute division between matter and spirit; Anthropological dualism which signifies the opposition of body and soul as distinct principles of being; *Psychological dualism* in which the contrast between good and evil is internalized and seen to be an opposition not between groups of people but between principles or impulses waging battle within man. According to this definition, J. Frey (294) suggests that the dualism of 1QS should be understood as creation-founded and eschatologically confined cosmic dualism with a subordinate ethical dualism, whereas, on the other hand Zoroastriarism should be denoted as *Metaphysical dualism* (282).

[151] Cf. Jub 2:2; 2 En 29:1; LAB 60:2-3. See our argument on the Jewish exegesis on the creation of the spirits (§ 2.1.1).

[152] Cf. Job 38:10; Ps 104:9; Prov 8:28-29; 1 En 69:18; 2 En 47:5; Sir 16, 33, etc.

And all his works serve him and *do not change*, but *all perform* his command . . . How the heavenly luminaries *do not change* . . . And *at their fixed seasons they appear,* and do not violate their proper order. Observe the earth and consider his works which have been wrought in it, that from the first to the last no work of God is changed[153]

Secondly, the idea of God's providence, which is prominent in the creation account of Sir 39:33 (cf. Sir 42:23; Pss 33, 104), can be seen in 1QS 3:17, 'God supports all in their need.'[154]

Sir 39:33
> Τὰ ἔργα κυρίου πάντα ἀγαθὰ καὶ πᾶσαν χρείαν ἐν ὥρᾳ αὐτῆς χορηγήσει
> The works of the Lord are all good, and he will supply every need in its time.

(B) מעשה אל כלם טובים לכל צורך בעתו יספוק
> All the works of God are good, he suffices for every need in their time.

Thirdly, 1QS 3:18 mentions the creation of human beings and the endowment of the spirits (Gen 1:26-28; 2:7). Concerning the endowment of the spirts, the wording of 1QS alludes to Isa 42:5[155]:

1QS 3:18
וישם לו שתי רוחות להתהלך בם
> And he *placed* in him two *spirits to walk* with them.

Isa 42:5
נתן נשמה לעם עליה ורוח להלכים בה
> who *gives* breath to its people and *spirit to those who walk* on it.

Sirach has a similar dualistic account on this issue. It is interesting that Sirach expands the account of the endowment of the spirit (Gen 2:7 or Isa 42:5) with a possible connection with the narrative of the tree of good and evil (Gen 3:1-7, 22).

Sir 16:16[156]
> τὸ φῶς αὐτοῦ καὶ τὸ σκότος ἐμέρισε τῷ Αδαμ.
> (The Lord) assigned his *light and darkness* to Adam.

Sir 17:7
> ἐπιστήμην συνέσεως ἐνέπλησεν αὐτοὺς καὶ ἀγαθὰ καὶ κακὰ ὑπέδειξεν αὐτοῖς.

---

[153] The translation of Knibb. Knibb (*The Qumran Community*, 97) notices that 1QS col. 3 may allude to 1 En 5:2.

[154] See our argument on Sir 39:12-35 (§ 3.15.1).

[155] Cf. 4 Ezra 3:5b; Ant 1:34; JosAsen 12:1.

[156] MS A, GII, Sir have vv. 15-16; GI or Lat do not have these verses. Cf. Di Lella, *The Wisdom of Ben Sira*, 270.

He filled them with the knowledge of intelligence and showed them *good and evil.*

Sir 33:10b-11

... καὶ ἐκ γῆς ἐκτίσθη Αδαμ. ἐν πλήθει ἐπιστήμης κύριος διεχώρισεν αὐτοὺς καὶ ἠλλοίωσεν τὰς ὁδοὺς αὐτῶν.

... and humankind was created out of the dust. In the fullness of his knowledge the Lord distinguished them and *appointed their different ways.*

ומן עפר נוצר אדם

(E) חכמ]ת יי תבדילם וישם אותם דרי האר]דמה] וישנ]ה] את דרכיהם

Thus the descriptive account of creation in 1QS col. 3 is relevant to the biblical and Jewish exegetical tradition of the Genesis creation account. The creation account in 1 Enoch and Sirach, as well as indirectly Ps 33 and Isa 42:5, may influence these texts.[157]

3.17.2 Thematic Considerations

God's Perfect Plan: as a Theological Basis

1QS 3:13-4:24 emphasizes how God dominates human history (תולדות) from the beginning to the end. The idea of the pre-established law of God before creation is seen in other biblical and Jewish writings: it means the order of the universe (e.g. Job chs. 37-38; Ps 104; 1 En 2:1-5:2; Sir 16:24-30; 42:15-43:33); it is connected to God's eschatological plan (e.g. 4 Ezra 6:6; 2 Bar 48:2; 54:1; 4Q402 frag. 4 1:12-14; 1 En 9:11); and it is expanded into the meaning of the predestination of human beings (Sir 18:1-3; 33:7-15; 1QS 11:11; 1QH[a] 7:17; 9:7-8, 19-20; 21:12-13; 4Q180 frag. 1:1). 1QS 3:15b-16 takes the last interpretation: strictly speaking, whereas 1QS follows the terminology of the creation account of 1 En 2:1-5:2 in some senses, it takes the understanding of תולדות, 'the predestination of human beings,' which appears elsewhere in Sirach. The idea of God's perfect design of תולדות is reinforced by the next statement, 'In his hand are the laws (משפט) of all things, and he provides (כול > יכלכלם) them in all their need (חפציהם)' (1QS 3:17).[158] Based on the ideas of God's perfect plan and his providence, 1QS explains the nature of human history (i.e. תולדות: the present reality of evil power and the expectation for the end time blessing) in order to encourage the community members to choose the way of life.

---

[157] It should be noted that the manuscripts of 1 Enoch and Sirach are found in the Qumran library (cf. 1Q23; 4Q201-212; 4Q530-531; 6Q8; 2Q18).

[158] See the similar expression, 'all their need,' in Sir 39:33 and 42:23.

Creation of Two Spirits: Dualism and Theodicy

1QS 3:18 states that God the Creator endowed two spirits on human beings. This term alludes to Isa 42:5, as previously shown. There seems to be relevance to Sirach's exegesis of the creation of human beings: i.e. Sirach (15:14; 17:7) may fuse the account of the bestowment of spirit on human beings (Gen 2:7; Isa 42:5) with a possible connection with the narrative of the tree of the truth and evil (עץ הדעת טוב ורע) (Gen 2:17; 3:1-24).[159] These two spirits are called, 'the spirits of truth and deceit' (רוחות האמת והעול) (1QS 3:19). 1QS cols. 3-4 highlights the rigid division of the two תולדות. There are three similar statements on the two תולדות in 1QS 3:18-21, and a summarized form appears at the end of col. 3 (1QS 3:25).

1QS 3:18
God placed on him the two spirits (שתי רוחות)
so that they walk with them (להתהלך בם) . . .

1QS 3:19
From the dwelling place of light (במעון אור[160])
(is) the generation of the truth (תולדות האמת).
From the fountain of darkness (ממקור חושך[161])
(is) the generation of the deceit (תולדות העול).

1QS 3:20
In the hand of the Prince of lights (ביד שר אורים)
(is) the dominion over all the sons of the truth
so that they walk (יתהלכו) on the paths of light (בדרכי אור).
In the hand of the Angel of darkness (ביד מלאך חושך)
(is) all dominion over the sons of deceit
so that they walk (יתהלכו) on the paths of darkness (בדרכי חושך).

1QS 3:25
He created (ברא) the spirits of light and darkness (רוחות אור וחושך),
and he established every deed on them,
every labour on their paths.

The first example (1QS 3:18) makes the topic clear, which is discussed in the following sections. 1QS 3:19 stresses the different origin of the two generations, whereas 1QS 3:20 argues that both are guided by the different

---

[159] See Di Lella's comment (*The Wisdom of Ben Sira*, 282) on Sir 17:7.

[160] Cf. the examples of the sense,'holy dwelling,' in Jer 25:30; Zech 2:17; Ps 68:5 [MT 68:6]; 2 Chr 30:27. See the simliar wordings: מעון קודש in 1QS 8:8, 10:1; 1QS^b 4:25; מעון כבוד in 1QS 10:3.

[161] Cf. the examples of the figurative use: Jer 2:13; 17:13; 51:36; Hos 13:15; Zech 13:1; Ps 36:9 (מקור חיים) [MT 36:10]; Prov 10:11; 13:14; 14:27; 16:22; 18:4 (מקור חכמה).

heavenly powers until the end time (עד מועד פקודתו in 1QS 3:18). In other words, the two תולדות were given the different destinies originally (1QS 3:19) and historically (1QS 3:20), by God the Creator. Also both the creation of the two spirits and the pre-establishment of human destiny are recalled in 1QS 3:25. These ideas are common in the Theodicy of the Jewish tradition. For example, Sirach applies the idea of the divisions of time and space to the argument of the division of human beings (or the distinctiveness of the chosen people) (e.g. Sir 33:7-15). 4 Ezra 6:38-54 and 2 Baruch 14:15-19 link the idea of the division of the creation to the argument of the original status of Israel. In order to argue why Israel suffers at the present time, they refer to the reality of evil powers. For instance, by referring to the demonic power (i.e. Mastema and his followers) (5:6; 10:1, 5, 8; 11:4; 12:20; 15:31, 32; 17:16; 18:9; 19:28; 48:2-49:4), the Book of Jubilees argues that God rules human history by controlling two kinds of spirit (demons and angels), and mentions that both can intervene in human history (esp. Jub chs. 17-18, 48-49). However, on the contrary, it is also said that the Lord gave evil spirits the authority to rule over the Gentiles (Jub 15:31), whereas the Lord did not permit them to touch Israelites (Jub 15:32).[162] In short, on the one hand the author of Jubilees understands that the evil power actually intervened in the history of Israel, whereas, on the other hand, he states that there is a clear division in the roles of the two kinds of spirits. This understanding is very similar to the idea of two spirits in 1QS 3:20-25: i.e. on the one hand, there is a division between the dominion of the prince of lights and the dominion of the angel of darkness (1QS 3:20-21), whereas, on the other hand, the angel of darkness can cause the fall and suffering upon the righteous by the end time (עד קצו) (1QS 3:22-24a; cf. 1QS 4:23). Although 1QS employs light/darkness imagery which reflect a strong dualistic idea,[163] the basic understanding can be found in the Second Temple Judaism.

Light and Darkness

Light/darkness imageries are employed to make clear the contrast between the two generations. The expression of 1QS 3:19, 'the dwelling place of light' (מעון אור), alludes to the astronomical accounts of 1QS 10:1-5 and 1QH[a] 20:4-10. 1QS 10:1-5 tells that the lights (מאורות) shine out from the holy vault (זבול קדוש) and retire to the dwelling place of glory (מעון כבוד), whereas God opens his store (אוצרו) for the watches of darkness (חושך

---

[162] See § 2.1.1.

[163] For example, Charlesworth ('Dualism in 1QS and John') is interested in the zurvan myth because its dualism contains a monotheistic view; Mansoor (*The Thanksgiving Hymns* [Leiden: E. J. Brill, 1961], 57-58) believes that Qumran dualism was derived from the old Iranian religion, and it was combined with Hebrew monotheistic doctrines of creation.

אשמורי), and darkness retires before light (מפני אור).[164] 1QHª states that each period of the dominion (ממשלת[165]) of light and darkness has been established in accordance with its regulation (לתכונו) or with the laws (לחוקות) of the great luminary (1QHª 20:4-10 [Sukenik col. 12]).   1QS 3:13-26 seems to apply typologically these astronomical phenomena (the storehouse of light and darkness; the period of dominion of light and darkness) to the understanding of human history (the present and end time).   In some cases, the metaphorical word pair, חושך and אור, are replaced by another word pair, העול (or צדך) and האמת (3:18, 20, 21, 22; 4:19, 21, 23).   The word pair, אור and חושך, is consistently employed to contrast the nature of האמת and העול. The word pair is also used for the names of the angels: שר אורים (or אמתו מלאך) (1QS 3:20, 25) and מלאך חושך (1QS 3:22).   However, the notion of אור and חושך does not necessarily imply a cosmic power as is prominent in Iranian Zoroastrianism.   Rather, it seems to be a simple application of a contrasted word pair, which is commonly used in several Jewish writings (e.g. Sirach, 1 Enoch, etc.) for theological arguments (e.g. the original status of the chosen people and their final reward, the reality of heavenly supports, and theodicy).

3.18 4Q392 (Liturgical Work from Qumran Cave 4) 1-9

3.18.1 Literary Considerations

Preliminary Remarks: Reconstruction of the Text

The right and left margins can be seen on the photo (PAM 42.150), but it is uncertain whether the top line of the fragment is the beginning of the text. Lines 4 to 7, which refer to the creation of light and darkness, are well preserved, while Lines 1 to 3 and 8 to 9 have lost a few words in each line.

RECONSTRUCTION OF 4Q392

[וממלכות]	1
[ ] ם[ ] [א]ור איש[166]ולי]יראה את א]להים ולא לסור ממן	2
שמים [ו] אלוהנים [ובבריתו תדבק נפשם ועשו א]ים דרריפיהו	3
ממעל ולחקר דרכי בני האדם [ל]אין סתר הוא ברא חשך] ואן]ור לו	4
ובמעונתו אור אורתם וכל אפלה לפנו נתה ואין עמו להבדיל בין האור	5
לחשך כי לבני [אד]ם הבדילם לאן]ור] יומם ובשמש לילה ירח וכוכבים	6

---

[164] The idea of 'the storehouse of lights' is common to Jewish astronomical accounts (e.g. 1 En chs. 72-75).

[165] Cf. ממשלת in 1QS 3:20-21, 23.

[166] Or another possible restoration is לאהבה Cf. Deut 11:22; 30:20.

כ]יא כופלים כל מעשי אל אנחנו   ועמו אור לאין חקר ואין לדעתנו   7

נפ]לאות ומ(פ)חתים לאין מספר   בשר הלוא נשכיל כמה עמנו ל[ ][8

מ]שרתי דבניר [ ] מלפנו יצאים המן   [מרים]   רו]חות וברקים]   9

THEMATIC FLOW OF 4Q392

1	] and kingdoms [

2   ] man [to fear G]od,
           and not to turn away from [
3   and to his covenant their soul adheres
           and [they] ob[serve ea]ch the words of h[is] mouth

3-4   Go[d   ] the heavens above
4   and to examine the paths of the sons of man,
           which have no secret for you.

      He created darkness [and li]ght for himself,
5   and in his dwelling the perfect light shines,
           and all the darkness leaves before him,
5-6   and he does not need to separate light from darkness
6   because (only) for the sons of [ma]n he separated them
               as the li[ght] at daytime with the sun,
                 at night the moon and the stars.
7   And with him there is a light which cannot be inspected
             nor can it be known
      [f]or all the creations of God are double.

7-8   We are flesh, which does not understand
           how many with us [won]ders
           and portents without number.
9   [wi]nds and lightning [
       the ser]vants of the holy of ho[lies] going out before him [

Context and Main Concern

It is uncertain whether the first word, which can be seen in the middle of Line 1, ממלכות 'kingdoms,' mentions the earthly kingdom (cf. 4Q392 frag. 2 3) or the heavenly kingdom (cf. 4Q400 frag. 1 1:2-3; 2:1; frag. 2 3,4; 4Q401 frags. 1-2 2; frag. 14 1:6; 4Q403 frag. 1 1:8, 32; 2:3, 10). The former rendering might suggest that the fragment mentions God's dominion over the kingdoms, whereas the latter suggests that it praises the Lord who dwells in the highest place. In some fragments from 4Q Songs of the Sabbath Sacrifice (4Q403 frag. 1 1:45-46; 2:1; 4Q404 frag. 5 4; 4Q405 frag. 4+ 14), the heavenly kingdom (שמי מלכות) appears with the perfect light (אורתם). It seems to suggest the latter rendering. In any case, the praise of God might come in the first line of the fragment. Lines 2 to 4a might mention God's mercy upon them who walk in righteousness (cf. Deut 11:22; 30:20). Lines 8 to 9 emphasize the sovereignty of God, by referring to the heavenly mysteries ('winds,' 'lightning,' 'angelic beings') (cf. Job chs. 37-38; Ps 104). Lines 4 to 7 refer to the creation of light and darkness. It is mentioned as a great mystery of God, which represents his magnificence.

Influence of Key Passages from the OT

As far as the creation account in 4Q392 is concerned, Lines 4b to 7 give an interpretation of the creation of light and darkness (cf. Gen 1:14-19). Reference to the creation of light and darkness in the context which emphasizes the sovereignty of God, as well as its wording, may allude to Isa 45:7. The idea that there is no darkness in the presence of God can be found in biblical tradition (cf. Ps 139:12; Dan 2:22).

3.18.2 Thematic Consideration: Creation of Light

The changing of the general word order, אור וחשך, to חשך ואור (frag. 1 4), attempts to focus on the creation of darkness. It was given through the division between light and darkness (frag. 1 5). 4Q392 argues that the division was given for the world of the sons of man (frag. 1 6), but there is no division in the realm of God's dwelling place (frag. 1 5). In other words, God created two different lights: one is perfect light (אורתם), which shines in the dwelling place of God (מעונת > מעון[167]) (frag. 1 4b-5, 7); the other is the luminaries, which were created for the sons of man (frag. 1 6). The word, כופלים 'double' (frag. 1 7), might allude to שנים שנים or δύο δύο in Sir 33:15, which is said to be the way of God's creation. In the context of 4Q392, the double might indicate the creation of light and darkness (v. 4); however, vv. 5-7a might suggest that it mentions the dual existence of the heavenly light (for God) and the luminaries (for human beings). Through this interpretation, 4Q392 emphasizes the distinctiveness of God's identity, by contrasting it to the lowliness of human beings (cf. frag. 1 8). The similar emphasis on God's distinctive nature, which employs light and darkness imageries, can be seen in the Old Testament as has been previously argued (cf. Ps 139:12; Dan 2:22). 4Q392 expands this tradition and applies it to the exposition of Gen 1:14-19. Consequently it may have produced the distinctive idea of the creation of two different lights (one being God's dwelling place; the other for human beings).

---

[167] In the sense of the dwelling place in heaven (cf. Deut 26:15).

3.19 4Q422 (Paraphrase of Gen and Exod from Qumran Cave 4) frag. 1 1-13

3.19.1 Literary Considerations

Preliminary Remarks: Reconstruction of the Text

Eleven tiny fragments, which were clearly written by the same hand, are now reconstructed into three columns, and they are called 4Q422 (4QParaGenExod).[168] It contains a paraphrase of the account of creation and the account of human rebellion (frag 1; Gen 1-4), the flood (frags. 2-6; Gen 6-9), and the Exodus event (frags. 10a-e; Exod 1-11 with Pss 78 and 105). It is assumed from the reconstruction of frags. 10a-e that the original columns have 12 to 13 lines, and that each line may contain 10 to 12 words. Fragment 1 contains 8 lines, in which three or four words are visible. This means that the fragment misses the first five lines and two thirds of the words in each.[169] The first words of fragment 1 refer to one of the creation formulae (the reference to the divine attribute), which usually appears in the first part of the creation account in the Jewish tradition (cf. 4Q381; 4 Ezra 6:38; PrMan 1:3; SibOr 3:20; 2 Bar 14:17; 21:4; 54:1; ApAbr 22:2; Sir 42:15, etc.). Thus this line (1:6) may be a part of the beginning of the creation account, whereas the five missing lines (1:1-5) may be an introductory section.[170] The reconstruction of col. 1 (frag. 1) is as follows.

RECONSTRUCTION OF 4Q422 frag. 1-13

השמים והארץ וכול[צבאם עשה]171כדנבר פיו   6

172אדם בצלמו[ן עשה ורוח קודשנו נפח באפיו   7

---

[168] See the works of T. Elgvin, 'The Genesis Section of 4Q422 (4QParaGenExod),' *DSD* 1 (1994) and E. Tov, 'The Exodus Section of 4Q422,' *DSD* 1 (2) (1994); '4QParaphrase of Genesis and Exodus,' in H. Attridge (DJD 13), 417-441.

[169] See Elgvin's reconstruction of fragment 1 (DJD 13, 421).

[170] Cf. Elgvin's comment (DJD 13, 422).

[171] See 4Q381 frag. 1 3 [צבאם כל] ובדבר פיו. Another possible reconstruction would be Elgvin's בדברו.

[172] It might be possible to assume that the fragment focuses on the creation of Adam, interpreting נשמת חיים 'the breath of life' (Gen 2:7 or Isa 42:5) as 'the holy spirit.' Sir 17:7 and 4Q504 frag. 8 5 seem to understand the spirit as 'the wisdom of God.' The letter before עשה is not necessarily ר, but rather ו (see the photo of PAM 41.478). 4Q504 frag. 8 4-5 clearly mentions this creation of Adam, before the account of the assignment of the human role. Another possible restoration is אור instead of בצלמו: the fragment might mention the construction of the heavenly realm; רוח קודש is considered to be in the perfect light (באור אורתם) in the heavenly sanctuaries (4Q403 frag. 1 44-45; 4Q404 frag. 5 1-8; 4Q405 frag. 6 11-15; frag. 14 1:5; frag. 23 2:8; 11Q17 8:1-10). The creation of light and

נתן לאדם לרדות בכול הנפ[ש החיה והרמש]ת על הארץ[173] 8

[174]שם האדם על האר[ץ המשילו לאכול פרני האדמה 9

[לו]בל]תי אכול מעץ הד[עת טוב ורע 10

ו]יקום עליו וישכחו] חוקיו 11

[ל] [ביוצר רע ולמעש]ני רשעה 12

[שלומן] 13

6   ] he made [the heavens and the earth and all] their hosts by [his] word. [
7   ] he made [Adam in his image and breathed his holy spirit into his nostrils.
8 he gave humankind dominion over every living creat]ure and what move[s on the earth.
9   he set humankind on the earth,] he set him in charge to eat the fru[it of the soil
10   ] that he shoul[d n]ot eat from the tree that gives know[ledge of good and evil.
11   ] he rose against him and they forgot [his laws
12   ] in evil inclination and for deed[s of injustice
13   ] peace [

Context and Main Concern

If our reconstruction is possible, then the fragment mainly focuses on the creation of Adam and his original status (his noble birth and assigned role as guardian over the created world). In spite of his godly origin, Adam sinned against his Creator and was inclined to do evil (1:11-12). The account of Adam's rebellion is followed by the narrative of the flood and the plagues in the Exodus event. It might be possible to assume a thematic continuity between the creation account and the rest of the narratives, which tells that the universe (or nature) which was originally created to serve human beings rose against them (in the form of the flood and plagues), because of Adam's rebellion.

Influence of Key Passages from the OT

The fragment is a retelling of Gen 1:26-28 and 2:7. Reference to the divine attributes in the work of creation (4Q422 frag. 1 6-7) may be influenced by Ps 33:6. If רוח קודשו is taken as a mediator of creation (rather than one of the list of created beings), Elgvin's comment may be right that the fragment assigns a more important role to God's holy spirit in the context of creation than Gen ch. 1 and Ps 33:6-9.[175]

---

divine spirits through the word of God might be mentioned (4Q404 frag. 4 1-2; 4Q405 frag. 6 3). Elgvin suggests another restoration by referring to Gen. 2:2:
.וישבות ביום השביעי מכול מלאכתו אש[ר
[173] Cf. Gen 1:21, 28.
[174] Cf. Gen 2:15-16; Ps 8:7; 4Q381 frag. 1 7-8.
[175] So Elgvin, 'The Genesis Section of 4Q422,' 195.

3.19.2 Thematic Consideration: the Word of God

The first sentence (v. 6) states that the work of creation was accomplished by
his word, with a possible reference to Ps 33:6. It is a shorter account of the
whole Genesis creation account (esp. Gen 1:1-25) which depicts the mighty
works of God, and it may also function as opening words for the retelling of
human history (esp. Gen 1:26 and thereafter).

3.20 4Q504 (Words of the Luminaries^a from Qumran Cave 4) frag. recto 8 4-10

3.20.1 Literary Considerations

Preliminary Remarks: Reconstruction of the Text

Two large fragments (frags. 1-2) and six middle size fragments (frags. 3-8), as
well as forty one tiny framents (frags. 9-49), are regarded as the collection of
daily prayers.[176] If fragment 8 belongs to the same group of fragments (such
as 1 and 2), each line of fragment 8 has lost more than half of its words. On
the back (verso) of fragment 8, the title for this collection is printed as המארות
דברי 'The words of Luminaries.' Because of this printing on the back and the
mentioning of the work of creation in it, fragment 8 (recto) shoud be
considered as the prayer of the first week.[177]

RECONSTRUCTION OF 4Q504 frag. 8 1-15

1   תפלה ביום הראישון זכור אדו]ח]נני [כיא ^{178}מענללי יה[179]
2   ]תנו ואתה ^{180}יח עולומים
3   ^{182}חשבתין נפלאות מקרם ונוראות^{181} נמשנות עולמים
4   אדם א]בינו יצרתה בדמות כבודנכה
5   נשמת חיים נפחתה באפו ובינה ודעת^{183} נמלאתה אותו
6   בגן עדן אשר נטעתה המשלתנה אותו

---

[176] Cf. Baillet (*Qumrân Grotte 4 III [4Q482-4Q520]* [DJD 7; Oxford: Clarendon Press,
1982]).

[177] So Baillet (DJD 7, 138).

[178] Baillet (DJD 7, 163) restores . . . מעמ with some hesitation. However, it might be
possible that Ps 77:10-11 is in the author's mind.

[179] See the similar opening formula in 4Q504 frags. 1-2 1:8; 7:4; frag. 3 2:5.

[180] Baillet (DJD 7, 163) reads יח with some hesitation; however the photo (PAM
43.626) suggests our reading. See 4Q504 frags. 1-2 5:8-9, אל חי לברדכה (cf. idiomatic
use אתה יהוה in the OT).

[181] So Baillet (DJD 7). Cf. Ps 77:5 [MT 77:6].

[182] Cf. Ps 77:5 [MT 77:6].

[183] So Baillet (DJD 7). Cf. Sir 17:7.

7   [ם ולתהלך בארץ כבוד א[

8   א[שמר ותקם עליו לבלתי ס[ור

9   [בשר הואה ולעפר ה[ן

10   [תו ואתה ידעתה]

11   [לדורות עולם[

12   [אל חי וידכה]

13   [האדם בדרכי]

14   למלוא אתהּ[חןמס[184 ולשפון] דם נקי

15   [ ] [לו[

1 Prayer for the first day. Remem]ber, Lord, because the deeds of the Lord
2] And you are the Lord for ev[er
3 I considered] the marvels of old and the portents
4 Adam,] our [fat]her, you fashioned in the image of [your] glory
5 the breath of life] you [b]lew into his nostril, and intelligence and knowledge [
6 in the gard]en of Eden, which you had planted. You made [him] govern [
7] and so that he would walk in a glorious land [
8] he kept. And you imposed on him not to tu[rn away

9] he is flesh, and to dust [
10] And you, you know [
11] for everlasting generations [
12] a living God, and your hand [
13] man on the paths of [
14] to fill the earth with violence and she[d innocent blood
15] to [

Context and Main Concern

The prayer recalls God's care for the father of Israel, Adam (frag. recto 8 4).
The last part of fragment 8 (recto) might mention the declared judgment of
God: that is the blessing upon the people who walk in the paths of
righteousness (cf. frag. 8 recto 10-13) and the curse upon the wicked (cf. frag 8
recto 14-15). Reflecting the sins of their fathers and God's punishment
against the people, they recall the forgiveness of God, which had been given to
them (cf. frags. 1-2 2:1-19; 3:10-21; 5:1-21). The prayer encourages the
people to strengthen their hearts, to walk on the paths of righteousness (cf.
frag. 4 12-13), and to hold a salvific expectation (cf. frags. 1-2 6:10-21).
Therefore, the creation of Adam is recalled in the examination of the history of
Israel (past, present, and future) with chronicles' point of view.[185]

Influence of Key Passages from the OT

The account of the creation of Adam in fragment 8 (recto) is a retelling of Gen
1:26 and 2:6-7 (or 5:1). The fragment expanded the account of the creation of

---

[184] So Baillet (DJD 7, 163). Cf. Gen 6:11, 13.
[185] Cf. Ant ch. 1; SibOr bks. 1-2.

Adam by interpreting נשמת חיים as the spirit of the divine wisdom (frag. 8 recto 5), or possibly by linking it to the account of the tree of knowledge.[186]

3.20.2 Thematic Consideration: Creation of Adam

Adam was fashioned in the image of God's glory ([בדמות כבוד]נכה), and was bestowed with the divine wisdom (lit. בינה ודעת 'intelligence and knowledge') (frag. recto 8 4-5). Adam was assigned to govern God's created world and was allowed to walk in a glorious land (בארץ כבוד) (frag. recto 8 6-8).[187] Thus the fragment emphasizes the glorious origin of Adam. It should be noted that Adam was called, 'our father' (א[ב]ינו) in this prayer, which means that the prayer focuses on the unique identity of Israel and God's special care for them.[188] This theme is repeated in the rest of the prayers:[189]

Frags. 1-2 3:3   כול הגוים כאין נגדכה
> All the peoples are [like not]hing.

Frag. 1-2 3:4-5   ולכבודכה ברתנו ובנים שמתנו לכה לעיני כול הגוים
> For your glory, you have created us, and you have established us as your sons in the sight of all the people.

Frag. 1-2 3:9-10   כיא אותנו בחרתה לכה [לעם מכול] הארץ
> For you chose us [to be your people among] all the earth.

Frag. 1-2 4:4-5   כיא אהבתה את ישראל מכול העמים
> For you loved Israel more than all the nations.

3.21 11QPs^a (The Psalms Scroll from Qumran Cave 11) 26:9-15

3.21.1 Literary Considerations

Preliminary Remarks: Reconstruction of the Text

From a palaeographic point of view, 11QPs^a seems to have been edited by one scribe. It contains forty one biblical psalms (Pss 93-150), seven apocryphal psalms (cols. 18, 19, 21, 22, 24, 26, 28), and a piece of prose about David's compositions (11QPs^a DavComp). Our text, which contains the poetic account of creation, and is now called 'The hymn to the Creator' (11QPs^a Creat), comes after the two paragraphs from Pss 149:7-9 and 150:1-6. The

---

[186] Cf. Sir 17:5-7; 4Q422 frag. 1 10.
[187] Cf. Wisd 9:2-3.
[188] Cf. 4 Ezra 6:38-54; 2 Bar 14:15-19.
[189] Cf. frag. 6 6, 10; frag. 4 5.

last two lines are partially damaged, but it can be reconstructed in accordance with Jer 10:12-13.

RECONSTRUCTION OF 11QPsª 26:9-15[190]

גדול וקדוש יהוה	(1)	9
קדוש קדושים לדור ודור		
לפניו הדר ילך	(2)	9-10
ואחריו המון מים רבים		
חסד ואמת סביב פניו	(3)	10-11
אמת ומשפט וצדק מכון כסאו		
מבדיל אור מאפלה	(4)	11-12
שחר הכין בדעת לבו		
אז ראו כול מלאכוו וירננו[191]	(5)	12
כי הראם את אשר לוא ידעו		
מעטר הרים תנובות	(6)	13
אוכל טוב לכול חי		
ברוך עושה ארץ בכוחו	(7)	13-14
מכין תבל בחוכמתו		
בתבונתו נטה שמים	(8)	14-15
ויוצא [רוח] מאו[נ]צרותיו		
[ברקים למט]ר עשה	(9)	15
ויעל ושיא[ני]ם מ[ן קצה [ארץ]		

LITERARY STRUCTURE OF 11QPsª 26:9-15

9	Opening	Great and holy is the Lord,
		the holy of holies to every generation.
9-10	Throne	In front of him Glory walks
	of	and behind him is the din of many waters.
10-11	God	Grace and truth surround his presence
		truth and justice and upright are the basis of his throne.
11-12	Creation	He separated light from darkness,
	of	the dawn he established by the knowledge of his mind.
12	Light	Then all his angels witnessed it and sang,
		for he showed them what they had not known.
13	Creation	He crowns the mountains with produce,
	on	good food for all the living.
13-14	the Earth	Blessed be he who made the earth with his power
		who established the world with his wisdom.
14-15	Creation	He spread out the heavens with his knowledge
	in	and brought out [the wind] from [his] st[orehouses].
15	the Heavens	He made [lightning for the rai]n,
		and made the mists rise [from] the end of [the earth].

---

[190] The reconstruction of the text is from J. A. Sanders (DJD 4, 89-90).

[191] The text writes אזראו.

Context and Main Concern

It is not certain whether there is a parallel between this apocryphal psalm and two citations from Pss 149:7-150:6. However, both psalms praise the Lord in the same way, by meditating on the mighty works of God. Following the opening praise (26:9a), the psalm pictures the heavenly throne of God, by using metaphorical words (26:9b-11a). The song of the angels (26:12) may be related to the previous description of the heavenly throne, and the psalm goes on to reflect upon the mighty work of creation (26:12-15).

Influence of Key Passages from the OT

11QPs^a 26:9-15 was composed by referring to (or alluding to) the biblical texts (mainly Ps 89 and Jer 10:12-13).

11QPs^a 26:9-15	Biblical Passages
Majesty precedes him (2a).	Grace and truth go before you (Ps 89:14b [MT 15b]
Behind him is the din of many waters (2b).	When he utters his voice, there is a tumult of waters in the heavens (Jer 10:13a; 51:16).
Grace and truth surrround his presence (3a).	Your truth surrounds you (Ps 89:8 [MT 9]).
Truth and justice and upright are the basis of his throne (3b).	Upright and justice are the basis of your throne (Ps 89:14a [MT 15]).
Blessed be he made the earth with his	It is he who made the earth with his power
power and established the world with his wisdom (7)	and who established the world with his wisdom (Jer 10:12ab).
He spread out the heavens with his knowledge (8a)	and with his knowledge he spread out the heavens (Jer 10:12c).
and brought out [the wind] from [his] st[orehouses] (8b)	and brought out the wind from his storehouse (Jer 10:13d)
He made [lightning for the rai]n,	He makes lightnings for the rain (Jer 10:13c)
and made the mists raise [from] the end	and he makes the mist rise from the ends of
of [the earth] (9).	the earth (Jer 10:13b).

Thus the first three verses of the apocryphal psalm are based on Ps 89:8 and 14, and the last three verses, which tell of God's work of creation, are grounded on Jer 10:12-13. It should be noted that the contexts of both Ps 89 and Jer ch. 10 describe the sovereignty of God that was sufficiently revealed in his work of creation (cf. Ps 89:5-13; Jer 10:6-7, 10-11).

Thematic Consideration: Monotheism

11QPs[a] 26:9-15 depicts the sovereignty of God, by employing several ideas and words from the biblical hymns. Firstly, the psalm illustrates the heavenly throne of God (26:9-11a): he is surrounded by grace and truth; majesty is in front; the dignity (in heavenly realm) is behind; truth, justice and upright are below. When God accomplished his first work of creation (the creation of light), the angels, who served him around his throne, praised the Creator (26:12).[192] Secondly, the psalm reflects on God's perfect nourishment for all the living beings (26:13).[193] Thirdly, the psalm reflects on the divine attributes (תבונתו, חוכמתו, כוחו) which are often used with monotheistic emphasis in the biblical and Jewish tradition. Fourthly, the psalm refers to the biblical accounts of the meteorological mysteries (26:8-9).

3.22 Summary (for Chapter 3)

Our findings from the early Jewish descriptive accounts of creation may be summarized as follows:

(1) The descriptive accounts of creation are shorter accounts which focus on particular events of creation. In other words, they make a selective reference to the Genesis creation account. Some creation accounts particularly refer to the creation in the heavenly realm or the astronomical and meteorological phenomena (1 En ch. 69; 2 En chs. 47-48; 4 Ezra 6:1-6; LAB 15:5-6; Sir 33:7-15; 4Q392 frag. 1-9; 11QPs[a] 24:11-15). Some accounts focus on the creation of human beings (2 En chs. 65-66; 4 Ezra 3:3-4; 2 Bar 14:16-19; Sir chs. 16-17; 4Q422 frag 1 1-13; 4Q504 frag 8 4-10). Some other accounts take a more compact form which generalizes the work of creation (2 Bar 21:4-8; 48:1-10; JosAsen 8:10-11; Sir 39:12-35; chs. 42-43). In general, the exposition of the Genesis creation account is a more interpretative than a narrative account.

(2) Like the narrative accounts, the descriptive accounts also find links between the Genesis creation account and other biblical creation accounts in accordance with their theological concern. The astronomical and meteorological accounts which highlight the mystic knowledge of God and God's providence over all creation hint at the reference to Job chs. 37-38 (1 En ch. 69; 2 En chs. 47-48; JosAsen 12:1-2; Sir chs. 42-43; 4Q392) and Ps 104:5-23 (2 En chs. 47-48; Sir chs. 16-17; 1QS 3:17; 4Q392). The unique identity of God as the Creator is depicted on the basis of these biblical references: Pss 33:6, 9 (2 Bar chs. 21, 48, 54; ApAbr 22:2; Sir ch. 39;

---

[192] Cf. Jub 2:2-3; 4QJub[a] 5. See § 2.1.2.
[193] Cf. 4Q381 frag. 1 9; 4Q422 frag. 1 9.

4Q422); 89:9, 14 (11QPs^a 24:11-15); 90:12 (2 En chs. 65-66); 119:73 (4 Ezra 3:4-5);139:2-8 (2 En chs. 65-66); Isa 42:5, 7 (2 En chs. 47-48; 4 Ezra 3:3-4; 1QS 3:18); Jer 10:12-13 (11QPs^a 24:11-15); Prov 8:22-29 (e.g. 4 Ezra 6:1-6; 1QS cols. 3-4). It should be noted that the Genesis creation account is linked to Isaiah 48:3, 13 and 55:11 and Ps 33:6-12, and their creational motifs are expanded in salvific and eschatological contexts.

ISAIAH AND PSALM IN THE CREATION ACCOUNTS

JEWISH CREATION ACCOUNTS	ISAIAH AND PSALM
Your word (*verbum*) accomplished the work (4 Ezra 6:38).	So shall my word be, . . . it accomplishes what I desire and makes succeed what I sent it (Isa 55:11).
Your word (*verbum*) went forth, and immediately the work was done (4 Ezra 6:43).	They (which were foretold) goes out of my mouth, . . .and I accomplish immediately, and they came to pass (Isa 48:3).
You . . . spoke (*w'emmart*) with the word (*bmeltā*) (2 Bar 14:17a); and at once (*sā'țē*) the works of your creation stood (*qāmw*) before you (2 Bar 14:17b).	he spoke, (Ps 33:9) . . .; with the word of the Lord the heavens were made (Ps 33:6); then at once I did (Isa 48:3); I call to them, they stand forth together (Isa 48:13; Ps 33:9).
O (Lord) one who made the earth, hear me, the one who fixed the firmament by the word (*bmelta*) and fastened the heaven by the spirit (*brūḥā*) (2 Bar 21:4a).	By the word of the Lord the heavens were established; and all the host of height of them by the spirit (וברוח) of his mouth. He spoke, and they were made (Ps 33:6).
The one who from the beginning of the world called (*daqrā* < *qr'*) that which did not yet exist, and they obeyed you (2 Bar 21:4b).	When I call (καλέσω [LXX]; *qōrē* < *qr'* [MT]) to them, they stand forth together (Isa 48:13).
You who commanded (*pqaḍt*) the air with your sign (*bremzāk*) and have seen the things which are to come (2 Bar 21:5). . .	and he commanded (*ziwwā*), and they were created (Ps 33:9).
You may create immediately (*barsā'țē*) all that you want (2 Bar 21:7b).	I (God) did immediately, and they (the events) came to pass (Isa 48:3).
You summon (*qārē*) the coming of the times, and they stand (*wqāimīn* < *qām*) before you (2 Bar 48:2a).	When I call (קרא) to them, they stand forth together (Isa 48:13); For he spoke, and it came to be; he commanded and it stood firm (Ps 33:9).
And with the word (*wamelta*) you raise that which does not exist (2 Bar 48:8a-b).	When I call to them, they stand forth (*mqīm*) (Isa 48:13).
You bring about (or summon) (*mayțē*) the things which will happen in the times by your word (*bmelțāk*) (2 Bar 54:1c).	They (what God declared) went out from my mouth, . . . then suddenly I did them, . . . and they came to pass (Isa 48:3).
The beginning of the ages serve (*mšamšīn*) the word (*lmelțāk*) (2 Bar 54:3).	so shall my word be, . . . it shall accomplish what I purpose (Isa 55:11).
All the works of the Lord are very good, and whatever he commands will be done at the appointed time (ἐν καιρῷ αὐτοῦ) (Sir 39:16).	The word of the Lord (דבר־יהוה) is right (ישׁר), and all his works (מעשׂהו) (are done) in faithfulness (באמונה) (Ps 33:4)

By his word (ἐν λόγῳ αὐτοῦ) the waters stood (ἔστη) like a heap of water and with the word of his mouth the reservoirs of water (ובמוצא פיו אוצרות) [B] [with the utterance of his mouth the reservoirs]) (Sir 39:17b).	By the word of the Lord (בדבר יהוה) the heavens were made; all their host by the breath of his mouth (וברוח פיו). He gathered the waters of the sea as in a bottle, and he put the depths in the reservoirs (באצרות) (Ps 33:6-7).
When he commands, his every will (is done) (ἐν προστάγματι αὐτοῦ πᾶσα ἡ εὐδοκία/ תחתנין רצונו יצליח [B] [In [his] place he makes his will prosper]) (Sir 39:18a).	For he spoke, and it came to be (ויהי); he commanded, and it stood firm (הוא אמר) (Ps 33:9).
This is my will as to what in the counsel (süvětŭ). . . I gave them a command by my word (slovomŭ moimŭ) and they came into existence. All the previously created you have seen stood (stawa) before me (ApAbr 22:2).	The counsel of the Lord (עצת יהוה) stands firm forever (Ps 33:11); He commanded, he spoke and it came to be (Ps 33:6, 9).

Isa 48:3 and 55:11 do not necessarily refer to creation, but rather illustrate how God will bring about his salvation by his word (or by his command). Nevertheless, 2 Baruch (cf. the narrative creation account in 4 Ezra ch. 6) exposes Isa 48:3 and 55:11 in both creational and eschatological contexts. This interpretation gives a more vivid picture of the eschatological works of God. That is to say, God who by the word accomplished the work of creation can bring about at once the eschatological works immediately by the same word. Interestingly, the word of God is personified when reference is made to Isa 55:11 (2 Bar 54:3; 56:4; cf. 4 Ezra 6:38, 43). Ps 33:6 is also interpreted in a similar way. Sir 39:16-18 reads Ps 33:6 (which is the description of the creational events) with Ps 33:9 (which is the general description of the way God works with his word). This reading associates the motif of the creative word with the salvific works of God. Sirach goes on to say that God, who completed the work of creation by the word of his mouth (Sir 39:17b), can bring about the salvific works (not necessarily with the eschatological emphasis) by the authority of his utterance (Sir 39:28-31). Similarly, ApAbr 22:2 reads Ps 33:9-12 with Ps 33:6-8, and its context indicates that the reality of the coming of the eschatological events is associated with the work of creation. The link between Isa 48:3, 13 and Ps 33:6, 9 occurs in 2 Baruch (14:17a; 21:4-7; 48:2). It is worth noting that Isa 48:3 corresponds to Ps 33:9, whereas Isa 48:13 corresponds to Ps 33:6. It may be one of the reasons for this interpretation.

(3) The creation accounts designate the identity of God who is unique (2 En 47:5, 6) and who is distinguished from other gods (2 En 47:3; 2 En 66:1-2, 5). He is the (sole) Creator (2 En 47:4-5; 4 Ezra 3:4-5; 6:6; 2 Bar 14:15-19; 21:4, 7; 54:2; Sir 18:1; 4Q392; 11QPs[a] 26:9-15) and the sole Ruler over all creation (2 Bar 21:6, 9; 48:3; 54:12-13; Sir 18:3; chs. 42-43). Some accounts

accompany a sapiential teaching 'to fear the Lord the Creator' (2 En chs. 47-48, 65-66; 4Q392).

(4) We have observed how the divine attributes function in the descriptive accounts of creation as well. First of all, the word of God (or its idea) is mentioned in the context where the sovereignty of God or his mighty works are highlighted (literal: 4 Ezra 3:4; 2 Bar 14:17; 48:2, 8; 54:1, 3; ApAbr 9:9; 22:2; JosAs 12:2; Sir 39:17; 42:15; 4Q422 frag. 1 6). The divine 'oath' (*māhlā*) (1 En 69:16-25; cf. 4Q381 frag. 1 3-4; Leg All 3:204) functions as the other expression of the creative word. J. Fossum holds that the creative and sustaining oath might come from the יהי 'let it be . . .' of Gen ch. 1. It might be possible that the name of God as 'I am who I am' (אהיה אשר אהיה; cf. Exod 3:14) is associated with the unique identity of God who is the origin of all things so that he alone can let everything be (exist). Thus, the name of God indicates his identity as the Creator. The 'sign' (*remzē*) also appears as a synonym of 'the word of God' in 2 Baruch (21:4-5; 48:8; 54:1-3). This motif may be linked to the divine command in the sense of an authorized signal by which a certain event will come about at once. So, the idea of 'sign' (*remzē*) is associated with the picture of Genesis ch. 1 (see a possible relation to the name of God [cf. PrMan 1:3 and LAB 60:2; Jub 36:7], as will be discussed in the next chapter). The idea of the eschatological word is built on the motif of the creative word, as has already been argued. As for the wisdom motif, it is mentioned in the context where God's providence over all creation (both space and time) is highlighted. Wisdom motif finds its link to God's thoughtful arrangement for all creation (2 En 48:4 [J]; 4 Ezra 6:6; 2 Bar 48:9; Sir 42:23-25), to the identity of God as the Ruler over the world (2 Bar 21:6; 54:13), to his sovereignty (11QPs^a 24:7-8), and to his perfect eschatological plan (2 Bar 21:8-12; 48:3-8; 54:1; ApAbr 22:2; 1QS cols. 3-4). The other imageries, God's hand(s) (4 Ezra 3:4-5; 2 Bar 54:13) and the power (2 Bar 48:8; 11QPs^a 24:7) appear in contexts where the mighty power of God is highlighted. Therefore, all these imageries of the divine attributes are associated with the description of the unique identity of God.

(5) The speculation on the unique identity of God, which was revealed in his work of creation, is developed in a salvific and a more eschatological context. The fulfillment (or realization) of the eschatological promise is strongly expected on the basis of the identity of the sovereign God (4 Ezra 6:6; 2 Bar 21:6-8; 48:2-10). In ApAbr 22:4-5, while being shown the sequence from the creational events to the eschatological events, Abraham affirms the sovereignty of God who has already made a plan for all creation. JosAsen 8:10-12 meditates on the Lord who 'gave life' (ζωοποιήσας) to all things and called (them) out from darkness to light in the context of creation (JosAsen 8:10a), and applies this motif to a salvic context by reiterating the language of new creation, such as ζωοποίησον (to give life), ἀνακαίνισον (to

renew), ἀνάπλασον (to form a new), and ἀναζωοποίησον (to make alive) (JosAsen 8:11a). When the life-giving motif is taken up again in JosAsen 12:1-3, it is interestingly associated with the motif of 'the word of creation': 'For you, Lord, spoke and they were brought to life (ἐλάλησας καὶ πάντα ἐζωογονήθησαν), because your word, Lord, is life for all your creatures' (JosAsen 12:2). This is an interpretation of the Genesis creation acccount in a salvific context. Similarly, several correspondences between the revealed identity of God as the Creator and the expected identity of God as the Fulfiller of the eschaton are explored:

THE CREATOR AND THE FULFILLER OF THE ESCHATON

GOD OF CREATION	GOD OF THE ESCHATON
These things were made through me alone, and not through another (4 Ezra 6:6a).	And the end [will come] through me and not through another (4 Ezra 6:6b).
God created at once (*barsā'ţē*) all that he wanted (2 Bar 21:7).	Not to postpone that which was promised (2 Bar 21:24).
God knows the number of the drops of rain (because he is the Creator of meteorological phenomena) (2 Bar 21:8a).	God knows the number of humankind (2 Bar 21:11); God knows the consummation of the times before they come (2 Bar 21:8); God knows where he preserves the end of those who sinned or the consummation of those who have been righteous (2 Bar 21:12).
You remember the beginning which you made (2 Bar. 48:7a).	And you do not forget the destruction that is to be (2 Bar 48:7b).
And with *the word* (*waḫmelţā* < *melţā*) you raise (*mqīm* < *qām*) that which does not exist (2 Bar 48:8a-b).	You *summon* (*qārē* < *qr'*) the coming of the times, and they stand (*wqāymīn* < *qām*) before you (48:2a); And you summon (*maytē*) the things which will happen in the times by *your word* (*bmeţţāḵ*) (2 Bar 54:1c); And it happened when *the word* (*melţā*) had gone out from him . . . and it was established in accordance with the abundance of the intelligence of him who let it go forth (2 Bar 56:4).
You are the one to whom both the depths and the heights come together (2 Bar 54:3a).	And the beginning of the ages (*rīšay 'ālmē*) serves (*mšamšin* < *šmš*) *the word* (*lmelţāḵ*) (2 Bar 54:3b).
With *signs* (*bremzē*) of fear and threat you *command* the flames, and they change into spirits (2 Bar 48:8a).	You are the one who easily performs all by a *sign* (*bremzā*) (2 Bar 54:2).
At *his word* (ἐν λόγῳ αὐτοῦ) the waters stood in a heap, and reservoirs of water at *the word* of his mouth (ἐν ῥήματι στόματος αὐτοῦ) (Sir 39:17b).	And whatever he *commands* (πᾶν πρόσταγμα) will be done at the appointed time (Sir 39:16b); When he *commands* (ἐν προστάγματι αὐτοῦ), his every purpose is fulfilled, and none can limit his salvation (σωτήριον αὐτοῦ) (Sir 39:18); When their (prepared instruments for the end time judgment) time comes they never disobey *the word* (λόγον) (Sir 39:31).

It should be noted that the motif of the creative word is expanded into the motif of a salvific (Sir 39:16, 18b, 31) and eschatological word (2 Bar 48:2; 54:1, 2, 3; 56:4). This interpretation of the Genesis creation account has been influenced by Isa 48:3, 13; 55:11 and Ps 33:4, 6-9.

(6) The Jewish creation accounts also focus on the creation of human beings (Gen 1:26-28; 2:7-24; Isa 42:5), and speculate on the identity of human beings (or Israel) and examine their position in history. They consider the relationship between God and the first human being (Adam), and affirm their status as the chosen people who were given special care from their Creator (4 Ezra 3:4-5; 2 Bar 21:24) and who were assigned a special role as guardians of all creation (2 Bar 14:18). In particular, they focus on the account of the giving of God's breath to Adam (Gen 2:7; Isa 42:5). For example, 4Q422 understands God's breath as the spirit, whereas Sir ch. 17 and 4Q504 interpret it as divine wisdom or knowledge. Since they possessed the divine wisdom and the law (Sinai event), they thought themselves to be in a special position from the beginning in order to rule over all creation. The Qumran sectarians (e.g. 1QS col. 3) interpret it in a more deterministic way, and understand that there were two kinds of spirits which were given to human beings: one for the chosen and the other for the Gentiles. They also develop Theodicy in several ways: 4 Ezra 3:7 acknowledges the responsibility of human beings for their sinful nature; 2 Bar 14:15-19 argues that God created two different worlds (this world for the nations; the coming world for the chosen); Sir 39:22-27 explains that God created good things for the good and bad things for the wicked; and 1QS col. 3 develops a dualistic world view as shown above. Therefore, speculating on the creation of human beings, they acknowledge that they live in a predetermined history, and they examine whether they are standing in the right position (both in an ethical sense and in a more deterministic sense). These speculations on the identity of human beings (or the people of God) are extended into the eschatological arguments as well. When they focus on God's special care for the chosen people, they also expect God to take immediate action for their restoration (4 Ezra ch. 3; 2 Bar ch. 14). And when they refer to a predetermined course, that idea comes from the expanded understanding of the division of the world (time and space). They examine at what stage they are living, and foresee the coming eschatological salvation behind the existing reality of their suffering (4 Ezra ch. 3; 2 Bar ch. 14; 2 En chs. 65-66; 1QS col. 3).

(7) Some Jewish creation accounts associate the identity of God with the life-giving motif: God is depicted as the life-giver (4 Ezra 3:5; 6:47-48; JosAsen 8:10-11) and life itself (ܚܝܐ: *ḥayā*) (2 Bar 21:9) or the Creator of life (ܒܪܝܐ ܚܝܐ: *bāryā ḥayyeh*) (2 Bar 23:5). He is the sole life-giver who alone has the authority to produce life *ex nihilo* (2 Bar 21:4; 4 Ezra 3:3-5; JosAsen 8:10-11). As has been observed in some creation accounts, this description of

the identity of God is associated with the motif of the divine attributes. For example, while wisdom is assigned to create Adam (2 En 30:8), 4 Ezra 7:69 emphasizes that God created human beings by his word. JosAsen chs. 8 and 12 meditate on the Lord who 'gave life' (ζωοποιήσας) to all things by his word which is defined as life (JosAsen 12:2). Moreover, the life motif may find a link to the account of the endowment of spirits (as discussed above), or to the motif of blessing (JosAsen chs. 8, 12, 15).

(8) As for the light imagery, firstly, light is considered a divine thing. In 4Q392 frag 1 4-5, light is described as a realm or sphere in which God dwells. Light finds its place beside God together with wisdom (2 Bar 54:13) or beside his throne (2 En 25:4 [J]), and light is thought to be brought out from God's treasuries (4 Ezra 6:40; cf. 2 Bar 59:11). Secondly, this light motif as divine is easily linked to the divine nature of the law (e.g. Ps 119:105; Prov 6:23; Isa 2:5; 42:21; 51:4; Sir 17:11; 2 Bar 17:4; 59:2; 77:13, 16; Wisd 18:4; T Lev 14:4). In particular, 2 Bar 59:2 seems to take Isa 9:2 as an account of the giving of the law at Mount Sinai. LAB 15:5-6 may suggest a typological correspondence between the two Exodus events (the miracle of the Red sea and the giving of the law) and the two creational events (the division of water on the third day and the creation of lights on the fourth day). It is an example of the association between the creation of lights and the giving of the law. The idea of the separation of light from darkness is taken in an ethical sense as well (2 Bar 18:1-2; JosAsen 8:10a; 1QS 3:19; cf. 2 En 30:15 [J]). Thirdly, like the life motif, light is counted as an eschatological blessing (2 En 65:10 [A]; 2 Bar 48:50; 51:1-3; cf. Isa 60:19-20; Jub 1:29; 2 En 65:7 [J]; LAB 3:10; 23:10; SibOr 2:315).

Chapter 4

Brief References to Creation

This chapter treats the shorter creation accounts which cannot come under the former categories (the narrative and descriptive accounts). It is a brief reference to the Genesis creation account, and in some cases the motif of creation plays a subsidiary role. Since there are many simple references to the Genesis creation, this chapter will select nine examples from early Jewish literature, which show a distinctive interpretation: Jub 12:4, 26; LAB 60:2-3; ApAbr 7:10-11; 9:3, 9; LadJac 2:10-14, 20; PrMan 1:2-3; Wisd 7:22; 8:5; 9:1-2, 9; 1 Bar 3:32-38; Sir 33:7-15.

4.1 The Book of Jubilees 12:4

4.1.1 Literary Considerations

Context and Main Concern

Jub ch. 11-23:8 is a retelling of the Abraham stories in Genesis, accompanied by a series of sapiential instructions. According to the Book of Jubilees, Abraham began to pray to the 'Creator of all' (*fāṭār kuĕl*) from his youth (Jub 11:17), and grieved at idolatry of his land so that wished to separate from the people and even from his father (Jub 11:14-16). One day, Abraham told Terah not to worship idols (Jub 12:2-5). In this conversation Abraham refers to God's work of creation to demonstrate the sovereignty of God, which is contrasted with the uselessness of other gods (i.e. the idols which were created by the hands of human beings).

Influence of Key Passages from the OT

Jub 12:2-5 mostly refers to Isaiah chs. 44 and 46 and Ps 135, which demonstrate a clear contrast between God and idols by referring to God's mighty work of creation. The literary correspondences between Jub 12:2-5 and the texts from Isaiah and Psalms are as follows:

Jub 12:2-5[1]	Isaiah and Psalms
What help and advantage do we get from these idols before which you *worship and bow down*?	and they *bow down* and *worship* it (Isa 46:6).
For there is *no spirit* in them,	. . . *no breath* (רוח) in their mouth (Ps 135:17)
for they are *dumb*, . . .	. . . *cannot speak* (Ps 135:16)
Worship the God of heaven (*'ǎmĕsāk sǎmāy*), who *makes the rain and dew* fall on the earth,	(cf. Ps 135:7)
and who *makes everything* upon the earth.	
He created everything *by his word* (*bǎḵālū*),[2]	(cf. Ps 33:6)
and every life (*wǎkuĕl ḥĕyyĕwǎt*) (comes) from him (or his presence) (*'ĕmmĕkĕdĕm gǎz*).[3]	
Why do you worship those things which *have no spirit* in them?	(Ps 135:7)
and they are *made by hands*,	made *by the hands* of men (Ps 135:15)
and you *carry* them *on your shoulders.* You receive *no help* from them,	they *lift* it to their *shoulders* and *carry* it . . . it *cannot save* him from his trouble (Isa 46:7).
but instead there is a great *shame* for those who made them, . . .	He and his kind will be put to *shame* (Isa 44:11; cf. 44:9)

4.1.2 Thematic Consideration: The Sovereignty of God

God is called 'the God of heaven (*'ǎmĕsāk sǎmāy*)' who sends down rain and dew upon the earth, and is depicted as the Creator (Jub 12:4). Several contrasts are made to highlight the sovereignty of God. That is to say, the idols are made 'by hands' (Jub 12:5), whereas God created everything 'by his word (or voice) (*bǎḵḵālū*)'; all life (*wǎkuĕl ḥĕyyĕwǎt*) comes from God, whereas there is no spirit in the idols. The term 'everything (*kuĕl*)' is repeated three times, and highlights the mighty works of God. It should be noted that in this context the divine attribute 'the word' (< *ḵāl*) and the life motif (i.e. God as the origin of all life) are mentioned to emphasize the sovereignty of God.

---

[1] English Translation is based on J. VanderKam (*The Book of Jubilees*, 69), while consulting his Ethiopic edition (J. VanderKam, *A Critical text*, 72).

[2] Or 'voice' (cf. S. Mercer, *Ethiopic*, 108).

[3] O. Wintermute (OTP II, 80) translates it 'all life is in his presence'; however, *'ĕmmĕkĕdĕm* should be translated as 'from the front' (cf. Ps 139:5 אחור ומקדם), otherwise, 'from east' (cf. Isa 9:11 מקדם).

4.2 The Book of Jubilees 12:26

4.2.1 Literary Consideration: Context and Main Concern

Jub 12:16-17 tells the stories of God's blessings and promises to Abraham (cf. Gen 11:31-12:3). Having finished the prayer to God, Abraham received the word of the covenant which promised that he would be a founder of a great nation (Jub 12:22-24). Following this narrative, the Book of Jubilees adds an account of the restoration of the Hebrew language (Jub 12:25-27). This account explains that Hebrew was a primordial language which had been used until the day of the Fall, and that God attempted to restore it in Abraham's mouth and thereafter. In this context, Jub 12:26 defines the Hebrew language as 'the tongue (or language) of creation' (*bälsān fēṭēt*).

4.2.2 Thematic Consideration: the Language of Creation

The former account is grounded on the understanding that the work of creation was done by the word of God. It is interesting that the restoration of the Hebrew language is mentioned in the context where the covenant is the focus. M. Rubin suggests that there is a Jewish tradition, called, '*Leshon Haqodesh*,' which was conceived in Palestine at the time of the national awakening during the second century BCE: '*Leshon Haqodesh*, in which the world which was created will prevail once more in the end of the days, when all nations will once again speak this primordial language in which the world was created.'[4] It is an eschatological speculation which is grounded on the Genesis creation account.

4.3 Liber Antiquitatum Biblicarum 60:2-3

4.3.1 Literary considerations

Context and Main Concern

The narrative of David begins from LAB ch. 59 in which David's two songs (LAB 59:4 and 60:2-3) are introduced. The former is the praise of David and the latter is the song which was sung when an evil spirit came upon Saul (60:1). Following the summary of the Genesis creation account, LAB focuses on the creation of the spirits (or evil spirits), which is hinted at in some Jewish literature (such as Jub 2:2; 2 En 29:1).

---

[4] M. Rubin, 'The Language of Creation or the Primordial Language: A Case of Cultural Polemics in Antiquity,' *JJS* (1998), 317.

Influence of Key Passages from the OT

As a whole, LAB 60:2 follows the narrative order of the Genesis creation
account but retells it in a shorter form: Line (b) alludes to Gen 1:3; Line (c)
alludes to Gen 1:6, 9; Lines (d) and (e) allude to Gen 1:8, 10; Line (g) alludes
to Gen 1:11-12.

(a) *Tenebre et silentium erat antequam fieret seculum,*
(b) *et locutum est silentium et apparuerunt tenebre*

(c) *Et factum est **tunc nomen** tuum in compaginatione extensionis*

(d) *quod appellatum est superius caelum,*
(e) *inferius vocatum est terra.*

(f) *Et preceptum est superiori ut plueret, secundum tempus eius,*
(g) *et inferiori preceptum est ut crearet escam homini qui factus est.*

(h) *Et post hec facta est tribus spirituum vestrorum* (LAB 60:2).[5]

Darkness and silence were before the world was made,
and silence spoke and the darkness came into sight.

Then *your name* was pronounced in the drawing together of what had been spread out.

The upper of which was called heaven,
and the lower was called earth.

And the upper part was commanded to bring down rain according to its season, and
the lower part was commanded to produce food for all things that had been made.

And after these was the tribe of your spirits made.

4.3.2 Thematic Consideration: Creation and Evil Spirit

David commands the evil spirit, who dwells in Tartarus (60:3), to bear in mind
that she was created on the second day of creation (60:2-3)[6] from a resounding
echo in the chaos (60:3). After a while Solomon the Exorcist[7] (lit. *lateribus
meis* 'my lions') was born to rule over her (60:3). It should be noted that God
does not appear except once (lit. 'your name' [*tunc nomen*]), but each work of
creation is described as born from chaos. However, it should be noted that
'the name' (*nomen*) is mentioned in the sense of the name which is
pronounced with the divine oath or command.[8] This may be associated with a

---

[5] The Latin Text is of Kisch's edition.
[6] See 2 En 29:1; cf. Jub 2:2 (spirits were created on the first day).
[7] See Harrington's note (OTP II, LAB).
[8] Cf. § 4.6.2.

Jewish tradition that the name of God is referred to in the context of creation (e.g. Jub 36:7; PrMan 1:3b; 1 En 69:13-15; cf. 3 En 42:1-7).

4.4 Apocalypse of Abraham 7:10-11; 9:3, 9

4.4.1 Literary Consideration: Context and Main Concern

The Apocalypse of Abraham can be divided into two parts (chs. 1-8 and chs. 9-32). The former section tells the story of Abraham's youth, and the latter describes the apocalyptic visions. While Abraham was discussing about idolatry with his father (ApAbr 7:1-12), God's voice came down from heaven, and commanded Abraham to go away from his father by saying, 'You are searching for 'the God of gods' (ва во: *va vo*) and 'the Creator (творца: *tvorca*) in the understanding of your heart'[9] (8:1-4). After Abraham left his father, Abraham heard the voice again, and this time God identified himself as the Creator with the descriptions of the work of creation. The creation motif is illuminated in the closing section which tells of the eschatological events (ApAbr 9:10).

4.4.2 Thematic Considerations

Identity of God

The self-identification of God as the Creator (ApAbr 9:3) seems to correspond to Abraham's previous description of God: 'who created all the gods, . . . who made the heavens crimson and the sun golden; who has given light to the moon and the stars with it; and who has dried the earth in the midst of the many waters' (ApAbr 7:10-11[10]). ApAbr describes how God responds to Abraham's faith in God the Creator. God identified himself with 'I am (азъ ѥсмь: *aзй jesmĭ*),' saying as follows.

> 'Here I am (азъ ѥсмь: *aзй jesmĭ*). Do not be afraid, for I am (азъ ѥсмь: *aзй jesmĭ*) before the age (преже вѣка: *preže vĕka*) (perhaps in the sense of 'the world') and the mighty God who created the light age (or the light of the age?) (свѣта вѣка: *svĕta vĕka*) in the past. And I am (азъ ѥсмь: *aзй jesmĭ*) the protector for you, and I am (азъ ѥсмь: *aзй jesmĭ*) your helper' (ApAbr 9:3-4).

It should be noted that God firstly refers to his pre-existence (преже вѣка: *preže vĕka*), and secondly to the creation of the heavens and the earth. In particular there is a focus on the creation of light (свѣта вѣка: *svĕta vĕka*)

---

[9] The Slavonic text is of N. S. Tikhonravov's edition.

[10] Our Slavonic text here follows S (Sil'vestrovskij, 14th AD) and some C (A Palaia, 16th AD) traditions (see OTP I, 692).

and the separation of the land from the waters.[11] Based on this description of the sovereign power of God, which was manifested in the work of creation, God demonstrates the reliability of his protection for Abraham.

The Word and Eschatology

God promises to show Abraham 'the great things which he has not seen' (ApAbr 9:6). It is the revelation concerning the ages which were founded by the word of God, and which were expected to be renewed: lit. 'I will show you these ages which were founded by the word (гломъ: *glomŭ*), and affirmed, created, and renewed (поновениia: *ponevenija*)' (9:9).[12] The idea of 'these ages' (ти вѣкы: *ti věkŭi*) may be associated with the apocalyptic vision which describes history from creation to the eschatological judgment (ApAbr 21:1-7).[13] The point is that the ages are considered to have been created by the word of God. This account follows the biblical and Jewish exegetical traditions, i.e. the creation by the word of God (cf. Ps 33:6). Secondly, the ages which were created in the past were expected to be renewed in the eschatological era (ApAbr 9:9). As it will be shown more clearly in ApAbr 21:1-7, Abraham is now allowed to view God's sovereign power over all ages from creation to the eschaton.

4.5 Ladder of Jacob 2:10-14, 20

4.5.1 Literary Consideration: Context and Main Concern

The Ladder of Jacob is a retelling of Jacob's dream at Bethel (Gen 28:11-22). Resting during his flight from Esau, Jacob had a dream of the ladder reaching from the earth to the heaven (LadJac 1:1-12). Jacob uttered a prayer asking God to interpret this dream (LadJac 1:6-22).[14] Then, God ordered the archangel Sariel to reveal to Jacob the apocalyptic meanings and to show the

---

[11] Cf. In Isaiah, 'I am saying' appears in the context which God's mighty work of creation is highlighted (e.g. 45:7 [the creation of light]; 45:8 [the Creator]; 48:12-13 [beginning and end], etc.).

[12] ти вѣкъ гломъ моимъ създаниia И оутверженіia сътворениia и поновениia: *ti věkŭi glomŭ moimŭ sŭzdanija i utverženija sŭtvorenija i ponevenija*. See § 3.10.2 for our translation of ApAbr 9:9.

[13] See § 3.11.2 (ApAbr 21:1-7).

[14] Recension B (e.g. K [Kolomna Palaia of 1406], M [Melec Monastry collection], P [Solovki Monastry collection]) does not have this text (from LadJac 2:3 through 5:1), but Recension A (S [Palaia of 1477], R [Rumiantsev Palaia of1494], U [Undolsky Palaia of 1517] has our text.

destiny of his descendants (LadJac 5:1-6:15[15]): i.e. the ladder indicates this age, and the twelve steps symbolize the periods of the age; the twenty four faces who are standing on both sides of the twelve steps indicate the kings of the godless nations who will try Jacob's descendants. In the prayer (LadJac 2:6-22) Jacob recalls the powerful and glorious figure of God, and asks him to be shown the interpretation of the dream (2:21-22). The creation accounts (LadJac 2:10-14, 20) appear in the context which depicts the identity of God as the glorious and fearful God.

THE STRUCTURE OF LADJAC 2:6-22

Prayer to the God of his fathers (v. 6)

>   A. God is fearful (vv. 7-9)
>   who was holding cherubim
>   bearing seraphim
>   carrying the whole world

>   B. *God is the Creator of heaven* (vv. 10-14)
>   who made the skies firm
>   for the glory of his name
>   stretching out the heaven which gleams under him
>   caused the sun to travel its course
>   destined the moon and stars to pass on

>   A'. God is fearful (vv.15-19)
>   whom seraphim are afraid of

>   B'. *God is the Ruler of the whole world* (v. 20)
>   who filled the heaven and the earth,
>   sea and abysses
>   all the ages
>   with his glory

Jacob's request to the mighty God of his fathers (vv. 21-22)

4.5.2 Thematic Consideration: Monotheism

In the prayer, Jacob combines a heavenly picture in which God is surrounded by the cherubim and seraphim (LadJac 2:7-8), receiving their ceaseless praise (2:15-19; cf. Isa 6:2) with a reciprocal picture of creation in which God made the heavens and filled the whole world with his glory (2:10-14, 20). LadJac 2:12-14 exhibits a particular account of the creation of luminaries: i.e. God conceals the sun during the night, and makes the moon wane, and destines the stars to pass on so that they might not seem to be gods. It is a monotheistic

---

[15] The account of LadJac is considered to be closed here, and ch. 7 is regarded as a Christian interpolation since it contains the description of the cross and suffering of the Messiah (vv. 30-35).

emphasis which may correspond to the ending words of Jacob's prayer: 'for you are a god who is mighty, powerful and glorious, a god who is holy . . .' (LadJac 2:22). A similar account of the creation of the luminaries appears in ApAbr 7:8-11a: 'But I will not call it (the sun) a god because when night comes it becomes murky with darkness, nor again shall I call the moon or the stars gods because they too at times during the night dim their light . . . but this is the true God who has made the heavens crimson . . .'[16] The context of ApAbr 7:8-11 thereby clearly exhibits monotheism.

4.6 The Prayer of Manasseh 1:2-3

4.6.1 Literary Consideration

Context and Main Concern

This short prayer is 'a penitential psalm, or individual lament of personal sin.'[17] The prayer can be divided into three parts: (1) an invocation: the praise to the Lord for his mighty work of creation (vv. 1-4) and the acknowledgment not only of the Lord's anger against sinners, but also his manifold mercies to them (vv. 5-7); (2) a confession of sins (vv. 8-10); and (3) a petition for forgiveness (vv. 11-13) which is followed by a concluding doxology (vv. 14-15).[18] Reference to the work of creation is made (vv. 2-3) in order to affirm God's mighty power (v. 4), which is associated with the identity of God (lit. 'the magnificence of his glory ($\dot{\eta}$ μεγαλοπρέτεια τῆς δόξης)' or 'the greatness of magnificence (or glory)' (ܕ ܐ [19]). That is to say, it is revealed as a fury against sinners (v.5), but also as a great compassion for them (vv. 6-7). Therefore, reference to the work of creation is made to affirm the unique identity of God which is the ground for the implied author's plea.

Influence of Key Passages from the OT

This prayer obviously depends on the narrative of Manasseh in 2 Chr 33:11-19, which tells of the king who humbled himself during the exile to Babylon and prayed to the Lord (vv. 11-13). The narrative tells that the Lord was moved by his prayer and brought him back to his kingdom, so that Manasseh

---

[16] Translation of Rubinkiewicz (OTP I, 692, Recension A, B, C, K).

[17] J. H. Charlesworth, OTP II, 625.

[18] Cf. J. H. Charlesworth, OTP II, 625.

[19] Syriac Text is of M. Baars and H. Schneider edition ('Prayer of Manasseh,' in *The Old Testament in Syriac: According to the Peshitta Version* [The Peshitta Insitute Leiden (ed.); Leiden: E. J. Brill, 1972]).

acknowledged that Yahweh is the true God (vv. 12-13). 2 Chr states that the prayer of Manasseh was written in the annals of the kings of Israel (v. 18) and in the records of Hozai (or the seers [τῶν ὁρώντων] [LXX] and ܣ) (v. 19). In particular, several terms of the prayer of Manasseh correspond to the records of 2 Chr as J. Charlesworth has rightly listed[20]:

2 Chr 33:11-19	PrMan 1:1-15
[Manasseh] . . . provoking his [Yahweh's] anger (v. 6)	I provoked your fury [or anger] (v. 10; cf.13)
[Manasseh] . . . placed . . . the idol . . . in the Temple (v. 7)	I set up idols (v. 10)
Manasseh with hooks, . . . in chains . . . led . . . away. . . (v.11)	I am ensnared (v. 9b) I am bent by a multitude of iron chains (v.10)
humbling himself deeply before	I am bending the knees of my heart before you (v. 11)
the God of his ancestors . . . (v. 12)	God of our fathers (v. 1)

The prayer of Manasseh may refer to Ps 51 (a penitential psalm): the prayer refers to God's right judgment against human transgressions (Ps 51:3-4; PrMan 1:9-10), to the abundant mercy of God (Ps 51:1; PrMan 1:7), and to the forgiveness and salvation of God (Ps 51:14-15; PrMan 1:15).[21]

Reference to the work of creation is frequently made in the biblical and Jewish traditions in order to highlight the sovereignty of God.[22] Similarly, PrMan prefixes a praise of the sovereign power of God the Creator to this penitential psalm (cf. Gen 1:1, 6-10; 2:1). The power (or authority) of God is depicted by the motif of the word (or command) of God and the motif of the authority of his divine name. The former frequently occurs in Ps 33:6[23] and in other Jewish creation accounts. The latter is associated with the former motif, as will be shown below.

---

[20] J. H. Charlesworth, OTP II, 628.

[21] Cf. Cf. J. H. Charlesworth, OTP II, 630.

[22] E.g. Pss 33:6-8; 89:11; 104:1-30; 135:7; 136:5-9; Job 36:22-38:38; Isa 40:28; 42:5; 44:24; 45:7; 48:12-13; Jer 10:12-13; Jub 12:4; SibOr bks. 1, 3, frag. 3; ApAbr 9:2; Wisd ch. 9; 1 Bar chs. 3-4; 2 En chs. 47-48, 65-66; 4Q176; 4Q381; 4Q392; 4Q403; 11QPsAp^a 2-3; 11QPs^a 24.

[23] Ps 33:6 is possibly referred to in SibOr bks. 1, 3; 4Q381; 2 Bar chs. 14, 21; ApAbr ch. 21; Sir ch. 39; 4Q422; Jub 12:4.

4.6.2 Thematic Considerations

The Word and Name of God in Creation

The creation account in PrMan consists of three sentences, and in particular the last two constitute a parallelism.

ܗܘ ܕܥܒܕ ܫܡܝܐ ܘܐܪܥܐ 2

ܥܡ ܟܠܗ ܨܒܬܗܘܢ

ܗܘ ܕܐܣܪ ܝܡܐ 3a

ܘܐܩܝܡܗ ܒܦܘܩܕܢܐ ܕܡܠܬܗ

ܗܘ ܕܐܚܕ ܬܗܘܡܐ 3b

ܘܚܬܡܗ ܒܫܡܗ ܕܚܝܠܐ ܘܫܒܝܚܐ

2 He created the heaven and the earth
with all their embellishment (or their order[24]).

3a He bound the sea
and made it firm (aphʿel < *qwm*) by the command of his word.

3b He closed the deep
and closed (< *ḥtm*; or sealed)[25] it by his powerful and glorious name.[26]

The above parallelism suggests that the idea of creation by the command of the word (of God) (ܒܦܘܩܕܢܐ ܕܡܠܬܗ) is associated with the idea of the creative and sustaining name (of God) (ܒܫܡܗ). Jub 36:7 refers to the name of God as the creative name:

> Now I will make you swear with the great oath (*bămăḥḥlā ʿabīyĕ*) - because there is no oath which is greater than it, by the praiseworthy, illustrious, and great, splendid, marvelous, powerful, and great *name* (*băsăm*) *which made the heavens and the earth and everything together* (or at once) - that you will continue to fear and worship him.[27]

J. Fossum observes that the connection between the name and creation appears frequently in later Rabbinical literature (TarJon Exod 28:30; y. Sanh 29; b. Suk 53b; b. Mak 11a).[28] In the creation account in 3 En 42:1-7, the power of the name of Yahweh functions as an agent to rule over the meteorological phenomena:

---

[24] κόσμῳ αὐτῶν (LXX).
[25] P. Smith, *Syriac English Dictionary*, 163-164,
[26] Lit. the noun 'name' precedes two adjectives.
[27] Translation of J. VanderKam (*The Book of Jubilees*, 238).
[28] J. Fossum, *The Name of God*, 250.

I saw water suspended in the height of the heaven of ʿArabot, *through the name Yah, I am who I am . . .* (בשם יה אהיה אשר אהיה[29]) (3 En 42:2).

The idea that the deep (ܐܬܗܘܡܐ; cf. תהום) was closed by the name of God might be associated with the motif of the divine oath which is also mentioned in the creation account of 1 En 69:16-21 (cf. 4Q381 frag. 1 3).

> And *by that oath (bămăḥḥlā) the depths are made firm*; they stand still and do not move from their places from the beginning (of creation); and forever (1 En 69:19).[30]

Referring to J. Fossum's observation that the creative and sustaining oath would have been the יהי 'let it be . . .' of Gen ch. 1,[31] S. McDonough argues that the name יהוה and the oath יהי were associated solely because of the similarity of their letters, and because one generally associates oath with name ('I swear by X').[32] According to Philo, the oath is a proof of the exceeding power of God, that whatever he says is sure to take place (Leg All 3:204). In short, the name of God, as well as the command of the word of God (PrMan 1:3) or the divine oath (1 En 69:19; cf. 4Q381 frag. 1 3), indicates the power of the divine authority of Yahweh, through which the heavens and the earth were made and sustained.

The Sovereignty of God

As discussed above, reference to the work of creation is made in vv. 2-3 in order to affirm God's mighty power (v. 4). In particular this power is expressed by the motif of the creative word and by his powerful and glorious name (v.3). All things fear and tremble before God since his command and his name exhibit the mighty power of God, which created and ruled the universe (v. 4).

---

[29] Hebrew text is of Odeberg's edition (*3 Enoch or the Hebrew Book of Enoch* [Cambridge: Cambridge University Press, 1928], נה [55]).

[30] Ethiopic Text is of M. Knibb's edition (*The Ethiopic Book of Enoch*, 204-205).

[31] J. Fossum, The Name of God, 78. Cf. Both TargNeo and TargJon to Exod 3:14 begin their explanation of the YHWH name by writing, 'The one who spoke and the world was . . .' (S. McDonough, 'The One who is,' 112; see also our discussion in § 3.1.2).

[32] S. McDonough, 'The One who is,' 112.

4.7 The Wisdom of Solomon 7:22; 8:5; 9:1-2, 9

4.7.1 Literary Consideration

Context and Main Concern

Although it is difficult to make a clear (literary and thematic) division in the Wisdom of Solomon, Wisd 6:12-10:21 can be distinguished from other sections, in which wisdom is personified, and the identity and the role of wisdom is the focus.[33] The creational motif occurs at least four times in this part, in relation to the description of the divine identity of wisdom.

Influence of Key Passages from the OT

Like other wisdom literature, the description of wisdom in the Wisdom of Solomon is grounded in Proverbs (e.g. 1:20-33; 3:13-20; 8:1-9:6). The author of Wisd shows a unique exposition of the narrative of Solomon in which King Solomon was given 'an understanding and wise heart' (καρδίαν φρονίμην καὶ σοφήν [1 Kgs 3:5-15 (LXX)]). Wisd 7:7 understood it as a bestowment of 'a spirit of wisdom' (πνεῦμα σοφίας). In the Old Testament, the connection of the divine wisdom to the spiritual activity of God is not uncommon: e.g. wisdom and all kinds of craftsmanship are brought to people through the spirit of God (Exod 31:3; 35:31); the spirit of the Lord brings wisdom, understanding, counsel, strength, knowledge, and the fear of the Lord (Isa 11:2). The Wisdom of Solomon expands this spiritual aspect of wisdom (e.g. Wisd 1:6; 7:7, 22b; 9:17) and depicts a more dynamic figure of wisdom (Wisd 7:23-24, 27; 8:1; 10:1-11:1) than other wisdom literature. Moreover, the role of (personified) wisdom as a mediator for the work of creation (Wisd chs. 7-9) is clearer[34] than in other wisdom literature.

4.7.2 Thematic Considerations

Wisdom

Wisd refers to the role of wisdom as an artificer (τεχνῖτις: feminine form of τεχνίτος) in God's work of creation (Wisd 7:22; 8:4-6; 9:1-2, 9), firstly in order to highlight the mystic aspect of wisdom which can tell of the cosmic order, the astronomical phenomena, and the nature of all living things (Wisd 7:17-22).[35] Secondly, Wisd argues that wisdom can make known the will of

---

[33] D. Winston (*The Wisdom of Solomon* [AB 43; New York: Doubleday, 1979], 10) includes 6:12-21 in the former part (1:1-6:21). However, the identity of divine wisdom is obviously the focus from 6:12.

[34] See § 7.1.2 (The Logos of Creation).

[35] See the connection of wisdom with the cosmic order in 1QH[a] 9:19; Sir 42:21.

God (τί ἀρεστὸν ἐν ὀφθαλμοῖς σου, καὶ τί εὐθὲς ἐν ἐντολαῖς σου) to the people since she was in close relationship to God from the beginning (Wisd 8:3-4; 9:4, 9-10; cf. Prov 8:27-30). King Solomon of Wisd expects to have wisdom since she is the one who was working with God and was initiated in the knowledge of God. Thirdly, Wisd focuses on the creative activity of wisdom: 'If understanding (φρόνησις) is productive, who more than she is the artificer of all that is?' (Wisd 8:6). Wisd thus argues that as all products are the works of the artificer who firstly had the idea in his (her) mind, wisdom could work and produce any virtue in human beings (Wisd 8:7). Wisd 9:2a mentions that God made human beings by his wisdom (cf. 2 En 30:8) in order that they could rule over the world according to the knowledge of God (Wisd 9:2b-3).[36] Wisdom had already been assigned the role as an instructor for human beings at the beginning of creation. The wish of Solomon to hold wisdom (Wisd 9:4-18) seems to be based on the original role of wisdom which had already been assigned at the beginning of creation. Therefore, there seems to be no problem in assuming that Wisd speculates about the divine role of wisdom (i.e. to reveal the will of God, and to guide the people to perfect knowledge) against the background of the motif of 'artificer' in the work of creation (an interpretation of אמון in Prov 8:30), and against the background of the exposition of the breath of life as 'the spirit of wisdom' (Gen 2:7).

The Sovereignty of God and the Word

The function of the creational account in Wisd 9:1 seems to be distinct from other creational accounts in Wisd (7:22; 8:4-6; 9:2-3, 9). It appears at the beginning of Solomon's prayer which simply mentions the unique identity of God in relation to the work of creation, like other Jewish prayers (e.g. PrMan 1:1-3; LadJac 2:6-22; 11QPs³ 24:11-15). Wisd 9:1-3 obviously follows the early Jewish exegetical tradition that mostly refers to the divine word and wisdom as an agent of the work of creation.[37] The motif of the creative word might have been employed here in order to emphasize the sovereignty of God.[38]

Light: Wisdom as a Reflection of the Identity of God

Although Wisd does not mention the connection of wisdom with the light imagery in the creational context, wisdom is modified by several light imageries in other contexts. For example, in Wisd 7:10, the term φέγγος

---

[36] Sir 17:1-14 understands the besowment of the breath of life as the divine knowledge (or wisdom), in which human beings are said to possess the knowledge of good and evil. Similarly, 4Q504 understands that wisdom is given to Adam in order to rule over the world.

[37] See the creation of human beings through personified wisdom in 2 En 30:8.

[38] Cf. Sir 42:15; 39:17; Jub 12:4; PrMan 1:3; 2 Bar 14:17; 21:4; 48:8; 54:1; 4 Ezra 3:4; 6:38; SibOr 1:19; 3:20; 4Q381; 4Q403.

('light' perh. in the sense of 'splendour' [LSJ]) is employed, which is
contrasted with φῶς (perh. in the sense of 'day light'). The sense of
'splendour' is suited to the context which demonstrates the superiority of
wisdom to any other treasures or health or beauty (Wisd 7:7-10, 13-14). In
Wisd 7:25-26, wisdom is depicted as 'the stream (ἀτμὶς) of the power
(δυνάμεως) of God,' 'a pure stream (ἀπόρροια) flowing from the glory (δόξης)
of the Almighty,' and 'an effluence (ἀπαύγασμα) of the everlasting light (φωτὸς
ἀϊδίου).' All three words are common in the sense of 'reflection' (ἀτμὶς,
ἀπόρροια, ἀπαύγασμα)[39] of the identity of God (as power, glory [cf. Wisd
9:11], and everlasting light which is paralleled with goodness [ἀγαθότητος]). In
Wisd 7:29-30, light (φῶς, in the sense of day light) is contrasted with night
(νὺξ), and this light/night opposition is paralleled by a wisdom/vice (κακία)
opposition. Thus, this light imagery displays an ethical contrast between
goodness and vice.

4.8 1 Baruch 3:32-38

4.8.1 Literary Considerations

Context and Main Concern

1 Baruch can be divided into three parts from its literary and thematic aspects:
(1) the introductory section which narrates the state of the writing of the book
(1:1-14); (2) the confession of sin (1:15-3:8); and (3) the praise of God's
wisdom (3:9-4:4) which is followed by the author's lamentation and comfort
(4:5-5:9).[40] The praise of wisdom questions where wisdom is to be found
(3:9-14; 29-31). It has not been found among the powerful rulers (3:15-21),
nor even among those who were reputed wise (3:22-23), but only in the
omniscient God (3:32). 1 Baruch closes the praise section, by suggesting that
God did not bestowed it on the giants so that they perished (3:26-28),[41] but
that he bestowed it on Jacob and Israel (3:37b-38) so that they could find life
(4:1-4). The structural understanding of 1 Bar 3:9-4:1 is as follows:

THE STRUCTURE OF 1 BAR 3:9-4:1

A.   the question as to where wisdom is to be found (3:9-14)

     B.   not among the powerful rulers (3:15-21)
          not among those who were reputed wise (3:22-23)

---

[39] See the parallel words, 'the unspotted mirror (ἔσοπτρον < εἴσοπτρον) of the power of
God,' and 'the image (εἰκὼν) of his goodness' (Wisd 7:26).

[40] Cf. Charles, APOT I, 569.

[41] Cf. Jub 5:1; 1 En ch. 7; Sir 16:7; Wisd 14:6.

  C. the description of the sovereign God as the mighty ruler (3:24-25)

    D. God did not bestow wisdom on the giants
      so that they perished (3:26-28)

A'. the question as to who can find wisdom (3:29-31)

  B'. but only in the omniscient God (3:32)

    C'. the description of the sovereign God as the Creator (3:33-37a)

      D'. God bestowed wisdom on Jacob and Israel
        so that they could find life (3:37b-4:4)

Thus the creation account (1 Bar 3:33-37b) is employed to describe the sovereignty of God, which was already mentioned in 1 Bar 3:24-25.

Influence of Key Passages from the OT

1 Baruch's sapiential hymn shares several ideas with Job 28:12-28 and 38:35:

1 Baruch ch. 3	Job chs. 28 and 33
Quest for wisdom (3:14)	Quest for wisdom (Job 28:12, 20)
Superiority of wisdom to any treasures (3:17-18, 30)	Superiority of wisdom to any treasures (Job 28:15-19)
Quest for wisdom in heaven and sea (3:29-30)	Quest for wisdom in the deep and the sea (Job 28:29-30)
God's dominion over the universe (3:24)	God's dominion over the earth and the heavens (Job 28:23-24)
God sent the light, and it obeyed (3:33-34)	God made the way for lightnings (Job 28:26) God sent lightnings, and they obeyed (Job 38:35)[42]

G. Sheppard comments that 1 Bar 3:32-35 expands the motifs of Job ch. 28 and ch. 38, with its own reflection of the Genesis creation account. Namely, 1 Bar expands the imagery of light, from lightnings in Job ch. 28 and ch. 38 to the primordial light (1 Bar 3:33) and luminaries (1 Bar 3:34-35) which appear

---

[42] G. Sheppard (*Wisdom as a Hermeneutical Construct: A Study in the Sapientializing of the Old Testament*, [BZAW 151; Berlin: Walter de Gruyter, 1980], 96) finds verbal correspondences between 1 Bar 3:33, 35 and Job 38:35: ὁ ἀποστέλλων τὸ φῶς . . . καὶ πορεύεται (1 Bar 3:33), ἀποστελεῖς δὲ κεραυνούς . . . καὶ πορεύσονται (Job 38:35 [LXX]); ἐκάλεσεν αὐγούς καὶ εἶπαν Πάρεσμεν (Bar 3:35), ἐδοῦσιν δὲ σοι Τί ἔσιν (Job 38:35 [LXX]).

in the Genesis creation account.[43]   1 Bar also alludes to the appearance of four-footed creatures on the earth in Gen 1:24-26, which is mentioned neither in Job ch. 28 nor in ch. 38.

4.8.2 Thematic Consideration: the Creation of Light

God is depicted as the God who alone knows wisdom (1 Bar 3:32a), in contrast with the rulers of the nations and with those reputed on the earth to be wise (1 Bar 3:15-23). In 1 Bar 3:32-36, the article ὁ leads three participial clauses (ὁ εἰδὼς τὰ πάντα, ὁ κατασκευάσας τὴν γῆν, ὁ ἀποστέλλων τὸ φῶς) which all depict the sovereignty of God. The subject of these participial clauses is summed up by οὗτος, and this description of God (vv. 32-36) is concluded by saying, 'This (οὗτος) is our God, and no other shall be given account in comparison with him' (1 Bar 3:36). In particular 1 Baruch seems to focus on the creation of light in order to depict the sovereign power of God over creation. 1 Bar 3:33-35 alludes to the Genesis creation account which narrates how the lights and luminaries were created by the command of God. The motif of obedience of light(s) is originally taken from Job 38:35 (as the obedience of lightnings), and is adapted to the picture of the Genesis creation account, i.e. the creation of light and luminaries (Gen 1:3-4, 14-19).[44] This picture thereby highlights the authority and creative power of the command of God.

4.9 Sirach 33:7-15

4.9.1 Literary Consideration: Context and Main Concern

Sir 24:1-33:18 comprises a large unit, which begins with the praise of wisdom (24:1-33), followed by some ethical disciplines (24:23-32:13). A contrast between the pious Jews and the wicked is depicted (32:14-33:6), and God's providence is affirmed (33:7-15). The creation account is employed in the arguments about God's providence (33:7-15).

4.9.2 Thematic Consideration: Creation and Theodicy

Sirach compares and contrasts the one who fears God (ὁ φοβούμενος κύριον) (Sir 32:14, 16; 33:1) with 'the sinner' (ἄνθρωπος ἁμαρτωλὸς) (33:17). The former is called 'the one who seeks the law' (ὁ ζητῶν νόμον) (32:15), 'a man of counsel' (ἀνὴρ βουλῆς) (32:18), 'the one who believes the law' (ὁ πιστεύων νόμῳ) (32:24), 'a wise man' (ἀνὴρ σοφὸς) (33:2), and 'intelligent person' (ἄνθρωπος συνετὸς) (33:3).   The latter is called, 'the hypocrite' (ὁ

---

[43] Sheppard, *Wisdom*, 96.

[44] Cf. Isa 40:26.

ὑποκρινόμενος) (32:15), 'an insolent and proud person' (ἀλλότριος καὶ ὑπερήφανος) (32:18), and 'the one who is hypocritical about it (the law)' (ὁ δὲ ὑποκρινόμενος ἐν αὐτῷ) (33:2).

To find an answer to the question of why there are two kinds of people (the good and evil) in this world (Theodicy), Sirach refers to the universal divisions (or the pairs of opposites, cf. 33:15) in time and space, which were given by 'God's knowledge' (ἐν γνώσει κυρίου) (33:8) and by 'the fullness of his knowledge' (ἐν πλήθει ἐπιστήμης) (33:11): surely the opposition is between hallowed days and ordinary days (33:7-9), the good and evil (τοῦ κακοῦ τὸ ἀγαθόν), life and death (τοῦ θανάτου ἡ ζωή), and the sinner and the pious (εὐσεβοῦς ἁμαρτωλός) (33:14). Sirach applies this notion of 'the universal division' to the understanding of human beings, arguing that although all the daylight in the year is from the same sun, one day is considered to be more important than another (33:7). Likewise, although all human beings have a common origin (from the clay of the earth), the Lord blessed some, exalted, made holy, and brought them near to God himself (33:10-12). Referring to the created universal order, Sirach thereby emphasizes how the destinies of human beings (or Israelite) are in the hands of the Creator (ἐν χειρὶ τοῦ ποιήσαντος αὐτοὺς) (33:13).[45]

4.10 Summary (for Chapter 4)

We may here sum up some of our findings in this chapter as follows:

(1) References are made, even briefly, to the work of creation in order to highlight the unique identity of God (Jub 12:4; ApAbr 9:3; LadJac 2:10-14, 20; PrMan 1:2-3; Wisd 9:1; 1 Bar 3:32-38; Sir 33:7-15): esp. Jub 12:4 depicts God as the origin of all life (lit. every life [wăkuĕl hĕyyĕwăt] from him) and as the Creator who completed his work of creation by his word; in ApAbr 9:3 God identifies himself as the Creator in a series of 'I am' sayings (ApAbr 9:3-4); Sir 33:7-15 emphasizes God's providence over all creation.

(2) The motif of the word of creation appears in contexts where the sovereign power of God is highlighted (PrMan 1:2-3; Wisd 9:2; ApAbr 9:9). Jub 12:26 expects the Hebrew language to be restored since Hebrew is thought to have been used by the Creator. In other words, the author thought Hebrew to be a primordial, powerful, and creative language. It should be noted that in PrMan 1:2-3 'the name of God' is paralled with 'the command of the word of God.' The name of God is referred to as a creative name in other Jewish creation accounts (Jub 36:7; LAB 60:2; 1 En 69:13-15; 3 En 42:1-7; cf. TarJon Exod 28:30; y. Sanh 29; b. Suk 53b; b. Mak 11a). It might be possible that the name of God as 'I am who I am' (אהיה אשר אהיה; cf. Exod 3:14) is associated

---

[45] 1QS develops this understanding into a more deterministic sense. See § 3.17.

with the unique identity of God who is the origin of all things so that he alone can let everything be (exist) (יהי 'let it be . . .' [Gen ch. 1]).

(3) The Wisdom of Solomon expands the spiritual aspect of wisdom (e.g. Wisd 1:6; 7:7, 22b; 9:17) and depicts a more dynamic figure of wisdom (Wisd 7:23-24, 27; 8:1; 10:1-11:1) than other wisdom literature. In the prayer, Solomon wished to possess wisdom (Wisd 9:4-18; 1 Kgs 3:5-15), hinting at the original role of wisdom which had been assigned in the beginning of creation (by interpreting the bestowment of the breath of life [Gen 2:7; Isa 42:5] as the spiritual wisdom). Thus the author speculates on the role of wisdom (i.e. to reveal the will of God, and to guide the people to knowledge) against the background of the exposition of the breath of life as 'the spirit of wisdom' (Gen 2:7; Isa 42:5) and the exposition of אמון in Prov 8:30 as 'artificer,' as well as a tradition that wisdom is linked to the spiritual activities of God (cf. Exod 31:3; 35:31; Isa 11:2).

(4) In Jub 12:4, God is depicted as the origin of all life as shown above. Thus it is possible that the life-giving motif is considered here to be one of the aspects of the unique identity of God.

(5) As for the light imagery, 1 Bar 3:33-35 demonstrates how the lights and luminaries were created by the command of God, by linking the meteorological account of Job ch. 28 (or ch. 38) with the account of the creation of light and luminaries (Gen 1:1-4, 14-19). ApAbr 9:3-4 also refers to the creation of light and luminaries in relation to the description of the sovereign power of God. In Wisd 7:7-30, which does not mention the Genesis creation account, light is depicted as the reflection of the identity of God (i.e. the power, glory, and the goodness of God).

(6) Sir 33:7-15 develops Theodicy (the origin of two kinds of people, the good and the evil), by referring to the universal order (i.e the division of time and space) (cf. 1QS col. 3).

Chapter 5

Summary and Conclusion (for Part I)

5.1 Literary Considerations

5.1.1 Classification of Early Jewish Creation Accounts

Our study has examined the creation accounts from early Jewish literature
which are generally dated between the 2nd century BC and the 1st century
AD. The classification is made in accordance with the way the creation
accounts are treated: (1) the narrative accounts of creation (Jub 2:1-16; 2 En
chs. 24-33; 4 Ezra 6:38-54; SibOr 1:5-35; 3:8-25; frag. 3; Ant 1:27-36; 1QM
10:8-18; 1QH^a 9:7-20; 4Q381 frag. 1 1-12); (2) the descriptive accounts of
creation (1 En 69:16-25; 2 En chs. 47-48; 65-66; 4 Ezra 3:3-4; 6:1-6; 2 Bar
14:15-19; 21:4-8; 48:2-10; 54:1-3, 13; ApAbr 21:1-22:2; LAB 15:5-6;
JosAsen 8:10-11; 12:1-2; Sir 16:24-17:14; 39:12-35; 42:15-43:33; 1QS 3:13-
4:1; 4Q392 frags. 1-9; 4Q422 frag. 1 1-13; 4Q504 frag. 8 4-10; 11QPs^a 26:9-
15); and (3) the brief references to creation (Jub 12:4, 26; LAB 60:2-3; ApAbr
7:10-11; 9:3, 9; LadJac 2:10-14, 20; PrMan 1:2-3; Wisd 7:22; 8:5; 9:1-2, 9; 1
Bar 3:32-38; Sir 33:7-15). The narrative account of creation is a long retelling
of the Genesis creation account, and it generally follows the narrative order of
Gen chs. 1-2 (Jub ch. 2; 2 En chs. 24-33; 4 Ezra ch. 6; Ant ch. 1; 4Q381),
whereas some creation accounts rearrange the order of the creation narrative in
accordance with their focus and point of view (SibOr bks. 1, 3, frag. 3; 1QM
col. 10; 1QH^a col. 9). The descriptive account of creation is a shorter account
which focuses on particular events of creation: some accounts refer to the
astronomical and meteorological phenomena (1 En ch. 69; 2 En chs. 47-48; 4
Ezra 6:1-6; LAB 15:5-6; Sir 33:7-15; 4Q392 frag. 1-9; 11QPs^a 24:11-15),
whereas others focus on the creation of human beings (2 En chs. 65-66; 4 Ezra
3:3-4; 2 Bar 14:16-19; Sir chs. 16-17; 4Q422 frag 1 1-13; 4Q504 frag 8 4-10).
They may develop their theological speculation, finding a link to other
canonical creation accounts, and take a more compact form which generalizes
God's work of creation (2 Bar 21:4-8; 48:1-10; JosAsen 8:10-11; Sir 39:12-35;
chs. 42-43). As for brief references to the Genesis creation in Jewish writings,
they usually take the more generalized or compact form of the creation
accounts. These types of creation accounts are sometimes combined and
appear in the same contexts.

CLASSIFICATION OF THE CREATION ACCOUNTS AND REFERENCES TO THE WORKS OF CREATION

Creation Account	Ast	Met	GH	Ear	GE	Hu	NB
(1) Narrative							
Jub 2:1-16	✓	✓		✓		✓	spirits
2 En chs. 24-33	✓			✓		✓	throne, angels, Paradise
4 Ezra 6:38-54	✓			✓		✓	
SibOr 1:5-35	✓			✓		✓	
SibOr 3:8-25	✓			✓		✓	springs, rivers, fire
SibOr f. 3	✓			✓		✓	
Ant 1:27-36	✓			✓		✓	
1QM 10:8-18	✓	✓		✓		✓	
1QHᵃ 9:7-20	✓	✓		✓		✓	powerful spirits
4Q381 f. 1 1-11	✓	✓		✓		✓	
(2) Descriptive							
1 En 69:16-25	✓	✓		✓			
2 En chs. 47-48	✓	✓		✓			visible and invisible
2 En chs. 65-66						✓	visible and invisible, ages
4 Ezra 3:3-4						✓	
4 Ezra 6:1-6		✓		✓		✓	paradise, angels, footstool
2 Bar 14:15-19					(✓)	✓	
2 Bar 21:4-8			✓		✓		
2 Bar 48:2-10			✓				
2 Bar 54:1-3, 13							ages, fountain of light
ApAbr 21:1-22:2				✓			torments, perdition
LAB 15:5-6	✓				✓		
JosAs 8:10-11			✓		✓		
JosAs 12:1-2		✓	✓		✓		
Sir 16:24-17:14						✓	
Sir 39:12-35			✓		✓		
Sir 42:15-43:33	✓	✓			✓		
1QS 3:13-4:1						✓	two spirits, generation
4Q392 f. 1-9	✓						darkness, light for God
4Q422 f. 1 1-13						✓	
4Q504 f. 8 4-10						✓	
11QPsᵃ 26:9-15	✓	✓					
(3) Brief							
Jub 12:4			✓	✓			
Jub 12:26							Hebrew language
LAB 60:2-3	✓	✓		✓			
ApAbr 7:10-11; 9:3, 9	✓			✓			ages
LadJac 2:10-14, 20	✓			✓			
PrMan 1:2-3			✓		✓		
Wisd 7:22; 8:5; 9:1-2, 9			✓		✓	✓	
1 Bar 3:32-38	✓			✓			
Sir 33:7-15	✓					✓	

* Ast: Ref. to Astronomical Phenomena; Met: Ref. to Meteorological Phenomena; GH: General Ref. of Heavenly things; Ear: Earthly things; GE: General Ref. of Earthly things; Hu: Human beings; NB: Non-Biblical

5.1.2 Focus and Main Concern

Focuses and theological concerns of the creation accounts differ according to each context:

(1) The creation accounts highlight the unique identity of God as the (sole) Creator (Jub 12:4; 4 Ezra 3:4-5; 6:6; 2 Bar 14:15-19; 21:4, 7; 54:2; ApAbr 9:3; LadJac 2:10-14, 20; PrMan 9:1; Wisd 9:1; 1 Bar 3:32-38; Sir 18:1; 33:7-15; 2 En 33:7-8; 47:3-6; 66:1-2, 5; SibOr bks. 1, 3; 1QM 10:8-9a; 4Q392; 11QPs[a] 26:9-15).

(2) The focus is given to the universal order (time and space) and the mystic knowledge of God, and God's providence over all creation is highlighted (4 Ezra 6:49-50; Sir 16:26-28; 42:15-43:33; 1 En 69:18; 2 En chs. 24-33; 47:5; JosAsen 12:1-2; 1QM col. 10; 1QS 3:17; 1QH[a] col. 9; 4Q392). The lowliness of human nature is contrasted with the great compassion of a merciful God (JosAsen chs. 8, 12; Sir chs. 16-17, 33).

(3) The speculation on the sovereignty of God accompanied a sapiential instruction 'to fear the Lord the Creator' (2 En chs. 47-48, 65-66; 4Q392; cf. 4Q176; 11QPsAp[a] 2-3) or 'to seek the sovereign God' (1 Bar chs. 3-4).

(4) The speculation on the unique identity of God which had been revealed in his work of creation was developed in a salvific and a more eschatological context (4 Ezra 6:6, 38-54; 2 Bar 21:6-8; 48:2-10; 54:1, 2, 3; 56:4; ApAbr 9:9; 22:4-5; JosAsen 8:10-12; SibOr bks. 1, 3. frag. 3; Sir 39:16, 18b, 31).

(5) The creation accounts also speculated on the identity of human beings and history which had been recorded in the books of Moses. They attempted to learn from history as to how the transgression of Adam brought human beings into a calamitous condition (Ant 1:49; SibOr 1:38).

(6) The focus was directed to the place of human beings or a more specific religious group (i.e. Israel or ideal Israel), and they attempted to affirm the unique relationship to God (4 Ezra chs. 3, 6; 2 Bar ch. 14; 1QS col. 3, etc.) or the original status of human beings (or Israel) as the rulers of all creation (4 Ezra 6:46, 54; SibOr frag. 3; 1QM col. 10; 1QH[a] col. 9; 4Q381 frag. 1 6-7). They also developed theodicy in relation to the understanding of the identity of human beings and their history (4 Ezra 3:7; 2 Bar 14:15-19; Sir 33:7-15; 39:22-27; 1QS col. 3).

(7) Finally, these examinations of the identity of human beings and their history were extended into the eschatological arguments. When they focused on God's special care for his created people, they expected God to take immediate action for their restoration (4 Ezra 6:38-54; 2 Bar ch. 14; 1QM col. 10; 1QH[a] col. 9). They referred to the predetermined course, and anticipated the coming eschatological salvation (4 Ezra ch. 3; 2 Bar ch. 14; 2 En chs. 65-66; 1QS col. 3).

5.1.3 Influence of Key Passages from the OT

In relation to their focus and concern, the Jewish creation accounts find some links between the Genesis creation account and other biblical creation accounts:

(1)   Several creation accounts refer to the following biblical texts in a context which highlights the unique identity of God as the Creator: Prov 8:22-29 (4 Ezra 6:1-6; 1QS cols. 3-4); Ps 33:6-12 (Jub 12:4; SibOr bks. 1, 3; 4Q381; 2 Bar chs. 21, 48, 54; ApAbr 9:3; 22:2; Sir chs. 33, 39; 4Q422); Ps 90:12 (2 En chs. 65-66); Ps 119:73 (4 Ezra 3:4-5); Ps 139:2-8 (2 En chs. 65-66); Jer 10:12-13 (11QPs^a 24:11-15); and Isa 45:7 (4Q392). Isa 40:18-26 is referred to in the context which makes a contrast between God and the idols (or other gods) (SibOr bks. 1, 3, frag. 3; 2 En 33:12).

(2)   The astronomical and meteorological accounts of Job chs. 38-43 (SibOr frag. 3; 1QH^a 9:8-13; 1 En ch. 69; 2 En chs. 47-48; JosAsen 12:1-2; Sir chs. 42-43; 4Q392) and Ps 104:5-23 (2 En chs. 47-48; Sir chs. 16-17; 1QS 3:17; 4Q392) are referred to as mystic knowledge in order to highlight God's providence.

(3)   When the Genesis creation account is linked to Isa 48:3, 13 and 55:11 (4 Ezra 6:38, 43; 2 Bar 14:17; 21:4, 7; 48:2, 8; 54:1, 3; 56:4), the creational motifs are expanded in salvific and eschatological contexts. Isa 48:3 and 55:11 do not necessarily refer to creation, but they illustrate how God will bring about his salvation by his word (or by his command). Nevertheless, 2 Baruch and 4 Ezra expose Isa 48:3 and 55:11 in both creational and eschatological contexts. This interpretation gives a more vivid picture of God who, by his word accomplished the work of creation, can alone bring about the eschatological works at once by the same word. Interestingly, when allusion is made to Isaiah 55:11, the personification of the word of God can be seen (4 Ezra 6:38, 43; 2 Bar. 54:3 and 56:4).

(4)   Ps 33:6 is also interpreted in a similar way. For example, Sir 39:16-18 reads Ps 33:6 (which is the description of the creational events) with Ps 33:9 (which is the general description of the way God works with his word). This reading associates the motif of the word of creation with salvific works, and depicts God as the Creator who has completed the work of creation by the word of his mouth (Sir 39:17b) and as the Savior who can bring about the salvific works (not necessarily with the eschatological emphasis) by the authority of his utterance (Sir 39:28-31). Similarly, ApAbr 22:2 reads Ps 33:9-12 with Ps 33:6-8, and its context indicates that the reality of the coming of the eschatological events is associated with the work of creation.

(5)   Ps 8:5-8 is referred to for the affirmation of human status as the ruler of all creation (SibOr frag. 3; 4Q381), whereas Isa 42:5 (Gen 2:7) is mentioned in the account of the bestowment of the breath of life (2 En chs. 47-48; 4 Ezra 3:3-4; 1QS 3:18; Wisd 9:2-3).

FOCUS AND THEOLOGICAL CONCERN OF EARLY JEWISH CREATION ACCOUNTS

Creation Account	Focus						Theological Concern					Key Scripture Ref.
	SG	PP	LU	PH	SN	No	GS	GE	HS	HE	No	
(1) Narrative												
Jub 2:1-16			✓							✓	(✓)	Gn 1-2
2 En chs. 24-33			✓				✓	✓		✓		Gn 1-2; Is 40
4 Ezra 6:38-54	✓			✓				✓				Is 48:3; 55:11
SibOr 1:5-35	✓				✓		✓					Ps 33:4-9,13;Is 40
SibOr 3:8-25	✓						✓					Ps 33:6;Is 40
SibOr f. 3	✓						✓	(✓)	✓			Ps 8:5-8;Is 40;Jb 38
Ant 1:27-36				✓				✓				Gn 1-2
1QM 10:8-18	✓		✓	✓							✓	Jb 38;Ps 104
1QH^a 9:7-20	✓		✓	✓			✓				✓	Jb 38-43
4Q381 f. 1 1-11	✓			✓			✓		✓			Pss 8,33
(2) Descriptive												
1 En 69:16-25			✓					✓				Jb 37-38
2 En chs. 47-48	✓						✓					Jb 38;Ps 139;Is 42:5
2 En chs. 65-66	✓						✓		✓			Pss 90; 139
4 Ezra 3:4-5				✓							✓	Jb10;Is 42:5;Ps119
4 Ezra 6:1-6	✓	✓					✓					Pv 8
2 Bar 14:15-19			✓				✓		✓			Is 48:3,13
2 Bar 21:4-8	✓						✓					Is 48:3,13; Ps 33
2 Bar 48:2-10	✓						✓					Is 48:13; Ps 33
2 Bar 54:1-3, 13	✓						✓					Is 48:13;55:11;Ps33
ApAbr 21-22	✓						✓					Ps 33:6-12
LAB 15:5-6	✓						✓					Ps18
JosAsen 8:10-11	✓			✓			✓					Gn 1
JosAsen 12:1-2	✓		✓	✓			✓					Gn 1;Jb38-43
Sir 16:24-17:14	✓		✓	✓			✓	✓				Ps 104:5-23
Sir 39:12-35	✓						✓	(✓)				Pss 33; 104
Sir 42:15-43:33	✓						✓					Jb 37-38; Is 40:13-
1QS 3:13-4:1	✓	✓	✓	✓	✓						✓	Pv 8;Ps104;Is42:5
4Q392 f. 1-9	✓						✓					Is 45:7;Jb 38;Ps 104
4Q422 f. 1 1-13				✓	✓				✓			Ps 33:6
4Q504 f. 8 4-10	✓			✓	✓				✓			Gen 1:26; 2:6-7
11QPs^a 26	✓						✓					Ps 89:8,14;Jer 10
(3) Brief												
Jub 12:4	✓						✓					Is 44, 46; Ps 33 135
Jub 12:26						✓					✓	Restoration of Hebr
LAB 60:2-3						✓					✓	Exorcist
ApAbr 7, 9	✓						✓					Ps 33:6
LadJac 2	✓		✓					✓				
PrMan 1:1-3	✓						✓					Ps 51;
Wisd 7-9	✓						✓					Pv 8;Gn 2:7;Is 42:5
1 Bar 3:32-38	✓						✓					Jb 28, 38; Gn 1
Sir 33:7-15	✓			✓						✓		Ps 33

* SG: Sovereignty of God; PP: Pre-existing Plan; LU: Law of Universe (time and space); PH: Place of Humanity; SH: Human Sinful nature; GS: God in Sapiential; GE: God in Eschatological; HS: Human in Sapiential; HE: Human in Eschatological; No: Non-Biblical.

5.2 Thematic Considerations

5.2.1 Theological Function of the Creation Account

Identity of God in a Sapiential Context

The creation accounts designate the identity of God who is unique (2 En 47:5, 6) and who is distinguished from other gods (Jub 12:4; SibOr 1:5-35; 3:8-25; frag. 3; 4Q403 frag. 1 1:34-36; 11QPsAp[a] 2:11-3:8; 2 En 47:3; 66:1-2, 5). He is the (sole) Creator (2 En 33:7-8; 47:4-5; 4 Ezra 3:4-5; 6:6; 1 Bar chs. 3-4; 2 Bar 14:15-19; 21:4, 7; 54:2; ApAbr 9:2; LadJac 2:10-14; PrMan 3:1; Wisd 9:1; SibOr bks. 1, 3, frag. 3; Sir 18:1; Sir 33:7-15; 4Q392; 1QM 10:8-9a; 11QPs[a] 26:9-15) and the sole Ruler over all creation (2 Bar 21:6, 9; 48:3; 54:12-13; Sir 18:3; chs. 42-43). In this context, God's greatness (PrMan 1:1-3; Wisd 9:1-2; 4Q381 frag. 1 1-11; 4Q392 frag. 1-9; 11QPs[a] 24:11-15) and his perfect dominion over time and space (Sir 39:12-35; 43:15-43:33; 1QH[a] 9:7-20) are recalled. In some contexts, it is accompanied by sapiential teaching, such as 'to fear the Lord of Israel' (2 En 47-48; 65-66; 4Q176 frags 16+ 1:2-3; 4Q392 frag. 1-9; 11QPsAp[a] 2:11-3:8) or 'to seek the Lord' (1 Bar 3:32-4:4).

Identity of God in an Eschatological Context

The speculation on the unique identity of God is expanded in a salvific (SibOr bks. 1, 3, frag. 3; JosAsen chs. 8:10-11;12:1-2; Sir 39:16-31) and a more eschatological context (4 Ezra 6:6, 38-54; 2 Bar 21:6-8; 48:2-10; ApAbr 9:9; 22:4-5). The fulfillment (or realization) of the eschatological promise is strongly expected on the basis of the identity of the sovereign God (4 Ezra 6:6, 38-54; 2 Bar 21:6-8; 48:2-10; 54:3). In this context, several typological correspondences between the revealed identity of God as the sole Creator and the expected identity of God as the fulfiller of the eschaton is explored (see § 3.2.2). In ApAbr 22:4-5, in the picture of creation and the eschaton, God's providence (i.e. perfect plan for all creation) is affirmed. JosAsen 8:10-12 meditates on the sovereign power of God who 'gave life' (ζωοποιήσας) to all things and called (them) out from darkness to light in the context of creation (JosAsen 8:10a), and asks for the new creation (ζωοποίησον [to give life], ἀνακαίνισον [to renew], ἀνάπλασον [to form anew], and ἀναζωοποίησον [to make alive]) (JosAsen 8:11a).

Identity of Humankind in a Sapiential Context

The creation accounts examine the identity of people and history, by retelling human history from the Genesis creation and thereafter (SibOr bks. 1-2; Ant ch. 1; 4Q422). Referring to the creation of Adam, they consider the relationship between God and the first human being (Adam), and affirm their status as the chosen people (4 Ezra 3:4-5; 2 Bar 21:24), and as rulers (or guardians) of all creation (4 Ezra 6:46, 54; 2 Bar 14:18; SibOr frag. 3; 1QM col. 10; 1QH^a col. 9; 4Q381 frag. 1 6-7). Some accounts focus on the giving of God's breath to Adam (Gen 2:7; Isa 42:5). For example, 4Q422 understands this breath of God as the spirit, whereas Sir ch. 17 and 4Q504 interpret it as the divine wisdom or knowledge. Since they possessed the divine wisdom and the law (Sinai event), they thought themselves to be in a special position from the beginning in order to rule over all creation. The Qumran sectarians (1QS) interpreted it in a more deterministic way, and understood that there were two kinds of spirits: one for the chosen and one for the Gentiles.

Identity of Humankind in an Eschatological Context

These examinations of the identity of people and history are expanded into the eschatological arguments. When they focus on God's special care for his created people, they also expect God to take immediate action for their restoration (4 Ezra ch. 3, 6; 2 Bar 14; 1QM col. 10; 1QH^a col. 9). And when they refer to a predetermined course, that idea comes from the expanded understanding of the division of creation and time; they examine at which stage they are living, and foresee the coming eschatological salvation behind the existing reality of their suffering (Jub ch. 2; 2 En chs. 24, 65-66; 1QS col. 3; 1QM col. 10; 1QH^a col. 9; 4Q180).

Summary

Jewish creation accounts depict the unique identity of God. This description of God is recalled in a sapiential context which instructs the people 'to fear the Lord' or 'to praise God the Creator.' When it is remembered in an eschatological context, the certainty and immediacy of the coming eschaton is expected, by displaying the typological correspondences between the revealed identity of God as the sole Creator and expected identity of God as the Fulfiller of the eschaton. They understand that they are living under the perfect dominion of a sovereign God, which is described by the idea of 'perfect design' or 'the predetermined course of the people.' They examine where they are standing (in an ethical sense and often in a fatalistic sense) and when they are living (in an eschatological sense); try to find the way of life (in a sapiential context) and also foresee the eternal life (in an eschatological context).

5.2.2 The Function of the Divine Attributes

The description of God's work of creation accompanies the divine attributes (i.e. the word of God [or command, oath], wisdom [or knowledge], right hand [or hands], name, and spirits). Each imagery seems to exhibit a particular sense or an aspect of the identity of God.

The word of God (or his command) seems to be associated with the description of the sovereign power in God's work of creation (2 En 33:4; 4 Ezra 3:4; 6:38, 43; 2 Bar 14:17; 48:2, 8; 54:1, 3; SibOr 1:19; 3:20; PrMan 1:2-3; Wisd 9:2; ApAbr 9:9; 22:2; JosAsen 12:2; Sir 39:17; 42:15; 4Q381 frag. 1 6-7; 4Q422 frag. 1 6). The divine 'oath' (*māḥlā*) (1 En 69:16-25; 4Q381 frag. 1 3-4; Leg All 3:204) functions like the other expressions of the word of creation. In PrMan 1:2-3 'the name of God' is paralleled with 'the command of the word of God.' The creative function of the name of God is significant in the Jewish creation accounts (Jub 36:7; LAB 60:2; 1 En 69:13-15; 3 En 42:1-7; cf. TarJon Exod 28:30; y. Sanh 29; b. Suk 53b; b. Mak 11a). The 'sign' also appears as a synonym of 'the word of God' in 2 Baruch (21:4-5; 48:8; 54:1-3). This motif may be linked to the divine command in the sense of an authorized signal by which a certain event will come about at once. Thus the idea of a 'sign' is associated with the picture of Genesis ch. 1. Influenced by Isa 48:3, 13 and 55:11, the motif of the creative word is expanded into a salvific or an eschatological word (4 Ezra and 2 Baruch). God, who by the word accomplished the work of creation at once, can bring about the salvific or eschatological works immediately by the same word.

Wisdom is mentioned in the context where God's providence over all creation (both space and time) is highlighted. Wisdom is associated with God's thoughtful arrangement for all creation (2 En 33:3-4; 48:4 [J]; 4 Ezra 6:6; 2 Bar 48:9; Sir 42:23-25; 1QH[a] 9:7, 14, 19), with the identity of God as the Ruler over the world (2 Bar 21:6; 54:13), with his sovereignty (11QPs[a] 24:7-8), and with his eschatological plan (2 Bar 21:8-12; 48:3-8; 54:1; ApAbr 22:2; 1QS cols. 3-4).

The word of God and wisdom appear simultaneously in some cases (2 En ch. 33; Sir ch. 42; Wisd ch. 9; 4Q403): esp. in 2 En 33:3-4, the former implies the perfect design or the plan of God, whereas the latter depicts the reality of God's deeds or his works. It should be noted that the creational word in 4 Ezra 6:38 and 43 is personified and depicted as an agent which produces life from lifeless things, whereas JosAsen 12:12 defines the word as 'life.'

The other imageries, 'God's hand(s)' (Jub 2:114 Ezra 3:4-5; 2 Bar 54:13) and 'the power' (2 Bar 48:8; 11QPs[a] 24:7) appear in contexts where the sovereign power of God is highlighted. Therefore, the divine attributes are deeply associated with the description of the unique identity of God.

DIVINE ATTRIBUTES IN EARLY JEWISH CREATION ACCOUNTS

Creation Account	Word Lit	Word Sy	Wisdom Lit	Wisdom Sy	Hands Lit	Hands Sy	Others
(1) Narrative							
Jub 2:1-16				✓	✓		
2 En chs. 24-33	✓		✓P				
4 Ezra 6:38-54	✓P						
SibOr 1:5-35	✓						
SibOr 3:8-25	✓						
SibOr f. 3							
Ant 1:27-36							
1QM 10:8-18							
1QH^a 9:7-20			✓	✓			
4Q381 f. 1 1-11	✓	✓					Spirit
(2) Descriptive							
1 En 69:16-25		✓					
2 En chs. 47-48			✓				
2 En chs. 65-66							
4 Ezra 3:4-5	✓	✓			✓		
4 Ezra 6:1-6				✓			
2 Bar 14:15-19	✓			(✓)			
2 Bar 21:4-8		✓		✓			spirit, sign
2 Bar 48:2-10	✓	✓		✓			power, sign
2 Bar 54:1-3, 13	✓P			✓	✓		
ApAbr 21:1-22:2	✓			✓			
LAB 15:5-6							
JosAs 8:10-11							
JosAs 12:1-2	✓						
Sir 16:24-17:14							
Sir 39:12-35	✓						
Sir 42:15-43:33	✓		✓				
1QS 3:13-4:1				✓			
4Q392 f. 1-9							
4Q422 f. 1 1-13	✓						spirit?
4Q504 f. 8 4-10			✓				spirit?
11QPs^a 24:11-15			✓	✓			power
(3) Brief							
Jub 12:4	✓						
Jub 12:26	✓						
LAB 60:2-3		✓					name?
ApAbr 9:2, 9	✓						
LadJac 2:10-14, 20							
PrMan 1:1-3	✓						God's name
Wisd.7:22; 8:5; 9:1-2, 9	✓		✓P				
1 Bar 3:32-38		(✓)					
Sir 33:7-15							

* Lit: Literal expression; Sy: Synonym; HS: the Holy Spirit; P: Personification;
?: Ambiguity.

5.2.3 The Life Imagery in Early Jewish Creation Accounts

The Genesis creation gives a picture of how God produces the living things by his word or by his utterance (Gen 1:11-12, 20-31). Some Jewish creation accounts focus on this aspect, and depict God as 'the life-giver' (4 Ezra 3:5; 6:47-48; JosAsen 8:10-11), 'the origin of all life' (wăkuĕl ḥĕyyĕwăt) (Jub 12:4), 'life' itself (ܚܝܐ: ḥayā) (2 Bar 21:9) or 'the Creator of life' (ܒܪܝܐ ܚܝܐ: bārya ḥayyeh) (2 Bar 23:5). He is the sole life-giver who himself has the authority to produce life ex nihilo (2 Bar 21:4; 4 Ezra 3:3-5; JosAsen 8:10-11).

The divine attributes also appear in the context where the identity of God as the sole life-giver is highlighted: e.g. wisdom is assigned to create Adam (2 En 30:8), whereas the word of God functions to produce human beings (4 Ezra 7:69). In JosAsen ch. 8, Joseph meditates on the Lord who 'gave life' (ζωοποιήσας) to all things, and expects God to provide Aseneth with new creational life. When the motif of 'God as the life-giver' is taken up again in JosAsen 12:1-3, it is interestingly linked to the word of God, and the word is called 'life.'

The motif of ζωή is prominent in the account of the creation of Adam as well (Gen 2:7). Isaiah gives an interpretation on this passage, by characterizing God as the life-giver who gives breath and spirit to the people (Isa 42:5). 4Q422 understands God's breath as the spirit, whereas Sir 17:1-14 and Wisd 9:2-3 and 4Q504 interpret it as divine wisdom or knowledge. Since they possessed divine wisdom and the law (Sinai event), they thought themselves to be in a special position from the beginning in order to rule over all creation. 1QS 3:18 develops this motif in a more dualistic way, and speculates on the origin of the division of two generations: e.g. two paths, humility and stubbornness toward the Torah (1QS 4:2-14), based on the understanding of the creation of human beings and the endowment of the spirits (1QS 3:18). Thus, in connection to the account of the endowment of spirits, the life motif is developed, particularly in the context which focuses on the status of the chosen people who possess the way of life (the Torah).

In short, on the one hand, the life motif is developed in the context which depicts the unique identity of God who alone can produce life ex nihilo, and bestows his breath of life on human beings. Based on the identity of God as the life-giver, people are encouraged to expect God to provide them with eternal life (as one of the end time blessings). On the other hand, the life motif is linked to the spirit or wisdom which was given to the first human being Adam, and the people were encouraged to seek for the way of life with wisdom and the law.

5.2.4 Light Imagery in Early Jewish Creation Accounts

Early Jewish creation accounts pay attention to the creation of light (אור and מארת) (e.g. Jub ch. 2; 1 En ch. 69; 2 En chs. 47-48, 24-33; 4 Ezra ch. 6; 1 Bar 3:33-35; ApAbr 9:3-4; SibOr bks. 1, 3, frag. 3; LAB ch. 60; Sir ch. 33; Ant ch. 1; 1QM col. 10; 1QH^a col. 9; 4Q381; 4Q392; 11QPs^a col. 26), and speculate on its theological meanings in various ways. Firstly, the creation of light may be taken as a manifestation of the sovereign power of God (e.g. 1 Bar 3:33-35; ApAbr 9:3-4; 11QPsAp^a 2:10-12). Secondly, light is considered to be a divine thing or good thing. For example, light is described as a realm or sphere in which God dwells: 'I (God), in the midst of the light (же средѣ свѣта: *že sredě světa*), moved around in the invisible things' (before creation) (2 En 24:4 [A]); 'I (God) was in the midst of light (азъ же срѣдѣ свѣта: *azĭ že sredě světa*)' (2 En 25:3 [J]); 'He created darkness [and li]ght for himself, and in his dwelling (במעונתו) the perfect light (אור אורתם) shines' (4Q392 frag 1 4-5). Light finds its place beside God together with wisdom (2 Bar 54:13), or beside his throne (2 En 25:4 [J]), and light is brought out from God's treasuries (4 Ezra 6:40; cf. 2 Bar 59:11).

This light imagery, as a divine or good thing, is linked to the divine nature of the Torah in the OT (e.g. Ps 119:105; Prov 6:23; Isa 2:5; 42:21; 51:4) and in early Jewish literature (Sir 17:11; 2 Bar 17:4; 59:2; 77:13, 16; Wisd 18:4; T Lev 14:4). In particular, 2 Bar 59:2 seems to take Isa 9:2 as an account of the giving of the Torah at Mount Sinai. LAB 15:5-6 may suggest a typological correspondence between the two Exodus events (the miracle of the Red Sea and the giving of the Torah) and the two creation events (the division of water on the third day and the creation of lights on the fourth day). It seems common in early Judaism, as well as later Rabbinic tradition (e.g. GenR 3:1, 5, 8) that the idea of the creation of light (i.e. the separation of light from darkness), is taken in an ethical sense as a contrast between righteousness and evil (2 Bar 18:1-2; 2 En 30:15; JosAsen 8:10a; 1QS 3:19).

Finally, like the life motif, light is counted as an eschatological blessing (Isa 60:19-20; Jub 1:29; 2 En 65:10 [J]; 2 Bar 48:50; 51:1-3; LAB 3:10; 23:10; SibOr 2:315), and regarded as a symbol of Paradise, whereas darkness is regarded as a symbol of Sheol (2 En 65:10 [A]; 2 Bar 48:50; 51:1-3). It should be noted that in both SibOr 2:315-317 and 2 En 42:6, light and life motifs appear in the same context, in the sense of the end time blessings.

Philo's Cosmogonic Account

Philo of Alexandria (ca. 20 BC to 45 AD) wrote a commentary of Genesis 1:1-2:7, 'On the Account of the World's Creation given by Moses' (ΦΙΛΩΝΟΣ ΠΕΡΙ ΤΗΣ ΚΑΤΑ ΜΩΥΣΕΑ ΚΟΣΜΟΠΟΙΙΑΣ), which is now called by the Latin title, *De Opificio Mundi* (abbreviated hereafter as Op Mund).[1] It is an account which basically attempts to make a link between Judaism and Hellenism.   Philo's   other   books   also   exhibit   several   cosmogonic understandings. While owing to the biblical and Jewish exegetical traditions, Philo takes several cosmogonic ideas from Greek philosophy (such as Platonism, Middle Platonism, Stoicism, Aristotelianism, and Pythagoreanism) and makes a complex arrangement of both traditions so that his creation account rather shows a distinction from other Jewish creation accounts. Therefore, this section will deal with Op Mund and other works independently.

1 Main Concern

Op Mund can be divided into three parts: (1) the prologue (1-12); (2) the interpretation of Gen 1:1-2:7 (13-169); and (3) the epilogue (170-172). In the second section, the creational events (from the 1st day to the sixth day) are interpreted in the same narrative order of Genesis. Philo's attempt to account for the creation of the world is stated in both the prologue and epilogue. Philo summarizes the point of his (or Moses') arguments as follows: (1) the deity has a real being (against the atheist); (2) God is one (against the polytheist); (3) the world really was created; (4) the world was one; and (5) God exercises forethought concerning the world (Op Mund 170-172). In the prologue, introducing an atheist's view, which admires the world itself rather than the Creator, and asserts that this world is unoriginate (Op Mund 8-9), Philo starts to explain how it could be said that there was an origin to this world (Op Mund 8). First of all, Philo presents the world view in which the universal law corresponds to this world, and the human beings were made to live in accordance with the law as citizens of this world (Op Mund 3). The relationship between the universal law and this world is explained in

---

[1] Our thesis uses LCL edition (F. H. Colson and G. H. Whitaker [eds.], *Philo* [LCL; Massachusets: Harvard University Press, 1929], 6-137).

philosophical language: i.e. 'active cause' (δραστήριον) and 'passive object' (παθητόν) (Op Mund 8). The former indicates 'the mind of the universe' (ὁ τῶν ὅλων νοῦς), whereas the latter indicates the objects which were fashioned by the former. This universal law is understood as God's providence as well (Op Mund 8-9). In the following interpretation of the Genesis creation account (Op Mund 13-169), Philo mainly argues that God (who is the invisible supreme cause) has a real relationship to the world (visible), by developing the idea of 'the divine Logos.'

2 Philo's Cosmogonic Understanding

2.1 Philo's Cosmogonic View

Philo's cosmogonic understanding has been influenced by Plato's cosmological account in Timaeus.[2] The parallel correspondences of the two cosmologies can be illustrated as follows:

PLATO		**PHILO**	
Creator god as	Tim	Creator God as	
ὁ δημιουργός	28a, 29a	δημιουργὸς ἀγαθός	OpM 18
ποιητὴς καὶ πατήρ	28c	ποιητὴς καὶ πατήρ	OpM 7,10, 21
Model or Plan for God's creation		God's Ideas or Model	
νοητός ζῷον	30c-31a	κόσμος νοητός	OpM 24, etc.
Cosmic Soul (mediator figure)	36-37	God's Mind	
ψυχή		ψυχή	OpM 18,20
The λόγος (as God's thought)		The λόγος (as God's forethought)	
λόγος καὶ διάνοια	38c	cf. προμηθεία	LegAll 1:24
The Reason (as God's Plan)		The Reason (as the laws in the city)	
λογισμός θεοῦ	34a	λογισμός	OpM 24
Craftsman gods, or Young gods		His Subordinate Powers (or 'angels')	
οἱ νέοι θεοί	41-42	συνεργός ἕτερος	Fug 68
		δύναμις	Fug 69
		ἕτερος δημιουργός	Fug 70
		πλῆθτος	Fug 71
		ἄγγελοι	Conf 174
		ὕπαρχοι	Conf 179
		οἰκεῖα	Conf 181

---

[2] Cf. D. Runia, *Philo of Alexandria and the 'Timaeus' of Plato* (Leiden: E. J. Brill, 1986), 524-527.

Both Plato and Philo describe God as a δημιουργός (craftsman), and both mention some subordinate existence for God's work of creation. These subordinate powers are called ἀγγέλοι in Conf 174 and 181, whereas they are depicted as subordinated to the divine Logos (λόγος θεῖος) in Fug 94-102:

> The word (λόγος) is, as it were, the charioteer of the powers (ἡνίοχος τῶν δυνάμεων), and he who utters (ὁ λαλῶν) it is the rider, who directs the charioteer how to proceed with a view to the proper guidance of the universe (101).[3]

Thus Philo distinguishes these powers which make direct contact with the visible world from the divine Logos, and the Logos is placed in the closest proximity to God, being called 'an image of God,' or 'the most ancient of all the objects of intellect in the whole world.'

2.2 The Pre-existent Plan as the Origin of the World

In Op Mund, Philo is interested in Plato's idea that God as the craftsman created the universe after a created model (παράδειγμα) (Tim 28b, 29b), and searches for a similar thought in Moses' creation account. Philo refers to Gen 1:26-27, 'he (Adam) was made in the image of God,' several times (Op Mund 24, 25, 69, 134, 139) as a ground text for the understanding of a pre-existent plan (as an origin). He interprets Gen 1:1 as follows: 'In the first place, from the model of the world, perceptible only by intellect, the Creator made an incorporeal (ἀσώματος) heaven, and an invisible earth' (Op Mund 29). The creation of light (Gen 1:1-5) is interpreted from the same point of view. Philo argues that the first created light which illuminates the image of God is invisible so that it is called the divine Logos (θεῖου λόγος), and that this creation preceded the creation of the visible lights (luminaries) (Op Mund 33).[4] Gen 2:4-5 is interpreted in the same way: 'before the earth was green, this same thing existed in the nature of things, and before the grass sprang up in the field, there was grass though it was not visible' (Op Mund 129). In Op Mund 17-24, Philo gives an illustration, by comparing the creation of the universe with the building of the city by the king. The king sketches out a model or plan for the building of the city, which is the νοητὴ (discernible by the intellect) πόλις and called ὁ τοῦ ἀρχιτέκτονος λογισμὸς (reason); likewise God must have a 'plan' for the creation of the universe beforehand in his mind or soul (ψυχή). The order in the universe is referred to as evidence for the existence of a supreme cause. Observing a perfect order in the heavens and the earth (Op Mund 33-63), Philo comments, 'operations are invariably carried out under ordinances and laws which God laid down in his universe as

---

[3] Based on Yonge's translation (C. D. Yonge [ed.] *The Works of Philo: New Update Edition* [Peabody: Hendrickson, 1993]).

[4] In Somn 1:75, referring to Ps 26:1, God and his Logos are mentioned as 'the first light,' and 'the archetypal pattern of every other light.'

unalterable' (Op Mund 61). The reason why Philo is interested in the Number (4 [Op Mund 48-52]; 7 [76-128]) seems to be related to the same concern (as a perfect design of the universe), as well as a possible influence from Pythagoreanism.

2.3 Monotheism against Polytheism

One of Philo's arguments is that God is one:

> God, with no counsellor to help him (who was there beside him?) (Op Mund 23).[5]

> He who really is is One (εἷς ὁ ὢν ὄντως ἐστι), and he has made the world (Op Mund 172).

However, he faced an exegetical problem in Moses' account of the creation of human beings, which hints at his fellow-workers: 'Let *us* make man in *our* image according to *our* likeness' (Gen 1:26). Philo understood this plurality as God's own (or subordinate) powers, to whom he had assigned the task of making the mortal part of human beings (Op Mund 75; Conf 175; Fug 69).[6] It should be noted that in the same context a monotheistic view is emphasized:

> Now it was most proper for God the universal Father to make those excellent things *by himself alone (δι' αὑτοῦ μόνον)* (Op Mund 74).

> In the first place, we must say that there is no existing being equal in honor to God, but there is *one only ruler and governor and king*, to whom *alone* it is granted to govern and to arrange the universe . . . There must be *one Creator*, and *one Father* and *one Master* of the one universe (Conf 170).

> It was not possible for any one to have an accurate view of all that had been created, *except for the Creator* (Mig 135).

In short, to contend against the polytheistic view, Philo employs the idea of subordinate powers (e.g. Op Mund 75; Conf 175; Fug 69). The figure of the Logos is also employed in the same way (as will be shown later).

2.4 Life and Light as God's Identity as Supreme Origin

The creation of light (e.g. Op Mund 29-35, 45-61; Som 1:75; Abr 156) and the life-giving motif (Op Mund 25, 30, 134-139, 144; Plant 19-20) are the focus in Philo's creation account.

---

[5] Cf. Isa 40:13.

[6] Philo uses the idea of subordinate powers in the context of theodicy: 'the successes of the intellect are attributed to God alone, but the errors of the being to his subordinate power' (Conf 179); 'to whom he has assigned the task of making the mortal part of our soul' (Fug 69); 'the one God alone is the sole Creator of the real man, who is the purest mind, whereas a plurality of workmen are the makers of that which is called man, the being compounded of external senses (Fug 71).

Referring (or alluding) to Gen 1:4, Philo mentions that light is preeminently beautiful (Op Mund 30) and the best of all things (Op Mund 53) since light is the first thing which is pronounced in the Sacred Scriptures to be good (Abr 156). Philo distinguishes the creation of light in Gen 1:4 from the creation of lights (luminaries), and defines the former light as the invisible and intelligible light which was created before the Sun (Op Mund 31).[7] Moreover, this invisible light is understood as an image of the divine Logos (θείου λόγου). In Som 1:75, Philo refers to Ps 26:1, 'For the Lord is my light and my Savior,' and states that God is the first light which is the archetypal pattern of every other light. In the same context, the Logos is also mentioned as 'light' in the sense of the model or image.

Philo mentions the giving of the breath of life to Adam on several occasions. In Plant 19-20, this breath is simply called 'the breath of life,' whereas elsewhere it is called, 'the divine breath,' 'immortal soul,' 'the sovereign Reason' (λογισμόν) (Op Mund 139), and 'the divine Spirit' (Op Mund 144; Leg All 1:36), through which human beings were made in the image of God (e.g. Op Mund 25; Plant 19-20), and in the image of the Logos (Op Mund 139).[8] In Op Mund 30, God is depicted as the author of life (ζωῆς θεὸς αἴτιος).[9]

In short, the identity of God as the supreme origin (possibly in the sense of Plato's idea) is modified or explained by the light and life imageries. That is to say, God is the supreme origin of light through which every light came about, whereas God is the author of life, through whom human beings received an immortal part, i.e. an immortal soul (as well as a mortal part [clay]; cf. Op Mund 134-139). It should be noted that the identity of God as the supreme originator of life and light is associated with the divine Logos (e.g. Op Mund 139; Som 1:75), which can be observed in early Jewish creation accounts.[10]

---

[7] See a similar division between the invisible and the visible in 2 En chs. 47-48, 65-66.

[8] The breath of life is understood in several ways in the early Jewish creation accounts (cf. Sir 17:1-14; Wisd 9:2; 1QS col. 3; 4Q422; 4Q504).

[9] The identity of God is associated with the life motif in the early Jewish creation accounts (4 Ezra 3:5; 2 Bar 21:9; 23:5; 6:47-48; JosAsen 8:10-11). Philo understands this life motif in accordance with his cosmogonic view.

[10] Cf. 2 En 33:4; 4 Ezra 3:4; 6:38, 43; 2 Bar 14:17; 48:2, 8; 54:1, 3; SibOr 1:19; 3:20; PrMan 1:2-3; Wisd 9:2; ApAbr 9:9; 22:2; JosAsen 12:2; Sir 39:17; 42:15; 4Q381 frag. 1 6-7; 4Q422 frag. 1 6.

3 Philo's Logos

3.1 The Logos as Plato's or Middle Platonic Model

Philo employs several parts of Plato's cosmological model (mainly from Timaeus), as previously observed. He goes on to reinterpret the book of Moses in accordance with this model. In the context where Philo considers some ontological subject (e.g. the relationship between the invisible God and the visible world), Plato's model is strongly highlighted and the Logos is defined as 'God's invisible model' or 'incorporeal plan.'[11] As has been observed, Philo is concerned with 'God's perfect plan,' or 'thought'[12] as an origin of this world. Philo calls it the λόγος θεοῦ. The Logos is compared with the law (νόμος θεῖος) or ordinances (θεομός) in Op Mund 143, which functions as 'a divine arrangement in accordance with which everything suitable and appropriate is assigned to every individual.' Philo emphasizes that it was settled in God's mind (Op Mund 17-18) or in his thought (cf. προμηθεία of Leg All 1:24) before the creation. The Logos is described in the rest of the book of Op Mund in the same sense: κόσμος νοητός (the world which is perceptible only by intellect) (Op Mund 24); ἀρχέτυπος σφραγίς (archetypal seal) (Op Mund 25).

Since wisdom in the Jewish tradition contains the motif of 'the divine thought,' wisdom may share an idea with Philo's Logos.[13] And since coincidentally Plato uses the Logos in the sense of 'the divine thought' at least once in Timaeus (Tim 38c3), it might have encouraged Philo to refer to the Logos, instead of wisdom.

3.2 The Logos applied to Allegorical Interpretation

Philo's Logos exhibits several distinctive aspects when it is associated with an allegorical interpretation.

(1) In Leg All 3:177-178, Philo gives an allegorical exegesis of Gen 48:15-16 to develop his argument about the relationship between God and the Logos (as heavenly food which nourishes the soul of human beings) (3:174-176).

---

[11] P. Borgen (*Philo, John and Paul: New Perspectives on Judaism and Early Christianity* [Atlanta: Scholars Press, 1987], 77) comments that Philo in his interpretation of Gen 1:3 moves from the uttered word of God to the concept of [the] Logos in an absolute sense, referring to Somn 1:75.

[12] H. Wolfson (*Philo: Foundation of Religious Philosophy in Judaism, Christianity and Islam, vol. 1* [Camgridge: Harvard, 1947], 233) defines it as 'a mind always in the act of thinking.'

[13] There are five examples where wisdom appears in the position of the divine Logos (Heres 199; Leg All 1:43, 65; 2:86; Fug 97; Somn 2:241-242).

> And he blessed them and said, 'the God in whose sight my fathers were well pleasing, even Abraham and Isaac, the God who continues to feed (ὁ τρέφων) me from my youth until this day; *the angel who delivers (ὁ ῥυόμενος) me from all evils*, bless these boys.
>   (Gen 48:15-16 [translation of the LXX])

Philo distinguishes the responsibility of God as nourisher of the people from that of the angel as the physician for his illness (ἰατρὸν κακῶν). He reads these texts by replacing the term, 'the angel,' with 'the λόγος,' whereas, ἰατρὸν is replaced by ἀπαλλαγὴν:

> The good things, namely food, he (God) gives to men by himself, but those which contain in them *a deliverance from evil (ἀπαλλαγὴν κακῶν)*, he gives *through his angels and his λόγων* (All Leg 3:177).

In this paraphrase, Philo juxtaposes the angels with the λόγος (and λόγους), and gives them a different task as deliverers from evil, not as physicians of illness. On account of the connection to the figure of the angel, the Logos (sg. in 177a; pl. in 177b and 178) takes a more personal figure or a mediator figure as the deliverer of the people from evil instead of a supreme God.

(2) In Fug 1-6, which is the allegorical exegesis of Gen 16:8-11 (a part of the Hagar narrative), Philo puts the Logos in the place of the angel who appears to Hagar.

Gen 16:8-11 [translation of the LXX]

> And *an angel of the Lord* found her by the fountain of water in the wilderness, by the fountain in the way to Sur. And the angel of the Lord said to her, 'Hagar, Sara's maid, where were you coming from? and are you going?' . . . And the angel said to her, 'Return. . .,' 'I will surely multiply your seed . . . ,' 'Behold . . .'

Philo replaces 'the angel' with 'the divine Logos' (θεῖον λόγον) (Fug 5a), and uses this text for his philosophical explanation of how the divine Logos relates to the human soul (Fug 5b-6). According to Fug 5-6, Hagar is a symbol of our causes for flight (i.e. hatred, fear, and shame), and the Logos of God is depicted as the comforter for the people to recommend, to encourage, to alarm, to comfort, and to restore the ignoble human soul (πάθος ψυχῆς). In this context, the divine Logos is given a mediator figure by means of the shadow of the angelic figure.

(3) In Quaest Exod 2:13, which is the exegesis of Exod 23:20-21, the Logos and the angel are connected together and they are called 'the minister of God,' 'judge,' and 'mediator' (μεσίτης) (although it is not necessarily clear whether Philo focuses on the Logos itself or the angel).

> And, behold, I send *my angel (τὸν ἄγγελον μου)* before your face, that he may *keep* you in the way, that he may bring you into the land which I have prepared for you. Take heed to yourself and listen to him, and disobey him not; for he will not give way to you, for *my name is on him* (Exod 23:20-21 [the translation of the LXX]).

As Philo says, it is one of the allegorical interpretations (ἀλληγορεῖται). According to Philo, the land which God has prepared for Israel is called 'philosophy' (φιλοσοφίαν). The angel is assigned to the position of 'an intellectual soul' (νοερὰ ψυχή), 'wholly mind (νοῦς), 'wholly incorporeal,' whereas the λόγος θεοῦ, which is appointed as 'judge' and 'mediator' (μεσίτης), is described as the one who helps the people to form their mind (τὸν νοῦν). In this context, Philo calls the angel 'an intellectual soul' or 'incorporeal mind,' and this motif is applied to the Logos as well.

(4) In Heres 203-205, Philo interprets 'the cloud,' which appears in the Exodus event (Exod 14:19), as the cloud which showers down wisdom on those minds study virtue, whereas the cloud pours forth punishments on the evil (204). The image of the water (e.g. 'the fountain' in Post 127 and 'the river' in Post 129, Somn 2:241, 246) is often allegorized as the divine Logos, so Philo may apply it to this context. Heres 205 depicts the divine Logos as God's 'archangelic (ἀρχαγγέλῳ) and most ancient (πρεσβυτάτῳ) λόγος.' Moreover, Philo understands the Logos here as 'the ambassador of the ruler' (πρεσβευτὴς τοῦ ἡγεμόνος) who is 'not created as God, nor as a human being, but as a hostage to both parties.' The Logos says, 'I stood in between the Lord and you.' It alludes to Num 16:48, in which Aaron stood in between the dead and the living.[14] The association of the Logos with the figure of Aaron may have something to do with the fact that Aaron is called Moses' mouth-piece, interpreter, and prophet who stands between God and the people (cf. Det 39). Although there is no clear mentioning of this association here, it seems possible that the mediator figure of the divine Logos is related to the figure of Aaron as an ambassador or the high priest.

(5) In Quaest Gen 4:110, Philo gives an allegorical interpretation of 'the bracelets of gold of ten drachmas' of Gen 24:22, and argues that the Number '10' is a sacred number. Then he assigns the Logos to the highest place, applying his understanding of 'the Number 10' to the construction of the universe:

> In the world, together with the number seven (of planets) and the eighth spheres of fixed stars and those sublunary things of one species which are changeable among themselves, *the divine Logos is the governor (κυβερνήτης) and administrator (οἰκονόμος)* of all things, since it has melodically harmonized the chorus of the nine musical (intervals).[15]

This framework is also applied to the construction of the human body:

---

[14] Aaron is actually allegorized as the Logos in Leg All 3:45.
[15] Trans. of R. Marcus (ed.), *Philo Supplement I* (LCL; Cambridge: Harvard University Press, 1987).

And in our body and soul there are also seven irrational parts and the mind, which is a single part. Now, *the divine Logos* is concerned with these nine (parts), being *the leader and ruler* of harmony, and by it the nine parts are harmonized.[16]

In those texts, the divine Logos is called 'the governor (κυβερνήτης) and administrator (οἰκονόμος)' of the universe and 'the leader and ruler' of the human body. The character of the divine Logos as the one who governs or rules the universal order is illustrated in other contexts that compare the Logos with the divine law (i.e. νόμος θεῖος): 'It supports and makes firm the foundation of the universe as boundary to all elements' (Plant 8-10); 'It holds all things together. . . and binds all the parts. . .' (Fug 112). Likewise, it seems reasonable to take the idea of 'the governor' or 'the leader' in Quaest Gen 4:110 as a figurative expression.

In summary, Philo's allegorical interpretation gives the Logos several distinctive meanings. In particular, Philo is interested in the angelic figures (Leg All 3:177-178; Fug 5-6; Quaest Exod 2:13) or other mediator figures, such as Aaron (Heres 205), or the metaphors which indicate the motif of nourishment (e.g. manna, or water). Then he finds the new features of the divine Logos as 'the healer of the soul' (Leg All 3:177-178), 'comforter' (Fug 5-6), 'mediator' (Quaest Exod 2:13), and 'ambassador' (Heres 205). And all this term seems to be just personification.

3.3 The Logos for Solving the Exegetical Problem

To solve the exegetical problem which seemingly indicates a polytheistic view, Philo expands the motif of the divine Logos.

(1) In Somn 1:227-230 (which is the interpretation of Gen 31:13), Philo does not take ἐν τόπῳ θεοῦ as the Greek translation of בֵית־אֵל (Beth'el), but literally as 'in the place of God.' Then he solves the problem of the text which seemingly indicates that there were two Gods (Somn 228). Philo explains that the former θεός takes an article so that it means the real God, while the latter does not take one so that it implies the divine Logos. While trying to solve the theological problem (of the polytheistic view), Philo takes up Gen 31:13 (the LXX rendering) and argues that the divine Logos should be placed beside God instead of the other autonomous substance. In other words, the divine Logos can be placed there because it is not considered to be an autonomous substance.

(2) The LXX reading of Gen 9:6 has a similar exegetical problem: '*I* made (ἐποίησα) man *in the image of God*,' unlike the Masoretic text, '*He* made (עשׂה) man in the image of God.' It seems to Philo that the text implies that there were some other Gods (Quaest Gen 2:62). In order to solve this problem, Philo thinks that the subject of this sentence is the supreme Father

---

[16] R. Marcus, *Philo*.

of the universe, and 'God' in the last phrase points to the divine Logos who is called τὸν δεύτερον θεόν (the second, or next God). Although he gives the title of τὸν δεύτερον θεόν to the Logos, the context of Quaest Gen 2:62 makes no allusion to any mediating role of the δεύτερος θεός. Thus it seems rather a paraphrase of Gen 9:6: 'I (God) made man in the image of the *next* God, not *the God.*'

(3) In Conf 146-147, while discussing the reason why the people can be called 'the sons of the Lord God' (Deut 14:1; cf. 32:18), Philo argues that even if there is no one who is worthy to be called a son of God, he can be assigned to the next position, that is 'the son of the divine Logos' 'the first born' (πρωτόγονος), 'the eldest' (πρεσβύτατου) of all his (God's) angels, as it were[17] 'an archangel' (ἀρχάγγελον).[18] In this context, Philo uses the motif of the divine Logos to solve the exegetical problem.

In short, to contend against the polytheistic view, Philo expands the motif of the Logos (e.g. Somn 1:227-230; Quaest Gen 2:62; Conf 146-147), and in this case, the Logos is called 'the second God' (Somn 1:227-230) or 'a God' (Quaest Gen 2:62) to sustain the monotheistic view since the divine Logos is not regarded as an autonomous being. However, because Philo was much influenced by Platonic view, Philo might have confused Jewish monotheism with Platonic 'monotheism' (one Supreme God but also lesser divine beings).[19]

3.4 The Logos as the Divine Word

There seems to be a certain association of Philo's Logos with the word of God in the biblical tradition as well.[20]

(1) Sacr 8: In order to prove the immortality of the human mind, Philo gives the example of Moses who departs to heaven when he is going to die. In this account, Philo emphasizes that through 'the word' (διὰ ῥήματος) of the supreme cause, by which the whole universe was formed (δι' οὗ καὶ ὁ σύμπας κόσμος ἐδημιουργεῖτο), Moses was summoned to heaven by God. Διὰ ῥήματος is replaced in the next sentence by τῷ αὐτῷ λόγῳ, so ῥῆμα and λόγος are used as synonyms. This account is based on Deut 34:5: 'So Moses the servant of the Lord died there in the land of Moab, according to the word of the Lord (διὰ ῥήματος κυρίου [LXX]).' Philo seems to take the genitive case of διὰ ῥήματος κυρίου as an expression of 'agent': i.e. 'by the power of his word,' not as 'according to the decision of the Lord.' Then, the account that the whole

---

[17] See the Greek expression, ὡς ἄν

[18] The one who is named as ἀρχή, ὄνομα θεοῦ seems to be Israel. See the Greek text.

[19] I am grateful to Prof. Bauckham for suggesting this point.

[20] Runia (*Philo*, 169-171) does not deny a possibility of the relation of Philo's Logos to the biblical texts, listing these motifs: (1) Moses' law; (2) Moses' παράδειγμα of the tabernacle; and (3) the word of YHWH (דבר יהוה).

universe was formed through 'the word' (ῥῆμα or λόγος) of the supreme cause (τοῦ αἰτίου μετανίσταται) seems to be based on the motif of the word of God. In Sacr 8 the Logos is paralleled with ῥῆμα ('utterance'), and the Logos is described in this context, not only as God's plan or model, but also as a real activity of God the Creator.[21] It should be noted that Moses was taken by the same Logos which operated in God's work of creation.

(2) Leg All 3:204: This is part of the exegesis of Gen 22:16: '"by myself have I sworn," said the Lord.' Philo states that God's oaths (ὅρκοι) are sure and are proofs of his exceeding power (τεκμήριον τῆς ἰσχυρότητος αὐτοῦ). He also writes that πάντες οἱ τοῦ θεοῦ λόγοι εἰσὶν ὅρκοι, paralleling the oath with the λόγοι τοῦ θεοῦ and νόμοι τοῦ θεοῦ (204).[22] Although both ὅρκοι and λόγοι τοῦ θεοῦ take a plural form here, each takes a singlar form in the same context.[23] So that, we can take λόγοι τοῦ θεοῦ as the same as the divine Logos. The idea, 'whatever he said comes to pass, and this is specially characteristic of an oath' (204), shares the idea of the word of God (e.g. Isaiah 55:11).

(3) Post 102: Philo gives an exegesis on Num 20:17, 'We (Moses and Israel) will go along the King's Highway,' with reference to Deut 28:14, 'You shall not turn aside from the word (ῥήματος [LXX]) which I commanded you this day.' Philo argues that 'the King's Highway' means 'genuine philosophy,' which should be distinguished from a secular one (102), and this royal road is called θεοῦ ῥῆμα καὶ λόγον and τὸ θεοῦ ῥῆμα. It is noteworthy that following the citation of Deut 28:14 (LXX), Philo takes the LXX rendering, θεοῦ ῥῆμα; however, he replaces it by λόγος. This pattern appears in Sacr 8 and Leg All 3:174-176 as well: i.e. διὰ ῥήματος κυρίου [LXX] → ῥῆμα τοῦ αἰτίου μετανίσταται (Sacr 8a) → τῷ αὐτῷ λόγῳ (Sacr 8b). In Post 102, ῥῆμα means God's command which he declared to Israel. Therefore, the Logos, called a 'genuine philosophy,' is related to the Logos as God's utterance.

(4) Leg All 3:174-178[24]: This is the exegesis of Deut 8:3.

> And He afflicted you and made you weak by hunger, and *fed* (ἐψώμισέν < ψωμίζω) you with *manna* (τὸ μάννα), which your fathers knew not, that he might make you know that man shall not live by bread (ἐπ' ἄρτῳ) alone, but *by every word* (ἐπὶ παντὶ ῥήματι) that goes forth out of the mouth of God man shall live (Deut 8:3 [translation of the LXX]).

Philo takes λόγος as an equivalent word to μάννα here, and interprets the passage as follows: 'God nourishes (διατρέφει) us by his most generic word

---

[21] Cf. Fug 95: 'the powers of Him who utters the word (λέγοντος), according to which the creator made the world with a word (λόγῳ).

[22] The connection between the oath and the λόγος can be seen in 1 En 69:16-25 and 4Q381 frag. 1 3-4.

[23] See Leg All 3:204 and 208.

[24] Cf. Det 118; Heres 79, 191.

(τὸ γενικώτατον αὑτοῦ λόγῳ), which is above all the world, and is the eldest (πρεσβύτατος) and most generic of created things' (175). It is also summarized in 176: 'The soul (ἡ ψυχὴ) of the most perfect is fed by the word (τῷ λόγῳ).' It is noteworthy that the λόγος τοῦ θεοῦ in this context has a similar character to the divine word: i.e. the character of the word seems to be God's utterance, because of the connection to the word ῥῆμα, and as the one which nourishes the soul of human beings, on account of the application to the metaphor, μάννα, a heavenly bread. These figures are rare in the former category (as an application to Plato's model), and have a certain connection to the divine word tradition.[25]

(5) Post 127-129: The Logos was linked to the water motif in several contexts.[26] In the exegesis of Gen 2:6 and 10, 'And a fountain went up from the earth, and watered all the face of the earth . . . And a river went out of Eden to water the Paradise,' the Logos takes the place of 'the fountain' in Post 127 and of 'the river' in 129.[27] In the former section, ὁ θεοῦ λόγος is described as ἀρχὴ and πηγὴ of noble conduct, whereas in the latter, ὁ θεῖος λόγος is assigned a divine task to increase and to nourish the souls of the ones who love God. It is interesting that Philo explains in detail how ὁ θεῖος λόγος can feed the soul of human beings, i.e. 'on account of the unceasing and everlasting flow of salutary words (λόγων) and doctrines' (δογμάτων) (129). In other words, ὁ θεοῦ λόγος is described as a source for the words as ordinances or instructions. This figure also seems to be nearer the word of God tradition than Plato's philosophical model.

In short, the Logos shows the nature of God's utterance: the word of creation (e.g. Sacr 8; Fug 95), the word of God in the prophetic tradition (Leg All 3:204), and in Deut 28:14 (Post 102). On account of the link of the Logos to the heavenly food 'manna' (Leg All 3:174-178; Det 118; Heres 79, 191) and to the 'fountain' or 'the river' of water (Post 127-129; Somn 2:241-242, 246), the Logos is assigned a divine task to increase and to nourish people's souls. Philo may depict a bridge between the Logos as God's plan (of the first category) and the Logos as the word of God, when he describes ὁ λόγος τοῦ θεοῦ as a source of the divine instructions (cf. Post 127-129).

---

[25] The similar connection of the λόγος τοῦ θεοῦ (or λόγος θεῖος) to μάννα is seen in Det 118 and Heres 79, 191.

[26] In Leg All 2:15-16 both manna and water are linked together, and they are mentioned as the λόγος of God: 'When they have been given *water* to drink, they are filled with *the manna*.' This is an allegorical exegesis of Deut 8:15-16.

[27] Cf. Somn 2:241-242, 246.

4 Summary and Conclusion

Philo's main concerns are summarized in the epilogue of Op Mund: (1) the deity has a real being (against the atheist); (2) God is one (against the polytheist); (3) the world really was created; (4) the world was one; and (5) God exercises forethought concerning the world. Notwithstanding, Philo cannot ignore some polytheistic expressions in Moses (e.g. Gen 1:26; 31:13; 9:6; particularly in the LXX translation). To solve the theological problem (in particular against polytheistic views), Philo employs several parts of Plato's cosmological model (mainly from Timaeus), and he goes on to reinterpret the book of Moses in accordance with the philosophical model. In this process, Philo might have confused Jewish monotheism with Platonic 'monotheism' (one Supreme God but also lesser divine beings). Moreover, on the one hand, in the context where Philo considers some ontological subject (e.g. the relation between the invisible God and the visible world), Plato's model is strongly emphasized and the λόγος is defined as 'God's invisible model' or 'incorporeal plan,' whereas on the other hand, in the context where Philo goes back to the biblical tradition, the Logos seems to have a different aspect from the former figure. It can have the nature of God's utterance (e.g. Sacr 8; Fug 95) and the divine word figure (Leg All 3:204; Post 102). In particular when the Logos is understood with some personal figures (e.g. angel [Leg All 3:177-178; Fug 5-6; Quaest Exod 2:13] or Aaron [Heres 205]) or other metaphors ('manna' [Leg All 3:174-178; Det 118; Heres 79, 191] or 'water' [Post 127-129; Somn 2:241-242, 246]), it appears as a divine mediator. In this context, the Logos is called 'the healer of the soul' (Leg All 3:177-178), 'comforter' (Fug 5-6), 'mediator' (Quaest Exod 2:13), and 'ambassador' (Heres 205). The Logos is assigned a divine task to increase and to nourish the souls of the people as well (Leg All 3:174-178; Det 118; Heres 79, 191; Post 127-129; Somn 2:241-242, 246) because of the connection to those metaphors. However, all this mediating figure seems to be a personification of the God's activities, not as a presentation of hypostatic being.

It is true that Philo attempts to defend Jewish monotheism from polytheistic and atheistic world views. However, while developing the idea of the Logos in Platonic or Middle Platonic philosophical models, Philo gradually moved from Jewish tradition (e.g. speculation on the divine word and wisdom). Philo 'sometimes' confuses Jewish monotheism with Platonic cosmogonical views which can include lesser divine beings, while emphasizing a philosophical notion (e.g. the Logos as 'Reason'). As will be shown in the next part, these ideas cannot be seen in the Johannine Logos, and these points make a disinction between Philo's Logos and the Johannine Logos which is all the way through concerned with Jewish monotheistic framework which speculates on the unique identity of God as the sole Creator and as the sole Fulfiller of the Eschatological hope.

Part II

The Johannine Prologue
in the Light of Early Jewish Creation Accounts
(ca. 2nd Century BC to 1st Century AD)

Chapter 6

Structural Analysis on the Johannine Prologue

Since the quest of Bultmann's work (1923) on the background of the Johannine prologue, several significant efforts have been made to identify the 'original hymn,' which has been understood to be the source of the prologue. On the other hand, there have been other efforts to describe the structure of the present form of the prologue. They attempt mainly to point out a chiastic structure by seeking a more developed refinement of the parallel correspondences in the prologue. This chapter will briefly assess the recent surveys of both source (diachronic) and structural (synchronic) analyses, and will propose a new structural understanding which will be the basis for later thematic analysis.

6.1 Source Analysis

6.1.1 Arguments

Although the first part of the original hymn (v. 1-5, 9-11) introduces the pre-existent λόγος, R. Bultmann[1] argues that the redactor understood that verse 14 and the phrase, τὸ φῶς ἐν τῇ σκοτίᾳ φαίνει in v. 5, refer to the Incarnation of the λόγος. He believes that the redactor added his own prosaic comments in vv. 6-8, and 15. Bultmann considers the literary style as another reason why an original hymn underlies the prologue. That is to say that on the one hand, the original hymn was composed in a poetical style which used in metaphorical terms, whereas, on the other hand the additional sections were composed in prosaic form.[2] He also points out that there is a contextual breaking or a sudden shift, which is especially seen in the section of the witness of John the Baptist (vv. 6-8, 15). Furthermore, he argues that vv. 12-13 is a later insertion which developed the notion of the τέκνα θεοῦ, and that v. 17 is an exegetical gloss on v. 16, whereas v. 18 is a note to stress the absoluteness of the revelation in Jesus.[3]

---

[1] R. Bultmann, 'Der religionsgesichtliche Hintergrund,' 3-26; idem, *John*, 16-17. He divided the prologue into two sections: A cultic community hymn and a later addition to or insertion into the original hymn.

[2] R. Bultmann, *John*, 16-18.

[3] R. Bultmann, *John*, 79.

E. Käsemann revises Bultmann's hypothesis, by observing that v. 10 links excellently with v. 5, and that v. 9 is inserted to link up with the hymn after the insertion of vv. 6-8.[4] He considers vv. 14-18 as an epilogue to the prologue which the Evangelist provided.[5] R. Schnackenburg accepts that the prologue is based on a song or hymn which was used for the beginning of the Gospel. He gives the following reasons: (1) the differences between the poetical sentences and the prose elements (vv. 6-8, 12, 13, 15, 17); (2) the breaks and sudden switches of structure and the movement of thought (vv. 6-8, 15); (3) the stylistic differences; and (4) the terminological and conceptual differences (e.g. ὁ λόγος, σκήνοω, ἴδιος).[6] E. Haenchen argues that the original hymn was composed on the basis of an old wisdom myth, and that this hymn was taken over by Judaism and put in the service of the Torah.[7] As for vv. 6-8, he argues that the interpolator might have understood v. 5 as an early reference to the incarnated Logos so that the interpolator might have attempted to put an account of John the Baptist prior to the appearance of Jesus.[8] Based on recent redaction analyses, R. Brown proposes two sets of additions: (1) the explanatory expansions of the lines of the Hymn (12c-13; 17-18); (2) the material pertaining to John the Baptist (6-9, 15).[9] He argues that vv.6-7 reads well before v. 19, since v. 7 says that John the Baptist came as a witness to testify, and v. 19 presents his testimony and the circumstances under which it was given.[10] He observes that the style of vv. 8-9 (the absence of καὶ and the use of subordination), and 12c-13 (the use of prosaic form) is different from the other poetic stanzas,[11] and that these verses also show explanatory features. Verse 5 is considered to be copied from v. 30, and vv. 17-18 repeats v. 16, in order to sustain each context.[12] However, scholars' opinions differ as to the point where the original hymn should be located in the prologue.[13]

---

[4] E. Käsemann, 'Structure,' 151.

[5] E. Käsemann, 'Structure,' 152.

[6] R. Schnackenburg, *The Gospel According to St. John vol. 1* (London: Burns & Oates), 224-226.

[7] E. Haenchen, *John*, 127-129.

[8] E. Haenchen, *John*, 116.

[9] R. E. Brown, *The Gospel According to John (I-XII)* (AB 29; New York: Doubleday, 1966), 22.

[10] R. E. Brown, *John*, 27.

[11] R. E. Brown, *John*, 9-11.

[12] R. E. Brown, *John*, 35-36.

[13] J. H. Bernard, *A Critical and Exegetical Commentary on the Gospel according to St. John* (Edinburgh: T & T Clark, 1928), 144; P. Gächter, 'Strophen im Johannesevangelium,' *ZTK* 60 (1936), 99; H. C. Green, 'The Composition of St. John's Prologue,' *ET* 66 (1954-1955), 291; J. T. Sanders, *The New Testament Christological Hymns: Their Historical Religious Background* (Cambirdge: Cambridge University Press, 1971), 20; W. Schmithals,

THE SOURCE ANALYSIS OF JOHN 1:1-18[14]

	1	2	3	4	5	6	7	8	9	10	11	12	13	14	15	16	17	18
Bultmann 1923						▨	▨	▨				▨	▨		▨		▨	▨
Bernard 1928						▨	▨	▨				▨	▨		▨		▨	▨
Gächter 1936						▨	▨	▨	▨	▨	▨		▨		▨		▨	▨
Green 1955			▨			▨	▨	▨	▨	▨	▨		▨		▨		▨	
Käsemann 1957		▨				▨	▨	▨	▨					▨	▨		▨	▨
Schnackenburg 1957		▨		▨		▨	▨	▨	▨			▨	▨			▨	▨	▨
Haenchen 1963						▨	▨	▨	▨			▨			▨		▨	▨
Brown 1966						▨	▨	▨				▨	▨	▨	▨	▨	▨	▨
Sanders 1971						▨	▨	▨			▨		▨	▨	▨	▨	▨	▨
Schmit-hals 1979						▨	▨	▨	▨	▨		▨			▨	▨		
Rochais 1985						▨	▨	▨		▨		▨	▨		▨		▨	▨

(The shadow indicates the sections regarded as the additions to the original hymn)

6.1.2 Assessment

Bultmann's earliest work on the Johannine prologue made a strong impact on later studies of the prologue. Since then, scholars have assumed an original hymn behind the prologue. This is based mainly on observations of literary style.[15] They argue that the original hymn was composed in poetical form, which uses metaphorical terms, whereas, on the other hand, the additional sections were composed in prosaic form. The question is whether the criteria, which scholars apply to the evaluation of the style of the prologue, can be suitable for understanding the style of the Fourth Gospel. For example, it seems subjective to judge the literary style. C. K. Barrett examines ancient poetic structure, and contends that it is impossible to draw this sort of

---

'Der Prolog des Johannesevangeliums,' *ZNW* 70 (1979), 16; G. Rochais, 'La Formation du Prologue (Jn. 1:1-18),' *SE* 37 (1985), 5-7.

[14] This table is based on Brown's survey (*John*, 22), and it is supplemented by E. Miller's summary (*Salvation-History in the Prologue of John: The Significance of John 1:3/4* [NovTSup 60; Leiden: E. J. Brill, 1989], 6).

[15] E. Käsemann ('Structure,' 141-142), R. Schnackenburg (*John*, 226) and R. Brown (*John*, 21-22) suggest that the difference of style should not be the criterion; however, they all seem to accept Bultmann's assumption.

division that might enable the readers to assign some verses to a source written in poetry, and others to a prose-writing evangelist.[16]

The source analysis also points out the contextual breaks or sudden shifts, which are especially seen in the sections of the witness of John the Baptist (vv. 6-8, 15).[17] There are some examples (see below) of the contextual breaks or sudden shifts in the other texts of the Fourth Gospel. However, these breaks do not necessarily show an awkward impression, but rather they can be observed as a literary pattern. It is noteworthy that 'the sentence break' is observed in Semitic languages as a literary device.[18]

The first example is from the narrative of the Samaritan woman (4:3-42).

(1) The Narrative of the Samaritan Woman (John 4:3-42)

```
A: Samaritan Woman and Jesus (3-26)        (1st part)
B:       Disciples came to them (27)                    (1st breaking)
A: Samaritan Woman and the People (28-30)  (2nd part)
B:       Disciples and Jesus (31-38)                    (2nd breaking)
A: Samaritan Woman and the People (39-42)  (3rd part)
```

In this narrative, on the one hand, three parts (vv. 3-26, 28-30, 39-42) focus on the Samaritan woman, whereas, on the other hand, two parts (vv. 27, 31-38) focus on the conversation with the disciples. In particular, the latter sections (vv. 27 and 31-38) seem to break the entire sequence of this narrative. However, it seems plausible to assume that the narrator unfolds two different scenes at the same time.

The second example is from the narrative of Jesus' arrest (18:12-40).

(2) The Narrative of Jesus' arrest (John 18:12-40)

```
A:     The Jews arrest Jesus (12-14)         (1st part)
B:           Peter denies Jesus (15-18)                  (1st breaking)
A:     The high priest questions Jesus (19-24) (2nd part)
B:           Peter denies Jesus, 2nd, 3rd (25-27)        (2nd breaking)
A:     Pilate questions Jesus (28-40)         (3rd part)
```

---

[16] C. K. Barrett, *The Prologue of St John's Gospel* (London: The Athlone Press, University of London, 1971), 13-17.

[17] Cf. R. Bultmann, *John*, 16-18; R. Schnackenburg, *John*, 225-226.

[18] T. D. Tsumura ('Literary Insertion [AXB Pattern] in Biblical Hebrew,' *VT* 33 [1983]) suggests one example of literary breakup system in Semitic language: 'A phenomenon of literary breakup has been noted in the "breakup of stereotype phrases by parallelism", first called to scholars' attention by E. Z. Melamed in 1961 and followed by schollars such as M. Dahood, D. N. Freedman, M. Z. Kaddari and others'; 'A and B stand for two words, phrases, clauses, or even discourses which constitute grammatically and/or semantically either a composite unit [AB] or a compound unit [A&B]; X is an affix, word, phrase, clause, or discourse which is inserted between A and B and yet limits the complex A-B *as a whole* grammatically or semantically' (468-469).

In this narrative, on the one hand, three parts (vv. 12-14, 19-24, 28-40) tell how Jesus was arrested and questioned by the high priest and Pilate, whereas, on the other hand, two parts (vv. 15-18, 25-27) tell the fact that Peter denied Jesus three times. To observe a grammatical aspect, the former parts begin with sentences which have οὖν; the latter parts begin with sentences which have δέ.

12:    Ἡ **οὖν** σπεῖρα καὶ . . .
15:       Ἠκολούθει **δὲ** τῷ Ἰησοῦ Σίμων πέτρος . . .
19:    ὁ **οὖν** ἀρχιερεὺς . . .
25:       Ἦν **δὲ** Σίμων πέτρος . . .
28:    Ἄγιουσιν **οὖν** . . .

Thus the narrator unfolds the passion narrative, clearly being aware of at least two different scenes.

In the two examples, the author unfolds the narrative, as if he expects the readers to watch two different scenes at the same time. Therefore, it seems possible to assume that a similar literary device might have been employed:

The Witness of John the Baptist in John 1:1-18

A: The Logos statement (1-5)
B: The Baptist's Witness (6-8)
A: The Logos (the Son) statement (9-14)
B: The Baptist's Witness (15)
A: The Son statement (16-18)

M. Hooker argues that references to John the Baptist occur as the turning-points of the context, based on her structural understanding of the prologue[19] :

A: (i) 1-5 (The Logos in relation to God; active in creation; as life which is light)

<6–8: Reference to John the Baptist>

(ii) 9-13 (The Light lightens men; but the world [created by him] did not accept him; those who did were made children of God through him)

B: (i) 14 (The incarnate Logos-his glory, full of grace and truth)

<15: Reference to John the Baptist>

(ii) 16-18 (Men have received of his fullness, and grace and truth have come through him; God, whom no one has seen, has been made known through him)

van der Watt rightly comments that the historical-critical interpreter might have interpreted the structural break between vv. 5 and 6 as an indication of different sources, while a structuralist might have seen it as an indication of a

---

[19] M. Hooker, 'John the Baptist and the Johannine Prologue,' *NTS* 16 (1970), 356-357.

shift in emphasis or as an indication of a dramatic event which is about to start.[20] C. K. Barrett also emphasizes the important theological function of the witness of John the Baptist in the prologue[21]:

> God, who, with his Logos, is eternally what he is, and is beyond definition, enters the world of time and space (and definition); first through a messenger, but secondly also in his own person... The word of verse 15 may be intended to convey the hint that Jesus before his public ministry had once been a follower of John, but they are so chosen as to express the subsequent emergence in time of one whose being spanned eternity before and after John... This means that the 'Baptist' verses were not an afterthought, thrown in injure the rival Baptist group, but part of a serious, connected, thought-out, theological purpose.[22]

The first statement about John the Baptist (vv. 6-8) indicates a shift in emphasis or a dramatic event which is about to start, and functions as a 'bridge' between the λόγος ἀσαρκός and the λόγος ἐνσαρκός. Furthermore, it functions to focus on the event of the coming of light, by making a clear distinction between true light (τὸ φῶς τὸ ἀληθινόν) and the Witness to it (οὐκ ἦν ἐηκεῖνος τὸ φῶς). The second statement about John the Baptist (v. 15) functions to remind the readers of the divine identity of the incarnated Logos (the pre-existence of the Son [πρῶτός μου ἦν]).[23]

The terminological and theological differences between the prologue and the rest of the Gospel have been considered as grounds for postulating later redactions.[24] However, our studies (ch. 8) will show a closer relationship between the prologue and the rest of the Fourth Gospel.[25]

6.2 Structural Analysis

6.2.1 Chiastic Structural Understanding

Efforts to describe the structure of the present form of the prologue have also been made apart from source analyses. N. W. Lund (1931) observes first a chiastic structure in the Johannine prologue.[26]

---

[20] J. van Der Watt, 'The Composition of the Prologue of John's Gospel: The Historical Jesus Introducing Divine Grace,' *WTJ* 57 (1995), 319-320.

[21] C. K. Barrett, *Prologue*, 22-25, 26-27.

[22] C. K. Barrett, *Prologue*, 23.

[23] See further discussions on the funcion of the statement of John the Baptist (§ 6.2.4.2).

[24] R. Schnackenburg, *John*, 225-226; R. Brown, *John*, 19.

[25] Cf. J. A. T. Robinson, 'The Relation of the Prologue to the Gospel of St. John,' *NTS* 9 (1962), esp. 122; E. Harris, *Prologue and Gospel: The Theology of the Fourth Evangelist* (JSNTSup 107; Sheffield: Sheffield Academic Press, 1994).

[26] N. W. Lund, 'The Influence of Chiasmus upon the Structure of the Gospels,' *ATR* 13 (1931), 42-46.

Lund's Chiastic Structural Understanding of John 1:1-18

A.   The eternal Logos and God (1-2)

  B.   The relationship of the Logos to the men of the OT (3-5, 9-10b)

    C.   The historical Logos rejected and received by men (10c-12)

      D.   True and false grounds of Sonship (13)

    C'.   The historical Logos dwelling among men and seen by them (14)

  B'.   The relationship of the Logos to believers in the NT (16-17a)

A'.   The eternal Logos in the bosom of the Father (17b-18)

He defines the nature of chiasmus as follows:

> 'According to its Greek origin the term designates a literary figure, or principle, which consists of "a placing crosswise" of words in a sentence. The term is used in rhethoric to designate an inversion of the order of words or phrases which are repeated or subsequently referred to in the sentence.'[27]

Since Lund's first observation, several scholars have attempted to seek a more reasonable list of parallel correspondences in the prologue.[28] Although Lunds omits vv. 6-8 and v. 15 from this list, recent scholars, who attempt to apply a chiastic structure to the prologue, consider these sections as important evidence of chiastic parallel correspondences.

The following Table shows the recent scholars' understanding of the chiastic structure in John 1:1-18 (the shadow indicates sections that are regarded as later additions of the original form of the prologue).

---

[27] N. W. Lund, *Chiasmus in the New Testament* (Chapel Hill: The University of North Carolina Press, 1942), 31.

[28] N. W. Lund, 'The Influence of Chiasmus,' 42-46; M. E. Boismard, *St. John's Prologue* (Westminster: Newman, 1957), 79-80; P. Lamarche, 'Le Prologue de Jean,' *RSR* 52 (1964), 529-532; A. Feuillet, *Le Prologue du Quatriéme Évangile* (Paris: Descleé de Brouwer, 1968), 160; P. Borgen, 'Observations on the Targumic Character of the Prologue of John,' 291; M. Hooker, 'John the Baptist and the Johannine Prologue,' *NTS* 16 (1969-1970), 357; R. A. Culpepper, 'The Pivot of John's Prologue,' *NTS* 27 (1980), 8; P. Ellis, *The Genius of John: A Composition -Critical Commentary on the Fourth Gospel* (Collegeville: Liturgical Press, 1984); J. Staley, 'The Structure of John's Prologue: Its Implication for the Gospel's Narrative Structure,' *CBQ* 48 (1986), 241-264; J. van der Watt, 'The Composition of the Prologue,' 330.

The Chiastic Structural Understandings of John 1:1-18

	1	2	3	4	5	6	7	8	9	10	11	12	13	14	15	16	17	18
Lund 1931	A		B			///	///	///		B		C	X	C'	///	B'		A'
Boismard 1953	A	B	C	D					E			X		E'	D'	C'	B'	A'
Lamarche 1964	A	B	C	D					E	X				E'	D'	C'	B'	A'
Feuillet 1968	A	B	C	D					E	F		F'		E'	D'	C'	B'	A'
Borgen 1970	A	B	C		C'					B'					A'			
Culpepper 1980	A	B	C	D					E	F		G[29]	F'	E'	D'	C'	B'	A'
P. Ellis 1984	A								B			X		B'		A'		
Staley 1986	A					B				C		X		C'	B'	A'		
Watt 1995	A		B			C			D					D'		C'		B'	A'

The possible parallel correspondences, which have been suggested by the chiastic structure, are as follows:

I. vv. 1 - 2: The eternal λόγος with God
 v. 18: The μονογενὴς θεὸς with the Father
 (Lund, Boismard, Lamarche, Feuillet, Culpepper, Ellis, Staley, Watt)

 vv. 1-2: ὁ λόγος - (ὁ) θεός
 vv. 14-18: ὁ λόγος - θεός
 (Borgen)

II. v. 4: The Logos as Life and Light
 v. 16: People received grace through the Logos
 (Lund, Boismard, Lamarche, Feuillet, Culpepper)

 v. 5: The primordial Light
 v. 6-9: The coming of the true Light
 (Borgen)

III. vv. 6-8: The Witness of John the Baptist
 v. 15: The Witness of John the Baptist
 (Boismard, Lamarche, Feuillet, Culpepper, Staley, Watt)

IV. v. 9b: The Logos as true light is coming to the world
 v. 14a: The Logos became flesh and dwelt in the world
 (Boismard, Lamarche, Feuillet, Culpepper, Ellis, Staley, Watt)

---

[29] This part is devided into three (g-h-g').

The correspondence between v. 1-2 and v. 18 has been suggested by many scholars. Both mention the intimate relationship between the Logos (the Son) and God (the Father). When P. Borgen sees the correspondence between vv. 1-2 and vv. 14-18, he may understand that the term 'Logos' itself indicates the motif of revelation. The proclamation of the Logos as God (v. 1) may be related to the revelation of the Father in the Son (or in the ministry of the Son) (v. 18). However, it should be noticed that each focus is different: i.e. the former presents 'the divine identity' of the Logos as God, whereas the latter argues 'the role' of the Son to reveal God (the Father). As far as these functions (the description of the divine identity, or the description of the role) are concerned, vv. 1-2 may find the other correspondences with vv. 10-11 and vv. 14cd-15. P. Borgen's structure is unique because it suggests the parallel between vv. 4-5 and vv. 6-9 (light motif). The parallel between vv. 4-5 and vv. 6-9 depicts a contrast between the scene of primordial light and the scene of the coming of light into history. However, if the light imagery (esp. τὸ φῶς τῶν ἀνθρώπων in vv. 4b, 6-9) exhibits the motif of saving revelation, then the topics (or contents) of revelation are mainly developed in vv. 14-18 (esp. vv. 16-18) (this will be discussed in our next chapter [ch. 7]).

Some other correspondences (see above list) do not seem certain. Firstly, as for the correspondence between v. 3 and v. 17,[30] πάντα δι᾽ αὐτοῦ ἐγένετο (v. 3) seems to correspond to ὁ κόσμος δι᾽ αὐτοῦ ἐγένετο (v. 10) and τὰ ἴδια (v. 11), since both refer to the work of creation, and allude to the relationship between the Logos and the world. As for the correspondence between vv. 4-5 and v. 16,[31] v. 5 should be separated from this correspondence, since there is no semantic correspondence between λαμβάνω (1:5) and καταλαμβάνω (1:16). Further, v. 5 gives a picture of the Genesis creation account that light shines in darkness, and it may allude to the relationship between the Logos as light and the world. Instead, it matches with the picture of the coming of the Logos as light into the world (vv. 9b, 14).

Concerning the absence of the correspondence to vv. 12-13, scholars have assumed these verses to be a pivot in the prologue: Lund locates the pivot in v. 13; Boismard, Ellis, and Stalay locate it in vv. 12-13; Lamarche locates it in vv. 10-13; and Culpepper locates it in v. 12c. However, it is still uncertain whether this section really functions as a pivot.[32] These problems occur

---

[30] Lund's parallel understanding is as follows: 'the relations of the Logos to the Cosmos and to the men of the OT' and 'the relations of the Logos to believers in the NT'; Boismard: 'His role of Creation' and 'Role of recreation'; J. Staley: 'Creation' and 'Re-Creation'; A. Culpepper: 'what came to be through the Word (Creation)' and 'what came to be through the Word (Grace and Truth)'; P. Ellis: 'all things made through him Life and Light,' and 'grace and truth through him grace and truth.'

[31] Lund, Boismard, Lamarche, Fevillet, Borgen, Culpepper.

[32] According to J. King's survey ('Prologue to the Fourth Gospel: Some Unsolved Problems,' *ET* 86 [1975], 372-375), there is little agreement as to the climactic section of

because they try to apply a perfect chiastic structure. As W. Watson suggests several types of chiasmus,[33] we should not necessarily attempt to find a perfect chiastic structure here.

6.2.2 Symmetric Parallel Structural Understanding

Not every scholar agrees that there is a chiastic structure in the Johannine prologue. R. Brown calls such a correspondence 'highly imaginative'[34]; M. Theobald judges previous chiastic approaches as 'zu gekünstelt'[35]; J. Louw also points out a tendency of chiastic approaches to obscure the real focus of the prologue.[36] Some have made efforts to determine another structural understanding of the prologue.

(1) W. Schmithals finds a symmetrical parallel correspondence between the former section (vv. 4-13) and the latter section (vv. 14-18).[37]

I. Prologue in Heaven 1 - 3					
II. Stanza on the Incarnated Logos	4 - 5	6 - 8	9 - 11	12a-b	12c - 13
III. Stanza on Incarnated Logos	14	15	16	17	18

However, this parallel correspondence seems rather partial, except the sections of vv. 6-8 and v. 15: e.g. vv. 4-5 indicates both the life and light motifs, and v. 14 partially corresponds; v. 18 and vv. 1-2 may constitute an *inclusio*. Since Schmithals is too much concerned with the order of the parallel correspondences, his model does not pay enough attention to syntactical cohesion of the text.

(2) M. Theobald divides the prologue syntactically into two (vv. 1-13; vv. 14-18) or three sections (vv. 1-5; vv. 6-13; and vv. 14-18).[38]

---

the prologue: Bernard, Morris locate it in v. 18; Hoskyns, in v. 17; Brown, in v. 16; Schnackenburg, March, Linders, in v. 14; and Barrett, in v. 13.

[33] W. G. E. Watson, *Classical Hebrew Poetry: A Guide to its techniques* (JSOT; Sheffield: Sheffield Academic Press, 1984), 202-203: E.g. 'mirror chiasmus' (a // -a); 'complete chiasmus' (A[a]B[b] // ba); 'split-member chiasmus' (ab-c // c'-a'b'); and 'partial chiasmus' (abc // c'b; ab-c // b'a'-c; a-bc // a-cb).

[34] R. Brown, *John*, 23.

[35] M. Theobald, *Im Anfang war das Wort. Textlinguistische Studie zum Johannesprolog* (Stuttgart: Katholisches Bibelwerk, 1983), 32.

[36] J. P. Louw, 'Christologiese himnes. Die Johannese Logos-Himne (John 1:1-18),' in J. H. Barkhuizen (ed.), *Hymni Christiani* (Pretoria: HTS, 1989), 41-42.

[37] W. Schmithals, 'Der Prolog des Johannesevangeliums,' 70 (1979), 41. Previously, Schmithals illustrates his structural understanding as follows: vv. 1-5 // v. 14 (Vorlage); vv. 6-8 // v. 15 (Täufer); vv. 9-11 // v. 16 (Dublette zur Vorlage); v. 12 ab // v. 17 (Vorlage); vv. 12c + 13 // v. 18 (Klimax) (31).

[38] M. Theobald, *Die Fleischwerdung des Logos. Studien zum Verhältnis des Johannesprologs zum Corpus des Evangeliums und zu 1 Joh* (Münster: Aschendorff, 1988), 182.

Teiltext 1									
	1			-		13		14	- 18

Teiltext 2									
	1	- 5	6		-	13		14	- 18

Teiltext 3									
	1 f	3 - 5	6	- 8	9	- 13	14	15	16 f	18

He supposes that the first part (vv. 1-5) functions as a prologue in the prologue[39]; the second section (vv. 6- 12 [13][40]) deals with the witness of John the Baptist and faith in Jesus[41]; and the third section (vv. 14-18) deals with the witness of the people who have faith in Jesus.[42] He illustrates his 'semantische Organisation' as follows[43]:

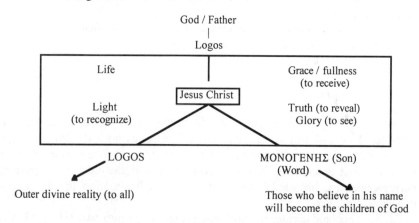

In this model, Theobald may suggest that the left side of the model indicates the aspect of vv. 1-12 [13]; the right side indicates the aspect of vv. 14-18 on the other.[44] Theobald also observes that this framework has already been alluded to in vv. 1-5,[45] while he includes vv. 1-5 in the former section as a whole.

---

[39] M. Theobald, *Fleischwerdung*, 211.

[40] M. Theobald (*Fleischwerdung*, 238-247) excludes v. 13 from the text.

[41] M. Theobald, *Fleischwerdung*, 229.

[42] M. Theobald, *Fleischwerdung*, 247.

[43] M. Theobald, *Fleischwerdung*, 262. This model is a revised one which is firstly presented in his former book, *Im Anfang war das Wort*, 37.

[44] In *Im Anfang* (31), Theobald suggests that the prologue can be divided into two main sections: I. A (vv. 1-2) ⇒ B (vv. 3-5) // C (vv. 6-8) // B' (vv. 9-13); II. D (v. 14) // C' (v. 15) // D' (vv. 16-17) ⇒ A' (v. 18).

[45] M. Theobald, *Fleischwerdung*, 216.

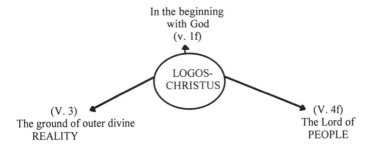

It seems quite admirable that Theobald does not necessarily attempt to seek perfect 'one-to-one' parallel correspondences between the former section (vv. 1-12 [13]) and the latter section (vv. 14-18), as Schmithals does (except between vv. 6-8 and v. 15, and between vv. 1-2 and v. 18). Rather he contrasts two different aspects of a christocentric argument. However, since he focuses on a 'theological structure,' his model cannot illustrate the literary sequence and the development of the plot in the prologue.

(3) M. Coloe's model[46] is similar to Schmithals'; however, she divides the former section (vv. 1-13) into four parts: A (vv. 1-2) = the word and God; B (vv. 3-5) = the story of the word's presence in the world; C (vv. 6-8) = prior witness of John the Baptist; and D (vv. 9-13) = the arrival of the word and response to the world. She observes that these four stories are repeated in order, as B' (v. 14) ⇒ C' (v. 15) ⇒ D' (vv. 16-17) ⇒ A' (v. 18). M. Coloe dismisses an arbitrary impression by presenting a looser correspondence between vv. 9-13 and vv. 16-17. However, it is still uncertain that v. 14 can be located in a direct correspondence to vv. 3-5.

6.2.3 Spiral Structural Understanding

It has been proposed by some scholars that the Johannine prologue consists of a three level spiral structure.[47]

(1) I. de la Potterie proposes 'La structure parallèle ou en spirale': i.e. the three progressive, or spiral developments in the prologue. In this structure, he observes parallel correspondences among the three divisions as follows[48]:

---

[46] M. Coloe, 'The Structure of the Johannine Prologue and Genesis 1,' *ABR* 45 (1997), 40-55.

[47] This idea is not necessarily new. See M. Lacan, 'Le Prologue de saint Jean. Ses thèmes, sa structure, son mouvement,' *LumVie*, 33 (1957), 91-110; M. Ridderbos, 'The Structure and Scope of the Prologue of the Gospel of John,' *NovT* 8 (1966), 180-201; S. Panimolle, 'Structura del Prologo,' in *Il Dono della Legge e la Grazia della Verità (Gv 1, 17)* (Roma 1973), 71-105.

[48] I. de la Potterie, 'Structure du Prologue de Saint Jean,' *NTS* 30 (1984), 358.

I	II	III
	THE BEGINNING	
A (vv.1-2) In the beginning was the word. The word was with God.	A (vv. 6-8) There was a man sent from God.	A (v. 15) He was before me.
	THE WORD SHINES PEOPLE	
B (vv. 3-5a) Life and Light of people.	B (v. 9) True light enlightens all people.	
	THE RESPONSE	
C (v. 5b) οὐ κατέλαβεν	C (vv. 10-12) οὐ παρέλαβον, ἔλαβον	C (v. 16) ἐλάβομεν
	THE OBJECT OF FAITH; THE FATHER'S ONLY SON	
	D (vv. 13-14) The word became flesh. The only Son came from the Father. Grace and Truth.	D (vv. 17-18) Jesus Christ. The only Son was in the bosom of the Father. Grace, Truth, Revelation.

Potterie observes, not double, but triple parallel correspondences. However, since he attempts to find an ideal symmetric parallel correspondence, his comparison sometimes becomes partial or inconsistent: e.g. vv. 1-2 and v. 15 are comparable on the correspondence of the theme of the pre-existence, and vv. 6-8 and v. 15 are comparable on the basis of reference to the witness of John the Baptist, while the relationship between vv. 1-2 and vv. 6-8 on the terminological correspondence (πρὸς τὸν θεόν; παρὰ θεοῦ)[49] seems partial; the correspondence between vv. 3-5a and v. 9 is partial; the semantic correspondence between λαμβάνω (1:5) and καταλαμβάνω (1:16) is ambiguous; and the division after v. 14 is rather artificial.

(2) G. Mlakuzhyil also considers the spiral structure of the prologue.[50] He proposes a unique pattern of sequence: a ⇒ b ⇒ c ⇒ b' ⇒ c'.

a*   *(1:1-5): The Divine, Creative, Revelatory Word*
a   (1-2): The divine Word with God
   b   (3ab): The mediation of the divine Word in creation
     c   (3c-5): The life-giving, revelatory Word opposed
  b*   *(1:6-8): The Baptist's Mission of Testimony to the Revelatory Word*
     c*   *(1:9-14): The Revelatory, Regenerative, Incarnate Word*
     c'   (9-11): The revelatory Word rejected

---

[49] De la Potterie, 'Structure,' 360.

[50] G. Mlakuzhyil, *The Christocentric Literary Structure of the Fourth Gospel* (Rome: Editrice Pontificio Istitute Biblico, 1987), 131-135.

d (12-13): The mediation of the revelatory Word in regeneration
  e (14): The incarnate, revelatory Word contemplated
b** *(1:15): The Baptist's Testimony to the Divine, Incarnate Word*
 c** *(1:16-18): The Incarnate, Revelatory, Divine Word*
  e' (16): The incarnate, revelatory Word participated
   f (17): The mediation of Jesus Christ in revelation
    g (18): The only divine revealer of God

Mlakuzhyil's model rightly suggests that the theme of vv. 3c-5 (the life-giving, revelatory Word) is developed in the two sections (vv. 9-14 and vv. 16-18). It is also noteworthy that two statements of the witness of John the Baptist (vv. 6-8 and v. 15) play an important role to introduce key sections (vv. 9-14 and 16-18): i.e. b (JB) ⇒ c (key) ⇒ b' (JB) ⇒ c' (key). However, it does not seem probable to link vv. 6-8 and v. 15 to v. 3. Moreover, it seems problematic to think that the opening section (vv. 1-2) does not have any correspondences.

6.2.4 Tripartite Parallel Structure: A Proposal

The attempt to see a chiastic structure and a symmetric structure tend to divide the Johannine prologue into two large units. However, it is possible for the parallel units to have more than two parts in the context. C. H. Giblin observes 'the tripartite narrative structure' in the Fourth Gospel.[51] Giblin divides the main part of the narrative of the Fourth Gospel into three parts (1:19-4:54; 5:1-10:42; 11:1-20:29), and argues that the author of the Gospel develops a given theological motif by successively restating it in three parts.[52] As E. Nida observes,[53] there seems to be a certain literary style in the Fourth Gospel, such as a 'tangential technique of spiraling,' or a 'successively restating of the themes.' Namely, the author of the Fourth Gospel might have used this technique to restate theological motifs in the three units. Several scholars (Lacan, Ridderbos, de la Potterie, Panimolle, Mlakuzhyil)[54] basically agree on the threefold dimensions, although each observation on the tripartite corrrespondences is varied.

The First Stanza: John 1:1-5

The literary character of John 1:1-5 is unique. It is composed of a terrace pattern parallelism (a word prominent in one line is taken up in the next line [often as subject or first word]), which gives a nimble rhythm to this part.

---

[51] C. H. Giblin, 'The Tripartite Narrative Structure of John's Gospel,' *Bib* 71 (1990), 449-68.

[52] C. H. Giblin, 'The Tripartite,' 463-465.

[53] E. A. Nida, 'Rhetoric and the Translator: With Special Reference to John 1,' *BT* 33 (1982), 327.

[54] M. Theobald's model does not disagree with the threefold dimension theory.

1-2 Ἐν ἀρχῇ ἦν ὁ λόγος,
  καὶ ὁ λόγος ἦν πρὸς τὸν θεόν,
    καὶ θεὸς ἦν ὁ λόγος.
      οὗτος ἦν ἐν ἀρχῇ πρὸς τὸν θεόν.
4-5 ἐν αὐτῷ ζωὴ ἦν,
  καὶ ἡ ζωὴ ἦν τὸ φῶς τῶν ἀνθρώπων·
    καὶ τὸ φῶς ἐν τῇ σκοτίᾳ φαίνει,
      καὶ ἡ σκοτία αὐτὸ οὐ κατέλαβεν.

In vv.1-2 there is a unique combination of chiastic structure and terrace pattern.

A	ἐν ἀρχῇ				
B		ἦν			
C1			ὁ λόγος,		
C2			καὶ ὁ λόγος		
D				ἦν	
E					πρὸς τὸν θεόν,
E'					καὶ θεὸς
D'				ἦν	
C2'			ὁ λόγος.		
C1			οὗτος		
B'		ἦν			
A'	ἐν ἀρχῇ				πρὸς τὸν θεόν.

The themes of the pre-existent Logos (ἐν ἀρχῇ ἦν [vv. 1a and 2a]) who is intimate with God (ἦν πρὸς τὸν θεόν [vv. 1b and 2b]) are restated in emphatic form. The divine nature of the Logos as θεὸς (v. 1c) is interestingly sandwiched by two πρὸς τὸν θεόν phrases. It may imply that while the focus is on the divine identity of the Logos as θεὸς, the identity of the Logos who is in intimate relationship with God is also affirmed.

Verse 3 refers to the relationship between the Logos and the world, and a mirror chiasmus emphasizes the lordship of the Logos as Creator.

A	πάντα	
B		δι' αὐτοῦ ἐγένετο
-B		χωρὶς αὐτοῦ ἐγένετο
-A		οὐδὲ ἕν ὃ γέγονεν[55]

---

[55] According to the text apparatus of NA [27], there are three readings for verse 3: 1) οὐδὲ ἕν is replaced by οὐδέν; 2) ὃ γέγονεν is joined with the preceding sentence; and 3) ὃ γέγονεν is joined with the following sentence. The UBS text apparatus includes reading Number One in both categories of the other two and mainly treats it as the punctuation problem, categorizing as follows: οὐδέν. ὁ γέγονεν ἐν; οὐδέν ˘ὁ γέγονεν ˘ ἐν; οὐδέν ὁ γέγονεν. ἐν. Reading Number One is supported by the earliest Alexandrian Manuscript: Π[55] [date:II] and Å* [(IV]. In the Fourth Gospel, there are fifteen examples where οὐδείς is used in the accusative case, and also it comes in the last part of the sentence (5:30; 6:63; 8:15 [οὐδένα], 23; 9:33; 10:41;

Verses 4-5 composes a terrace pattern parallelism as previously observed. However, v. 4 and v. 5 should be distinguished since the former takes the verb εἰμί and states the role of the Logos as life and light for the people (τῶν ἀνθρώπων). The latter illustrates a picture of the Logos which shines its glory in darkness. It seems to be an illustration of the glorious existence of the Logos (perhaps in pre-existent stage).

John 1:1-5 has a Logos-centric literary structure which argues that (1) before the creation of the world, the Logos existed (pre-existence); (2) the Logos was in intimate relationship with God (the intimacy with God); (3) through the Logos, the whole world came into existence (Creator); (4) in the Logos there is life (the motif of the life-giver); (5) the Logos holds the role as light; (6) the Logos is radiating its glory in darkness; (7) the darkness has never overcome it.[56] The first three themes (1-4a) focus on the divine identity of the Logos (the pre-existence, the intimacy with God, the lordship as Creator, and life). The life motif (4) may also depicts the role of the Logos (as the life-giver). The light in vv. 4-5 seems to have several functions in the context: i.e. the light in v. 4b depicts 'the role' of the Logos as light for the people (in the meaning of revelation), whereas v. 5 describes a scene that light (primordial light) shines in darkness, alluding to the Genesis creation account (Gen 1:3-5). It is a picture of the glorious existence of the Logos (in the pre-existent stage). This picture (light in the pre-existent stage) seems to be contrasted with the picture of the incarnation of light in vv. 6-9. Thus the thematic structure of John 1:1-5 can be illustrated as follows:

11:49; 12:19; 14:30; 15:5; 16:23; 18:9 [οὐδένα], 20,31 [οὐδένα]; 21:3). Thus reading Number One is one of the strong candidates; however, it makes no difference to its meaning. The important problem here is whether ὃ γέγονεν should be joined with the preceding sentence or with the following sentence. Another textual problem, that is the replacement of ἦν to ἐστίν, is also related to this problem. If the scribe chose reading Number Three, he would change the tense from ἦν to ἐστίν. In this case the subject of ἦν becomes ὃ γέγονεν, so that it is natural to take the present tense. However, ἦν is supported by many strong evidences(Π[66, 75], A [V], B [IV], C[V]); and its translation, 'what came into being was life in him' is awkward, since if 'what came into being' were 'the Life,' it would not match well with the next statement,'the Life was the light of men.' Although reading Number Two has only two early MSS (bo [IV]; Å[c] [VI]), this reading is the best reading in the literary context.

[56] As for the translation of καταλαμβάνω, there are two main understandings: (1) 'to comprehend' or 'to receive' (Cyril of Alexandria, the Latin tradition); and (2) 'to overcome' (Origen and the majority of the Greek Fathers). In the NT, καταλαμβάνω is used 14 times. On the one hand, when it means 'to comprehend,' it seems to take the middle voice: Acts 4:13; 25:25; Eph 3:18. On the other hand, when it means 'to overcome' or 'to win,' it takes the active or passive voice (John 8:3, 4; 12:35; 1Cor 9:24; Phil 3:13; 1Th 5:4). Bauer (412-413) also classified its meaning by its voice. The nuance of 12:35 is similar to that of John 1:5: 'darkness may not overtake you.' John 6:17 has a variant which replaced σκοτία ἤδη ἐγεγόνει by κατέλαβεν δε αὐτοὺς ἡ σκοτία (א, D). It has also the same nuance just as, 'the darkness may not overtake someone.' Namely, ἡ σκοτία αὐτὸ οὐ κατέλαβεν (1:5b) can be translated as 'darkness has not overcome it.'

DIVINE IDENTITY:
Pre-existence of the Logos (1a, 2a)
Intimacy of the Logos with God (1b, 2b)
Lordship of the Logos (Creator) (3-4a)

    ROLE:
    (a) The Logos as LIFE (4a)
    (b) The Logos as LIGHT (4b)

        SCENE:
        The Light shines in Darkness (universe) (5a)
        The superiority of Light against the Darkness (5b)

The Second Stanza: John 1:6-13

The second stanza begins with a historical narrative form (e.g. Judg 13:2; 19; 1 Sam 1:1)[57] which is rather distinct from previous section. It may indicate a shift from primordial narrative to history in emphasis or a dramatic event which is about to start. After the description of the Genesis creation account, the Johannine prologue refers to the coming of John the Baptist. It should be noted that John 1:19-37 dramatically describes how the focus shifts from John the Baptist to Jesus. The prologue attempts to mention the coming of John the Baptist because historically John came before Jesus, while Jesus is said to be preexistent and therefore 'before' John (vv. 1-3, 15). Therefore, it is possible to assume that the statement of John the Baptist functions as a 'bridge' between the λόγος ἀσαρκός and the λόγος ἐνσαρκός.[58] There is another function of the statement that we must not ignore. That is a function to specify the meaning of φῶς (vv. 4b-5). First of all, the figure of John the Baptist may be understood by the readers along the lines of the Isaianic prophecy (e.g. John 1:23 [Isa 40:3]; cf. John 1:29, 36 [Isa 53:7]). Secondly, while the relationship between ὁ λόγος and John the Baptist is given a focus, φῶς is defined as a messianic figure or as saving revelation: i.e. οὐκ ἦν ἐκεῖνος (personal figure) τὸ φῶς, ἀλλ᾽ ἵνα μαρτυρήσῃ περὶ τοῦ φωτός (personal figure, contrasted to ἐκεῖνος) (John 1:8).[59] This definition of φῶς governs the character of ὁ λόγος in the rest of the prologue.

The historical event of the coming of John the Baptist in v. 6 (cf. Isa 40:3) is in contrast with the event of the coming of the true light in v. 9 (cf. Isa 40:5

---

[57] R. Brown, *John*, 27.

[58] Cf. van Der Watt, 'The Composition,' 320.

[59] In Isaiah, the Servant of Yahweh is already associated with the image of light (42:6; 49:6; 51:4. Cf. Isa 9:1-7 [Matt 4:12-16]; 42:6-7 [Luke 4:18; cf. Acts 13:47]; 60:1-3 [Eph 5:6-14].

[LXX]⁶⁰; 9:1-7 [Matt 4:12-16]; 60 [Eph 5:6-14]).⁶¹ Both v. 6 and v. 9 begin with the intransitive verb without a conjunction (ἐγένετο [v. 6]; ἦν . . . ἐρχόμενον [v. 9]). The former takes an aorist, and the latter is constructed as a periphrastic imperfect,⁶² which may indicate a past action of duration. Secondly, both John the Baptist and the light are said to have come (ἦλθεν εἰς μαρτυρίαν [v. 7]; ἐρχόμενον εἰς τὸν κόσμον [v.9]); however, of the former it is said that he was not light, but bore witness to the light (v. 7-8), while the latter is modified by τὸ ἀληθινόν (v. 9), which emphasizes the distinction between the light and its Witness (John the Baptist). Thirdly, John came into the world, so that πάντες πιστεύσωσιν (v. 7b). On the other hand, true light came to shine on πάντα ἄνθρωπον (v. 9b). Thus the historical event of the coming of John the Baptist (vv. 6-8) is obviously contrasted with the other event of the coming of the true light (v. 9). Moreover, this description of the two historical events seems to be contrasted with the previous description of the Logos as a primordial light, which shines in the darkness (perhaps in pre-existent stage) in v. 5 (i.e. it is a contrast between the λόγος ἀσαρκός and the λόγος ἐνσαρκός).

The subject of v. 10 may be the same as v. 9 (i.e. τὸ φῶς); however, αὐτόν (masculine) of v. 10 indicates that the real subject is still ὁ λόγος, or John may already have been thinking of alluding to the incarnate Christ.⁶³ The prologue looks back to the divine identity of the Logos (vv. 10ab, 11a), with an expanded meaning of previous statements (vv. 1-3). That is, the pre-existence of the Logos (ἐν τῷ κόσμῳ ἦν, v. 10a)⁶⁴ and the lordship of the Logos as the Creator (ὁ κόσμος δι' αὐτοῦ ἐγένετο, v. 10b) are recalled, and are contrasted with the people's unfaithful response (vv. 10c, 11b).⁶⁵ There is a shift in the mentioning of the world (e.g. πάντα) from v. 3 to vv. 10-11 as follows:

v. 3	πάντα	The totality of creation
v. 10a	ὁ κόσμος	The created world, including human beings
v. 10b	ὁ κόσμος	The created world, focusing on human beings
v. 11ab	οἱ ἴδιοι	His people

---

⁶⁰ Isa 40:3 [LXX]: Καὶ ὀφθήσεται ἡ δόξα κυρίου καὶ ὄψεται πᾶσα σάρξ τὸ σωτήριον τοῦ θεοῦ ὅτι κυρίου ἐλάλησεν. The Masoretic text does not have the phrase, 'the salvation of God.'

⁶¹ Cf. J. Painter, 'Christology and the History of the Johannine Community in the Prologue of the Fourth Gospel,' *NTS* 30 (1984), 469.

⁶² Cf. Zerwick, 362.

⁶³ L. Morris, *The Gospel According to John* (NICNT; Grand Rapids: Eerdmans, 1971), 95.

⁶⁴ The εἰμί verb with an imperfect tense implies the continuous existence of the Logos as the Light from the beginning (cf. vv. 1a and 5a).

⁶⁵ See the contrast between God's grace and people's unfaithfulness in the prophetic tradition (Hos 11:1; Jer 3:19; Isa 1:2, 4; 30:1; 45:11-12; 63:8-10, 16; 64:8), as well as in the wisdom tradition (Prov. 1:20-32; Job 28; Sir 24:7; Bar 3:10-13, 29-36; 1 En 42:1-3).

The focus clearly shifts to the incarnated Logos and people's response to the coming of the Logos (αὐτὸν οὐκ ἔγνω [v. 10]; αὐτὸν οὐ παρέλαβον [v. 11]; δὲ ἔλαβον αὐτόν [v. 12]). Δέ (v. 12), after two negative sentences (vv. 10-11), indicates a shift of the focus into a climactic statement. That is to say, the prologue tells of the new creation or the new birth of people as the children of God (v. 12-13). The point is that this new creation is made available by the name (of the Son) (v. 12), and that this new birth is from God (v. 13). The phrase 'he gave power to become children' (ἔδωκεν αὐτοῖς ἐξουσίαν) (v. 12) indicates that it was revealed as an (eschatological) gift to the people. Moreover, the prologue states that it was given through the name of the Son (Logos) (v. 12) who had been given the authority to give life to them (cf. v. 4). Thus, it is possible to say that the new creation is associated with the description of the role of the Logos as life.

SCENE:
The coming of the witness to Light (6-8)
is contrasted to
the coming of True Light (9b)

DIVINE IDENTITY:
Pre-existence of the Logos (10a) and
Lordship of the Logos (as Creator)
    are contrasted to
the people's unfaithful response (10-11)

GIFT: New Creation through the Name of the Son
New birth of the children of God.
through the revealed name of the Son (12-13)

The Third Stanza: John 1:14-18

Verse 13 functions as a supplement to the climactic statement (v. 12), with an emphasis on the divine begetting (ἐκ θεοῦ ἐγεννήθησαν),[66] and its emphatic form (οὐκ ... οὐδὲ ... οὐδὲ ... ἀλλ'; cf. v. 8) gives the readers an impression that the narrative sequence should stop here. A new stanza, therefore, begins from verse 14, with a description of the historical event of the coming and dwelling of the Logos among people.[67] There seems to be a shift in the scenes which describe the way the Logos exists, and the response of the world (v. 5 ⇒ v. 9 ⇒ v. 14):

SCENE in the 1st Stanza:
(a) The Logos gloriously exists in darkness (in the picture of Genesis ch. 1) (5a);
(b) Darkness has never overcome it (5b).

---

[66] John highlights some important statements with supplemental sentences (cf. vv. 2, 3b, 5b, 8, 13, 14cd).

[67] If verse 14 is read with vv. 12-13, it may lose a grammatical coordinate clause of ὅτι clauses of vv. 16-17.

SCENE in the 2nd Stanza:
(a) True light was coming to the world (9b);
(b) John bore witness to the light (6-8).

SCENE in the 3rd Stanza:
(a) The Logos became flesh and historically dwelt among the people (14a);
(b) People saw his glory (14b).

The prologue reminds the readers of the divine identity of the incarnated Logos again (vv. 14cd and 15; cf. vv. 1-3 and v. 10), and it is declared in the testimonies of both believers (vv. 14cd) and John the Baptist (v. 15).[68]

DIVINE IDENTITY in the 3rd Stanza:
(b) Believers' testimony: Intimate relationship between the Son and the Father (ἐθεασάμεθα ... δόξαν ὡς μονογεοῦς [v. 14cd]).
(a) Baptist's testimony: Pre-existence of the Son (πρῶτός μου ἦν [v. 15]).

Cf.   *DIVINE IDENTITY in the 1st Stanza:*
(a) Pre-existence of the Logos (1a, 2a)
(b) Intimacy of the Logos with God (1b, 2b)
(c) Lordship of the Logos (Creator) (3)

DIVINE IDENTITY in the 2nd Stanza:
(a) Pre-existence of the Logos (10a)
(c) Lordship of the Logos (as Creator) (10b).

It is interesting to observe how the three topics of the divine identity of the Logos in the first stanza (a, b, c) are developed in the other two sections: i.e. the second stanza focuses on (a) and (c); the third stanza deals with (b) and (a). The last two stanzas, therefore, restate perfectly all the three topics which appear in the first stanza:

1st Stanza: (a)
                       (b)
                              (c)
2nd Stanza: (a)
                              (c)
3rd Stanza: (b)
                  (a)

The description of the glory of the Son as πλήρης χάριτος καὶ ἀληθείας in v. 14 is expanded or developed in vv. 16-18,[69] particularly in the picture of the

---

[68] Most of the Johannine scholars have tried to find a correspondence between vv. 6-8 and v. 15; however, it seems better to consider the thematic functions of both statements of John the Baptist (vv. 6-8 and v. 15) in each context. The former functions to highlight the coming of the True Light with historical narrative form; the latter functions to recall the divine identity of the incarnated Logos.

theophany in the Exodus event,[70] which has already been alluded to in the beginning of the third stanza (ἐσκήνωσεν ἐν ἡμῖν, v. 14).

In the last three verses, the prologue climactically states the role (or earthly mission) of the Son of God to reveal the Father, i.e. 'full of grace and truth' (vv. 16-17) and to make the Father known (v. 18). The motif of the 'revelation' may be associated with the light motif (τὸ φῶς τῶν ἀνθρώπων in v. 4b) which presents the role of the Logos.[71] The parallels (as an *inclusio*) between v. 1 and v. 18 can be observed: 'with God' is parallel to 'in the bosom of the Father'; 'the proclamation of the Logos as God' may be parallel to 'the role of the Son to reveal the Father.' The former proclaims that the Logos was God as a description of the divine identity of the Logos (v. 1), whereas the latter argues the Son (and his ministry) was the perfect revelation of the Father (v. 18). The phrase 'from his fullness have we all received' (ἐκ τοῦ πληρώματος αὐτοῦ ἡμεῖς πάντα ἐλάβομεν) (v. 16) indicate that this revelation of grace and truth, or glory, was given as an (eschatological gift) to the people. Moreover, the prologue states that it was given through Jesus Christ (διὰ Ἰησοῦ Χριστοῦ) (v. 17) who is in the bosom of the Father. Thus, vv. 16-18 refers to the role of the Son as saving revelation, as well as to the gift which was brought through his ministry. Therefore, vv. 12-13 and vv. 16-18 indicate a parallel correspondence: i.e. both make statements on the eschatological gifts, and on the role of the Logos (the Son) to make them available to believers. Therefore, the thematic flow of the third stanza can be illustrated as follows:

SCENE:
The Logos became Flesh and dwelt among people.
People saw the glory of the Son (v. 4ab)

DIVINE IDENTITY:
b) Believers' testimony: the intimate relationship between the Son and the Father (ἐθεασάμεθα . . . δόξαν ὡς μονογεοῦς [v. 14cd]).
a) Baptist's testimony: the pre-existence of the Son (πρῶτός μου ἦν [v. 15]).

GIFT: Perfect Revelation of God through the Sonship
The perfect revelation of grace and truth in the (Glory) Son,
in contrast with the giving of the Mosaic Law (vv. 16-17).

The only Son of God
who is in the bosom of the Father

revealed the Father (18).

---

[69] See how three words (πλήρης, χάριτος, ἀληθείας) in v. 14 are restated in order in vv. 16-17 (πληρώματος, χάριν ἀντὶ χάριτος, ἡ χάρις καὶ ἡ ἀλήθεια).

[70] Cf. A. Hanson, 'John 1.14-18 and Exodus xxxiv,' *NTS* 23 (1976-1977), 90-101.

[71] The parallel between the light imagery and the motif of the revelation is suggested by several scholars (e.g. Lund, Boismard, Lamarche, Feuillet, Culpepper, Watt).

6.3 Summary and Conclusions

The main points, which have been suggested by our structural understanding of the Johannine prologue, are as follows:

(1) It seems probable to observe a threefold division in the prologue, as several scholars have already suggested (e.g. Lacan, Ridderbos, de la Potterie, Panimolle, Mlakuzhyil), rather than a twofold division (according to Lund, Boismard, Lamarche, Fevillet, Borgen, Culpepper, P. Ellis, Staley, Schmithals, Watt, Theobald, Coloe). The description of the divine identity of the Logos (the pre-existence of the Logos; the intimacy of the Logos with God [or oneness motif]; the lordship of the Logos as the Creator) is clearly restated three times (a-b-c [vv. 1-3] ⇒ a-c [v. 10] ⇒ b-a [v. 14cd-15]). The description of the existence of the Logos and the response of the world are also depicted three times (v. 5 ⇒ v. 9 ⇒ v. 14).

(2) Some scholars (e.g. Hooker, van der Watt, Barrett) have pointed out that references to John the Baptist occur at what may be described as the turning-points of the text. Our structural understanding makes their functions clearer. Namely, the first statement about John the Baptist (vv. 6-8) indicates a shift in emphasis or a dramatic event which is about to start, and functions as a 'bridge' between the λόγος ἀσαρκός and the λόγος ἐνσαρκός. It specifies the meaning of φῶς along the lines of the Isaianic prophecy (vv. 4b-5). Furthermore, it functions to focus on the event of the coming of light, by making the distinction clear between true light (τὸ φῶς τὸ ἀληθινόν) and the Witness to it (οὐκ ἦν εηκεῖνος τὸ φῶς). The second statement about John the Baptist (v. 15) functions to remind the readers of the divine identity of the incarnated Logos (the pre-existence of the Son [πρῶτός μου ἦν]), accompanying another reminder of an intimate relationship between the Son and the Father (μονογενοῦς παρὰ πατρός), which is given by believers' testimony (v. 14cd). The statement of John the Baptist in v. 15 also has a literary effect in keeping the balance in the parallelism of the descriptions of the divine identity of the Logos (a-b-c [vv. 1-3] ⇒ a-c [v. 10] ⇒ b-a [v. 14cd-15]). Therefore, while keeping the scene of the testimony of John the Baptist open (v. 6-8 ⇒ v. 15 ⇒ v. 19-34), the prologue assigns different functions to each statement (vv. 6-8 and v. 15).

(3) Scholars differ at the point where the climactic statement is to be found in the Johannine prologue: in v. 12 (and v. 13) (Barrett, Lund, Boismard, Lamarche, Ellis, Staley, Culpepper); in v. 14 (Schnackenburg, Marsh, Lindars); in v. 16 (Brown); in v. 17 (Hoskyns), and in v. 18 (Bernard, Morris). However, our structural understanding suggests that key themes which occur in the first stanza (vv. 1-5) gradually are expanded and developed in the two other stanzas (vv. 6-13; vv. 14-18). In particular, the last two stanzas (vv. 6-13; vv. 14-18) take the same literary sequence (as will be shown in the

following diagram): the scene of the coming of the Logos is described (vv. 6-9; v. 14ab), the divine identity of the Logos (the Son) is affirmed (vv. 10-11; vv. 14cd-15), and the gifts which were made available through the Logos (the Son) are climactically described twice (vv. 12-13; vv. 16-17) in the prologue.

APPENDIX: TRIPARTITE PARALLEL STRUCTURE

I. First Stanza (John 1:1-5)

    A¹. DIVINE IDENTITY:
Pre-existence of the Logos (1a, 2a)
The Logos as God (1c)
Intimacy of the Logos with God (1b, 2b)
Lordship of the Logos, Life (Creator) (3-4a)

        B¹. ROLE:
        (a) The Logos as LIFE (4a)
        (b) The Logos as LIGHT (4b)

            C¹. SCENE:
            Light shines in darkness (universe) (5a);
            The superiority of Light against the darkness (5b).

II. Second Stanza (John 1:6-13)   Shift: λόγος ἀσαρκός to λόγος ἐνσαρκός

            C². SCENE:
            The coming of the witness to the Light (6-8)
            is contrasted to the coming of the True Light (9b).

    A². DIVINE IDENTITY:
Pre-existence of the Logos (10a).
The Lordship of the Logos (as Creator) is contrasted to
the people's unfaithful response (10-11).

    B². GIFT: New Creation through the Name of the Son
New birth of the children of God
through the revealed name of the Son (12-13).

III. Third Stanza (John 1:14-18)

            C³. SCENE:
            The Logos became Flesh and dwelt among people.
            People saw the glory of the Son (14ab).

    A³. DIVINE IDENTITY:
b) The Believers' testimony: Intimate relationship between the Son and the Father
(ἐθεασάμεθα . . . δόξαν ὡς μονογεοῦς [v. 14cd]).
a) Baptist's testimony: Pre-existence of the Son (πρῶτός μου ἦν [v. 15]).

        B³. GIFT: Perfect Revelation of God through the Son
        The perfect revelation of God in the Son (Glory)
        in contrast with the revelation through Moses (16-17).

The only Son of God
who is in the bosom of the Father

    revealed the Father (18).

Chapter 7

Thematic Analysis on the Johannine Prologue

This chapter attempts a thematic analysis of the Johannine prologue, based on the results of our research of early Jewish creation accounts (chs. 2-5) and our literary structural understanding of the prologue (ch. 6). Since previous scholarship has searched for a figure equivalent to the personified Logos in the Johannine prologue, scholars have ignored the background of the Genesis creation account. Our question is, however, 'Are there not any theological significance in John when he refers to the Genesis creation account?,' 'Have we not lost central theological concern of the Johannine prologue when we ignore the background of the Genesis creation account?'

Our previous research shows that in early Jewish tradition, references are often made to the Genesis creation account, and that these references play a very important role in each theological context. Therefore, this new chapter attempts to find a correspondence between the way the Genesis creation account is referenced in early Jewish tradition and John's attempt to depict the identity of the Son in the Johannine prologue.

7.1 John 1:1-5

7.1.1 ὁ λόγος and ἀρχή

It is widely accepted that the opening words, ἐν ἀρχῇ (John 1:1), correspond to the beginning words of the Genesis creation account, בְּרֵאשִׁית (Gen 1:1; ἐν ἀρχῇ [LXX]).[1] The term, 'beginning' (ἀρχή in Greek), often appears in contexts where reference is made to God's work of creation (Gen 1:1; Prov 8:22; Sir 24:9; 39:25; Jub 2:2; 4 Ezra 3:4; 6:38 cf. 6:1-6; 2 En 24:2; Ant ch. 1; Mt 19:4; 24:21; Mk 10:6; 13:19; 2 Pet 3:4; Heb 1:10; Rev 3:14).

In Jewish creation accounts, reference is made to 'the beginning' (רֵאשִׁית) of Genesis 1:1 in contexts where the sovereignty of God is the focus. 4 Ezra 6:6 retells the Genesis creation account, by stating, '*In the beginning* (*Initio*) of the circle of the earth, . . . I thought (*cogitavi*), and these things were made *through me alone* (*per me solum*), *and not through another*.' In this context,

---

[1] In the Fourth Gospel, the combination of ἐν and ἀρχή appears only here, while in other cases, ἐξ and ἀπό are attached to ἀρχή (6:64; 8:25, 44; 15:27; 16:4). In the NT, there are two examples of ἐν ἀρχῇ (Acts 11:15; Phil 4:5).

both the idea of 'the beginning' and 'the sole Creator' are equally essential to the description of the unique identity of God. 2 Bar 21:4 states that God is the Creator 'who *from the beginning* of the world called that which did not yet exist and they obey him.' The term 'the beginning' is related to the idea of 'creation *ex nihilo*.' 2 En 24:2 [J] also focuses on the unique identity of God, who produces the creatures *ex nihilo*: 'Before (прѣже: *prěže*) anything existed, *from the beginning* (нспръва: *nsprŭva*), whatever exists I created from the non-existent, and from the invisible into the visible.'

The term, 'the beginning,' is related to the divine attributes in some contexts. Jewish wisdom tradition (cf. Sir 24:9; Wisd 9:9) describes the sovereignty of God who providentially planned and produced creatures *ex nihilo*, by focusing on the divine nature of the pre-existent wisdom. In other contexts, reference to 'the beginning' is related to the idea of the word of creation.

> O sovereign Lord, *did you not speak at the beginning* (*ab initio*) when you formed the earth? (4 Ezra 3:4).

> O Lord, you *spoke at the beginning* (*ab initio*) of creation, and said on the first day (*in primo*), 'Let heaven and earth be made,' and *your word* (*verbum*) accomplished the work (4 Ezra 6:38).

On the one hand, with relation to the idea of 'the beginning,' the divine wisdom focuses on God's providential plan, while, on the other hand, the divine word highlights the mighty power (or action) of God. Thus, the term, 'the beginning,' easily reminds the readers of Genesis 1:1, while it is related to the description of the unique identity of God.

In the Johannine prologue, the narrative begins with ἐν ἀρχῇ, and it tells that there was the word before all things happened. It seems to correspond to the claim of the narrative of the very first day of the Genesis creation account that ויאמר אלהים יהי אור ויהי אור. As the Jewish creation accounts speculate on the divine identity in the term of 'the beginning,' or 'the beginning of all creation,' the Johannine prologue might be concerned with the divine identity of the Logos, by rendering ἐν ἀρχῇ, which would remind readers of Genesis 1:1. It is also common in Jewish creation accounts that the motif of 'the word of creation' is combined with the term, 'the beginning' (the description of the beginning of the world). Therefore, at the beginning of the narrative, John starts to describe the divine nature of the Logos on the ground of the Genesis creation account.

It is also worth considering M. Hengel's suggestion that the very beginning, before the six days of creation (John 1:1) corresponds to the last day of Christ, the Cross.

> 'At the beginning of Jesus' prayer for the disciples we read: "I have finished the work (*ergon*) that you gave me to do (*poiein*)." (17:4) There is a clear allusion with all this to

Gen 2:2 (LXX): "And on the sixth day God finished his work (*erga*) which he had done (*epoiesen*)." God's works of Creation and Salvation, which begins with ἐν ἀρχῇ in Gen 1:1 and John 1:1, is "finished" in the death of the Son on Golgotha at evening of the sixth day. There follows, according to John 19:31, the enigmatic "great Sabbath" - for the dead Jesus, it is a "day of rest" in the grave.' [2]

The God, who had begun the creation of the world with his word, finished his salvific work with the cross of the Son. It should not be ignored that the expanse of idea from Creation to Salvation depicts the scope of the sovereignty of God. It is symbolic that the last day or the completion of the earthly ministry of the Son was the day before 'the great Sabbath.' In addition, J. Frey observes a typological correspondence between Gen 1:1-2:4 and John 1:19-2:11.[3] It is an interesting point that, if the manifestation of his glory in John 2:11 is relevant to the work of the sixth day (Gen 1:24-31), then the narrative of the rest at Capernaum may correspond to the Sabbath (Gen 2:1-3).[4] In any case, the Johannine prologue seems to present a typological correspondence between the work of creation in Genesis and the ministry of the Son.

7.1.2 ὁ λόγος and θεός

The Relationship between the Logos and God

The next claim of the Johannine prologue is the intimate relationship between the Logos and God: καὶ ὁ λόγος ἦν πρὸς τὸν θεόν (1:1b). It is restated in 1:2: οὗτος ἦν ἐν ἀρχῇ πρὸς τὸν θεόν., and forms a chiastic parallelism (John 1:1-2).[5] In the Genesis creation account, the relationship between God and the word is not necessarily the focus; rather, the focus is the uniqueness of his mighty work of creation: his word and his command produce the universe. However, in the Jewish creation accounts of the second temple period, the divine attributes (such as wisdom[6] and the word of God[7]) are highlighted. Scholars have found a link to the Jewish wisdom tradition, since the personified wisdom is prominent in their narratives of creation, and is described as being closely related to God the Creator (cf. Prov ch. 8). R. Bauckham introduces two texts (1 En 84:2-3; Wisd 9:4) in which wisdom is represented as sharing

---

[2] M. Hengel, 'The Old Testament in the Fourth Gospel,' *HBT* 12 (1990), 33-34.

[3] J. Frey, *Die johanneische Eschatologie II: Das johanneische Zeitverständnis* (WUNT 110; Tübingen: Mohr Siebeck, 1998), 195-196.

[4] J. Frey, *Die johanneische Eschatologie II*, 195.

[5] See § 6.2.4.

[6] Cf. 2 En 33:3-4; 48:4 [J]; 4 Ezra 6:6; 2 Bar 48:9; Sir 42:23-25; 1QH[a] 9:7, 14, 19.

[7] Cf. 2 En 33:4; 4 Ezra 3:4; 6:38, 43; 2 Bar 14:17; 48:2, 8; 54:1, 3; SibOr 1:19; 3:20; PrMan 1:2-3; Wisd 9:2; ApAbr 9:9; 22:2; JosAsen 12:2; Sir 39:17; 42:15; 4Q381 frag. 1 6-7; 4Q422 frag. 1 6.

God's throne.[8] He argues that the picture of God's wisdom seated beside him as his adviser does not create a tension with the monotheistic emphasis on God's rule over all things, because wisdom is not someone other than God.[9] Moreover, it should be noted that in 2 En 33:3-4 [J], both the word of God and wisdom are employed in order to highlight the unique identity of God as the sole Creator and sole Ruler: 'There is no adviser and no successor to my creation. . . because wisdom is my adviser and my word is an agent (lit. 'doer,' or 'deed')' (мысль моа съвѣтникъ ецть, и слово мое дѣло есть: *m̆iisl̆i moê s̆uvĕtnik̆u est̆i i slovo moe d̆ilo est̆i*) (2 En 33:3-4 [J]).[10] Therefore, not only wisdom, but also the word of God are depicted as being closely related to God the Creator. When John asserts the intimate relationship between the Logos and God (John 1:1, 2), he does not ignore the Jewish understanding (canonical and non-canonical) of the divine attributes which are related to the Genesis creation account.[11]

The Identification with God

The proclamation of the Logos as θεός (v. 1c)[12] is highlighted in a chiastic structure, sandwiched by the two identical statements (πρὸς τὸν θεόν).[13]

A	ἐν ἀρχῇ			
B		ἦν		
C1		ὁ λόγος,		
C2		καὶ ὁ λόγος		
D			ἦν	
E				πρὸς τὸν θεόν,
E'				**καὶ θεὸς**
D'			ἦν	
C2'		ὁ λόγος.		
C1		οὗτος		
B'		ἦν		
A'	ἐν ἀρχῇ			πρὸς τὸν θεόν.

---

[8] R. Bauckham, 'Throne of God,' 54.

[9] R. Bauckham, 'Throne of God,' 54.

[10] Cf. Isa 40:13-14; Sir 42:21; 1 En 14:22. The Torah is regarded as closely related to wisdom (Jer 8:8-9; Ps 37:30-31; 1 Chr 22:12; Sir 15:1; 19:20; 21:11; Bar 4:1), and moreover, the Torah often replaces the position of Wisdom in the Rabbinic tradition. See E. Epp's list ('Wisdom,' 133): 'The Torah lay on God's bosom' (Aboth of Rabbi Nathan 31 [8b]); 'rested on God's knee' (Midrash on Psalms 90 § 12); 'I (God) cannot be separated from her' (ExodR 33 [94a]), etc.

[11] See R. Bauckham, *God Crucified*, 39-40; 'The Throne of God,' 43-69.

[12] It seems true that θεός has no article here because of the grammatical reason: predicate nouns are generally anarthrous (BDF, § 273). John 1:1-2 composes a chiastic structure (see § 6.2.4), and because of this structure, the predicate noun θεός should come before the subject ὁ λόγος. So that, the article might have been taken from θεός in order to make clear which the subject is.

[13] See § 6.2.4.

This proclamation of the deity of the Logos is clearly associated with the other descriptions of the identity of the Logos. As previously discussed, it is an intimation of its divine identity that the Logos was in the beginning before all creation (John 1:1). Furthermore, the Logos is depicted as the Creator (John 1:3) and the life-giver (John 1:4). Both are considered to be related to the unique identity of God in the theological framework of the Jewish creation accounts. Thus, the proclamation of the deity of the Logos (as θεός) in John 1:1 is, in a sense, a summary of the first part of the prologue. It may also be true that this description of the identity of the Logos as God is associated with the final argument of the prologue, that the role of the Son was to reveal the perfect identity of the Father (v. 18). In the rest of the Fourth Gospel, it is emphasized that any one who has seen the Son has seen the Father (John 12:45; 14:7, 9; cf. 15:24). The Son's work (John 6:38; 8:29; 9:33; 10:32, 37; 14:10, 31) and his word (John 3:11; 8:26, 28; 12:49; 14:24; 17:14) were nothing less than the work of the Father, which were revealed in his perfect unity with the Father. The Son also shares the glory of the Father (John 11:4, 40; 13:31, 32; 17:5, 24). Therefore, the proclamation of the Logos as God (v. 1) may be associated, not only the divine identity of the Son, but also with the description of the role (or the work) of the Son (i.e. the perfect revelation of the Father, v. 18).

The Logos of Creation

God's spoken 'word' is a preeminent motif of Genesis' affirmation concerning God as the Creator. The Jewish traditions refer to the word of God in the context of creation (2 En 33:4; 4 Ezra 3:4; 6:38, 43; 2 Bar 14:17; 48:2, 8; 54:1, 3; SibOr 1:19; 3:20; PrMan 1:2-3; Wisd 9:2; ApAbr 9:9; 22:2; JosAsen 12:2; Sir 39:17; 42:15; 4Q381 frag. 1 6-7; 4Q422 frag. 1 6). The Psalmist expands it as, 'by the word of the Lord (בדבר יהוה; τῷ λόγῳ τοῦ κυρίου [LXX]) the heavens were made' (Ps 33:6a); Ps 33:6 is often alluded to in early Jewish creation accounts (Jub 12:4; SibOr bks. 1, 3; 4Q381; 2 Bar chs. 21, 48, 54; ApAbr 9:3; 22:2; Sir chs. 33, 39; 4Q422).

John describes the Logos as the Creator, and emphasizes the lordship of the Logos over the whole world, or over his people (e.g. πᾶς [John 1:9; 2:24; 5:28]; πάντα ἄνθρωπον [1:9; 2:10]; ἡμεῖς πάντες [1:16] πάσης σαρκός [17:2]). A word pair, ארץ and שמים, appears in the Scriptures to describe the totality of creation in the sense that 'the heaven and the earth' are the most basic foundation which contains everything that God has created (Gen 14:19, 22; Exod 31:17; Isa 37:16; 51:13; Pss 89:11; 102:25[MT 26]; 121:2; 124:8; 134:3; Prov 3:19). The totality of the creation is also depicted by the idea of 'all (e.g. πᾶς)' (Jub 12:4; 2 En 33:8; 66:4, 5; JosAsen 12:1; SibOr 1:7-8; 3:20).

Wisdom is mentioned in the creation context (Prov 3:19; 8:30; 2 En 33:4; 1QH[a] 9:19; 11QPs[a] 26:13-14; Sir 42:21; Wisd 7-9), and in both 2 En 33:4 and Wisd 7-9, wisdom is personified and described as a co-worker of God's work. It seems to be an expanded interpretation of Prov 8:30.

As for the meaning of אָמוֹן in Prov 8:30, the major translations (e.g. NIV, NASB, RSV, NRSV, NJV) take it as 'craftsman' or 'master workman,' by accepting the commonly held derivation from Akkadian *ummiānu, ummānu* (a skilled craftsman).[14] However, scholars' views vary as follows:

אָמַן 'binding' 'uniting.'[15]
אָמֹן 'mother official' 'counselor.'[16]
אָמוּן 'darling' or אָמוּן 'ward' of Yahweh.[17]
אָמוּן or אָמָן (feminine form), 'artificer' or 'one who is skilled in making things.'[18]

אָמָן 'joiner' 'Established' (LXX, Origen, ἁρμόζουσα < ἁρμόζω; Symmachus,
    Theodotion   ἐστηριγμένη < στηρίζω).
אָמוּן 'ward' (Aquila, τιθηνουνένη < τιθηνέομαι).

According to the context of Prov 8:22-31, Proverbs does not seem to stress the role as a co-worker of God's creation, but simply says, 'she was established' (8:23), 'she was brought forth' (8:24, 25), 'she was there' (8:27), 'when heaven and the earth were created by God's hand' (8:26, 27, 28, 29). Although a possibility still remains to render אָמוֹן as 'craftsman,'[19] the focus is not on the idea of a co-worker of God's creation, but rather on her divine nature as pre-existent (8:22-29) and her intimate relationship with God (8:30-31).

Since the Wisdom of Solomon finds a link between wisdom and the revelatory activities of the spirit of God (Wisd 1:6; 7:7, 22; 9:17), its wisdom may possess a more dynamic figure than in other creation accounts. Thus, the description of the divine attributes (both the word of God and wisdom), which appear in the creation context (both canonical and non-canonical), may

---

[14] W. von Soden, *Akkadisches Handwörterbuch III*, 1981, 1415-16. Garrett (*Proverbs*, 109-110) notes on אָמוֹן "craftsmen" in Jer 52:15. Whybray (*Proverbs*, 136) states that the late Wisdom of Solomon 7:21 (22) and 8:5 (6) refer to Wisdom as the (female) "artificer of all things" in a passage which is clearly based on Prov 8:30.

[15] R. B. Y. Scott, 'Wisdom in Creation: The ʾAMON of Proverbs VIII 30,' *VT* 10 (1960), 213-23. However, if אָמֹן were a participle, it ought to be in a feminine form.

[16] P. A. H. de Boer, 'The Counsellor,' in M. North (ed.),*Wisdom in Israel and in the Ancient Near East* (VTSup 3; Leiden: Brill, 1955), 69-71.

[17] McKane, *Proverbs*, 357.

[18] Whybray, *Proverbs*, 136. He takes the view that it should mention God himself, not Wisdom: 'then I was beside him, (that is), the Creator.'

[19] GenR 1 takes the meaning of אָמוֹן in Prov 8:30 as 'workman' with some hesitation, listing several possibilities: (1) tutor (Num 11:12); (2) covered (Lam 4:5); (3) hidden (Est 2:7); (4) great (Nah 3:8); and (5) workman.

be behind the motif of the Logos of creation in John 1:1-5. One of the reasons why the prologue chooses the Logos (or the word) rather than wisdom will be discussed later, in relation to the motif of the eschatological Logos.

The Eschatological Logos

Sir 39:16-18 reads Ps 33:6 (which is a description of the events of creation) with Ps 33:9 (which is a general description of the way God works with his utterance), and links the motif of the creative word to the mighty works of his salvation. Sirach goes on to the eschatological argument that God, who completed the work of creation by the word of his mouth (Sir 39:17b), can realize and accomplish the eschatological works by the authority of his utterance (Sir 39:28-31). ApAbr 22:2 also reads Ps 33:9-12 with Ps 33:6-8, and its context implies that the reality of the coming eschatological events is linked to God's work of creation.

Isaiah also develops this motif of the creative word, and gives a vivid picture of God's redemptive works by means of his word:

(1) Isa 44:24-28:

24		כה־אמר יהוה גאלך	Thus says the Lord, your Redeemer,
		ויצרך מבטן	who formed you in the womb,
		אנכי יהוה	I am the Lord,
		עשׂה כל	who made all things
		נטה שׁמים לבדי	who stretched out the heavens alone
		רקע הארץ מי אתי ...	who spread out the earth by myself
26	(A)	האמר לירושׁלם תושׁב	who says to Jerusalem, 'Be inhabited'
		ולערי יהודה תבנינה	(who) to the city of Judah, 'Be rebuilt'
		וחרבותיה אקומם	and I will raise up their ruins
27	(B)	האמר לצולה חרבי	who says to the deep, 'Be dry'
		ונהרתיך אוביש	and I will dry up your rivers
28	(B)'	האמר לכורשׁ רעי	who says to Cyrus, 'Be my shepherd'
		וכל חפצי ישׁלם	and he accomplishes all my will
	(A)'	ולאמר לירושׁלם תבנה	(who) saying, to Jerusalem, 'Be rebuilt'
		והיכל תוסד	'Temple! Be laid.'

God is depicted here as the Redeemer (גאלך, your Redeemer) and the one who formed Israel (lit. ויצרך מבטן) (44:24); after the aspect of creation is mentioned (44:26a), God commands, as he did in the work of creation, saying, 'Jerusalem is to be inhabited, and Judah to be rebuilt' (26b), which is restated chiastically in 28b. In vv. 27-28, 'the drying up of the water[20]' (27), which is used as a metaphor to indicate God's mighty works of redemption, is paralleled with the calling of Cyrus (28a). And both are expected to obey God's command.

(2) Isa 45:7-8:

7	יוצר אור ובורא חשך	I form light and create darkness
	עשה שלום ובורא רע	I make weal and create woe
(A)	אני יהוה עשה כל־ארה	I am the Lord who creates all these things
8	חרעיפו[21] שמים ממעל	Shower, O heavens, from above
(B)	ושחקים יזרו־דרק	and let clouds shower righteousness
	תפתח[22]־ארץ	Let the earth open
(B)'	ויפרו־ישע[23]	and let salvation spring up
	וצדקה תצמיח יחד	and let righteousness grow together
(A)'	אני יהוה בראתיו[24]	I am the Lord who has created it.

This section follows a framework similar to the previous one. It states first that God created light and darkness (45:7a), and that God declared himself twice as the one who creates everything (45:7b, 8b). Two sets of parallel lines, i.e. the former being the command to heaven, the latter being the command to the earth, are sandwiched by them. The language of redemption (i.e. the giving of righteousness and salvation) is woven into the framework of creation.

(3) Isa 46:8-13:

9	זכרו ראשבות מעולם	Remember the former things of old
	כי אנכי אל	For I am God,
	ואין עוד אלהים	and there is no other God
	ואפס כמוני	and none like me
10	מגיד	the one who makes known
	מראשית אחרית	the end from the beginning
	ומקרם אשר לא־נעשׂו	and from ancient times things that have not happened

---

[20] See its redemptive motif (cf. Isa 42:15; 50:2-3; Ps 60:6).

[21] Cf. The LXX renders εὐφρανθήτω, 'Rejoice.'

[22] Cf. The LXX renders ἀνατειλάτω, 'Bring forth.'

[23] Cf. The LXX renders ἔλεος, 'grace'; 1QIsa[a] takes ישׁע.

[24] Cf. The LXX renders σε, 'you'; In 1QIsa[a] this sentence is omitted but sufficient space is left for its insertion (cf. DJD 15, 64).

	אמר	the one who says,
	עצתי תקום	'My purpose shall stand'
	וכל־חפצי אעשה[25]	then I will accomplish all my will
11	קרא	the one who calls
	ממזרח עיט	a bird of prey from the east
	מארץ מרחק איש עצתו	a man of my will from the far land
	אף־דברתי אף־אביאנה	Indeed I said, then I will bring it about
	יצרתי אף־אעשנה	I planned, then I will accomplish it.

God is represented as the one who makes plans (Isa 46:11b), and who makes them known (46:10a), and brings them about by his utterance (46:11). When God speaks, his purpose shall stand, and all his will shall be accomplished (46:10). This expression is similar to Isa 48:13b, קרא אני אליהם יעמדו יחדו, as well as 46:11b, אף־דברתי אף־אביאנה.

(4) Isa 48:12-15:

12b	אני־הוא אני ראשון אף אני אחרון	I am He, I am the first, and I am the last
13	אף־ידי יסדה ארץ	My hand laid the foundation of the earth
	וימיני טפחה שמים	and my right hand spread out the heavens
	קרא אני אליהם	When I summon them
	עמדו[26] יחדו . . .	they stand together
15	אני אני דברתי	I, indeed, I have spoken
	אף קראתיו הביאתיו	and I called him, brought him
	והצליח דרכו	he will succeed in his mission

God who calls himself the first (ראשון) and the last (אחרון) (48:12), and who is mentioned as the Creator of heaven and earth (48:13), spoke (דברתי) and called Cyrus (קראתיו); God also let Cyrus succeed in his mission (48:15).

(5) Isa 48:3:

	הראשנות מאז הגדתי	I foretold the former things long ago
(A)	ומפי יצאו[27]	They came from my mouth
(B)	ואשמיעם[28]	I made them known
(B)'	פתאם עשיתי	I immediately accomplished them
(A)'	ותבאנה[29]	and they came to pass

---

[25] Cf. 1QIsa[a] takes 3rd m sg (יעשה).

[26] Cf. 1QIsa[a] (ויעמדו); 4QIsa[c] (ויעמדו); 4QIsa[d] (ויעמדו).

[27] Cf. The LXX takes 3rd sg. (ἐξῆλθεν).

[28] Cf. The LXX takes 3rd sg. (ἀκουστὸν ἐγένετο).

It is interesting to observe that two sentences in the first person (i.e. God as an actor to reveal and accomplish his plan) are sandwiched at the same time between two other sentences which are written in the third person (that allude to what God said).

(6) Isa 55:11 (cf. Isa 45:22-23a):

כֵּן יִהְיֶה דְבָרִי	So was my word
אֲשֶׁר יֵצֵא מִפִּי	that goes out from my mouth
לֹא־יָשׁוּב אֵלַי רֵיקָם	it shall not return to me empty
כִּי אִם־עָשָׂה אֶת־אֲשֶׁר חָפַצְתִּי[30]	until it shall accomplish what I will
וְהִצְלִיחַ אֲשֶׁר שְׁלַחְתִּיו	and succeed in that for which I send it.

[Cf. Isa 45:22-23a]

בִּי נִשְׁבַּעְתִּי	By myself I have sworn,
יָצָא מִפִּי צְדָקָה דָּבָר	the word went in truth from my mouth
וְלֹא יָשׁוּב	and it will not return.

Isa 55:11 is read in the same framework. A similar expression appears in Isa 45:22-23.

This Isaianic exegesis of the Genesis creation account, or an application of its framework to a salvific context, appears in the 1st century apocalyptic literature (such as 4 Ezra and 2 Baruch) with an important expansion. That is to say, in the context of Isaiah, neither 48:3 nor 55:11 necessarily mention the events of creation, but rather illustrate how God will bring about his redemptive works by his utterance. Nevertheless, 4 Ezra and 2 Baruch expand Isa 48:3 and 55:11 in the context of both creation and eschatology. This interpretation of Isaiah 48:3 and 55:11 gives a more vivid picture of the realization of the eschatological events. God, who, by the word accomplished the work of creation, can also bring about the eschatological works immediately by the same word. Interestingly, when reference is made to Isaiah 55:11, the personification of the divine word can be seen (4 Ezra 6:38, 43; 2 Bar 54:3 and 56:4). It should be noted that Isa 55:11 is alluded to in John 6:27-71, where the divine role of the Son of God is claimed (this will be shown later).

Therefore, the Johannine Logos shows an important link to the motifs of the creative word and the eschatological word, which are prominent in the creation accounts of 4 Ezra and 2 Baruch. In early Christian tradition, reference to the divine word (ὁ λόγος τοῦ κυρίου, or ῥῆμα θεοῦ) also occurs in

---

[29] Cf. The LXX takes 3rd sg. (ἐπῆλθεν).

[30] In the LXX, the subject is not the word of God but 'what God wished' with passive voice: συντελεσθῇ ὅσα ἠθέλησα.

the contexts of the creation and the new creation (2 Pet 3:5-7; cf. Jas 1:18; 1 Pet 1:23). However, the Johannine prologue is unique in that this motif is employed to depict the divine identity and role of the Son of God. While wisdom (in Prov 8 and in Jewish wisdom tradition) may characterize one aspect of the Johannine Logos, an eschatological interpretation of the Genesis creation account (through Isaianic exegesis of the Genesis creation account) may provide the Johannine Logos with the other aspect; i.e. the eschatological word. It may be one of the reasons that the prologue keeps the figure of the divine word (ὁ λόγος) rather than wisdom. It is not an issue of gender, but rather a more theological matter.

7.1.3 ὁ λόγος *and* ζωή

The Genesis creation account describes how God produces the living things by his word or by his utterance (Gen 1:11-12, 20-31). Several Jewish creation accounts focus on this aspect, and depict God as 'the life-giver' (4 Ezra 3:5; 6:47-48; JosAsen 8:10-11), 'the origin of all life' (*wăkuël hĕyyĕwăt*) (Jub 12:4), 'life' itself (ܚܝܐ: *hayā*) (2 Bar 21:9), and 'the Creator of life' (ܚܝܐ ܒܪܝܐ: *bāryā hayyeh*) (2 Bar 23:5). He is 'the sole life-giver' who himself has the authority to produce life *ex nihilo* (2 Bar 21:4; 4 Ezra 3:3-5; JosAsen 8:10-11).

The divine attributes appear in the context where the identity of God as the sole life-giver is highlighted; e.g. wisdom is assigned to create Adam (2 En 30:8), the word of God functions to produce human beings (4 Ezra 7:69). JosAsen ch. 8 meditates on the Lord who 'gave life' (ζωοποιήσας) to all things, and applies this to a salvific context, by reiterating the language of the new creation, such as ζωοποίησον (to give life), ἀνακαίνισον (to renew), ἀνάπλασον (to form anew), and ἀναζωοποίησον (to make alive) (JosAsen 8:11a). When the motif of 'God as the life-giver' is taken up again in JosAsen 12:1-3, interestingly it refers to the motif of 'the word of creation': 'For you, Lord, spoke and all things were brought to life' (ἐλάλησας καὶ πάντα ἐζωογονήθησαν); 'Because your word, Lord, is life for all your creatures' (JosAsen 12:2).

The motif of ζωή is prominent in the account of the creation of Adam as well: 'Then the Lord God formed man from the dust of the ground, and breathed into his nostrils the breath of life (נשמת חיים: πνοὴν ζωῆς [LXX]); and the man became a living being (נפש חיה; ψυχὴν ζῶσαν [LXX]) (Gen 2:7). Isaiah gives an interpretation of this passage, by characterizing God as the life-giver who gives breath and spirit to the people: 'Thus says God, the Lord, who created the heavens and stretched them out, who spread out the earth and what comes from it, who gives breath (נשמה: πνοὴν [LXX]) to the people upon it and spirit (רוח: πνεῦμα [LXX]) to those who walk in it (Isa 42:5).' It is interesting that the breath of life is associated with the spirit (4Q422 frag. 1;

1QS col. 3) and divine wisdom or knowledge (Sir 17:1-14; 4Q504 frag. 8; cf. Wisd 9:2-3).

Therefore, whereas the life motif is developed in the context which depicts the unique identity of God who alone can produce life *ex nihilo* and who alone can provide eternal life, it is linked to the spirit or wisdom through which the first human being was created and through which the people were guided to the way of life with wisdom and the Torah (as the revelation of divine wisdom).

John states in the prologue that ἐν αὐτῷ ζωὴ ἦν (John 1:4a). First of all, it may remind the readers of the sovereignty of God as the sole life-giver which appears in the creation context. Secondly, the exegesis of the life-giving motif is linked to the divine attributes (wisdom [e.g. 2 En 30:8] or the word of God [4 Ezra 7:69; JosAsen 8, 12]). Thirdly, in the Johannine prologue, the Logos finds its location within the unique identity of God. This notion is developed in the rest of the Fourth Gospel in contexts where the Father bestows authority on his Son to give life to the world (John 3:15-16, 36; 5:21, 26; 6:57).[31] Finally, the life motif in John 1:4a seems to be opened to later eschatological discussion; i.e. those who believe in the name of the Logos (or the Son of God from John 1:14) will be given a new birth as the children of God (John 1:12).

7.1.4 ὁ λόγος *and* φῶς

The Genesis creation account seems to pay attention to the creation of light (אור in the first day; מארת in the fourth day). The Genesis creation narrative has two poles; i.e. heaven and earth, and its focus moves from the heavens to the earth. However, at the fourth creation day (vv. 14-19) the order is changed or reversed. Moreover, the Genesis creation account refers to the role of light (אור and מארת) with an emphatic form (chiastic structure) (vv. 14-19), while the account gives no special emphasis to the other created objects.[32]

>   A. to divide the day from the night (14a)
>   B. for signs, for fixed times, for days and years (14b)
>   C. to give light on the earth (15)
>   D. to rule the night (16a)
>   D'.to rule the night (16b)
>   C'.to give light on the earth (17)
>   B'.to rule the day and the night (18a)
>   A'.to divide the light from the darkness (18b)

Early Jewish creation accounts also pay much attention to the creation of light (אור and מארת) (e.g. Jub ch. 2; 1 En ch. 69; 2 En chs. 47-48, 24-33; 4 Ezra ch. 6; SibOr bks. 1, 3, frag. 3; LAB ch. 60; Sir ch. 33; Ant ch. 1; 1QM

---

[31] In these contexts, a more individualistic salvation is in view.

[32] G. J. Wenham, *Genesis 1-15* (WBC 1; Waco: Word Books Publisher, 1987), 5-10.

col. 10; 1QH[a] col. 9; 4Q381; 4Q392; 11QPs[a] col. 26), and speculate on its theological meanings. For example, the creation of light may be taken as a manifestation of the sovereign power of God (e.g. 1 Bar 3:33-35; ApAbr 9:3-4; 11QPsAp[a] 2:10-12), whereas light is considered as a divine thing (2 En 24:4 [A]; 25:3 [J]; 4Q392 frag. 1 4-5). Light finds its place beside God together with wisdom (2 Bar 54:13), or beside his throne (2 En 25:4 [J]), and light is brought out from God's treasuries (4 Ezra 6:40; cf. 2 Bar 59:11). This light imagery is linked to the divine nature of the Torah in the OT (e.g. Ps 119:105; Prov 6:23; Isa 2:5; 42:21; 51:4) and in early Jewish literature (Sir 17:11; 2 Bar 17:4; 59:2; 77:13, 16; LAB 15:5-6; Wisd 18:4; T Lev 14:4).[33] It seems also common in early Judaism, as well as later Rabbinic tradition,[34] that the idea of the creation of light (i.e. the separation of light from darkness) is taken in an ethical sense, contrasting righteousness with evil:

> He (Moses), who was lighted, took from the light (*nūhrā*), . . . but many whom he illuminated took from the darkness (*yesukē*) of Adam and did not rejoice in the light of the lamp (*bnūhrā dasrāgā*) (2 Bar 18:1-2).

> And I gave him (Adam) his free will and I pointed out to him the two ways - light and darkness (свѣ и тьмѫ, *svě i tǐmô*) (2 En 30:15 [J]).

> You called (them) out from darkness to light (ἀπὸ τοῦ σκότους εἰς τὸ φῶς) (JosAsen 8:10a).

> From the dwelling place of light (במעון אור) (is) the generation of the truth (האמת תולדות); from the fountain of darkness (ממקור חושך) (is) the generation of the deceit (תולדות העול) (1QS 3:19).[35]

Like the life motif, light is counted as an eschatological blessing (Isa 60:19-20; Jub 1:29; 2 En ch. 65 [J]; 2 Bar 48:50; 51:1-3 LAB 3:10; SibOr 2:315), and regarded as a symbol of Paradise (2 En 65:10 [A]; 2 Bar 48:50; 51:1-3). It should be noted that in both SibOr 2:315-317 and 2 En 42:6, light and life motifs appear in the same context, in the sense of the end time blessings.

---

[33] See later Rabbinic traditions (e.g. GenR 3:1; 3:5, 8; b. Meg 99; b. Ab 21; DeutR 7:3 [204a]; Ketub 111b; Ab 6:7; SifNum 6:25; NumR 11 [63d]).

[34] E.g. 'The light which God gave us is for our understanding' (GenR 3:1a); 'The opening of God's words gives light' (GenR 3:1b). According to GenR 3:8, the utterance, 'Let there be light,' refers to the deeds of the righteous; 'God divided between the light and the darkness' means that he divided between the deeds of the righteous and the deeds of the wicked.' GenR 3:5 demonstrates how the light, which was created in the first day of creation, matched the five books of the Torah.

[35] The notion of אור and חושך does not necessarily imply a cosmic power as it is prominent in Iranian Zoroastrianism; rather, it seems to be a simple application of the contrasted word pair, which is commonly used in Judaism. See our discussion on the dualistic expression of 1QS 3 (§ 3.17.1).

As for the use of light imagery in the Johannine prologue, first of all, it reminds the readers of the event of the giving of light in the Genesis creation account. In early Judaism, reflecting its divine character, light is understood in both an ethical and religious sense. Moreover, the creation of light is typologically applied to the event of the giving of the Torah in early Judaism and later Rabbinic tradition. Thus, when John 1:4 argues that in the Logos was life and it was light for the people, it may imply a revelatory activity of God, which is often typologically correlated with the creation of light.

7.2 John 1:6-13

7.2.1 τὸ φῶς τὸ ἀληθινόν

After the description of creation, the Johannine prologue refers to the coming of John the Baptist, and makes a contrast between true light and the witness to the light (vv. 6-8). Verse 9 states that the primordial light (v. 5) was coming into the world. The figure of John the Baptist (John 1:6-8) may remind the readers of Isaianic prophecy[36] which opens the meaning of φῶς (vv. 4b-5) toward the Isaianic use of the light imagery,[37] though it is not necessarily clear in the first stanza (John 1:1-5). We should notice that while the relationship between ὁ λόγος and John the Baptist is mentioned, φῶς is treated as a personal figure; i.e. οὐκ ἦν ἐκεῖνος (John the Baptist) τὸ φῶς, ἀλλ' ἵνα μαρτυρήσῃ περὶ τοῦ φωτός (a personal figure) (John 1:8). P. Borgen is skeptical about the reading of the Messiah's light, but rather emphasizes the idea of the primordial light with the lawgiving of Moses.[38] However, this does not necessarily seem inconsistent with the use of the light imagery. In Isaiah, the Servant of Yahweh is already associated with the image of light (42:6; 49:6; 51:4),[39] and especially in Isa 51:4 (cf. Isa 2:3-5) it is linked to the

---

[36] Cf. John 1:23 which alludes to Isa 40:3; John 1:29 and 36 which allude to Isa 53:7.

[37] Isaianic light imagery appears in salvific contexts in the NT, and it is regarded as a symbol of the coming of salvation: 'The people who walked in darkness have seen a great light (אוֹר גָּדוֹל); those who dwelt in a land of deep darkness, on them has light (אוֹר) shined' (Isa 9:2 in Matt 4:12-16); 'to open the eyes that are blind, to bring out the prisoners from the dungeon, from the prison those who sit in darkness' (Isa 42:17 in Luke 4:18); 'Arise, shine; for your light (אוֹרֵךְ) has come, and the glory of the Lord (יהוה כְּבוֹד) has risen upon you; for behold, darkness shall cover the earth, and thick darkness the peoples, but the Lord will arise upon you, and his glory (כְּבוֹדוֹ) will be seen upon you' (Isa 60:1-2 in Eph 5:14): see the LXX translation: ἐπὶ δὲ σὲ φανήσεται Κύριος, καὶ ἡ δόξα οὐτοῦ ἐπὶ σὲ ὀφθήσεται (Isa 60:2); πᾶν γὰρ τὸ φανερούμενον φῶς ἐστιν. διὸ λέγει . . . καὶ ἐπιφαύσει σοι ὁ Χριστός (Eph 5:14).

[38] P. Borgen, 'Creation, Logos and the Son: Observations on John 1:1-18 and 5:17-18,' *Ex Auditu* 3 (1987), 93-94.

[39] R. Schnackenburg, *John*, vol. 2, 190.

revelation of the law (תורה) or justice (משפט) (cf. the word of God [דבר־יהוה] in Isa 2:3-5[40]). The light imagery, soon afterward, appears in the context: 'O house of Jacob, come, let us walk in the light of the Lord (יהוה באור)' (Isa 2:5).[41] The light is thus easily understood as a symbol of 'saving revelation.'

Thus, while based on the light imagery, which is presented in the creation context with the idea of God's revelatory activities (perhaps contrasted with the lawgiving of Moses), a contrast between τὸ φῶς τὸ ἀληθινόν and the witness to φῶς in John 1:6-9 seems to open the meaning of φῶς (vv. 4b-5) toward a messianic understanding of light (saving revelation). It is a reminder of a fulfillment of the Isaianic hope of the coming of the Torah or the word of God in a salvific sense.

7.2.2 The Pre-existence and the Lordship of the Logos as Creator

The Johannine prologue looks back to the divine identity of the Logos (vv. 10ab, 11a), and refers to the pre-existence (v. 10a) and the lordship of the Logos as the Creator (v. 10b). The Old Testament and early Jewish traditions recall their God as the Creator of Israel, and a special relationship between God and his people is referred to (Isa 43:1-7; 45:11-13; 64:8; 4 Ezra 6:55-59; 8:45; 2 Bar 14:15-19; 4Q504 frag. recto 8, 4-10; cf. frags. 1-2 3:3, 4-5, 9-10; 4:4-5). Reference to the lordship of God as the Creator is often made in an eschatological context in which the restoration of God's people is expected (esp. Isa 43:1-7; 45:11-13; 64:8; 4 Ezra 6:55-59; 8:45; 2 Bar 14:15-19). Namely, Israel was created for the world as the first-born (*primogenitum*), only begotten of God (*unigenitum æmutatorem*), so that they would be restored and possess their world in the end time.[42] In John 1:10-13, this idea of the relationship between God the Creator and his people with a hope of their restoration may be relevant to the idea of the new creation of τέκνα θεοῦ. However, the prologue's view is different from early Judaism, particularly in that the prologue refers to the divine lordship as the Creator (John 1:10-ab, 11a) in order to highlight Israel's unfaithful response to it (John 1:11b; cf.

---

[40] Isa 2:2-5 may be alluded to in John 4:21-24 as a prophecy of the coming of the Messiah in the end time. For example, the Samaritan woman mentioned Jerusalem as the place where the worshippers gather (John 4:20; Isa 2:2), although Jesus presented a new perspective that in the time of salvation there would be no regional division (Isa 2:2-3a; John 4:20-21). Jesus mentioned that the place where the salvation or savior would appear was Zion or Jerusalem (John 4:22; Isa 2:3b). The Samaritan woman mentioned that the coming messiah would teach the way (Isa 2:3a; John 4:25-26).

[41] Cf. Isa 42:21.

[42] It is interesting that 4 Ezra 6:56 and 4Q504 frag. 1-2 3:3 refer to Isa 40:15-17 in order to emphasize the superiority of the people of Israel to other nations.

10c),[43] and the prologue proclaims that the hope of the restoration of God's people can only be realized through faith in the Logos of God (εἰς τὸ ὄνομα αὐτοῦ) (John 1:12-13).

7.2.3 New Creation: τέκνα θεοῦ

The Restoration of God's People as an Eschatological Hope

John 1:12-13 deals with the eschatological hope of being τέκνα θεοῦ, perhaps in relation to the reference to the lordship of the Logos as the Creator.

Although the phrase, τέκνα θεοῦ, does not occur, the concept is well established in the Old Testament.[44] The people of Israel are called υἱός πρωτότοκος μου (Exod 4:22 [LXX]; בני בכרי [MT]), υἱοὶ κυρίου τοῦ θεοῦ (Deut 14:1 [LXX]; בנים ליהוה [MT]), and their God is called σου πατήρ (Deut 32:6 [LXX]). David and his line are also called υἱός to God ὁ πατήρ (2 Sam 7:14 [LXX]; Ps 2:7) and πρωτότοκος, 'first-born' (Ps 89:26 [LXX 88:27]). The prophetic tradition appeals to this relationship in lamentation, in which God's love is contrasted to people's unfaithfulness:

> When Israel was a child, I loved him, and out of Egypt I called my child (בני; τὰ τέκνα αὐτοῦ [LXX[45]]), but the more I called them, the more they went from me (Hos 11:1).

> How gladly would I treat you like children (בבנים; cf. τάξω σε εἰς τέκνα [LXX]) . . . I thought you would call me 'Father (אבי)' . . . you have been unfaithful to me, O house of Israel (Jer 3:19).

> I reared children (בנים; υἱοὺς [LXX]) and brought them up, but they have rebelled against me' (Isa 1:2; cf. 1:4; 30:1); 'Thus says the Lord, the Holy One of Israel, and its Creator, "Will you question me about my children (בני; υἱῶν μου [LXX]). . . I made the earth and created humankind upon it . . . (Isa 45:11-12).

> Surely they are my people, children (τέκνα [LXX]) who will not be false to me . . . , but they rebelled and grieved his holy spirit' (Isa 63:8-10 [16]).

> Yet, O Lord, you are our Father, we are the clay, and you are our potter; we are all the work of your hand (Isa 64:8).

---

[43] People's rejection of the divine word is regarded as a fulfillment of Isaianic prophecy in the NT: Isa 6:9-10 in Matt 13:14-17; Isa 29:13 in Matt 15:7-9; Isa 53:1 in John 12:38; Isa 6:10 in John 12:40; Isa 6:9-10 in Acts 28:25-28. Bultmann (*John*, 22) and other scholars find a similarity between the motif of rejected Logos and rejected Wisdom (cf. Prov. 1:20-32; Job 28; Sir 24:7; 1 Bar 3:10-13, 29-36; 1 En 42:1-3). It may be safe to say that both prophetic tradition and Jewish wisdom tradition deal with the same theme of Israel's unfaithfulness to God (cf. Isa 29:13-16).

[44] Cf. Culpepper, 'Pivot,' 17-19.

[45] The LXX renders τὰ τέκνα αὐτοῦ, perhaps mentioning the offspring of Israel.

In John 1:10-13, the motif of people's unfaithfulness is contrasted to the motif of the lordship of the Creator.

This motif of the relationship between God and his people is referred to in an eschatological context as well:

> In the place where it was said to them, 'You are not my people,' it shall be said to them, 'Children of the living God (υἱοὶ θεοῦ ζῶντος [LXX 2:1]; בְנֵי אֵל־חָי)' (Hos 1:10).

> Bring my sons (υἱούς μου [LXX]; בָּנַי) from afar and my daughters (θυγατέρας μου) from the end of the earth - everyone who is called by my name, whom I created (κατεσκεύασα) for my glory, whom I formed (ἔπλασα) and made (ἐποίησα) (Isa 43:6-7).

Likewise, the promise to be τέκνα θεοῦ in John 1:12 can also be understood in line with the eschatological expectation for the restoration of God's people. The phrase 'he gave power to become children' (ἔδωκεν αὐτοῖς ἐξουσίαν) (v. 12) indicates that it was revealed as 'eschatological gift' to the people.

The Revelation of the Name

According to John 1:12-13, the right (ἐξουσία) to become τέκνα θεοῦ is said to be given through faith in the name of ὁ λόγος (John 1:12c). The expression, δίδωμι with ἔξουσια, is used to emphasize that the authority comes from God, or from above (Matt 9:8; 21:23 [Mark 11:28; Luke 20:2]; 28:18; John 5:27; 17:2; Rev 2:26; cf. Sir 17:2; 45:17; Dan LXX 7:14). John 1:12-13 carefully states that τέκνα θεοῦ was born (ἐγεννήθησαν) from God (ἐκ θεοῦ) (John 1:13b), and through faith in the name of ὁ λόγος (John 1:12c). In other words, the new birth (or new creation of his people) will happen by the authority of ὁ λόγος (cf. John 1:4a, ἐν αὐτῷ ζωὴ ἦν).[46] This role of the Logos (John 1:12-13) seems to correspond to the role of the Logos as life (John 1:4a).

Concerning the reference to his name (John 1:12), W. Dumbrell suggests a possible allusion to the context of Exod chs. 33-34.[47] When he was asked by Moses to reveal his glory (33:18), the Lord declared his name (33:19), which may have been a reminder of the original revelation of his name (אֲשֶׁר אֶהְיֶה אֶהְיֶה) (Exod 3:14). W. Dumbrell thereby argues that in the Sinai event, 'glory' represents the unique feature of divine majesty, whereas 'the name' provides the content of its revelation. Similarly, the prologue mentions the

---

[46] It is important to notice that faith in the Son is based on the fact of the bestowment of divine authority on his Son (although it is not stated clearly in the prologue): ὁ πατὴρ ἀγαπᾷ τὸν υἱὸν καὶ πάντα δέδωκεν ἐν τῇ χειρὶ αὐτοῦ. ὁ πιστεύων εἰς τὸν υἱὸν ἔχει ζωὴν αἰώνιον· (John 3:35-36a); ἀλλὰ τὴν κρίσιν πᾶσαν δέδωκεν τῷ υἱῷ, . . . ὁ τὸν λόγον μου ἀκούων καὶ πιστεύων τῷ πέμψαντί με ἔχει ζωὴν αἰώνιον καὶ εἰς κρίσιν οὐκ ἔρχεται (John 5:22-24; cf. 5:27).

[47] W. J. Dumbrell, 'Law and Grace: The Nature of the Contrast in John 1:17,' EQ 58 (1986), 29-30.

name of the Son which makes the restoration of God's people possible (John 1:12), while it also refers to the revelation of glory which is obviously grounded against the background of the Sinai event (John 1:14). In short, the revelation of the name (John 1:12) is paralleled with the revelation of glory (John 1:14). Both are important ingredients of saving revelation of the eschatological Logos (or light).[48]

7.3 John 1:14-18

7.3.1 The Son as the Incarnated Logos

The Johannine prologue shows a dramatic shift in the way the Logos exists or the place of the Logos (I to II), and a different angle on the incarnation (II to III) throughout the prologue (v. 5 ⇒ v. 9 ⇒ v. 14).

   I. The Logos was shining in pre-existent stage (v. 5).

   II. The Logos as Light was coming to his world (v. 9).

   III. The Logos dwelt in the world as the Son of God (v. 14).

This scene indicates that the Logos, which was pre-existent with God and created the world (John 1:3, 10-11), historically came into the world and dwelt among the people. The same Logos that accomplished the work of creation came and dwelt in his world for the purpose of executing a new mission. The prologue quoted the testimony of John the Baptist (v. 15; cf. v. 30) in order to affirm the divine identity of the Son[49]: οὗτος ἦν ὃν εἶπον ἔμπροσθέν μου γέγονεν, ὅτι πρῶτός μου ἦν. First of all, the Baptist claims that the prophecy which he had proclaimed (ὃν εἶπον) was fulfilled.[50] The existence of the Son (οὗτος in John 1:15) had been known in the prophecy, in the word of God. The Baptist did not know who the Son was (John 1:31, 33), but he knew that the Son was in the word of God. The Son was become (γέγονεν) before (ἔμπροσθέν) the Baptist, and he was before (πρῶτός) the Baptist.[51] The statement not only contrasts the status of the Son and John the Baptist, expressing the absolute primacy of the Son. It also points to the temporal relationship between the two. The audience who had understood that John

---

[48] Cf. the creative role of the divine name in the Jewish tradition (Jub 36:7; LAB 60:2; 1 En 69:13-15; 3 En 42:1-7; cf. TarJon Exod 28:30; y. Sanh 29; b. Suk 53b; b. Mak 11a).

[49] See § 6.2.4.

[50] Cf. Luke 3:2: ἐγένετο ῥῆμα θεοῦ ἐπὶ Ἰωάννην τὸν Ζαχαρίου υἱὸν ἐν τῇ ἐρήμῳ. Luke clearly describes the ministry of John the Baptist as prophecy.

[51] Both ἔμπροσθέν and πρῶτός have the similar temporal meaning, but the former includes the aspect of absolute primacy (cf. Carson, *John*, 131).

the Baptist came before Jesus faced at a crisis which forced them to think of the pre-existence of the Son. The first reader may have read this statement in connection with vv. 1-2 and v. 9. In addition, it should be noted that the coming of the תורה or דבר־יהוה is expected in an eschatological context (Isa 2:3-5; cf. 51:4-5; Mic 4:1-3).[52] John 4:22 understands that Isa 2:3 was fulfilled by the coming of the Son of God. John 6:45 also argues that Isa 54:13 (i.e. an eschatological hope that his people shall be taught by God[53]) was fulfilled. Interestingly, John 6:45 is followed by a similar expression in John 1:18: 'No one has ever seen the Father except him who is from God; he has seen the Father' (οὐχ ὅτι τὸν πατέρα ἑώρακέν τις εἰ μὴ ὁ ὢν παρὰ τοῦ θεοῦ, οὗτος ἑώρακεν τὸν πατέρα).

7.3.2 The Son as a Fulfillment of an Eschatological Hope

The coming of the Son is also described as a fulfillment of the eschatological hope of the dwelling of God in the end time. The hope of the restoration of God's people (i.e. that they would be the children of God), which is the focus in the second stanza, is often linked to the hope that God might dwell in the midst of his people in the prophetic traditions:

'*I will dwell among the people of Israel*, . . . and they shall know that I am *the Lord their God* (אֲנִי יהוה אֱלֹהיהֶם) (Exod 29:45-46).

'So you shall know that I am *the Lord your God* (ἐγὼ κύριος ὁ θεὸς ὑμῶν [LXX]), *who dwell* (κατασκηνῶν [LXX]) in Zion' (Joel 3:17).

'For, behold, I will come and *dwell* (κατασκηνώσω [LXX]) *in the midst of you*. And many nations shall join themselves to the Lord in that day, and shall be *my people* (ἐγὼ ἔρχομαι καὶ κατασκηνώσω ἐν μέσῳ σου [LXX]) (Zech 2:10-11).

'*My dwelling place* (ἡ κατασκήνωσίς μου [LXX]) shall be with them; and I will be *their God*, and they shall be *my people*' (Ezek 37:27).

The verb, σκηνόω,[54] occurs only five times in the New Testament (once in John; four times in Rev); Rev 7:15 and 21:3 mention the dwelling of God in the midst of his people in the end time, with reference to Isa 25:8; 49:10; Ezek

---

[52] See § 7.2.1.

[53] John seems to take the LXX rendering here: καὶ πάντας τοὺς υἱούς σου διδακτοὺς θεοῦ, καὶ ἐν πολλῇ εἰρήνῃ τὰ τέκνα σου.

[54] Cf. Barrett (*John*, 165): 'the word σκηνοῦν was chosen here with special reference to the word δόξα which follows. It recalls, in sound and in meaning, the Hebrew שׁכן, which means 'to dwell'; the verb is used of the dwelling of God with Israel (e.g. Exod 25:8; 29:46; Zech 2:14), and a derived noun שׁכינה was used (though not in the OT) as a periphrasis for the name of God himself.'

37:27; and 48:35.[55] John 1:14 means no more than that the Logos took up a temporary dwelling;[56] however, that John finds a link to this Jewish eschatological hope may be indicated by several allusions to the narrative of the theophany in the Exodus event.[57]

THE EXODUS EVENT	JOHN 1:14-18
The glory of the Lord (δόξης κυρίου) filled the tabernacle (ἡ σκηνή), when God came down to the Tent of meeting (Exod 40:34-35).	They saw the glory as the Son of God (δόξαν ὡς μονογενοῦς παρὰ πατρός), when the Logos came and dwelt among the people (1:14).
God declared that he was full of grace and truth (ורב־חסד ואמת) in the revelation (Exod 34:6).	The Son was full of grace and truth (πλήρης χάριτος καὶ ἀληθείας) (John 1:14); Out of his fullness (πληρώματος) believers received grace in place of grace (χάριν ἀντὶ χάριτος) (1:16).
The Law was given through Moses (Exod 34:28).	Grace and Truth (ἡ χάρις καὶ ἀλήθεια) came through Jesus Christ (1:17).
Moses was allowed to see God, but partially (Exod 33:20; cf. 33:11).	The only Son, who is in the bosom of the Father, he has made him known (1:18).

As the people of Israel saw the glory of God (Exod 40:34) and bore witness to his fullness of grace and truth in the Exodus event (Exod 34:6), believers saw the glory (John 1:14) and the fullness of grace and truth (John 1:16) in the event of the coming of the Son of God.[58] It is also stated as a climactic revelation of God, whom no one has ever seen (John 1:18), which is contrasted with the encounter which allowed Moses to see God partially (Exod 33:20; cf. 33:11). Thus, the coming and the dwelling of the Son of God is depicted against the background of the epiphany of God in Mount Sinai.

In short, the role (or the ministry) of the Son is depicted not only against the background of the Jewish wisdom tradition, but also against the background of an eschatological hope of the coming of the Torah and the hope of God's dwelling (or epiphany of God) among the people in the end time.

---

[55] Κατασκηνόω is not used in the sense of eschatological dwelling of God in the NT (Matt 13:32; Mark 4:32; Luke 13:19; Acts 2:26).

[56] Barrett, *John*, 165-166.

[57] Cf. A. Hanson, 'John 1.14-18 and Exodus xxxiv,' *NTS* 23 (1976-1977), 90-101.

[58] Cf. J. K. Elliott, 'John 1:14 and the New Testament's Use of πλήρης,' *BT* 28 (1977), 151-153; W. Dumbrell, 'Law and Grace,' 25-37; R. B. Edwards, 'χάριν ἀντὶ χάριτος (John 1:16): Grace and the Law in the Johannine Prologue,' *JSNT* 32 (1988), 3-15.

7.3.3 The Son as the Climactic Revelation of God

The final statement of the prologue (John 1:18) makes one of the roles of the Son of God clear; i.e. to reveal the Father: 'No one has ever seen God; the only Son, who is in the bosom of the Father, he has made him known (ἐξηγήσατο).'

The role of the Logos is depicted by the light imagery as 'saving revelation' (John 1:4 [τὸ φῶς τῶν ἀνθρώπων]; cf. 1:9 [τὸ φῶς τὸ ἀληθινόν]), and the rest of the prologue focuses on its contents. While alluding to the narrative of the theophany in the Exodus event (Exod chs. 33-34), the prologue mentions the revelation of glory (1:14b) and 'full of grace and truth' (1:14c; 16-17), as well as the name through which the restoration of God's people is made (1:12). F. F. Bruce comments that the glory seen in the incarnated Word was the glory which was revealed to Moses, and that it has been manifested on earth as 'the fullness of grace and truth.'[59] The prologue proclaims that believers witnessed the glory of the Son of God (δόξαν ὡς μονογενοῦς παρὰ πατρός), and that this glory was also the revelation of 'the fullness of grace and truth.'[60] Since the revelation of 'grace and truth (ἡ χάρις καὶ ἡ ἀλήθεια)' is contrasted with the event of the giving of the Torah in John 1:17, the glory which the believers witnessed in the Son was the Father's. Thus, the glory of the Son is the revelation of the Father. The Fourth Gospel describes that the Son shares the glory of the Father (John 11:4, 40; 13:31, 32; 17:5, 24), and it is difficult to make a distinction between them. Although it is not clearly stated in the prologue,[61] the rest of the Fourth Gospel proclaims that the glory of the Son (and also it is the Father's) was climactically revealed at the cross and the exaltation of the Son (John 7:39; 12:16, 23; 13:31-32).

Therefore, in John 1:4b-9, the role (or the ministry) of the Logos was depicted as light (i.e. saving revelation), and the rest of the prologue demonstrated how the revelation of God had been accomplished in the ministry of the Son (or his sonship).[62]

---

[59] F. F. Bruce, *The Gospel of John* (Grand Rapids: Eerdmans 1983), 42.

[60] D. A. Carson (*John*, 129) takes 'the fullness of grace and truth' as a modifier of 'glory.'

[61] However, it may be alluded to in John 1:17-18; i.e. the statement, 'grace and truth' came (ἐγένετο) through Jesus Christ (John 1:17), may suggest a completion of the ministry of the Son; the present tense in the statement, 'the only Son who is (ὢς) in the bosom of the Father' (John 1:18), may suggest the exalted Son.

[62] See the note (§ 6.2.4) for the understanding of the parallelism between v. 1 and v. 18.

7.4 Summary and Conclusions

The main points, which have been suggested by our thematic understanding of the Johannine prologue in the light of early Jewish creation accounts (and other related sources), are as follows:

(1) The Genesis creation account had been the subject of speculation in various ways in the Old Testament and Jewish traditions. Consulting these exegetical traditions, we have found how the Johannine prologue developed Christology on the basis of the exposition of the Genesis creation account.

(2) In early Jewish creation accounts, there is speculation on God's work of creation in the context where the sovereignty of God and the absoluteness of his existence is highlighted. God is the sole Creator who made a perfect plan *in the beginning*, and who created *the very beginning* of the world; He produced creatures *ex nihilo*; He is the only God who has the authority to produce *Life and Light*. Surprisingly, the Johannine prologue proclaims that the Logos was the beginning, God, Creator, life, and light. That is to say, the prologue modifies the Logos with the terms which clearly refer to the Genesis creation account, and also which indicate the divine identity of God in first century Judaism. It should be noted that, in the Jewish exegetical traditions, only the word and wisdom can be depicted to be the agents of God's work of creation. Moreover, these figures emphasize the sovereignty of God. Therefore, Jewish monotheism was not put in danger when the Logos was modified with these terms. In other words, the prologue attempted to develop Christology on the basis of the exegetical traditions of the Genesis creation account, in which Jewish monotheism was carefully preserved.

(3) This speculation on the sovereignty of God, which had been manifested in the work of creation, was expanded in the prophetic tradition and also in later eschatological discussions. In these contexts, the sovereign power of God, which was believed to assure the coming eschaton, was greatly expected to be shown. In particular, the motif of the creative word (esp. Ps 33:6 and 9 and Isaiah 48:3 and 55:11) is expanded and developed in the eschatological context (e.g. Sir ch. 39; ApAbr chs. 21-22; 4 Ezra ch. 6; 2 Bar chs. 14, 21, 48, 54; 2 Pet 3:5-7; cf. Jas 1:18; 1 Pet 1:18). Contrasted with the agency of the divine word which accomplished the work of creation, the new agency of the divine word was greatly expected to accomplish the eschatological works. When the prologue employed the Logos language in Christology (firstly in the context of creation [John 1:1-5] and secondly in the eschatological discussion which was associated with the motif of the sonship [John 1:6-18]), the motif of the eschatological word may have been in both the author's and the first readers' minds. Therefore, while wisdom (in Prov 8 and in Jewish wisdom tradition) may characterize one aspect of the Johannine Logos, the motif of

the eschatological word may provide the Johannine Logos with the other aspect.

(4) The early Jewish creation accounts (e.g. 2 Bar 21:4; 4 Ezra 3:3-5; JosAsen 8:10-11) depicted God to be the sole life-giver, who alone could produce life, and in some creation accounts, the divine attributes (both wisdom [e.g. 2 En 30:8] and the word of God [4 Ezra 7:69; JosAsen 8, 12]) work as agents to give life to human beings. In the Johannine prologue, the life motif appears first in the creation context (John 1:3-4a). Since the Logos found its place within the unique identity of God (based on the Jewish exegetical tradition of the Genesis creation account), the Logos was depicted as the Creator and the one who possessed life in himself. This motif (the Logos as the Creator and the life-giver) appears in John 1:10-13 in the eschatological context, in which the role of the Logos is to give birth the children of God (esp. vv. 12-13).

(5) Early Jewish creation accounts (as well as Genesis itself) paid attention to the creation of light, and speculated on its theological meanings in various ways.[63] It is important to notice that the light imagery was associated with the description of a revelatory activity of God. The light imagery appears in the description of the Torah (Sir 17:11; 2 Bar 17:4; 59:2; 77:13, 16; Wisd 18:4; T Lev 14:4) or of the event of the giving of the Torah (e.g. 2 Bar 59:2; LAB 15:5-6, etc.). It is also interesting that the light imagery appears in the eschatological context as a symbol of an eschatological blessing (as a revelation in a more salvific sense) (Jub 1:29; 2 En 65:10 [J]; LAB 3:10; SibOr 2:315).

Similarly, the Johannine prologue describes how the light which appeared first in the context of creation (John 1:4b-5) visited the world as 'true light' (τὸ φῶς τὸ ἀληθινόν). The figure of John the Baptist (John 1:6-8) may remind the readers of Isaianic prophecy which opens the meaning of φῶς (vv. 4b-5) toward the Isaianic use of the light imagery. In Isaiah, the Servant of Yahweh is already associated with the image of light (42:6; 49:6; 51:4), and especially in Isa 51:4 (cf. Isa 2:3-5) it is linked to the revelation of the law (תורה) or justice (משפט) (cf. the word of God [דבר־יהוה] in Isa 2:3-5). Thus, the light imagery is easily understood as a symbol of 'saving revelation.' The contents of its 'revelation' are mainly dealt with in the rest of the prologue (the revelation of the name, glory, fullness of grace and truth, and God the Father), and the revelation is said to have been accomplished in the ministry of the Son (or his sonship).

(6) Key motifs (of the descriptions of the divine identity and the role of the Logos) which occur in the first stanza (vv. 1-5) are gradually expanded and developed in the rest of the prologue. The Johannine Christology in the prologue is developed on the basis of the exposition of the Genesis creation

---

[63] See § 7.1.6.

account. Therefore, it is no exaggeration to say that the Johannine prologue presents a christological exegesis of the Genesis creation account.

Chapter 8

The Relation of the Prologue to the Rest of the Gospel

The relation of the prologue to the rest of the Gospel is one of the questions which has been seriously examined ever since Harnack's first effort (1892).[1] Since then, this question has been critically argued, mainly by source analyses which focus on identifying the original independent hymn (Christian or non-Christian) behind the prologue.[2] They have argued that several theological concepts and terms in the prologue (e.g. the concept of the incarnation of ὁ λόγος; the tent dwelling of the Son [σκηνόω] in contrast with the dwelling in the Temple; the concepts of πλήρης χάρις καὶ ἀληθείας, and οἱ ἴδιοι), as well as prologue's unique literary style are scarcely reflected in the rest of the Gospel.[3] On the other hand, there are scholars who have pointed out several motifs shared by the prologue and the rest of the Gospel. J. A. T. Robinson suggests that the prologue was written as an introduction to the body of the Gospel, just after the writing of the Johannine Epistles and that this is why similar symbolic terms appear in 1 John 1:1-2.[4] He also lists 12 themes which are shared by the prologue and the rest of the Gospel.[5] E. Harris attempts a more systematic study of this question and reaches the conclusion that the description of the role of the Logos is deliberately subsumed in the Gospel by the terms 'the Son of Man' and 'the Son of God,' and the phrase

---

[1] A. von Harnack, 'Über das Verhältnis des Prologs des vierten Evangeliums zum ganzen Werk,' *ZTK* 2 (1892), 189-231.

[2] See § 6.1.

[3] E.g. R. Bultmann, *John*, 13-18; R. Schnackenburg, *John*, 225-226; R. Brown, *John*, 18-21.

[4] J. A. T. Robinson, 'The Relation of the Prologue to the Gospel of St. John,' *NTS* 9 (1962), 123-124.

[5] The pre-existence of the Logos or Son (1:1; 17:5); the life motif (1:4; 5:26); the relation between life and light (1:4; 8:12); the rejection of light by darkness (1:5; 3:19); the victory of light over darkness (1:5; 12:35); the coming of light into the world (1:9; 3:19; 12:46); the rejection of Christ by his own (1:11; 4:44); being born of God and not of flesh (1:13; 3:6; 8:41); seeing his glory (1:14; 12:41); the only-begotten Son (I:14, 18; 3:16); truth in Jesus Christ (1:17; 14:6); the statement that no one has seen God, except the one who comes from God's side (1:18; 6:46) (Robinson, 'Relation,' 122). He also referred to B. T. D. Smith's work ('The Johannine Theology,' in F. Jackson [ed.], *The Parting of the Roads* [1912], 256) which suggested that the description of Christ which was presented in the prologue gives a framework for the rest of the Gospel (Robinson, 'Relation,' 122-123).

ἐγώ εἰμί.[6] Although the fuller study of this question lies outside the scope of our thesis, this chapter will show that several key christological motifs which appear in the Johannine prologue are expanded in the rest of the Fourth Gospel. As has been observed in the prologue, several motifs in the first stanza (John 1:1-5) are developed into the portrayal of the Son of God (μονογενής) in the rest of the prologue. Furthermore, the plot of the narrative gradually unfolds and develops these motifs in christological contexts of the Gospel. This chapter will mainly focus on examining how the descriptions of 'the divine identity' and 'the role' of the Son (Logos) in the prologue are associated with later christological statements in the Gospel.

8.1 The Description of the Divine Identity of the Son (Logos)

8.1.1 Pre-existence

The motif of the pre-existent Logos is one of the prominent motifs in the Johannine prologue (John 1:1, 10, 15), and it is also essential to the Johannine Christology.[7] In the rest of the Fourth Gospel, the focus clearly shifts from the pre-existent Logos (John 1:1-5) to the incarnated Logos, which means the dwelling of the Son of God on the earth.   However, the motif of the pre-existence is taken over in the description of the 'Son of God.'

John 1:30

The Fourth Gospel begins after the prologue with two episodes of John's testimony (John 1:19-34). In the second episode, John the Baptist cries, ἴδε ὁ ἀμνὸς τοῦ θεοῦ ὁ αἴρων τὴν ἁμαρτίαν τοῦ κόσμου (John 1:29; cf. 36), which alludes to Isa 53:7. He claims that the prophecy of Isaiah and the prophecy told him by the one who sent him (John 1:33) was fulfilled: οὗτός ἐστιν ὑπὲρ οὗ ἐγὼ εἶπον (John 1:30). John emphasizes that the testimony belongs to God's mystery. There was none who knew him (John 1:26), and John the Baptist did not know him either until God revealed it to him (John 1:31, 33). The Son had been known in the prophecy (in the word of God) before it happened. The prophecy was fulfilled, the mystery was revealed, and the testimony that he who came after (ὀπίσω) John was the Son of God (ὁ υἱὸς τοῦ θεοῦ) was presented (John 1:34). John 1:30 presents an enigmatic statement that the one who came after (ὀπίσω) John was before (ἔμπροσθέν and πρῶτος) him. The temporal aspect is seen in the term ἔμπροσθέν, since it is used in

---

[6] E. Harris, *Prologue.* She also observes the connection between the prologue and the Gospel concerning the witness of John.

[7] R. Schnackenburg, *Jesus in the Gospels: A Biblical Christology* (O. Dean [tr.]; Kentucky: Westminster John Knox Press, 1993 [1995]), 287.

contrast to the antithetic word ὀπίσω. It may be true that ἔμπροσθέν μου also indicates Jesus' priority of status over John. However, the statement is supported by the next announcement that indicates Jesus' priority in time (πρῶτος μου). The audience who had understood that John the Baptist came before Jesus, might have been amazed and guided into understanding the revealed mystery that the Son was pre-existent. The same testimony has already been quoted in the prologue (v. 15), in which the pre-existence of the Logos and light (vv. 1-5, v. 9) is the focus. Therefore, the first readers would have easily associated it with the description of the incarnated Logos.

John 8:58

The assertion of the Son's pre-existence is also made in John 8:58: 'I am (ἐγὼ εἰμι) before Abraham was (γενέσθαι).' This is the climactic statement of the long dialogue between the Jews and Jesus (John 8:12-59),[8] in which Jesus' identity is hotly debated.[9] It is pointed out that there are several absolute 'I am' sayings in the Fourth Gospel (e.g. John 8:24, 28, 58) (which seem to be based on a series of such sayings in Isaiah), and that the ἐγὼ εἰμι sayings in John 8:58 was based on the ἐγὼ εἰμι sayings in Isaiah (esp. Isa 43:10, 13) (LXX; אני הוא [MT]) in which YHWH claims exclusive divinity.[10] If this is the case, then the claim of pre-existence in the ἐγὼ εἰμι saying in John 8:58 may possibly be linked to the proclamation of the deity of Yahweh in Isaiah 43.[11] It should be noticed that the motif of God's eternal existence is emphasized in connection with the claim of Yahweh's divinity in Isaiah 43:10 and 13.

Isa 43:10 . . . ἔμπροσθέν μου οὐκ ἐγένετο ἄλλος θεὸς καὶ μετ' ἐμὲ οὐκ ἔσται

---

[8] D. Ball (*'I Am' in John's Gospel: Literary Function, Background and Theological Implications* [JSNTSup 124; Sheffield: Sheffield Academic Press, 1996], 80-81) suggests that John 8:12-59 should be regarded as a literary unit since the ἐγὼ εἰμι saying in the first and third sections form an inclusio. Cf. Kern's chiastic structural understanding (W. Kern, 'Der symmetrische Gesamtaufbau von Joh. 8, 12-58,' *ZTK* 78 [1956], 451-454).

[9] M. Hengel ('The Old Testament in the Fourth Gospel,' 26 and 39) refers to the Jewish tradition which tells of Abraham as a Witness to the Messiah and the day of salvation (i.e. ApAbr 9:1-10; ApLao frag. 48).

[10] P. Harner (*The 'I am' of the Fourth Gospel*, Facet Books [Philadelphia: Fortress, 1970], 37-45) discussed a connection of the reference to Abraham (John 8:31-56) with the Targumic interpolation of Abraham into Yahweh's words in Isaiah, in which Abraham was described with the theme of deliverance and salvation; D. Ball (*'I Am,'* 185-198) finds both linguistic and thematic correspondence between Isa 43:10 and the ἐγὼ εἰμι saying in Jesus' mouth. See these correspondences: the role of Jesus as the 'witness' (John 8:18; Isa 43:13); the identity of Jesus as the life-giver (John 8:24, 28; Isa 43:10, 25) (D. Ball, *'I Am,'* 185-194).

[11] M. Davies (*Rhetoric and Reference in the Fourth Gospel* [JSNTSup 69; Sheffield: Sheffield Academic Press, 1992], 84-86) argues that Jesus' saying is no more than a claim to superiority over Abraham. But this is not the case if we consider the background of Isa 43.

Isa 43:13 ἔτι ἀπ᾽ ἀρχῆς καὶ οὐκ ἔστιν ὁ ἐκ τῶν χειρῶν μου ἐξαιρούμενος
ποιήσω καὶ τίς ἀποστρέψει αὐτό

Thus, Jesus' claim of pre-existence (John 8:58) speaks of an intimate identification with the exclusive God of Isaiah, as D. Ball has rightly commented.[12] The Jews understood this saying as an assertion of the pre-existence of Jesus (John 8:57), and presumably as something related to the proclamation of deity (John 8:59).[13]

John 17:5, 24b

The assertion of the Son's pre-existence is made also in the prayer of Jesus (John 17:1-26).

καὶ νῦν δόξασόν με σύ, πάτερ, παρὰ σεαυτῷ τῇ δόξῃ ᾗ εἶχον πρὸ τοῦ τὸν κόσμον εἶναι παρὰ σοί (John 17:5).

ἵνα θεωρῶσιν τὴν δόξαν τὴν ἐμήν, ἣν δέδωκάς μοι ὅτι ἠγάπησάς με πρὸ καταβολῆς κόσμου (John 17:24b).

When Jesus knew that his hour (ἡ ὥρα αὐτοῦ) had come (John 17:1; cf. 12:27; 13:31), he prayed that the glory of the Father should be perfectly manifested (John 17:5; cf. 12:28; 13:31). Both John 17:5 and 17:24 emphasize that the Son possessed the glory before the world was created: πρὸ τοῦ τὸν κόσμον εἶναι (17:5); πρὸ καταβολῆς κόσμου (17:24), and that the glory was given in the intimate relationship with the Father: παρὰ σοί (17:5); ὅτι ἠγάπησάς με (17:24). According to the prologue, the glory is depicted as μονογενοῦς παρὰ πατρός, and it was manifested in the event of the incarnation of the Logos (John 1:14). That means that the glory which was manifested in the Son was pre-existent in the same sense.

John summarizes the earthly ministry of the Son as being to reveal the glory of the Father. The Son manifested the glory of the Father, having accomplished the work which the Father gave him to do (John 17:4). The Fourth Gospel understands the words and works of the earthly Jesus as manifestations of the glory (John 2:11; 8:54; 11:4; 17:4), and the cross as a climactic revelation of glory of the Father (John 7:39; 12:16, 23; 13:31-32). John 17:4 seems to mention that this glorification of the Son would never be diminished after Jesus' departure (return to the Father, or to the world above) (John 17:5, 24), since the phrase, 'to glorify in your presence (παρὰ σεαυτῷ),' seems to imply the glorification of the exalted Son in heaven, which is

---

[12] D. Ball, *'I Am,'* 191.

[13] Stoning was prescribed for blasphemy (e.g. Lev 24:16; m. Sanh 7:4 [D. A. Carson, *John,* 358]).

contrasted with the glory which was manifested in the earthly mission of the Son (i.e. to glorify the Father on earth [John 17:4; cf. 12:28; 13:31]). That is to say, on the one hand, the prologue describes the coming of the Son to the world as the revelation of the glory (John 1:14), whereas, on the other hand, Jesus' prayer, which has been considered an epilogue to the farewell discourse (John chs. 13-17),[14] describes Jesus' departure to the Father in order to share the Father's glorification.[15] Furthermore, in Jesus' prayer, the ultimate hope of the Son is that believers would witness the glory of the Son in the presence of the Father (παρὰ σεαυτῷ) at the end time (John 17:24; cf. 14:1-3). Thus, the eternity of the glory of the Son is an important claim of the Johannine Christology.

8.1.2 Intimacy with the Father

In the early Jewish creation accounts, the divine attributes (such as the word of God and wisdom) appear in contexts where the sovereignty of God is highlighted. On the one hand, they are personified and function as agents for the work of creation (and also for the eschatological work); on the other hand, they never jeopardize the monotheistic framework but rather support the understanding of the unique identity of God. Based on this notion of the God-attribute relationship, the unique relationship of the Logos and God is remarkably expressed in John 1:1-2. It should be noted that this oneness motif is totally subsumed into the other notion of the Father-Son relationship in John 1:14-18, since the focus shifts from the pre-existent Logos to the incarnated Logos, which means the coming of the Son of God. The motif of the intimate relationship of the Son and the Father is prominent in the rest of the Fourth Gospel as well. The Son shares the lordship of the Father (e.g. John 5:21, 26; 10:28-29), the Father's work (John 6:38; 8:29; 9:33; 10:32; 14:10, 31), the Father's word (John 3:11; 8:26, 28; 12:49; 14:24; 17:14), and the Father's glory (John 11:4, 40; 12:28; 13:31-32; 17:1). Jesus' divine status was climactically proclaimed in the confession of Thomas, ὁ κύριός μου καὶ ὁ θεός μου (John 20:28). M. Hengel states that the confession of the divinity of Christ stands at the beginning (John 1:1) and the end of the Fourth Gospel.[16]

John 5:17-18

John 5:14-18 records one of the dialogues between Jesus and the Jews on the sabbath law. Jesus answered, 'My Father is working (ἐργάζεται) until now,

---

[14] E.g. R. G. Hamerton-Kelly, *Pre-Existence, Wisdom, and the Son of Man: A Study of the Idea of Pre-existence in the New Testament* (Cambridge: Cambridge University Press, 1973), 215; C. H. Dodd, *Interpretation*, 420; C. K. Barrett, *John*, 417.

[15] Cf. M. L. Appold, *The Oneness Motif in the Fourth Gospel* (WUNT 1; Tübingen: J. C. B. Mohr [Paul Siebeck], 1976), 31.

[16] M. Hengel, *Studies in Early Christology* (Edinburgh: T&T Clark, 1995), 367.

and I am working (ἐργάζομαι)' (5:17). In other words, God has never ceased his activities even after the work of creation, but is still working (ἐργάζεται) for its completion.[17] The point is that Jesus referred to the ceaseless activity of the Father (possibly the creational works and the eschatological works) as the reason the Son was working on the sabbath. The Jewish audience could not accept this because the Jews clearly understood these words as a claim to equality with God the Father (ἴσον ἑαυτὸν ποιῶν τῷ θεῷ) (John 5:18).

John 5:19-30

The Jews' objection to Jesus' claim of equality with God in John 5:18 leads to the other arguments about the divine authority of the Son (John 5:19-30). In John 5:19-20 Jesus argued that the Son was doing his works in *oneness* with the Father, and that the Son was *entrusted* with the Father's works:

οὐ δύναται ὁ υἱὸς ποιεῖν ἀφ᾽ ἑαυτοῦ οὐδὲν ἐὰν μή τι βλέπῃ τὸν πατέρα ποιοῦντα (5:19b).

ἃ γὰρ ἂν ἐκεῖνος ποιῇ, ταῦτα καὶ ὁ υἱὸς ὁμοίως ποιεῖ (5:19c).

ὁ γὰρ πατὴρ φιλεῖ τὸν υἱὸν καὶ πάντα δείκνυσιν αὐτῷ ἃ αὐτὸς ποιεῖ (5:20a).
καὶ μείζονα τούτων δείξει αὐτῷ ἔργα (5:20b).

The oneness motif is developed into the eschatological context that mentions the end time life and judgment (5:21-22):

ὥσπερ γὰρ ὁ πατὴρ ἐγείρει τοὺς νεκροὺς καὶ ζῳοποιεῖ, οὕτως καὶ ὁ υἱὸς οὓς θέλει ζῳοποιεῖ (5:21).

οὐδὲ γὰρ ὁ πατὴρ κρίνει οὐδένα, ἀλλὰ τὴν κρίσιν πᾶσαν δέδωκεν τῷ υἱῷ (5:22)

J. Frey rightly comments that John 5:23 implies the climactic goal for the oneness of the Son and the Father: that is to say, that all may honor the Son

---

[17] R. Bauckham (in his comment on this part of my work) suggests that the most relevant Rabbinic text for John 5:17-18 is b. Ta'an 2a: God gives life on the Sabbath and God judges the dead on the Sabbath. Cf. P. Borgen's focus ('Creation,' 89) on the role of the Son as a mediator of the completion of the work of creation ('Creation,' esp. 92-93). See GenR 11: God works on the Sabbath by punishing or rewarding people (cf. H. Odeberg, *The Fourth Gospel* [2nd (ed.); Amsterdam: B. R. Grüner, 1968], 202); M. Hengel (*Studies in Early Christology*, 362) contrasts between the Old creation and New creation, showing correspondences between the Genesis creation account (Gen chs. 1-2) and the Johannine Christology: Gen 1:1 (beginning) to John 1:1; Gen 2:1 (accomplishment) to John 19:28; Gen 2:7 (breathing a breath of life) to John 20:21. He ('The Old Testament,' 33) also suggests that the Fourth Gospel begins with ἐν ἀρχή, the very beginning, before the six days of creation, and that Jesus dies in the evening of the sixth day of the week thereby finishing God's word.

as they honor the Father.[18] The argument of John 5:19-23 is repeated in John 5:26-30.[19] The Son was entrusted with authority to give eternal life (v. 26) and judgment (v. 27). John 5:28-29 highlights the eschatological aspects of the divine authority entrusted to the Son.[20]

John 8:12-30

The Pharisees argue against the authenticity of the Son's testimony, by saying, 'your testimony is not true, because you are bearing witness to yourself' (v. 13). Jesus answered that his testimony was true (ἀληθής) because he was bearing witness to himself (v. 14). That is to say, he expresses his divinity in that he is the one who needs no one to bear witness to himself. His self-recognition of his (divine) origin (πόθεν ἦλθον) and goal (ποῦ ὑπάγω) (v. 14) warrant his testimony. Secondly, by making reference to the legal rule that the testimony of two men is true (v. 18), Jesus answered that his testimony was also true because the Father who sent him bore witness to the Son (v. 18). It is God the Father who is bearing witness to Jesus. In other words, Jesus shows his unique relationship with the Father. The next concern of the Pharisees is, therefore, 'Where is your Father who bears witness to you?' (v. 19), in other words, 'How can we make sure of the testimony of the Father?' It is a hopeless question, because the Father could be known only through the revelation of the Son (v. 19): εἰ ἐμὲ ἤδειτε, καὶ τὸν πατέρα μου ἂν ἤδειτε. Another reason they could not understand the words of Jesus is that Jesus was in a different realm.

The next dialogue (v. 21 ff.) contrasts the two realms. They cannot come where Jesus goes (v. 21); they are from below (ἐκ τῶν κάτω), and Jesus is from above (ἐκ τῶν ἄνω)[21]; they are of this world (ἐκ τούτου τοῦ κόσμου), and Jesus is not of this world (v. 23). While the different origins of the Jews and Jesus is suggested, Jesus also mentioned the difference in position between the two: the Jews would die in their sins (vv. 21, 24), while on the contrary, Jesus is (ἐγώ εἰμι) the one who would give life (v. 24) and judge (κρίνειν) (v. 26). The Jews could not help asking of his identity, 'Who are you?' (v. 25a). This is what Jesus attempted to tell from the beginning (v. 25b). Thus, the main concern of the dialogue and the aim of these contrasts is to exhibit the divine identity of the Son, who is from above, and his unique relationship with the Father: Jesus is always with the Father (v. 29), and he is entrusted with authority to reveal the words of the Father (vv. 26, 28).

---

[18] J. Frey, *Die johanneische Eschatologie* III, 354.

[19] According to J. Frey's structural understanding (*Die johanneische Eschatologie* III, 322-335), v. 19 and v. 30 form an *Inclusio*, while there are parallelisms between vv. 21-23 and v. 26, as well as between v. 24 and 28.

[20] See J. Frey, *Die johanneische Eschatologie* III, 381-391.

[21] Cf. John 3:31 (ἄνωθεν); 3:3, 7; 19:11.

John 10:22-39

At the Feast of Dedication, there was a dialogue between the Jews and Jesus, concerning the identity of Jesus. Jesus did not hesitate to claim oneness with the Father (v. 30) (ἐγὼ καὶ ὁ πατὴρ ἕν ἐσμεν.) in having authority to rule his people (v. 28-29).[22] No one is able to snatch them out of Jesus' hand, and no one shall snatch them out of the Father's hand (vv. 28-29). There is a parallelism to exhibit an equality in the divine role between the Father and the Son. The Jews understood Jesus' claims of oneness with the Father in the context as identification with God, and took up stones to punish him for blasphemy (v. 33): σὺ ἄνθρωπος ὢν ποιεῖς σεαυτὸν θεόν. Against their condemnation, Jesus argues that the works (τὰ ἔργα) that he does in his Father's name bear witness to him (v. 25) because the works are the testimony that the Father is in him and that Jesus is in the Father (v. 38).

John 14:5-11

In the first part of the farewell discourse with the disciples, Jesus mentioned his destination again (vv. 2-3). In the dialogue with the Jews (John 8:12-30), Jesus said to them that they did not know the destination (8:14). On the contrary, he advises his disciples that they know the way (τὴν ὁδόν) (v. 4). Namely, it is the way to the Father (πρὸς τὸν πατέρα) (v. 6). In the former dialogue with Thomas (vv. 1-5), the destination itself is the focus; however, in the latter discussion, the focus shifts to the role of the Son as the way (ἡ ὁδὸς) which guides his disciples to the Father (vv. 6-11). When Jesus designates himself as the way through which the people can come to see the Father, Jesus suggests that he is the perfect revelation of the Father.[23] In this sense, Jesus could say that he who has seen the Son has seen the Father (vv. 7, 9). The unique relationship between the Father and the Son is restated: the Son is in the Father and the Father is in the Son, and the Father dwells in the Son and does his works (vv. 10-11).

John 17:5

In the prayer of Jesus (John 17:1-26), while the earthly ministry of the Son is summarized as the revelation of the glory of the Father (vv. 1, 4-5, 10, 22, 24), the ultimate goal of salvation is spelled out as believers being one, as the Father and the Son are one (ἵνα ὦσιν ἓν καθὼς ἡμεῖς) (v. 11; cf. vv. 21-23, 24, 26). Eternal life is now depicted as the inauguration of the unique (intimate) relationship among believers and the Father and the Son (v. 3); i.e. to know the Father and the Son (γινώσκωσιν σὲ τὸν μόνον ἀληθινὸν θεὸν καὶ ὃν ἀπέστειλας Ἰησοῦν Χριστόν). That is to say, believers are invited into the divine

---

[22] It is also related to the description of the lordship of the Son (see § 8.1.4).

[23] The revelation would be completed in that day (ἐν ἐκείνῃ τῇ ἡμέρᾳ) (John 14:20).

community, which was revealed through the ministry of the Son. Jesus and the Father are one, so that they shared glory before the world was created (v. 5). Now it is expected that believers would become perfectly one (ὦσιν τετελειωμένοι εἰς ἕν) (v. 23), so that the glory which the Father and the Son shared would be witnessed by believers at the end time (v. 24).

8.1.3 The Lordship of the Son: Life and Judgment

It is common in early Judaism to think that God is the sole life-giver who has authority to produce life. Life clearly belongs to God himself and to his divine identity. The life-giving motif can only be shared with divine attributes, such as the word of God and wisdom (e.g. 2 En 30:8; 4 Ezra 7:69; JosAsen 12:2). The Logos in the Johannine prologue is also described as the divine agent through whom all things were made (John 1:3, 10), and in his name (i.e. in the authority which was given to him), the new creation of τέκνα θεοῦ was made (John 1:12). In the rest of the Gospel, the lordship of the Son is mentioned in several contexts.

John 3:35-36

After the testimony of John the Baptist (John 3:22-30), the Gospel presents christological statements that depict the divine authority which was bestowed the Son by the Father (John 3:31-36).

> He who comes from above (ἄνωθεν) is above all (ἐπάνω πάντων).
> He who comes from heaven (ἐκ τοῦ οὐρανοῦ) is above all (ἐπάνω πάντων).
> It is not by measure that he gives the Spirit.
> The Father loves the Son, and has given all things into his hand (ἐν τῇ χειρὶ αὐτοῦ).
> He who believes in the Son has eternal life.
> He who does not obey the Son shall not see life, but the wrath of God rests upon him.

The Son is ἐπάνω πάντων, since he comes ἄνωθεν or ἐκ τοῦ οὐρανοῦ (v. 31). God gives the Son the Spirit without measure (v. 34) and has given all things (πάντα) into the hand of the Son (ἐν τῇ χειρὶ αὐτοῦ) (cf. John 13:3). The phrase, ἐν τῇ χειρὶ, expresses the idea that the Son was given authority to rule over the world (cf. John 17:2; Matt 28:18). The eschatological judgment (life or the wrath of God) is also mentioned to have been entrusted to the Son (v. 36).

John 5:21-22, 26-27

When the lordship of the Son is mentioned, the Fourth Gospel clarifies its particular aim and its direction; i.e. to give eternal life to believers (John 3:36; 5:21, 24-29; 17:2) and to judge all (John 3:36; 5:22, 27).[24] According to early

---

[24] However, the Gospel emphasizes that the role or the ministry of the Son is to give life (for salvation) rather than to judge the world (John 3:17; 8:15;12:47).

Jewish creation accounts (and also eschatological accounts), God is often described as the sole life-giver who alone has authority to produce life (e.g. 2 Bar 21:4; 4 Ezra 3:3-5; JosAsen 8:10-11). This idea is exhibited in John 5:21-22 and 26-27:

> The Father raises the dead and gives them Life (ζῳοποιεῖ) (5:21a),
> so also (οὕτως) the Son gives Life (ζῳοποιεῖ) to whom he will (5:21b).

> The Father has Life in himself (ἔχει ζωὴν ἐν ἑαυτῷ) (5:26a),
> so also (οὕτως) he has granted (ἔδωκεν) the Son to have Life in himself (ζωὴν ἔχειν ἐν ἑαυτω) (5:26b).[25]

> He has given him authority (ἐξουσίαν) to execute judgment (κρίσιν ποιεῖν) (5:27).

It should be noted that firstly the Father is depicted as the life-giver (vv. 21a, 26a), and secondly the Son is depicted to have been entrusted by the Father with authority to give life to all things (vv. 21b, 26b). The Son is also entrusted with authority (ἐξουσίαν) to execute eschatological judgment (v. 27; cf. v. 30).

John 17:2

The lordship of the Son is remembered in the prayer of Jesus (vv. 1-26).

> Since you (the Father) have given him (the Son) power (ἐξουσίαν) over all flesh (πάσης σαρκός),
> in order that he (the Son) would give eternal life to all whom you (the Father) have given him (the Son) (v. 2).

The Father has given the Son power (authority) over all flesh, and this power (ἐξουσίαν) is entrusted to the Son to give eternal life to believers. In addition, Jesus emphasizes in the prayer that prior to this eschatological blessing (eternal life), the Father will have already entrusted his people into the hands of the Son (vv. 2, 6, 7, 9, 10, 24). Therefore, the Gospel's Christology asserts that the Son has been entrusted authority not only to give eternal life, but also to rule over his people until the end time. Considering Jewish understanding that the authority to do these things (life giving and ruling power) belong to God, the Son is clearly described as being involved in the unique identity of God in the rest of the Fourth Gospel.[26]

---

[25] See J. Frey's detailed analysis on John 5:19-30 in *Die johanneische Eschatologie III: Die eschatologische Verkündigung in den johanneischen Texten* (WUNT 117; Tübingen: Mohr Siebeck, 2000), 322-391.

[26] The Synoptic Gospels make a statement on the authority of Jesus to forgive sins in the narrative of the healing of a paralytic (Matt 9:6; Mark 2:10; Luke 5:26). Both Mark and Luke quote the question of the scribes, 'Who can forgive sins but God alone (εἰ μὴ εἷς ὁ

8.2 The Description of the Role of the Son (Logos)

8.2.1 The Eschatological Logos

The Johannine prologue hints at the eschatological Logos. This suggests a new agency of the word of God to accomplish the eschatological works of God, in contrast with the old agency of the word of God in accomplishing the works of creation. This motif is actually stated in the rest of the Gospel. In the dialogues between Jesus and the Jews on the sabbath law (John 5:17-18), Jesus referred to the ceaseless activity of the Father (possibly the creational works and the eschatological works) as the reason why the Son was working on the sabbath.[27] The Gospel repeats again and again that the Son was doing the works of the Father (John 6:38; 8:29; 9:33; 10:32, 37; 14:10, 31) and that the Son was sent to accomplish (τελειόω) the work (or the will) of the Father (John 4:34; 5:36; 17:4).

John 4:34

In John 4:34, Jesus said, 'My food is to do (ποιήσω) the will of him who sent me, and to accomplish (τελειώσω) his work.' The word combination, 'to do (ποιέω)' and 'to accomplish (τελειόω),' occurs only three times in the New Testament (John 4:34; 5:36; 17:4), and all examples are interestingly related to the ministry of the Son of God. In the Old Testament, this word combination occurs six times (Ps 37:7; Dan 8:12, 24; 11:36; Isa 55:11; 2 Chr 31:21), and in particular Isa 55:11 (ποιέω for עשה and τελειόω for צלח[28]) is the only example which refers to the work of God. Moreover, John 4:34 and Isa 55:11 have an interesting similarity as follows:

> My food is *to do* (ἵνα ποιήσω) *the will* of him who *sent* me, and *to accomplish* (τελειώσω) his work (John 4:34).

> It (Word) shall *do* (עשה) that which *I will*, and *accomplish* (והצליח) the thing for which I *sent* it (Isa 55:11).[29]

John 4:34 depicts the ministry of the Son as the food (βρῶμα), which may be contrasted to the water in John 4:14 (see John 6:35).[30] The motifs of both food and water appear in Isa 55:1-2 and 10 as the things which God would offer to the people in the end time. It should be noted that similarly, the

---

θεός)?' This means that the people in the Gospels considered the authority, which had been given to the Son, clearly to belong to the divine identity of God.

[27] See § 8.1.2.

[28] The LXX renders συντελέω as צלח.

[29] The LXX rendering amplifies the differences with the wording of John 4:34.

[30] Jesus is echoing Deut 8:3. However, the focus does not seem to be on the aspect of the word as the Torah, but on the aspect of the word that carries out the will of God.

ministry of the word of God (which is personified) in Isa 55:11 is depicted by the imagery of food and water (Isa 55:10). Therefore, it is possible to conclude that the description of the ministry of the Son of God in John 4:34 may allude to the figure of the word of God in Isa 55:11.

John 6:33, 38

Allusion to Isa 55:11 is also made in John 6:22-58. D. Burkett lists literary and thematic correspondences between Isa 55:1-11 and John 6:27-71.[31]

ISAIAH 55:1-11	JOHN 6:27-71
Two types of food are contrasted, that which does not satisfy and that which does (1-2).	Two types of food are contrasted, that which perishes and that which remains (27).
One should not pay money or one's labor for the food which does not satisfy (2).	One should not work for the food which perishes (27).
One should buy the food which satisfies, which is given without a price (1).	One should work for the food which remains, which the Son will give (27).
To buy and eat the food which satisfies is to listen (receptively) to the word of God (2).	To work for the food which remains is to believe in the one whom God sent (28-29).
'Incline your ear and come to me' (3).	'Everyone who has heard from the Father and learned comes to me (45: cf. 35, 37, 44, 65).
If one listens to God's word (eats the bread which satisfies), one's soul will live (3).	If one eats the bread of life one will live forever (27, 33, 35, 40 etc.).
Listening to the word of God satisfies both hunger and thirst (1-2).	'He who comes to me shall not hunger and he who believes in me shall never thirst' (35, cf. 53-56).
The word of God is sent by God (11).	Jesus, the living bread, is sent by God (29, 38, 39, 44, 57).
The word of God, like the rain and snow, descends from heaven (10-11).	The bread of God is that which descends from heaven and gives life to the world (33).
The word of God, like the rain and snow, gives bread to eat (10-11).	Jesus, or the Father, gives bread (27, 32, 51).
The word of God does the will of God, who sent it (11).	'I have come down from heaven not to do my own will, but the will of the one who sent me' (38).
The word of God returns to God in heaven (10-11).	The Son of the Man ascends to where he was before (62).

---

[31] D. Burkett, *The Son of the Man in the Gospel of John* (JSNTSup 56; Sheffield: Sheffield Academic Press, 1991), 131-132.

First of all, the motifs of food and water (Isa 55:1-2) can be seen in John 6:27 and 35 (cf. John 6:53-56), whereas the descent motif (Isa 55:10-11) appears in John 6:33, 38, 50-51 and 58. The figure of descending Manna in Ps 78:23-25 might be linked to this motif. Scholars have observed that Deut 8:3 is also the background for the life-giving motif in John 6:33.

> [Deut 8:3 (LXX)]
> Man shall not live by bread alone, but by every word (παντὶ ῥήματι) that comes out from the mouth of God shall man live.[32]

> [Isa 55:11a]
> So (as the rain comes down from heaven, and gives bread to the eater [Isa 55:10]) shall my word be that goes out from my mouth.

This linking to the Manna motif may be related to a later account of the word of Jesus, which is designated as life (John 6:63; cf. 6:68). That is to say, the ministry of the Son is considered to have superseded the Mosaic law, which is often linked to the Manna motif in early and later Jewish traditions. However, this life-giving motif in John ch. 6 seems to imply a more dynamic aspect of the ministry of the Son of God. As previously observed, Isa 55:11 is the key in the creation accounts of 4 Ezra and 2 Baruch, and it presents the reality and certainty of the eschatological work of God. The personified word appears in both creational and eschatological contexts, and it is described as an agent to accomplish the will of God (4 Ezra 6:38, 43; 2 Bar 54:3 and 56:4). The Gospel repeatedly implies that the will of the Father is to give life to the world (John 3:16; 6:39-40; 12:50; cf, 5:21, 26), and the ministry of the Son is said to accomplish it; i.e. 'I have come down from heaven, not to do my own will, but the will of him who sent me' (John 6:38). Therefore, the motif of Isa 55:11 (the eschatological word), which is employed in the creation and eschatological accounts of 4 Ezra and 2 Baruch, seems to be an important background for the description of the ministry of the Son of God, particularly in John 4:34, 6:33 and 38.

8.2.2 The Revelation of the Father through the Ministry of the Son

The Work of the Son: the Revelation of the Father's Glory

In the prologue, the glory of the Son, as of the only Son from the Father (ὡς μονογενοῦς παρὰ πατρός) was witnessed by believers (John 1:14), and the only Son of God (μονογενὴς θεὸς) was said to have revealed the Father (John 1:18). In the rest of the Fourth Gospel, the ministry of the Son was said to carry out the work of the Father on earth (John 5:19; 5:20, 30; 6:38; 8:29; 10:32). The Son was always doing the Father's work (John 5:17-20; 8:16), and the Father

---

[32] The MT rendering, עַל־כָּל־מוֹצָא פִי־יהוה, alludes to the word of God as well.

was working in the Son (John 5:22, 27, 36; 8:28; 12:49; 17:4). Thus it could be said that any one who had seen the Son's work had seen the Father (John 12:45; 14:10; 15:24). In other words, the Son revealed the Father through his work which the Father gave him to accomplish on earth.

The earthly ministry of the Son was to reveal the Father's glory (11:40). The works revealed the Son's glory (John 2:11), and through them the Father was also glorified (John 11:4, 40; 13:31, 32). The Gospel proclaims that the Son's glory had been climactically revealed at the cross and exaltation of the Son (John 7:39; 12:16, 23, 28; 13:31-32; 17:1), and that this glorification was not only of the Son, but also of the Father (John 13:31-32; 17:1, 4). In other words, the Son climactically revealed the Father's glory through the cross and his exaltation. Although there is no clear mention of the cross in the prologue, the words, 'grace and truth came (ἐγένετο) through Jesus Christ' (John 1:17), may allude to the completion of the revelation of the Father's glory, that is the cross. If this is the case, then the prologue and the rest of the Gospel share an important motif of the Johannine Christology; i.e. the perfect glorification of the Father through the cross.[33]

The Word of the Son: the Revelation of the Father's Word

The Son of God is depicted not only as an agent who carries out the work of the Father, but also as a revealer of the word (or wisdom) of the Father. The Son speaks the words of God (τὰ ῥήματα τοῦ θεοῦ) (John 3:34; 14:24; 17:14), since the Son told what he had heard from the Father, and what he had been taught and commanded by the Father (John 3:11; 8:26, 28; 12:49).[34] It is noteworthy that John 14:10 states that, when the Son spoke his words (τὰ ῥήματα), the Father who dwelt in the Son did his works (τὰ ἔργα).

What the Son revealed to the world is the word of truth (ἀλήθεια) (John 8:40, 45, 46; cf. 18:37),[35] which the Son heard from the Father (John 8:40). It is the word concerning (eternal) life (John 6:63, 68; 12:50; 8:51-52; 10:18), which belongs to the Father's commandment (ἡ ἐντολὴ αὐτοῦ) (John 12:50). The Son spoke the word of love (John 13:34; 15:12, 17), which belongs to the Father's commandment (John 15:10). The Son revealed the Father's name (τὸ ὄνομα) (John 17:6), which the Father gave to him (John 17:11, 12) to make known (ἐγνώρισα [aorist] and γνωρίσω [future]) to believers (John 17:26). In the Exodus event (esp. Exod chs. 33-34), the Lord declared his name (33:19), which may have been a reminder of the original revelation of his name (אהיה

---

[33] The Gospel expands this role into the revelation of the glory of the Son and the Father, and entrusts it to later revelatory activity of the Spirit (John 16:4), and also to the works of believers (John 14:13; 15:8; cf. 21:19).

[34] Cf. Deut 18:18. The prophet is expected to tell the word of God and every thing which God will command.

[35] In John 8:45-46, truth is paralleled with the words of God (τὰ ῥήματα τοῦ θεοῦ).

אֲשֶׁר אֶהְיֶה) (Exod 3:14), when he was asked to reveal his glory by Moses (33:18). W. Dumbrell thus suggests that 'glory' represents the unique feature of divine majesty, whereas 'the name' provides the content of its revelation; similarly, the Father's name and glory are brought together in the person of Jesus.[36] Interestingly, in John ch. 17 the revelation of glory (John 17:1, 4) is paralleled with the revelation of the name of God (John 17:6, 11-12). Similarly, the prologue mentions the name of the Son which makes the restoration of God's people possible (John 1:12), while it also refers to the revelation of glory which is obviously grounded against the background of the Sinai event (John 1:14). Thus, the revelation of the name (John 1:12) is paralleled with the revelation of glory (John 1:14).

According to the Gospel, it is an important message of the Son that he was sent from the Father (John 5:36, 38; 6:29; 7:28, 29; 8:18, 42; 16:30; 17:3, 8, 21, 23, 25). In other words, these salvific messages of God (i.e. truth, life, love and revelation of God) are made available to those who know (or believe) that the Son was sent from the Father to make him known to the world. This revelation is made available through the Son, who alone heard the Father's voice (φωνὴν) and saw his form (εἶδος) (cf. John 5:37; cf. 3:32) and knew the Father (John 7:28-29; 8:19, 55). This understanding clearly corresponds to the prologue (John 1:18).

8.2.3 The Light for the World

The Fourth Gospel states that the Son came into the world as light (ἐλήλυθεν εἰς τὸν κόσμον) (John 3:19; 12:46) and dwelt temporarily in the world (John 9:5; 12:35, 36).[37] The words 'came into' may suggest that light which had pre-existed in the world above came into the world below. This motif of the coming of the pre-existent light is identical with the description of light in the prologue (John 1:5-9).

The Servant of Yahweh is already associated with the image of light in Isaiah (42:6; 49:6; 51:4),[38] and especially in Isa 51:4 (cf. Isa 2:3-5) it is linked to the revelation of the law (תורה) or justice (מִשְׁפָּט) (cf. the word of God [דבר־יהוה] in Isa 2:3-5). The light is thus easily understood as a symbol of 'saving revelation.' Similarly, when it refers to the earthly ministry of the Son in the Gospel, the light imagery indicates 'saving revelation,' which guides people in a proper direction or to a proper goal (John 12:35) with hope of

---

[36] W. Dumbrell, 'Law and Grace,' 29-30.

[37] *While I am in the world* (ὅταν ἐν τῷ κόσμῳ ὦ), I am the light of the world (9:5); The light is with you *for a little longer* (ἔτι μικρὸν χρόνον) (12:35); *While you have the light* (ὡς τὸ φῶς ἔχετε), believe in the light (12:36). These examples allude to the death of Jesus (cf. John 9:4; 12:33).

[38] R. Schnackenburg, *John*, vol. 2, 190.

eternal life.[39]   The expression 'the light of the world' (τὸ φῶς τοῦ κόσμου) (John 8:12) should be understood as 'the light for the world (i.e. the objective genitive), through which believers will not walk in darkness, but will have the light of life (τὸ φῶς τῆς ζωῆς). This description of believers, who walk in the light, may be contrasted with the other picture of unbelievers, who belong to this world below so that they will die in their sin (John 8:21-24).   In this sense, the world below (John 8:21-24) may become co-extensive with darkness as the sphere in which the way is lost (12:35).[40]   The Son came into this world below as light, as the revealer of salvific knowledge, through which believers are guided into the right direction or to the right goal with hope of eternal life (8:12; cf. 8:21-24).   In John 9:5, Jesus' claim to be the light of the world is grounded on the symbolism that (spiritual) blindness is contrasted with sight in the narrative of the healing of the blind (John 9:1-41).[41]   Jesus' claim to be light thereby indicates that it is the Son who gives sight (or light) to the spiritual blindness of the world.[42]   The healing of the blind (Isa 42:7, 16), or their enlightening (Isa 60:19-20; Jub 1:29; 2 En 165:7 [J]; LAB 3:10; SibOr 2:315), is counted as an eschatological blessing in the biblical and early Jewish tradition.   If it is background for the Johannine symbolism, then the Son is depicted as an eschatological light which guides the blind in the end time and opens their eyes with his saving revelation (cf. Isa 6:10; 42:21).   In the prologue, the Logos is depicted to be 'true light' (John 1:9), which is 'for human beings' (John 1:4b).   The figure of John the Baptist (John 1:6-8) hints at the Isaianic use of light imagery as a symbol of 'saving revelation.'   The Johannine prologue claims that the revelation has been accomplished through the Son; i.e. the Son reveals the name (1:12), glory (1:14a), the fullness of grace and truth (1:14b, 16-17) and God the Father (1:18).

8.2.4 The Life Motif

The prologue proclaims that in him (ἐν αὐτῷ [the Logos]) was life (John 1:4a). This statement seems to correspond to John 5:39-40:

> You search the scriptures, since you think that in them (ἐν αὐταῖς) you have eternal life; and it is they that bear witness to me. Yet you refuse to come to me that you may have *life.*

---

[39] R. Schnackenburg, *John*, vol. 2, 191.

[40] H. Schneider, 'The Word Was Made Flesh,' *CBQ* 31 (1969), 345.

[41] See other references to the contrast between sight and blindness (John 8:12; 11:9-10; 12:35-36, 40, 46). Cf. R. Schnackenburg, *John*, vol. 2, 255.

[42] The idea of contrast between spiritual blindness and sight (Isa 6:10; 42:18-20; 43:8) is also an important Isaianic message. Isa 6:10 is cited to depict Jewish stubbornness in John 12:40.

As previously discussed, the Gospel emphasizes that the Father has given all things (πάντα) into the hand of the Son (ἐν τῇ χειρὶ αὐτοῦ) (John 3:35; cf. John 10:28-29; 13:3). When the lordship of the Son is mentioned, it clarifies its particular aim and direction; i.e. to give eternal life to believers (John 3:36; 5:21, 24-29; 17:2), as well as to judge all (John 3:36; 5:22, 27). The only way to have life is announced in the Gospel: to believe in the name of the Son (John 3:16, 36; 5:24; 6:40, 47 [cf. 6:50-58]; 8:12; 8:51; 11:25; [cf. 14:6]; 20:31).

The dialogue with Nicodemus (John 3:1-12) discusses the new birth or new creation. Jesus argues that unless one is born from above (ἄνωθεν), he cannot see the kingdom of God (John 3:3; cf. 3:7). The expression 'to be born from above' is expanded as being begotten of water and Spirit (v. 5); moreover, its nature is explained by the contrast of flesh and Spirit (John 3:6): τὸ γεγεννημένον ἐκ τῆς σάρξ and τὸ γεγεννημένον ἐκ τοῦ πνεύματος. The Gospel obviously describes Jesus (and his word) as the one who made life (salvation) available to believers through the fullness of his Spirit[43]:

He on whom you see *the Spirit* descend and remain, this is *he who baptizes with the Holy Spirit* (John 1:33).

It is *the Spirit that gives life*, the flesh is of no avail. *The words* that I have spoken to you are *Spirit and life* (John 6:63).

He who believes in me, as the scripture has said, 'Out of his heart shall flow rivers of living water.' Now this he said about *the Spirit*, which *those who believed in him* were to receive (John 7:38-39a).

Concerning the bestowment of the Spirit on believers, the Gospel comments that it would happen after Easter (John 7:39). When the risen Lord met his disciples, in associating them with his continuing mission on earth, he bestowed the Spirit on them with a symbolic action of breathing on them (ἐνεφύσησεν < ἐμφυσάω) (John 20:22). This action may have reminded the readers of the breathing of the breath of life (נשמת חיים) in the Genesis creation account (Gen 2:7), which is understood as the spirit (רוח) in Isaiah 42:5.[44] The Johannine symbolism (i.e. Jesus' bestowment of the Spirit on the disciples) may suggest the new creation of human beings through Jesus' fullness of the Spirit and his word (the fullness of salvific revelation) (cf. John 6:63, 68).

The prologue proclaims that all who believed in the name of the Son were given power to become children of God (ἐξουσίαν τέκνα θεοῦ γενέσθαι) (John 1:12) and to be born from God (ἐκ θεοῦ ἐγεννήθησαν) (John 1:13). These

---

[43] Cf. R. Schnackenburg, *John*, 386.

[44] Sir 17:1-14 and 1QS 3:18 focus on the bestowment of the spirit in the context of the creation of human beings.

words correspond to the idea of new birth from above (ἄνωθεν) or new creation in John 3:1-12. The Gospel states that it actually happened after Easter. That is to say, the risen Christ carefully instructed the disciples that the Father of the Son should be called 'your Father' and 'your God' (John 20:17). This is the inaugurated eschatological fulfillment of the restoration (or new creation) of God's people.

8.3 Summary and Conclusions

In the Johannine prologue, the divine identity and role of Jesus are dramatically expressed by the motif of the relationship between the Logos and God (esp. John 1:1-5), and by the motif of the relationship between the Son and the Father (or Jesus' sonship) (esp. John 1:14-18). In particular the latter christological motif (sonship) is obviously expounded in the rest of the Fourth Gospel, while hinting at the motif of the eschatological Logos as well.

(1) The motif of the pre-existent Logos (John 1:1-2) or the Son (John 1:14) is seen in the rest of the Fourth Gospel (esp. John 1:30; 8:58; 17:5, 24). The first statement is given through the Baptist's testimony (John 1:30), which has been already quoted in the prologue (John 1:15). The second assertion of the pre-existent Son is made in the ἐγώ εἰμι saying (John 8:58), which is considered by scholars to be associated with an exclusive claim of divinity by Yahweh (esp. Isa 43:10, 13). That is to say, the claim to pre-existence uttered by Jesus (John 8:58) speaks of an intimate identificaton with the exclusive God of Isaiah. The third assertion of the pre-existent Son is made in Jesus' prayer (John 17:1-26). The restoration of pre-existent glory (John 17:4, 24) seems to be in contrast to the description of the Logos which was shining in darkness (John 1:5) and the glory which was witnessed by believers when the pre-existent Logos was made incarnate (John 1:14).

(2) The oneness of the Logos and God is remarkably expressed in the Johannine prologue, and it is totally subsumed in the other notion of the Father-Son relationship in John 1:14-18 and in the rest of the Fourth Gospel. The Son shares the lordship of the Father because of the unique relationship the Son shares with the Father: i.e. they are one (ἐγὼ καὶ ὁ πατὴρ ἕν ἐσμεν) (John 10:30; 17:22). The Son had life in himself like his Father (John 5:21, 26). The Son's work (e.g. John 6:38; 8:29; 9:33; 10:32; 14:10, 31), word (John 3:11; 8:26, 28; 12:49; 14:24; 17:14) and glory (John 11:4, 40; 12:28; 13:31-32; 17:1) display the oneness of the Son and the Father. Jesus' ἐγώ εἰμι saying also claims an intimate identificaton with the exclusive God, and this was climactically manifested in the confession of Thomas, ὁ κύριός μου καὶ ὁ θεός μου (John 20:28).

(3) The Johannine prologue hints at the eschatological Logos. It displays a new agency of the word of God to accomplish the eschatological works of God, which is contrasted with the old agency of the word of God which accomplished the creational works. In John 4:34, Jesus refers to the ceaseless work of the Father (possibly the creational work and the eschatological work; cf. the Jewish exegetical tradition on the seventh day of creation) as the reason the Son was working on the sabbath. The terms and contexts of John 4:34 and 6:33, 38 may allude to Isa 55:11, which presents the reality and certainty of the eschatological work through the word of God.

(4) The work of the Son was the revelation of the Father's work (John 5:19; 5:20, 30; 6:38; 8:29; 10:32) and glory (11:4, 40; 13:31, 32). Although there is no clear mention of the cross in the prologue, the words, 'grace and truth came (ἐγένετο) through Jesus Christ' (John 1:17) may allude to the completion of the revelation of the Father's glory (John 7:39; 12:16, 23, 28; 13:31-32; 17:1); that is, the cross. The word of the Son is also the revelation of the word (or wisdom) of the Father (John 3:11, 34; 8:26, 28; 12:49; 14:24; 17:14). It is the word of life (John 6:63, 68; 12:50; 8:51-52; 10:18), the love command (John 13:34; 15:12, 17) and the revelation of the Father's name (τὸ ὄνομα) (John 17:6, 11, 12, 26). These revelations are made available through the Son who alone heard the Father's voice (φωνὴν) and saw his form (εἶδος) (cf. John 5:37; cf. 3:32) and knew the Father (John 7:28-29; 8:19, 55). This understanding clearly corresponds to the claim of the prologue, 'the only Son, who is in the bosom of the Father, he has made him known' (John 1:18).

(5) The Fourth Gospel states that the Son came into the world as light (John 3:19; 12:46). This motif of the coming of the pre-existent light is obviously identical with the description of light in the prologue (John 1:5-9). The Son came into this world as light, as the revealer of the salvific knowledge, through which believers are guided in the right direction or to the right goal with the hope of eternal life (8:12; cf. 8:21-24).

(6) The Gospel states that the Son was given authority to give life to people (John 3:36; 5:21, 24-29; 17:2), and that the only way to have life is to believe in the name of the Son (John 3:16, 36; 5:24; 6:40, 47 [cf. 6:50-58]; 8:12; 8:51; 11:25; [cf. 14:6]; 20:31). The prologue also proclaims that all who believed in the name of the Son were given power to become children of God (ἐξουσίαν τέκνα θεοῦ γενέσθαι) (John 1:12), and to be born from God (ἐκ θεοῦ ἐγεννήθησαν) (John 1:13). These words correspond to the idea of the new birth from above (ἄνωθεν) or the new creation through the spirit in John 3:1-12. The Gospel states that it actually happened after Easter (John 20:17), and Jesus' symbolic action of breathing on the disciples (John 20:22) may hint at a typological correspondence with the breathing of the breath of life (חיים נשמת) in the Genesis creation account (Gen 2:7), alluding to the new creation of human beings through the Son.

Chapter 9

Summary and Conclusion

This thesis has been concerned with the theological background of the Johannine Christology in the prologue, by focusing on the early Jewish exegetical traditions of the Genesis creation account (ca. the 2nd century BCE to the 1st century CE).

The first part of this thesis (chs. 2-5) has observed the ways the creation accounts were employed. Firstly, there are several ways by which the creation accounts were referred: (1) the narrative account of creation (a longer retelling of the Genesis creation account); (2) the descriptive account of creation (a shorter or a more interpretative account which focuses on particular events of creation); and (3) the brief reference to creation (a more generalized form of the creation accounts).

Secondly, we have observed the theological function of the creation account. First of all, the creation account highlights the unique identity of God as the (sole) Creator. Speculation on the sovereignty of God in some creation accounts accompanies a sapiential instruction, while it was also developed in a salvific and a more eschatological context, in which the revealed identity of God as the sole Creator corresponded typologically with the expected identity of God as the Fulfiller of the eschatological work. The focus was also directed to the identity of human beings or a more specified religious group (i.e. Israel or ideal Israel) to affirm their unique relationship to God or their original status as rulers of the earth. They examined where they were standing (in an ethical sense and often in a fatalistic sense) and when they were living (in an eschatological sense), and tried to find the way of life (in a sapiential context), as well as to foresee the immediate coming of salvation (for their restoration) and eternal life (in an eschatological context).

Thirdly, early Jewish creation accounts found some links between the Genesis creation account and other biblical creation accounts. They were concerned with the biblical speculation on the divine identity of God as the Creator (Prov 8:22-29; Ps 33:6-12; 90:12; 119:73; 139:2-8; Jer 10:12-13; Isa 40:18-26; 45:7). The astronomical and meteorological accounts of Job chs. 38-43 and Ps 104:5-23, which highlight God's providence, are often mentioned. When the Genesis creation account was linked to Isa 48:3, 13 and 55:11 (2 Baruch and 4 Ezra), or linked to Ps 33:6-9 (Sirach and ApAbr), the creational motifs were expanded in a more salvific and eschatological context.

Fourthly, the description of the unique identity of God as the Creator often accompanies the divine attributes (i.e. the word of God [or command, oath], wisdom [or knowledge], right hand [or hands], name, and spirits). Each imagery exhibits a particular sense or aspect of the unique identity of God. The divine word (or his command) seems to be associated with the description of the sovereign power of God in his creational works. Influenced by Isa 48:3, 13 and 55:11 (and Ps 33:6-9), the creational word is expanded into a salvific or an eschatological word (esp. 4 Ezra and 2 Baruch; cf. JosAsen, ApAbr, and Sir). Wisdom is mentioned in the context where God's providence over all creation (both space and time) is highlighted. Both the divine word and wisdom appear simultaneously in some cases (2 En ch. 33; Sir ch. 42; Wisd ch. 9; 4Q403), and generally the former implies the reality of God's deed or his works, whereas the latter depicts the perfect design or plan of God.

Fifthly, this thesis has observed that the life motif is deeply associated with the unique identity of God as well. God is the sole life-giver who himself has the authority to produce life *ex nihilo*. The divine attributes are linked to this description: wisdom is assigned to create Adam (2 En 30:8), whereas the divine word functions to produce human beings (4 Ezra 7:69); in JosAsen 12:1-2, the word is called 'life.'

Finally, our study has observed that the creation accounts speculated on the theological meanings of the creation of light(s) (אור and מארת). The creation of light was understood as a manifestation of the sovereign power of God, whereas light was considered to be a divine thing. This light motif as a divine thing was easily linked to the divine nature of the Torah or the salvific revelation. It is noteworthy that both life and light motifs were counted as eschatological blessings.

In accordance with our findings in early Jewish creation accounts, Part II (chs. 6-8) has attempted to provide literary and thematic analyses of the Johannine prologue. First of all, Chapter 6 has proposed a tripartite parallel structural understanding of the prologue which suggests that the key themes (the identity and the role of the Logos) which occur in the first stanza (John 1:1-5) are gradually expanded and developed in two other stanzas, with the relationship between the Logos and God being subsumed into the relationship between the Son and the Father (John 1:6-13 and 1:14-18).

Chapter 7 has observed that the Johannine Christology in the prologue was developed on the exposition of the Genesis creation account. Based on the understanding that there is speculation on the work of creation in the description of the unique identity of God, and that only the divine word, as well as wisdom, can be an agent of the creational work, the Johannine prologue claims that the Logos (Son) was obviously associated with the unique identity of God. Thus the prologue carefully attempted to develop Christology on the basis of the exegetical traditions of the Genesis creation account in which Jewish monotheism was carefully preserved.

In addition, the motif of the creative word (esp. Ps 33:6 and 9 and Isaiah 48:3 and 55:11) was expanded and developed into the eschatological word in early Jewish and Christian tradition (e.g. Sir ch. 39; ApAbr 21-22; 4 Ezra ch. 6; 2 Bar chs. 14, 21, 48, 54; 2 Pet 3:5-7; cf. Jas 1:18; 1 Pet 1:18). In contrast with the agency of the divine word which accomplished the creational work, the new agency of the divine word to accomplish the eschatological work was greatly expected. When the prologue employed the Word (ὁ λόγος) in the contexts of both creation (John 1:1-5) and eschatology (John 1:6-18), the motifs of the (creational and eschatological) word may have been in both the author's and the first readers' minds. Therefore, the divine word provides the Johannine Logos with an important aspect.

Moreover, the Johannine prologue modifies the Logos with the life motif which was often employed to depict the identity of God as the sole life-giver in early Jewish creation accounts. In the prologue, the Logos was depicted as the Creator and the one who possessed life in himself. This motif may be associated with the authority (τὸ ὄνομα αὐτοῦ) which was given to the Logos through which the children of God would be born (esp. vv. 12-13).

In relation to the life motif, the Johannine prologue claims that the Logos was light, and describes how the light which appeared firstly in creation (John 1:4b-5) visited the world as 'the true light' (τὸ φῶς τὸ ἀληθινόν). In the Jewish tradition, the creation of light is typologically applied to the revelation of the Torah. Thus, the light imagery is easily understood as a symbol of 'saving revelation.' The contents of its 'revelation' are mainly considered in the rest of the prologue (i.e. the revelation of the name, glory, fullness of grace and truth, and God the Father). In summary, we have observed that the description of the identity and the role of the Logos (the Son) were made on the basis of the exegetical tradition of the Genesis creation account. Therefore, we have reached the conclusion that the Johannine prologue presented a christological interpretation of the Genesis creation account.

The final attempt of our thesis (Chapter 8) was to observe that the descriptions of the divine identity and the role of the Son (Logos) in the prologue are associated with the christological statements in the rest of the Fourth Gospel. Firstly, the motif of the pre-existence (John 1:1-2, 15) is found in the Baptist's testimony (John 1:30), in Jesus' 'I am saying' (John 8:58) which alludes to an exclusive claim of the divinity of Yahweh (esp. Isa 43:10, 13), and in Jesus' prayer (John 17:4, 24) which alludes to the pre-existent glory in John 1:5. Secondly, the oneness motif (John 1:1-2, 18) is prominent in the rest of the Fourth Gospel (John 10:30; 17:22). The Son's work (John 6:38; 8:29; 9:33; 10:32; 14:10, 31), word (John 3:11; 8:26, 28; 12:49; 14:24; 17:14), and glory (John 11:4, 40; 12:28; 13:31-32; 17:1) also display the oneness of the Son and the Father. An intimate identification of Christ with the only God (John 1:1) is climactically manifested in the confession of Thomas, ὁ κύριός μου καὶ ὁ θεός μου (John 20:28). Thirdly, the motif of the eschatological word (which is hinted at in the Johannine Logos) can be observed in John 4:34 and 6:33 and 38. These contexts may allude to Isa 55:11. Fourthly, the role of the Son as the revelation of God (John 1:16-17, 18) is an important message in the rest of the Gospel. The work of the Son was the revelation of the Father's work (John 5:19; 5:20, 30; 6:38; 8:29; 10:32) and glory (11:4, 40; 13:31, 32), as well as the Father's name (τὸ ὄνομα) (John 17:6, 11, 12, 26). Although there is no clear mention of the cross in the prologue, 'grace and truth' which came or was accomplished (ἐγένετο) through Jesus (John 1:17) may allude to the completion of the revelation of the Father's glory (John 7:39; 12:16, 23, 28; 13:31-32; 17:1), that would be the cross. The Son's word is also the revelation of the word (or wisdom) of the Father (John 3:11, 34; 6:63, 68; 8:26, 28, 51-52; 10:18; 12:49-50; 13:34; 14:24; 15:12, 17; 17:14). Fifthly, the life motif which depicts the identity of the Logos (the Son) in the prologue shares its idea with the rest of the Gospel. The Son was given the authority to give life to the world (John 3:36; 5:21, 24-29; 17:2), and the only way to have life is to believe in the name of the Son (John 3:16, 36; 5:24; 6:40, 47 [cf. 6:50-58]; 8:12; 8:51; 11:25; [cf. 14:6]; 20:31). The claim of the prologue that all who believe in the name of the Son would be born from God (ἐκ θεοῦ ἐγεννήθησαν) (John 1:13) may correspond to the idea of new birth from above (ἄνωθεν) or the new creation (John 3:1-12). Jesus' symbolic action of breathing on the disciples after Easter (John 20:22) may hint at a typological correspondence with the breath of life in the Genesis creation account (Gen 2:7). Finally, the light motif which depicts the role (or the ministry) of the Logos (the Son) in the prologue appears in the Gospel as well. The Son came into the world as light (John 3:19; 12:46), and as the revealer of salvific knowledge through which believers are guided to the right direction or goal with a hope of eternal life (8:12; cf. 8:21-24). Therefore, the descriptions of 'the divine identity' and 'the role' of the Son (Logos) in the prologue are associated with later christological statements in the Fourth Gospel. In other words, the prologue functions as a christologically oriented introduction which is deeply associated with the description of the identity and the ministry (the role) of the Son of God in the rest of the Fourth Gospel.

Reflection on our observations may give a new light to several debated issues. Firstly, our conclusion will challenge and refute Bultmannian assumption that the Johannine Logos cannot be understood on the basis of the OT. Once the Johannine prologue is carefully compared with early Jewish creation accounts, it becomes clear how John develops Christology on the basis of the exposition of the OT (especially Pentateuch and Isaiah). The thesis emphasizes that the (creative and salvific) motifs of the divine word (e.g. in Genesis, Psalms, and Isaiah) were much focused and expanded in a more eschatological speculation in first century Judaism (e.g. 4 Ezra, 2 Baruch; cf. JosAsen, ApAbr, Sir). Secondly, this thesis challenges recent christological discussions which have searched for some mediator figures in or outside biblical and Jewish literature in order to find a divine position for Christ. This thesis argues that the Johannine prologue claims that the right place for Christ (the Son) should be found in the unique identity of God (within the context of Jewish monotheism), which was revealed in his work of creation and in the eschatological hope. Finally, this thesis challenges recent Johannine scholarship which has so strongly emphasized the Jewish wisdom tradition that has easily ignored the context in which the Genesis creation account is the focus. Admitting a possible influence from the personified figure of divine wisdom, this thesis argues that the (creative and eschatological) figures of the divine word play a primary role in the Johannine prologue which is concerned with the eschatological events inaugurated in the revelation of the identity and the ministry of the Son of God.

Bibliography

Ackerman, J. S. 'The Rabbinic Interpretation of Psalm 82 and the Gospel of John: John 10:34.' *HTR* 59 (1966), 186-191.

Albright, W. F. 'The Bible After Twenty Years of Archeology.' *RL* 21 (1952), 549.

Allegro, J. M. *The Dead Sea Scrolls* (Baltimore: Vallentine, Mitchell, 1956).

Andersen, F. I. '2 (Slavonic Apocalypse of) Enoch.' in J. Charlesworth (ed.), *The Old Testament Pseudepigrapha*, vol. 1 (New York: Doubleday, 1983), 91-221.

Appold, Mark L. *The Oneness Motif in the Fourth Gospel* (WUNT II/1; Tübingen: J. C. B. Mohr [Paul Siebeck], 1976).

Argall, R. A. *1 Enoch and Sirach: A Comparative Literary and Conceptual Analysis of the Themes of Revelation, Creation and Judgment* (Atlanta: Scholars Press, 1995).

Ashton, John. 'The Transformation of Wisdom: A Study of the Prologue of John's Gospel.' *NTS* 32 (2) (1986), 161-186.

_____. *Understanding the Fourth Gospel* (Oxford: Oxford University Press, 1991).

Atkinson, K. M. T. 'The Historical Setting of the "War of the Sons of Light and the Sons of Darkness.' *BJRL* 40 (1957), 286.

Attridge, Harold. (ed.) *Qumran Cave 4, VIII, Parabiblical Texts*, part 1 (DJD 13; Oxford: Clarendon Press, 1994).

Baars, W. and Schneider, H. 'Prayer of Manasseh.' in The Peshitta Institute Leiden (ed.), *The Old Testament in Syriac: According to the Peshitta Version* (Leiden: E. J. Brill, 1972).

Baillet, Maurice. (ed.) *Qumrân Grotte 4 III* (4Q482-4Q520) (DJD 7; Oxford: Clarendon Press, 1982).

Ball, David Mark. *'I Am' in John's Gospel: Literary Function, Background and Theological Implications* (JSNTSup 124; Sheffield: Sheffield Academic Press, 1996).

Bardtke, Hans. 'Die Loblieder von Qumran.' *TLZ* 81 (1956), 149-153.

Barrett, C. K. *The Gospel according to St. John* (2nd [ed.]; Philadelphia: Westminster Press, 1978).

_____. *The Prologue of St John's Gospel* (London: The Athlone Press, University of London, 1971).

Bauckham, Richard. *The Climax of Prophecy: Studies on the Book of Revelation* (Edinburgh: T. & T. Clark, 1993).

_____. *God Crucified: Monotheism and Christology in the New Testament* (Carlisle: Paternoster Press, 1999).

_____. *Jesus and Identity of God* (forth-coming).

_____. 'The Liber Antiquitatum Biblicarum of Pseudo-Philo and the Gospels as "Midrash."' in R. T. France (ed.), *Gospel Perspectives III* (Sheffield: Sheffield Academic Press, 1983), 33-76.

_____. 'Qumran and the Fourth Gospel: Is There a Connection?.' in S. Porter and C. A. Evans (eds.), *The Scrolls and the Scriptures* (JSPSup 26; Sheffield: Sheffield Academic Press, 1997).

_____. 'The Relevance of Extra-Canonical Jewish Texts to New Testament Study.' in J.Green (ed.), *Hearing the New Testament: Strategies for Interpretation* (Grand Rapids: Eerdmans, 1995), 90-108.

_____. 'The Sonship of the Historical Jesus in Christology.' *SJT* 31 (1978), 245-260.

_____. 'The Throne of God and the Worship of Jesus.' in J. Davila and C. Newman (eds.) *The Jewish Roots of Christological Monotheism: Papers from the St. Andrews Conference on the Historical Origins of the Worship of Jesus* (Leiden: E. J. Brill, 1999), 43-69.

Becker, Heinz. *Die Reden des Johannesevangeliums und der Stil der Gnostischen Offenbarungsrede* (Göttingen: Vandenhoeck & Ruprecht, 1956).

Bensly, Robert L. (ed.) *The Missing Fragment of the Latin Translation of the Fourth Book of Ezra, Discovered and Edited with an Introduction and Notes* (Cambridge: Cambridge University Press, 1875).

Bernard, J. H. *A Critical and Exegetical Commentary on the Gospel according to St. John* (Edinburgh: T & T Clark, 1928).

Black, Matthew. (ed.) *The Book of Enoch or I Enoch: A New English Edition with Commentary and Textual Notes* (Leiden: E. J. Brill, 1985).

Boismard, M. E. *St. John's Prologue* (Westminster: Newman, 1957).

Borgen, Peder. 'Creation, Logos and the Son: Observation on John 1:1-18 and 5:17-18.' *Ex Auditu* 3 (1987), 88-97.

_____. *Logos was the True Light and other Essays on the Gospel of John* (Trondheim, Norway: Tapir Publishers, 1983).

_____. 'Observations on the Targumic Character of the Prologue of John.' *NTS* 16 (1970), 288-295.

_____. *Philo, John and Paul: New Perspectives on Judaism and Early Christianity* (Atlanta: Scholars Press, 1987).

Böttrich, Christfried (ed.) *Apokalypsen: Das slavische Henochbuch* (JSHRZ V/7; Gütersloher Verlagshaus, 1995).

Box, G. H. 'IV Ezra.' in Charles (ed.), *The Apocrypha and Pseudepigrapha of the Old Testament in English.* vol. 2 (Oxford: Clarendon Press, 1913).

Brooks, E. W. (ed.) *Historia Ecclesiastica Zachariae Rhetori Vulgo Adscripta I* (CSCO 38; Louvain: Imprimerie Orientaliste L. Durbecq, 1953).

_____. *Historia Ecclesiastica Zachariae Rhetori Vulgo Adscripta I: Interpretatus est* (CSCO 41; Louvain: Imprimerie Orientaliste L. Durbecq, 1953).

Brown, Raymond E. *The Gospel According to John (I-XII)* (AB 29; New York: Doubleday, 1966).

Bruce, F. F. *The Gospel of John* (Grand Rapids, Michigan: Eerdmans Publishing Co., 1983).

Bultmann, R. 'Der religionsgeschichtliche Hintergrund des Prologs zum Johannesevangelium.' in H. Schmidt (ed.), *EYXAPISTHPION: Studien zur Religion und Literatur des Alten und Neuen Testaments* (Göttingen: Vandenhoeck & Ruprecht, 1923), 3-26.

_____. 'Die Bedeutung der neuerschlossenen Mandäischen Quellen für das Verständnis des Johannesevangeliums.' *ZTK* 24 (1925), 100-146.

_____. *The Gospel of John: A Commentary,* tr. G. R. Beasley-Murray (Philadelphia: The Westminster Press, 1971) = *Das Evangelium des Johannes* (Göttingen: Vandenhoeck & Ruprecht, 1964).

Burchard, C. (ed.) *Unterweisung in erzählender Form, Joseph und Aseneth* (JSHRZ 2; Gütersloh: Gütersloher Verlagshaus Gerd Mohn, 1983).

Burkett, D. *The Son of the Man in the Gospel of John* (JSNTSup 56; Sheffield: Sheffield Academic Press, 1991).

Carmignac, Jean and Guilbert, P. (eds.) *Les Textes de Qumran* (Paris: Letouzey et Ané, 1961).

Carson, D. A. *The Gospel according to John* (Leicester: Inter-Varsity Press).

Carter, Warren. *'The Prologue and John's Gospel: Function, Symbol and the Definitive Word'* (JSNT 39; Sheffield: Sheffield Academic Press, 1990), 35-58.

Charles, R. H. (ed.) *The Book of the Secrets of Enoch: Translated from the Slavonic by W. R. Morfill* (Oxford: Clarendon Press, 1896).

_____. (ed.) *The Apocrypha and Pseudepigrapha of the Old Testament in English.* 2 vols. (Oxford: Clarendon Press, 1913).

Charlesworth, J. H. 'The SNTS Pseudepigrapha Seminars at Tübingen and Paris on the Books of Enoch.' *NTS* 25 (1979), 315-323.

_____. 'A Critical Comparison of the Dualism in 1QS 3:13-4:26 and the "Dualism" Contained in the Gospel of John.' in J. H. Charlesworth (ed.), *John and the Dead Sea Scrolls* (New York: Crossroad, 1990), 76-106.

_____. (ed.) *The Dead Sea Scrolls: Hebrew, Aramaic, and Greek texts with English translations* (The Princeton Theological Seminary Dead Sea Scrolls Project 2; Tübingen: J. C. B. Mohr, 1995).

_____. and R. A. Culpepper. 'The Odes of Solomon and the Gospel of John.' *CBQ* 35 (1973), 298-322.

_____. (ed.) *John and the Dead Sea Scrolls* (New York: Christian Origins Library, 1990).

_____. (ed.) *Graphic Concordance to the Dead Sea Scrolls* (Tübingen: J. C. B. Mohr [Paul Siebeck], 1991).

Clementis, VIII. (ed.) *Biblia Sacra* (Paris: Apud Garnier Fratres, Bibliopolas, 1868).

Collins, J. J. 'Sibylline Oracles.' in Charlesworth (ed.), *The Old Testament Pseudepigrapha,* vol. 1 (New York: Doubleday, 1983), 317-472.

Coloe, Mary. 'The Structure of the Johannine Prologue and Genesis 1.' *ABR* 45 (1997), 40-55.

Colson, F. H. and Whitaker, G. H. (eds.) *Philo* (LCL; Massachusets: Harvard University Press, 1929).

Cook, Joan E. 'Creation in 4 Ezra: The Biblical Theme in Support of Theology,' in R. Clifford and et. al. (eds.) *Creation in the Biblical Traditions* (Washington, DC: Catholic Biblical Association of America, 1992).

Cross, F. M. *The Ancient Library of Qumran* (New York: Anchor Books, 1961).

_____. 'The Development of the Jewish Scripts.' in G. E. Wright (ed.), *The Bible and the Ancient Near East: Essays in Honor of William Foxwell Albright* (Garden City, New York: Anchor Books A431, 1965), 170-264.

Culpepper, R. A. 'The Pivot of John's Prologue.' *NTS* 27 (1980), 1-31.

Davies, Margaret. *Rhetoric and Reference in the Fourth Gospel* (JSNTSup 1; Sheffield: England: Sheffield Academic Press, 1992).

Davis, Peter. 'Divine Agents, Mediators, and New Testament Christology.' *JTS* 45(2) (1994), 479-503.

Davis, Philip. *The Literary Structure of 1QM* (Ph. D. Thesis St. Andrews: University of St. Andrews, 1973).

de la Potterie, Ignace. 'Structure du Prologue de Saint Jean.' *NTS* 30 (1984), 354-381.

Dillmann, August. *Ethiopic Grammar* (London: Williams & Norgate, 1907).

Díez Macho, A. (ed.) *Neofiti I. Targum Palestunense. MS dela Biblioteca Vaticana.* 5 vols. (Madrid-Barcelona: Consejo Superior de Investigationes Científicas, 1968).

Dodd, C. H. *The Interpretation of the Fourth Gospel* (Cambridge: Cambridge Unversity Press, 1965).

Driver, G. R. *The Judaean Scrolls* (Oxford: Basil Blackwell, 1965).

Dumbrell, William J. 'Law and Grace: The Nature of the Contrast in John 1:17.' *EQ* 58 (1) (1986), 25-37.

Dunn, J. D. G. *Christology in the Making: A New Testament Inquiry into the Origin of the Doctrine of the Incarnation* (London: SCM Press, 1980).

Dupont-Sommer, A. *The Essene Writings from Qumran* (New York: Meridan Books, 1962).

_____. (ed.) *Le Livre des Hymnes découvert près de la mer Morte (1QH).* (Semitica 7; Paris: Librairie d'Amérique et d'Orient Adrien Maisonneuve, 1957).

Edwards, Ruth B. 'χάριν ἀντὶ χάριτος (John 1:16): Grace and the Law in the Johannine Prologue.' *JSNT* 32 (1988), 3-15.

Elgvin, Torleif. *The Genesis Section of 4Q422 (4QParaGenExod)* (DSD 1; Oxford: Clarendon Press, 1994), 180-196.

Elliott, J. K. 'John 1:14 and the New Testament's Use of πλήρης.' *BT* 28 (1977), 151-153.

Ellis, P. *The Genius of John: A Composition-Critical Commentary on the Fourth Gospel* (Collegeville: Liturgical Press, 1984).

Ensor, Peter W. *Jesus and His Works* (WUNT II/85; Tübingen, J. C. B. Mohr [Paul Siebeck], 1996).

Epp, Eldon J. 'Wisdom, Torah, Word: The Johannine Prologue and the Purpose of the Fourth Gospel.' in G. F. Hawthorne (ed.), *Current Issues in Biblical and Patristic Interpretation: Studies in Honor of Merrill C. Tenny Presented by his Former Students* (Grand Rapids: Eerdmans, 1975), 128-146.

Eshel, E. and et al. (eds.) *Qumran Cave 4. VI: Poetical and Liturgical Texts.* Part 1 (DJD 11; Oxford: Clarendon, 1998).

Evans, Craig A. *Word and Glory: on the Exegetical and Theological Background of John's Prologue* (JSNTSup 89; Sheffield: Sheffield Academic Press, 1993).

Fossum, Jarl E. *The Name of God and the Angel of the Lord* (WUNT 36; Tübingen: J. C. B. Mohr [Paul Siebeck], 1985).

Frey, Jörg. 'Different Patterns of Dualistic Thought in the Qumran Library: Reflections on their Background and History' in M. Bernstein, F. García Martínez, and J. Kampen [eds.] *Legal Texts and Legal Issues* [Leiden: Brill], 1997], 275-335.

_____. *Die johanneische Eschatologie II: Das johanneische Zeitverständnis* (WUNT 110; Tübingen: Mohr Siebeck, 1998).

_____. *Die johanneische Eschatologie III: Die eschatologische Verkündigung in den johanneischen Texten* (WUNT 117; Tübingen: Mohr Siebeck, 2000).

Fritsch, C. T. *The Qumrân Community* (New York: Anchor Books, 1956).

Gardiner, S. C. *Old Church Slavonic: An Elementary Grammar* (Cambridge: Cambridge University Press, 1984).

Geffcken, Joh. (ed.) *Die Oracula Sibyllina* (Leipzig: J. C. Hinrichs'sche Buchhandlung, 1902).

Giblin, C. H. 'The Tripartite Narrative Structure of John's Gospel.' *Bib* 71(4) (1990), 449-468.

Green, H. C. 'The Composition of St. John's Prologue.' *ET* 66 (1954-1955), 291-294.

Gächter, Paul. 'Strophen im Johannesevangelium.' *ZKT* 60 (1936), 99-111.

Haenchen, Ernst. *John 1* (Hermeneia; Philadelphia: Fortress Press, 1984).

_____. 'Probleme des Johanneischen "Prologs".' *ZTK* 60 (1963), 16-34.

Hamerton-Kelly, R. G. *Pre-Existence, Wisdom, and the Son of Man: A Study of the Idea of Pre-existence in the New Testament* (Cambridge: Cambridge University Press, 1973).

Hanson, A. 'John 1.14-18 and Exodus xxxiv.' *NTS* 23 (1976-1977), 90-101.

Harnack, A. von. 'Über das Verhältnis des Prologs des vierten Evangeliums zum ganzen Werk.' *ZTK* 2 (1892), 189-231.

Harner, Philip. *The 'I am' of the Fourth Gospel* (Facet Books Philadelphia: Fortress, 1970).

Harrington, D. J. 'Pseudo-Philo.' in Charlesworth (ed.), *The Old Testament Pseudepigrapha* vol. 2 (New York: Doubleday, 1985), 297-377.

Harris, Elizabeth. *Prologue and Gospel: The Theology of the Fourth Evangelist* (JSNTSup 107; Sheffield: Sheffield Academic Press, 1994).

Hayward, Robert. 'Memra and Shekhina: A Short Note.' *JJS* 31 (1981), 210-213.

_____. 'The Memra of YHWH and the Development of Its Use in Targum Neofiti 1.' *JJS* 25 (1974), 412-418.

Hengel, Martin. 'The Old Testament in the Fourth Gospel.' *HBT* 12 (1990), 19-41.

_____. *Studies in Early Christology* (Edinburgh: T&T Clark, 1995).

Hooker, M. 'John the Baptist and the Johannine Prologue.' *NTS* 16 (1969-1970), 40-58.

Hurtado, L. *One God, One Lord: Early Christian Devotion and Ancient Jewish Monotheism* (Philadelphia: Fortress Press, 1988).

Janssens, Y. 'The Trimorphic Protennoia and the Fourth Gospel.' in A. H. B. Logan and A. J. M. Wedderburn (eds.), *The New Testament and Gnosis* (Edinburgh: T. & T. Clark, 1983), 229-244.

Kee, H. C. '"The Man" in fourth Ezra: Growth of a Tradition.' *SBLASP* 20 (1981), 199-208.

Kern, W. 'Der symmetrische Gesamtaufbau von Joh. 8, 12-58.' *ZTK* 78 (1956), 451-454.

King, J. S. 'Prologue to the Fourth Gospel: Some Unsolved Problems.' *ET* 86 (1975), 372-375.

Kisch, Guido (ed.) *Pseudo-Philo's Liber Antiquitatum Biblicarum* (Notre Dame, Indiana: University of Notre Dame, 1949).

Kittel, Bonnie Pedrotti. *The Hymns of Qumran: Translation and Commentary* (Missoula, MT: Scholars Press, 1980).

Kmosko, M. (ed) *Epistola Baruch Filli Neriae* (Patrologia Syriaca Paris: Instituti Franciti Typographi, 1907).

Knibb, Michael A. (ed.) *The Ethiopic Book of Enoch: A New Edition in the Light of the Aramaic Dead Sea Fragments* (Oxford: Clarendon Press, 1978).

_____. *The Qumran Community* (Cambridge: Cambridge University Press, 1987).

Kuhn, K. G. 'Die Sektenschrift und die iranische Religion.' *ZTK* 49 (1952), 296-315.

Kurfess, C. A. 'Sibylline Oracles.' in R. McL. Wilson (ed.), *New Testament Apocrypha* vol. 2 (Philadelphia: Westminster Press, 1963-1964).

Käsemann, Ernst. 'Aufbau und Anliegen des Johanneischen Prologs.' in Ernst Käsemann (ed.), *Libertas Christiana, Festschrift für F. Delekat* (München: 1957); (English version) 'The Structure and Purpose of the Prologue to John's Gospel.' in E. Käsemann (ed.), *New Testament Question of Today* (Philadelphia: Fortress Press, 1969), 138-167.

Lacan, M. 'Le Prologue de saint Jean. Ses thèmes, sa structure, son mouvement.' *LumVie* 33 (1957), 91-110.

Lamarche, P. 'Le Prologue de Jean.' *RSR* 52 (1964), 529-532.

Lange, Armin. *Weisheit und Prädestination: Weisheitliche Urordnung und Prädestination in den Textfunden von Qumran* (STDJ 18; Leiden: E.J. Brill, 1995).

Leaney, A. R. C. *The Rule of Qumran and its Meaning: Introduction, translation and commentary* (London: SCM Press, 1966).

Licht, Jacob. (ed.) מגילת ההודיות (Jerusalem: Bialik Institute, 1957).

Longenecker, Bruce W. *Eschatology and the Covenant: A Comparison of 4 Ezra and Roman 1-11* (JSNTSup 57; Sheffield: Sheffield Academic Press, 1991).

Louw, J. P. 'Christologiese himnes. Die Johannese Logos-Himne (John 1:1-18).' in J. H. Barkhuizen (ed.), *Hymni Christiani* (Pretoria: HTS, 1989), 35-43.

Lund, Nils Wilhelm. *Chiasmus in the New Testament* (Chapel Hill: The University of North Carolina Press, 1942).

_____. 'The Influence of Chiasmus upon the Structure of the Gospels.' ATR 13 (1931), 41-46.

Lunt, H. 'The Apocalypse of Abraham.' in Charlesworth (ed.), *The Old Testament Pseudepigrapha* vol. 1 (New York: Doubleday, 1983), 689-705.

MacRae, G. W. 'The Jewish Background of the Gnostic Sophia Myth.' *NovT* 12 (1970), 86-101.

Mansoor, M. *The Thanksgiving Hymns* (Leiden: E. J. Brill, 1961).

Marcus, Ralph (ed.) *Philo Supplement I* (LCL; Cambridge, MA: Harvard University Press, 1987).

Martínez, F. G. (ed.) *The Dead Sea Scrolls Translated: The Qumran Texts in English* (Leiden: E. J. Brill, 1996).

_____. (ed.) *The Dead Sea Scrolls Study Edition*, vol. 1 (Leiden: E. J. Brill, 1997).

_____. and Barrera, J. T. *The People of the Dead Sea Scrolls: their writings, beliefs and practices, transl. by W. G. E. Watson* (Leiden: E. J. Brill, 1995 (1993).

McDonough, Sean M. *The One who is and who was and who is to come: Revelation 1:4 in its Hellenistic and Early Jewish Setting* (Ph. D Thesis; University of St. Andrews, 1997); now published, *YHWH at Patmos: Rev. 1:4 in its Hellenistic and Early Jewish Setting* (WUNT II/107; Tübingen: Mohr Siebeck, 1999).

McNamara. 'Logos of the Fourth Gospel and Memra of the Palestinian Targum (Ex. 12.42).' *ET* 79 (1968), 115-117.

_____. *Targum and Testament. Aramaic Paraphrases of the Hebrew Bible. A Light on the New Testament* (Granad Rapids/Shannon: Eerdmans/Irish University Press, 1972).

_____. (ed.) *Targum Neofiti 1: Genesis* (The Aramaic Bible 1A; Wilmington, Delaware: Michael Glazier, Inc., 1992).

Metzger, B. 'The Fourth Book of Ezra.' in J. Charlesworth (ed.), *The Old Testament Pseudepigrapha* vol. 1 (New York: Doubleday, 1983), 517-559.

Milik, J. T. "Prière de Nabonide' et autres écrits d'un cycle de Daniel: Fragments araméens de Qumrân 4.' *RB* 63 (1956), 407-415.

_____. and Black, M. (eds.) *The Book of Enoch. Aramaic Fragments of Qumran Cave 4* (Oxford: Clarendon, 1976).

Miller, ED. L. *Salvation-History in the Prologue of John The Significance of John 1:3-4* (NovTSup; Leiden, The Netherlands: E. J. Brill, 1989).

Mlakuzhyil, George. *The Christocentric Literary Structure of the Fourth Gospel* (Rome: Editrice Pontificio Istitute Biblico, 1987).

Moeller, Henry, R. 'Wisdom Motifs and John's Gospel.' *BETS* 6 (1963), 92-100.

Moore, G. F. 'Intermediaries in Jewish Theology.' *HTR* 15 (1922), 41-85.

Morris, Leon. *The Gospel According to John* (NICNT; Grand Rapids, Michigan: Eerdmans Publishing Co., 1971).

Munoz, Domingo. *Gloria de la Shekina en los Targumim del Pentateuco* (Madrid: Consejo Superior de Investigaciones Científicas. Instituto 'Francisco Suarez,' 1977).

Murphy-O'Connor. 'Community, Rule of the, (1QS).' in David Noel Freedman et al. (eds.), *Anchor Bible Dictionary*, vol. 1 (New York: Doubleday, 1992), 1110-1112.

Myers, Jacob, M. *I and II Esdras: Introduction, Translation and Commentary* (Garden City, NY: Doubleday, 1974).

Nida, E. A. 'Rhetoric and the Translator: With Special Reference to John 1.' *BT* 33 (1982), 324-328.

Odeberg, Hugo. (ed.) *3 Enoch or the Hebrew Book of Enoch* (Cambridge: Cambridge University Press, 1928).

_____. *The Fourth Gospel* (Amsterdam: B. R. Grüner, 1968).

Painter, John. 'Christology and the History of the Johannine Community in the Prologue of the Fourth Gospel.' *NTS* 30 (1984), 460-474.

Panimolle, S. 'Structura del Prologo,' in *Il Dono della Legge e la Grazia della Verità* (Gv 1, 17) (Roma 1973), 71-105.

Philonenko, Marc (ed.). *Joseph et Aséneth: Introduction Texte Critique Traduction et Notes* (Leiden: E. J. Brill, 1968).

Rahlfs, Alfred. (ed.) *Septuaginta* (Germany: Deutsche Bibelgesellschaft Stuttgart, 1979).

Ridderbos, M. 'The Structure and Scope of the Prologue of the Gospel of John,' *NovT* 8 (1966), 180-201.

Ringgren, H. *The Faith of Qumran* (Philadelphia: Fortress Press, 1963).

Robinson, G. 'The Trimorphic Protennoia and the Prologue of the Fourth Gospel.' in J. E. Goehring (ed.), *Gnosticism and the Early Christian World* (Sonoma: Polebridge Press, 1990), 37-50.

Robinson, J. A. T. 'The Relation of the Prologue to the Gospel of St. John.' *NTS* 9 (1962), 120-129.

Rochais, Gérard. 'La Formation du Prologue (Jn. 1:1-18).' *SE* 37 (1985), 5-7.

Rubin, Milka. 'The Language of Creation or the Primordial Language: A Case of Cultural Polemics in Antiquity.' *JJS* (1998), 306-333.

Rubinkiewicz, R. 'Aporalypse of Abraham.' in Charlesworth (ed.), *The Old Testament Pseudepigrapha* vol. 1 (New York: Doubleday, 1983), 681-688.

Ruiten, van J. T. A. G. M. *Primeval History Interpreted: The Rewriting of Genesis 1-11 in the book of Jubilees* (JTSSup 66; Leiden: Brill, 2000).

Runia, David. *Philo of Alexandria and the 'Timaeus' of Plato* (Leiden: E. J. Brill, 1986).

Sanders, J. A. (ed.) *The Psalms Scroll of Qumran Cave 11* (DJD 4; Oxford: Clarendon, 1965).

_____. 'Nag Hammadi, Odes of Solomon, and NT Christological Hymns.' in J.E. Goehring (ed.), *Gnosticism and the Early Christian World: In Honor of James M Robinson* (Sonoma: Polebridge Press, 1990), 51-66.

_____. *The New Testament Christological Hymns: Their Historical Religious Background* (Cambirdge: Cambridge University Press, 1971).

Schenke, H. 'Die Neutestamentliche Christologie und der Gnostische Erlöser.' in K. Tröger (ed.), *Gnosis und Neues Testament: Studien aus Religionswissenschaft und Theologie* (Berlin: Evangelische Verlangsanstalt, 1973), 205-229.

Schmithals, Walter. 'Der Prolog des Johannesevangeliums.' *ZNW* 70 (1979), 16-43.

Schnackenburg, Rudolf. *The Gospel according to St. John* (London; Burns & Oates, 1980); (orig. ed.) *Das Johannesevangelium* (Freiburg: Herder, 1965).

_____. *Jesus in the Gospel: A Biblical Christology* (Kentucky: Westminster John Knox Press, 1993 [1995]).

Schneider, Herbert. 'The Word Was Made Flesh.' *CBQ* 31 (1969), 344-356.

Schuller, E. M. '4Q380 and 4Q381: Non-Canonical Psalms from Qumran.' in D. Dimant and U. Rappaport (ed.), *The Dead Sea Scrolls: Forty Years of Reserch* (STDJ 10; Leiden: E. J. Brill, 1992), 241-256.

Schweizer, Eduard. *Ego Eimi: Die Religionsgeschichtliche Herkunft und Theologische Bedeutung der Joh. Bildreden* (Göttingen: Vandenhoeck & Ruprecht, 1965).

Scott, R. B. Y. 'Wisdom in Creation: The 'ĀMON of Proverbs VIII 30.' *VT* 10 (1960), 213-23.

Segal, M. H. 'The Qumran War Scroll and the Date of its Composition.' in Ch. Rabin and Y. Yadin (eds.), *Aspects of the Dead Sea Scrolls* (ScrHie 4; Jerusalem: Magnes, 1965), 138-143.

Sheppard, Gerald T. *Wisdom as a Hermeneutical Construct: A Study in the Sapientializing of the Old Testament* (BZAW 151; Berlin: Walter de Gruyter, 1980).

Skehan, P. W. 'Jubilees and the Qumran Psalter,' *CBQ* 37 (1975), 343-47.

_____. (ed.) *The Wisdom of Ben Sira* (AB 39; New York: Doubleday, 1987).

Slotki, Judah J. *Midrash Rabbah* (London: Soncino Press, 1939).

Smith, B. T. D. 'The Johannine Theology.' in F. J. Foakes Jackson (ed.), *The Parting of the Roads* (1912), 239-282.

Smith, J. Payne (ed.) *A Compendious Syriac Dictionary* (Oxford: Clarendon Press, 1903).

Sokolov, M. I. (ed.) *Slavyanskaya kniga Enoha Pravednage Tekst latinskij perevod i izsledovanie* (Moscow: The Inperial Society for Russian History and Antiquities, 1910).

Soulen, Richard N. *Handbook of Biblical Criticism* (Atlanta: John Knox Press, 1981).

Staley, J. 'The Structure of John's Prologue: Its Implication for the Gospel's Narrative Structure.' *CBQ* 48 (1986), 241-264.

Stone, M. E. *Fourth Ezra: A Commentary on the Book of Fourth Ezra* (Minneapolis: Fortress Press, 1990).

Sukenik, E. L. (ed.) *The Dead Sea Scrolls of the Hebrew University* (Jerusalem: Magnes, 1955).

Thackeray, H. (ed.). *Josephus* (LCL; London: William Heinemann Ltd, 1926).

Theobald, M. *Die Fleischwerdung des Logos. Studien zum Verhältnis des Johannesprologs zum Corpus des Evangeliums und zu 1 Joh* (Münster: Aschendorff, 1988).

_____. *Im Anfang war das Wort. Textlinguistische Studie zum Johannesprolog* (Stuttgart: Katholisches Bibelwerk, 1983).

Tikhonravov, N. S. (ed.) *Pamjatniki ostrec\cennoj russkoj literatury* (St. Petersburg, 1863) (C. H. van Schooneveld [rep.], *Slavistic Printings and Reprintings* [Paris: Mouton, 1970]).

Tov, E. (ed.) *The Dead Sea Scrolls on Microfiche: A Comprehensive Facsimile Edition of the Texts from the Judean Desert: Companion Volume* (Leiden: E. J. Brill and IDC, 1993).

_____. 'The Exodus Section of 4Q422.' *DSD* 1(2) (1994), 197-209, 419-424.

Treves, M. 'The Date of the War of the Sons of Light.' *VT* 8 (1958).

Tsumura, Toshio D. 'Literary Insertion (AXB Pattern) in Biblical Hebrew.' *VT* 33 (1983), 468-480.

Vaillant, A. (ed.) *Le Livre des Secrets D' Hénoch* (Paris: Institut D' 'Etudes Slaves: Texte Slave et Traduction Française, 1952).

VanderKam, James C. (ed.) *The Book of Jubilees* (CSCO 511; Louvain: Peeters, 1989).

_____. (ed.) *The Book of Jubilees: A Critical Text* (CSCO 510; Louvain: Peeters, 1989).

_____. 'Biblical Interpretation in 1 Enoch and Jubilees.' in J. Charlesworth (ed.), *The Pseudepigrapha and Early Biblical Interpretation* (JSPSup 14; Sheffield: Sheffield Academic Press, 1993), 96-125.

_____. and Milik, J. T. (eds.) *Qumran Cave 4* (DJD 13 Oxford: Clarendon Press, 1994).

Vattioni, Francesco. *Ecclesiastico: Testo ebraico con apparato critico e versioni greca, latina e siriaca* (Napoli: Istituto Orientale di Napoli, 1968).

Vermes, Geza (ed.) *The Dead Sea Scrolls in English* (London: Penguin Books, 1995).

_____. 'Preliminary Remarks on Unpublished Fragments of the Community Rule from Qumran Cave 4.' *JJS* 42 (1991), 250-255.

Vermes, Pamela. 'Buber's Understanding of the Divine Name related to Bible, Targum and Midrash.' *JJS* 24 (1973), 147-66.

von der Osten-Sacken, P. *Gott und Belial* (Göttingen: Vandenhoeck & Ruprecht, 1969).

Watson, W. G. E. *Classical Hebrew Poetry: A Guide to its techniques* (JSOTSup; Sheffield: Sheffield Academic Press, 1984).

Watt, Jan G. van Der. 'The Composition of the Prologue of John's Gospel: The Historical Jesus Introducing Divine Grace.' *WTJ* 57 (1995), 311-332.

Wenham, Gordon J. *Genesis 1-15* (WBC; Waco, Texas: Word Books Publisher, 1987).

Wenthe, Dean O. 'The Use of the Hebrew Scriptures in 1QM.' *DSD* 5 (3) (1999), 290-319.

Wernberg-Møller. 'An Inquiry into the Validity of the Text-Critical Argument for an Early Dating of the Recently Discovered Palestinian Targum.' *VT* 12 (1962), 312-330.

Willett, Tom W. *Eschatology in the Theodicies of 2 Baruch and 4 Ezra* (JSPSup 4 Sheffield: JSOT Press, 1989).

Winston, D. 'The Iranian Component in the Bible, Apocrypha, and Qumran: A Review of the Evidence.' *HR* 5 (1966), 183-216.

_____. (ed.) *The Wisdom of Solomon* (AB 43; New York: Doubleday, 1979).

Wise, Michael and et. al. (eds.) *The Dead Sea Scrolls: A New Translation* (London: Harper Collins, 1996).

Witherington, Ben. *John's Wisdom* (Louisville: Westminster/J. Knox, 1995).

Wintermute, O. S. 'Jubilees' in J. Charlesworth (ed.), *The Old Testament Pseudepigrapha* vol. 2 (New York: Doubleday, 1985), 35-142.

Wolfson, H. A. *Philo: Foundation of Religious Philosophy in Judaism, Christianity and Islam*, vol. 1 (Camgridge, MA: Harvard, 1947).

Yadin, Y. *The Scroll of the War of the Sons of Light against the Sons of Darkness* (Oxford: Oxford University Press, 1962).

Yagi, S. (ed.) *The Old Testament Pseudepigrapha* (Apocrypha and Pseudepigrapha 3; Tokyo: Kyobunkan, 1976) (Japanese).

Yamauchi, Edwin M. 'Gnostic Ethics and Mandaean Origins.' HTS 24 (1970).

_____. 'Jewish Gnosticism? The Prologue of John, Mandaean Parallels, and the Trimorphic Protennoia.' in R. van den Brock and M.J. Vermaseren (eds.), *Studies in Gnosticism and Hellenistic Religions* (EPRO; Leiden: Brill, 1981), 467-497.

_____. *Pre-Christian Gnosticism: A Servey of the Proposed Evidences* (Grand Rapids, Michigan: Eerdmans Publishing Co., 1973).

Yonge, C. D. (ed.) *The Works of Philo: New Update Edition* (Peabody, MA: Hendrickson, 1993).

York, A. 'The Dating of the Targumic Literature.' *JSJ* 5 (1974), 49-62.

Zaehner, R. C. *The Dawn and Twilight of Zoroastrianism* (London: Weidenfeld and Nicolson, 1961).

Zaehner, R. C. *Zurvan: A Zoroastrian Dilemma* (Oxford: Clarendon Press, 1955).

Index of Sources

Old Testament

New Testament

Jewish Texts

Josephus:

Targumim:

Other Text

Index of Names

Index of Subjects

292   *Indexes*

Wissenschaftliche Untersuchungen zum Neuen Testament

Alphabetical Index of the First and Second Series

Byrskog, Samuel: Story as History – History as Story. 2000. *Volume 123.*

Cancik, Hubert (Ed.): Markus-Philologie. 1984. *Volume 33.*

Capes, David B.: Old Testament Yaweh Texts in Paul's Christology. 1992. *Volume II/47.*

Caragounis, Chrys C.: The Son of Man. 1986. *Volume 38.*

– see *Fridrichsen, Anton.*

Carleton Paget, James: The Epistle of Barnabas. 1994. *Volume II/64.*

Carson, D.A., O'Brien, Peter T. and *Mark Seifrid* (Ed.): Justification and Variegated Nomism: A Fresh Appraisal of Paul and Second Temple Judaism. Volume 1: The Complexities of Second Temple Judaism. *Volume II/140.*

Ciampa, Roy E.: The Presence and Function of Scripture in Galatians 1 and 2. 1998. *Volume II/102.*

Classen, Carl Joachim: Rhetorical Criticsm of the New Testament. 2000. *Volume 128.*

Crump, David: Jesus the Intercessor. 1992. *Volume II/49.*

Dahl, Nils Alstrup: Studies in Ephesians. 2000. *Volume 131.*

Deines, Roland: Jüdische Steingefäße und pharisäische Frömmigkeit. 1993. *Volume II/52.*

– Die Pharisäer. 1997. *Volume 101.*

Dietzfelbinger, Christian: Der Abschied des Kommenden. 1997. *Volume 95.*

Dobbeler, Axel von: Glaube als Teilhabe. 1987. *Volume II/22.*

Du Toit, David S.: Theios Anthropos. 1997. *Volume II/91*

Dunn, James D.G. (Ed.): Jews and Christians. 1992. *Volume 66.*

– Paul and the Mosaic Law. 1996. *Volume 89.*

Dunn, James D.G., Hans Klein, Ulrich Luz and *Vasile Mihoc* (Ed.): Auslegung der Bibel in orthodoxer und westlicher Perspektive. 2000. *Volume 130.*

Ebertz, Michael N.: Das Charisma des Gekreuzigten. 1987. *Volume 45.*

Eckstein, Hans-Joachim: Der Begriff Syneidesis bei Paulus. 1983. *Volume II/10.*

– Verheißung und Gesetz. 1996. *Volume 86.*

Ego, Beate: Im Himmel wie auf Erden. 1989. *Volume II/34*

Ego, Beate and *Lange, Armin* with *Pilhofer, Peter (Ed.):* Gemeinde ohne Tempel – Community without Temple. 1999. *Volume 118.*

Eisen, Ute E.: see *Paulsen, Henning.*

Ellis, E. Earle: Prophecy and Hermeneutic in Early Christianity. 1978. *Volume 18.*

– The Old Testament in Early Christianity. 1991. *Volume 54.*

Endo, Masanobu: Creation and Christology. 2002. *Volume 149.*

Ennulat, Andreas: Die 'Minor Agreements'. 1994. *Volume II/62.*

Ensor, Peter W.: Jesus and His 'Works'. 1996. *Volume II/85.*

Eskola, Timo: Messiah and the Throne. 2001. *Volume II/142.*

– Theodicy and Predestination in Pauline Soteriology. 1998. *Volume II/100.*

Fatehi, Mehrdad: The Spirit's Relation to the Risen Lord in Paul. 2000. *Volume II/128.*

Feldmeier, Reinhard: Die Krisis des Gottessohnes. 1987. *Volume II/21.*

– Die Christen als Fremde. 1992. *Volume 64.*

Feldmeier, Reinhard and *Ulrich Heckel* (Ed.): Die Heiden. 1994. *Volume 70.*

Fletcher-Louis, Crispin H.T.: Luke-Acts: Angels, Christology and Soteriology. 1997. *Volume II/94.*

Förster, Niclas: Marcus Magus. 1999. *Volume 114.*

Forbes, Christopher Brian: Prophecy and Inspired Speech in Early Christianity and its Hellenistic Environment. 1995. *Volume II/75.*

Fornberg, Tord: see *Fridrichsen, Anton.*

Fossum, Jarl E.: The Name of God and the Angel of the Lord. 1985. *Volume 36.*

Frenschkowski, Marco: Offenbarung und Epiphanie. Volume 1 1995. *Volume II/79* – Volume 2 1997. *Volume II/80.*

Frey, Jörg: Eugen Drewermann und die biblische Exegese. 1995. *Volume II/71.*

– Die johanneische Eschatologie. Volume I. 1997. *Volume 96.* – Volume II. 1998. *Volume 110.*

– Volume III. 2000. *Volume 117.*

Freyne, Sean: Galilee and Gospel. 2000. *Volume 125.*

Fridrichsen, Anton: Exegetical Writings. Edited by C.C. Caragounis and T. Fornberg. 1994. *Volume 76.*

Garlington, Don B.: 'The Obedience of Faith'. 1991. *Volume II/38.*

– Faith, Obedience, and Perseverance. 1994. *Volume 79.*

Garnet, Paul: Salvation and Atonement in the Qumran Scrolls. 1977. *Volume II/3.*

Gese, Michael: Das Vermächtnis des Apostels. 1997. *Volume II/99.*

Gräbe, Petrus J.: The Power of God in Paul's Letters. 2000. *Volume II/123.*

Gräßer, Erich: Der Alte Bund im Neuen. 1985. *Volume 35.*

– Forschungen zur Apostelgeschichte. 2001. *Volume 137.*

Green, Joel B.: The Death of Jesus. 1988. *Volume II/33.*

Gundry Volf, Judith M.: Paul and Perseverance. 1990. *Volume II/37.*

Hafemann, Scott J.: Suffering and the Spirit. 1986. *Volume II/19.*

– Paul, Moses, and the History of Israel. 1995. *Volume 81.*

Hannah, Darrel D.: Michael and Christ. 1999. *Volume II/109.*

Hamid-Khani, Saeed: Relevation and Concealment of Christ. 2000. *Volume II/120.*

Hartman, Lars: Text-Centered New Testament Studies. Ed. von D. Hellholm. 1997. *Volume 102.*

Hartog, Paul: Polycarp and the New Testament. 2001. *Volume II/134.*

Heckel, Theo K.: Der Innere Mensch. 1993. *Volume II/53.*

– Vom Evangelium des Markus zum viergestaltigen Evangelium. 1999. *Volume 120.*

Heckel, Ulrich: Kraft in Schwachheit. 1993. *Volume II/56.*

– see *Feldmeier, Reinhard.*

– see *Hengel, Martin.*

Heiligenthal, Roman: Werke als Zeichen. 1983. *Volume II/9.*

Hellholm, D.: see *Hartman, Lars.*

Hemer, Colin J.: The Book of Acts in the Setting of Hellenistic History. 1989. *Volume 49.*

Hengel, Martin: Judentum und Hellenismus. 1969, ³1988. *Volume 10.*

– Die johanneische Frage. 1993. *Volume 67.*

– Judaica et Hellenistica. Volume 1. 1996. *Volume 90.*

– Volume 2. 1999. *Volume 109.*

Hengel, Martin and *Ulrich Heckel* (Ed.): Paulus und das antike Judentum. 1991. *Volume 58.*

Hengel, Martin and *Hermut Löhr* (Ed.): Schriftauslegung im antiken Judentum und im Urchristentum. 1994. *Volume 73.*

Hengel, Martin and *Anna Maria Schwemer:* Paulus zwischen Damaskus und Antiochien. 1998. *Volume 108.*

– Der messianische Anspruch Jesu und die Anfänge der Christologie. 2001. *Volume 138.*

Hengel, Martin and *Anna Maria Schwemer* (Ed.): Königsherrschaft Gottes und himmlischer Kult. 1991. *Volume 55.*

– Die Septuaginta. 1994. *Volume 72.*

Hengel, Martin; Siegfried Mittmann and *Anna Maria Schwemer* (Ed.): La Cité de Dieu / Die Stadt Gottes. 2000. *Volume 129.*

Herrenbrück, Fritz: Jesus und die Zöllner. 1990. *Volume II/41.*

Herzer, Jens: Paulus oder Petrus? 1998. *Volume 103.*

Hoegen-Rohls, Christina: Der nachösterliche Johannes. 1996. *Volume II/84.*

Hofius, Otfried: Katapausis. 1970. *Volume 11.*

– Der Vorhang vor dem Thron Gottes. 1972. *Volume 14.*

– Der Christushymnus Philipper 2,6-11. 1976, ²1991. *Volume 17.*

– Paulusstudien. 1989, ²1994. *Volume 51.*

– Neutestamentliche Studien. 2000. *Volume 132.*

– Paulusstudien II. 2002. *Volume 143.*

Hofius, Otfried and *Hans-Christian Kammler:* Johannesstudien. 1996. *Volume 88.*

Holtz, Traugott: Geschichte und Theologie des Urchristentums. 1991. *Volume 57.*

Hommel, Hildebrecht: Sebasmata. Volume 1 1983. *Volume 31* – Volume 2 1984. *Volume 32.*

Hvalvik, Reidar: The Struggle for Scripture and Covenant. 1996. *Volume II/82.*

Joubert, Stephan: Paul as Benefactor. 2000. *Volume II/124.*

Jungbauer, Harry: „Ehre Vater und Mutter". 2002. *Volume II/146.*

Kähler, Christoph: Jesu Gleichnisse als Poesie und Therapie. 1995. *Volume 78.*

Kamlah, Ehrhard: Die Form der katalogischen Paränese im Neuen Testament. 1964. *Volume 7.*

Kammler, Hans-Christian: Christologie und Eschatologie. 2000. *Volume 126.*

– see *Hofius, Otfried.*

Kelhoffer, James A.: Miracle and Mission. 1999. *Volume II/112.*

Kieffer, René and *Jan Bergman (Ed.):* La Main de Dieu / Die Hand Gottes. 1997. *Volume 94.*

Kim, Seyoon: The Origin of Paul's Gospel. 1981, ²1984. *Volume II/4.*

– "The 'Son of Man'" as the Son of God. 1983. *Volume 30.*

Klein, Hans: see *Dunn, James D.G..*

Kleinknecht, Karl Th.: Der leidende Gerechtfertigte. 1984, ²1988. *Volume II/13.*

Klinghardt, Matthias: Gesetz und Volk Gottes. 1988. *Volume II/32.*

Köhler, Wolf-Dietrich: Rezeption des Matthäusevangeliums in der Zeit vor Irenäus. 1987. *Volume II/24.*

Korn, Manfred: Die Geschichte Jesu in veränderter Zeit. 1993. *Volume II/51.*

Koskenniemi, Erkki: Apollonios von Tyana in der neutestamentlichen Exegese. 1994. *Volume II/61.*

Kraus, Thomas J.: Sprache, Stil und historischer Ort des zweiten Petrusbriefes. 2001. *Volume II/136.*

Kraus, Wolfgang: Das Volk Gottes. 1996. *Volume 85.*
– see *Walter, Nikolaus.*
Kreplin, Matthias: Das Selbstverständnis Jesu. 2001. *Volume II/141.*
Kuhn, Karl G.: Achtzehngebet und Vaterunser und der Reim. 1950. *Volume 1.*
Kvalbein, Hans: see *Ådna, Jostein.*
Laansma, Jon: I Will Give You Rest. 1997. *Volume II/98.*
Labahn, Michael: Offenbarung in Zeichen und Wort. 2000. *Volume II/117.*
Lange, Armin: see *Ego, Beate.*
Lampe, Peter: Die stadtrömischen Christen in den ersten beiden Jahrhunderten. 1987, ²1989. *Volume II/18.*
Landmesser, Christof: Wahrheit als Grundbegriff neutestamentlicher Wissenschaft. 1999. *Volume 113.*
– Jüngerberufung und Zuwendung zu Gott. 2000. *Volume 133.*
Lau, Andrew: Manifest in Flesh. 1996. *Volume II/86.*
Lee, Pilchan: The New Jerusalem in the Book of Relevation. 2000. *Volume II/129.*
Lichtenberger, Hermann: see *Avemarie, Friedrich.*
Lieu, Samuel N.C.: Manichaeism in the Later Roman Empire and Medieval China. ²1992. *Volume 63.*
Loader, William R.G.: Jesus' Attitude Towards the Law. 1997. *Volume II/97.*
Löhr, Gebhard: Verherrlichung Gottes durch Philosophie. 1997. *Volume 97.*
Löhr, Hermut: see *Hengel, Martin.*
Löhr, Winrich Alfried: Basilides und seine Schule. 1995. *Volume 83.*
Luomanen, Petri: Entering the Kingdom of Heaven. 1998. *Volume II/101.*
Luz, Ulrich: see *Dunn, James D.G..*
Maier, Gerhard: Mensch und freier Wille. 1971. *Volume 12.*
– Die Johannesoffenbarung und die Kirche. 1981. *Volume 25.*
Markschies, Christoph: Valentinus Gnosticus? 1992. *Volume 65.*
Marshall, Peter: Enmity in Corinth: Social Conventions in Paul's Relations with the Corinthians. 1987. *Volume II/23.*
McDonough, Sean M.: YHWH at Patmos: Rev. 1:4 in its Hellenistic and Early Jewish Setting. 1999. *Volume II/107.*
McGlynn, Moyna: Divine Judgement and Divine Benevolence in the Book of Wisdom. 2001. *Volume II/139.*

Meade, David G.: Pseudonymity and Canon. 1986. *Volume 39.*
Meadors, Edward P.: Jesus the Messianic Herald of Salvation. 1995. *Volume II/72.*
Meißner, Stefan: Die Heimholung des Ketzers. 1996. *Volume II/87.*
Mell, Ulrich: Die „anderen" Winzer. 1994. *Volume 77.*
Mengel, Berthold: Studien zum Philipperbrief. 1982. *Volume II/8.*
Merkel, Helmut: Die Widersprüche zwischen den Evangelien. 1971. *Volume 13.*
Merklein, Helmut: Studien zu Jesus und Paulus. Volume 1 1987. *Volume 43.* – Volume 2 1998. *Volume 105.*
Metzler, Karin: Der griechische Begriff des Verzeihens. 1991. *Volume II/44.*
Metzner, Rainer: Die Rezeption des Matthäusevangeliums im 1. Petrusbrief. 1995. *Volume II/74.*
– Das Verständnis der Sünde im Johannesevangelium. 2000. *Volume 122.*
Mihoc, Vasile: see *Dunn, James D.G..*
Mittmann, Siegfried: see *Hengel, Martin.*
Mittmann-Richert, Ulrike: Magnifikat und Benediktus. *1996. Volume II/90.*
Mußner, Franz: Jesus von Nazareth im Umfeld Israels und der Urkirche. Ed. von M. Theobald. 1998. *Volume 111.*
Niebuhr, Karl-Wilhelm: Gesetz und Paränese. 1987. *Volume II/28.*
– Heidenapostel aus Israel. 1992. *Volume 62.*
Nielsen, Anders E.: "Until it is Fullfilled". 2000. *Volume II/126.*
Nissen, Andreas: Gott und der Nächste im antiken Judentum. 1974. *Volume 15.*
Noack, Christian: Gottesbewußtsein. 2000. *Volume II/116.*
Noormann, Rolf: Irenäus als Paulusinterpret. 1994. *Volume II/66.*
Obermann, Andreas: Die christologische Erfüllung der Schrift im Johannesevangelium. 1996. *Volume II/83.*
Okure, Teresa: The Johannine Approach to Mission. 1988. *Volume II/31.*
Oropeza, B. J.: Paul and Apostasy. 2000. *Volume II/115.*
Ostmeyer, Karl-Heinrich: Taufe und Typos. 2000. *Volume II/118.*
Paulsen, Henning: Studien zur Literatur und Geschichte des frühen Christentums. Ed. von Ute E. Eisen. 1997. *Volume 99.*
Pao, David W.: Acts and the Isaianic New Exodus. 2000. *Volume II/130.*
Park, Eung Chun: The Mission Discourse in Matthew's Interpretation. 1995. *Volume II/81.*

Park, Joseph S.: Conceptions of Afterlife in Jewish Insriptions. 2000. *Volume II/121.*

Pate, C. Marvin: The Reverse of the Curse. 2000. *Volume II/114.*

Philonenko, Marc (Ed.): Le Trône de Dieu. 1993. *Volume 69.*

Pilhofer, Peter: Presbyteron Kreitton. 1990. *Volume II/39.*

– Philippi. Volume 1 1995. *Volume 87.* – Volume 2 2000. *Volume 119.*

– Die frühen Christen und ihre Welt. 2002. *Volume 145.*

– see *Ego, Beate.*

Pöhlmann, Wolfgang: Der Verlorene Sohn und das Haus. 1993. *Volume 68.*

Pokorný, Petr and *Josef B. Souček:* Bibelauslegung als Theologie. 1997. *Volume 100.*

Porter, Stanley E.: The Paul of Acts. 1999. *Volume 115.*

Prieur, Alexander: Die Verkündigung der Gottesherrschaft. 1996. *Volume II/89.*

Probst, Hermann: Paulus und der Brief. 1991. *Volume II/45.*

Räisänen, Heikki: Paul and the Law. 1983, ²1987. *Volume 29.*

Rehkopf, Friedrich: Die lukanische Sonderquelle. 1959. *Volume 5.*

Rein, Matthias: Die Heilung des Blindgeborenen (Joh 9). 1995. *Volume II/73.*

Reinmuth, Eckart: Pseudo-Philo und Lukas. 1994. *Volume 74.*

Reiser, Marius: Syntax und Stil des Markusevangeliums. 1984. *Volume II/11.*

Richards, E. Randolph: The Secretary in the Letters of Paul. 1991. *Volume II/42.*

Riesner, Rainer: Jesus als Lehrer. 1981, ³1988. *Volume II/7.*

– Die Frühzeit des Apostels Paulus. 1994. *Volume 71.*

Rissi, Mathias: Die Theologie des Hebräerbriefs. 1987. *Volume 41.*

Röhser, Günter: Metaphorik und Personifikation der Sünde. 1987. *Volume II/25.*

Rose, Christian: Die Wolke der Zeugen. 1994. *Volume II/60.*

Rüger, Hans Peter: Die Weisheitsschrift aus der Kairoer Geniza. 1991. *Volume 53.*

Sänger, Dieter: Antikes Judentum und die Mysterien. 1980. *Volume II/5.*

– Die Verkündigung des Gekreuzigten und Israel. 1994. *Volume 75.*

– see *Burchard, Christoph*

Salzmann, Jorg Christian: Lehren und Ermahnen. 1994. *Volume II/59.*

Sandnes, Karl Olav: Paul – One of the Prophets? 1991. *Volume II/43.*

Sato, Migaku: Q und Prophetie. 1988. *Volume II/29.*

Schaper, Joachim: Eschatology in the Greek Psalter. 1995. *Volume II/76.*

Schimanowski, Gottfried: Weisheit und Messias. 1985. *Volume II/17.*

Schlichting, Günter: Ein jüdisches Leben Jesu. 1982. *Volume 24.*

Schnabel, Eckhard J.: Law and Wisdom from Ben Sira to Paul. 1985. *Volume II/16.*

Schutter, William L.: Hermeneutic and Composition in I Peter. 1989. *Volume II/30.*

Schwartz, Daniel R.: Studies in the Jewish Background of Christianity. 1992. *Volume 60.*

Schwemer, Anna Maria: see *Hengel, Martin*

Scott, James M.: Adoption as Sons of God. 1992. *Volume II/48.*

– Paul and the Nations. 1995. *Volume 84.*

Siegert, Folker: Drei hellenistisch-jüdische Predigten. Teil I 1980. *Volume 20* – Teil II 1992. *Volume 61.*

– Nag-Hammadi-Register. 1982. *Volume 26.*

– Argumentation bei Paulus. 1985. *Volume 34.*

– Philon von Alexandrien. 1988. *Volume 46.*

Simon, Marcel: Le christianisme antique et son contexte religieux I/II. 1981. *Volume 23.*

Snodgrass, Klyne: The Parable of the Wicked Tenants. 1983. *Volume 27.*

Söding, Thomas: Das Wort vom Kreuz. 1997. *Volume 93.*

– see *Thüsing, Wilhelm.*

Sommer, Urs: Die Passionsgeschichte des Markusevangeliums. 1993. *Volume II/58.*

Souček, Josef B.: see *Pokorný, Petr.*

Spangenberg, Volker: Herrlichkeit des Neuen Bundes. 1993. *Volume II/55.*

Spanje, T.E. van: Inconsistency in Paul? 1999. *Volume II/110.*

Speyer, Wolfgang: Frühes Christentum im antiken Strahlungsfeld. Volume I: 1989. *Volume 50.*

– Volume II: 1999. *Volume 116.*

Stadelmann, Helge: Ben Sira als Schriftgelehrter. 1980. *Volume II/6.*

Stenschke, Christoph W.: Luke's Portrait of Gentiles Prior to Their Coming to Faith. *Volume II/108.*

Stettler, Christian: Der Kolosserhymnus. 2000. *Volume II/131.*

Stettler, Hanna: Die Christologie der Pastoralbriefe. 1998. *Volume II/105.*

Strobel, August: Die Stunde der Wahrheit. 1980. *Volume 21.*

Stroumsa, Guy G.: Barbarian Philosophy. 1999. *Volume 112.*

Stuckenbruck, Loren T.: Angel Veneration and Christology. 1995. *Volume II/70.*

Stuhlmacher, Peter (Ed.): Das Evangelium und die Evangelien. 1983. *Volume 28.*
- Biblische Theologie und Evangelium. 2002. *Volume 146.*

Sung, Chong-Hyon: Vergebung der Sünden. 1993. *Volume II/57.*

Tajra, Harry W.: The Trial of St. Paul. 1989. *Volume II/35.*
- The Martyrdom of St.Paul. 1994. *Volume II/67.*

Theißen, Gerd: Studien zur Soziologie des Urchristentums. 1979, ³1989. *Volume 19.*

Theobald, Michael: Studien zum Römerbrief. 2001. *Volume 136.*

Theobald, Michael: see *Mußner, Franz.*

Thornton, Claus-Jürgen: Der Zeuge des Zeugen. 1991. *Volume 56.*

Thüsing, Wilhelm: Studien zur neutestamentlichen Theologie. Ed. von Thomas Söding. 1995. *Volume 82.*

Thurén, Lauri: Derhethorizing Paul. 2000. *Volume 124.*

Treloar, Geoffrey R.: Lightfoot the Historian. 1998. *Volume II/103.*

Tsuji, Manabu: Glaube zwischen Vollkommenheit und Verweltlichung. 1997. *Volume II/93*

Twelftree, Graham H.: Jesus the Exorcist. 1993. *Volume II/54.*

Urban, Christina: Das Menschenbild nach dem Johannesevangelium. 2001. *Volume II/137.*

Visotzky, Burton L.: Fathers of the World. 1995. *Volume 80.*

Wagener, Ulrike: Die Ordnung des „Hauses Gottes". 1994. *Volume II/65.*

Walter, Nikolaus: Praeparatio Evangelica. Ed. von Wolfgang Kraus und Florian Wilk. 1997. *Volume 98.*

Wander, Bernd: Gottesfürchtige und Sympathisanten. 1998. *Volume 104.*

Watts, Rikki: Isaiah's New Exodus and Mark. 1997. *Volume II/88.*

Wedderburn, A.J.M.: Baptism and Resurrection. 1987. *Volume 44.*

Wegner, Uwe: Der Hauptmann von Kafarnaum. 1985. *Volume II/14.*

Welck, Christian: Erzählte 'Zeichen'. 1994. *Volume II/69.*

Wiarda, Timothy: Peter in the Gospels . 2000. *Volume II/127.*

Wilk, Florian: see *Walter, Nikolaus.*

Williams, Catrin H.: I am He. 2000. *Volume II/113.*

Wilson, Walter T.: Love without Pretense. 1991. *Volume II/46.*

Wisdom, Jeffrey: Blessing for the Nations and the Curse of the Law. 2001. *Volume II/133.*

Wucherpfennig, Ansgar: Heracleon Philologus. 2002. *Volume 142.*

Yeung, Maureen: Faith in Jesus and Paul. 2002. *Volume II/147.*

Zimmermann, Alfred E.: Die urchristlichen Lehrer. 1984, ²1988. *Volume II/12.*

Zimmermann, Johannes: Messianische Texte aus Qumran. 1998. *Volume II/104.*

Zimmermann, Ruben: Geschlechtermetaphorik und Geschlechterverhältnis. 2000. *Volume II/122.*

For a complete catalogue please write to the publisher
Mohr Siebeck • P.O. Box 2030 • D–72010 Tübingen/Germany
Up-to-date information on the internet at www.mohr.de